Theories of **Per*f*ormance**

To my teachers Paul H. Gray and Beverly Long Chapin

Theories of **Performance**

Elizabeth Bell
University of South Florida

SAGE Publications
Los Angeles • London • New Delhi • Singapore

For information:

Sage Publications, Inc.
2455 Teller Road
Thousand Oaks, California 91320
E-mail: order@sagepub.com

Sage Publications India Pvt. Ltd.
B 1/I 1 Mohan Cooperative Industrial Area
Mathura Road, New Delhi 110 044
India

Sage Publications Ltd.
1 Oliver's Yard
55 City Road
London EC1Y 1SP
United Kingdom

Sage Publications Asia-Pacific Pte. Ltd.
33 Pekin Street #02-01
Far East Square
Singapore 048763

Printed in the United States of America

Library of Congress Cataloging-in-Publication Data

Bell, Elizabeth, 1953—
Theories of performance / Elizabeth Bell.
    p. cm.
Includes bibliographical references and index.
ISBN 978-1-4129-2637-9 (cloth)
ISBN 978-1-4129-2638-6 (pbk.)
    1. Performance. I. Title.

BF481.B375 2008
302'.1—dc22   2007036498

This book is printed on acid-free paper.

08   09   10   11   12   10   9   8   7   6   5   4   3   2   1

Acquisitions Editor:	Todd R. Armstrong
Editorial Assistant:	Katie Grim
Production Editor:	Astrid Virding
Copy Editor:	Jamie Robinson
Typesetter:	C & M Digitals (P) Ltd.
Proofreader:	Scott Oney
Cover Designer:	Candice Harman
Marketing Manager:	Carmel Withers

Contents

List of Boxed Features

CAUGHT LOOKING

MAKE A LIST

Preface

The rationale for this book is a simple one: *Theories of Performance* is the first textbook in performance theory written specifically for an undergraduate audience, funded by performance scholarship from Communication Studies, and dedicated to pedagogies that invite critical discoveries. Each of the operative phrases in that sentence is a goal for this book.

First, *Theories of Performance* is a textbook written for undergraduate students. Performance Studies is a rich and vibrantly diverse arena, and our scholarship appears in journals, collections, and books aimed at our colleagues. When we cobble together these articles and chapters for our students, we have to work very hard to underscore basic principles, trace historical shifts, define key terms, translate complexities, and draw connections across academic traditions. *Theories of Performance* does all of this groundwork. The first goal of this textbook is *to create theoretical common ground* between students and teachers of performance. With this common ground, students are primed to create, explore, and hone a critical awareness of performances all around us.

Second, *Theories of Performance* draws from foundational theories of performance central to the discipline of Communication. While performance has traditionally been theorized, studied, and practiced in a wide range of academic disciplines, scholarship in Communication is often overlooked, underrepresented, or misunderstood in Performance Studies. *Theories of Performance* corrects these tendencies, featuring scholarship in Communication that richly accounts for performance as constitutive of identities, relationships, organizations, cultures, and technologies. The second goal of this textbook is *to start at the intersection of communication and performance* to make theoretical, historical, critical, and methodological connections. These connections move outward to the disciplines of Theatre, Anthropology, Folklore, Sociology, English, Psychology, Philosophy, and the Fine Arts; these connections move inward to areas of Communication—rhetoric, interpersonal communication, organizational communication, health communication, intercultural communication, media studies, gender studies, queer theory, cultural studies, and mass communication.

Third, *Theories of Performance* takes the undergraduate classroom seriously as a productive site to engage theory, performance, communication, and lives. Too often the word "theory" is coded in three ways in the undergraduate classroom: it's the cue for students to vacate the classroom in body, mind, and spirit; it's a signal that students will endure reading, writing, and lectures as the primary modes of learning; and it's a pretty good indicator that students will have to strain for relevant connections to their lives. *Theories of Performance* challenges this code, featuring a range of student-centered activities, examples, illustrations, and prompts for performance, research, fieldwork, analysis, and criticism. The third goal of this textbook is *to invite students to demonstrate, apply, extend, and share their discoveries* in the classroom, on the streets, across media, and in their lives.

If these three goals have been realized, then my hope is that *Theories of Performance* is elastic enough to account for many versions of Performance Studies, comprehensive enough to capture its diverse vibrancy, and useful enough to benefit students and teachers in the classroom.

Acknowledgments

Years ago, my friend Laura Sells said to me, "Never write a textbook. It will consume your life." For years, I successfully followed Laura's advice. Then Todd Armstrong of Sage just about pestered me to death with phone calls, e-mails, and letters. Thinking a face-to-face "No!" would put an end to this, I agreed to have lunch with him.

"Writing a textbook is easy," Todd said. "A chapter is . . . what? . . . twenty-five pages? You can write 25 pages! A book is . . . what . . . nine chapters? You can write nine chapters!"

Both Laura and Todd were right. This book has consumed my life, and I have produced pages and chapters. These three years of consumption and production, however, have been the most rewarding of my life. An opportunity not to be missed to harvest the many gifts I have received from my discipline, my colleagues, my students, and my family. And at harvest time, one gives thanks.

I thank the kind folks at Sage. Todd Armstrong, Deya Saoud, Sarah Quesenberry, Katie Grim, Astrid Virding, and Jamie Robinson are a pleasure to work with and to know. I thank my disciplinary colleagues in Performance Studies in Communication across the United States who worked very hard reviewing this book at each stage of the process. Their fingerprints show up on every page: Bryant Keith Alexander (California State University, Los Angeles); Michael S. Bowman (Louisiana State University); Judith Hamera (Texas A&M University); Mercilee M. Jenkins (San Francisco State University); E. Patrick Johnson (Northwestern University); Amy L. Kilgard (San Francisco State University); Kristin M. Langellier (University of Maine); Lesa Lockford (Bowling Green State University); Christie Logan (California State University, Northridge); Denise A. Menchaca (Bowling Green State University); Tony Perucci (University of North Carolina at Chapel Hill); Elyse Lamm Pineau (Southern Illinois University at Carbondale); and Keith C. Pounds (Hofstra University).

I thank Marcy Chvasta and Stacy Holman Jones, my colleagues in Performance Studies at the University of South Florida, who gave their talents, ideas, and teaching acumen to every page of this textbook. I am grateful for their coauthorship of Chapters Eight and Nine.

I thank my department chair, Ken Cissna, for making my academic home a wonderful place to work and to play. And I thank my colleagues in Communication—Jay Baglia, Elissa Foster, Kim Golombisky, Krista Hirschmann, Janna Jones, Jane Jorgenson, Christine Kiesinger, Michael LeVan, Shane Moreman, Mark Neumann, David Payne, Gil Rodman, and Fred Steier. I am grateful for their suggestions, libraries, "test drives" of chapters, and constant good cheer.

I thank the students who volunteered their time, energy, and talents for this book. Jaclyn Lannon is responsible for all the beautiful images—the hunting, gathering, and corresponding with photographers—as well as taking many photographs herself. Richard P. Johnson and Chris Sorenson are responsible for the Web site companion to this book; they hunted, gathered, and composed on the computer screen rather than through the lens of a camera, but the results, too, are beautiful ones. Laura Bergeron, Daniel Blaeuer, Katherine Bzura, and Bob Gonzalez all offered their time and talents throughout this project. I am grateful to all for their generous gifts to me.

All the folks above blur the lines among students, friends, colleagues, and family, many of whom have sat around David's bountiful table with Miranda, Daniel, Meredith, Will, and me. I am grateful for the sustenance this family offers me each and every day.

CHAPTER 1

Introducing Theories of Performance

Theory in Perspective: Can You See the Forest for the Trees?

Welcome to the world of performance, and a fascinating world it is. Here, we have the privilege of watching, interacting, creating, critiquing, and thinking about performances around us. Theories of performance help in the accomplishment of this work.

This book will introduce you to theories that take performance as the entry point for studying texts, drama, culture, social roles, identity, resistance, and technologies. Each chapter will attempt to do three things: *survey* theories that are foundational to understanding performance as a mode of communication; *translate* these theories from their sometimes complex claims for their lived and felt experiences in your life; and *illustrate* these theories with relevant examples from performances all around us. Each chapter will ask you to think more, think harder, and think differently about how you are a performer, an audience member, and a member of many communities coalescing in and around performances.

Each chapter begins with a "Theory in Perspective" section to put the specific theories covered in each chapter in conversation with history, with claims about the self, and with changing ideas of what knowledge is and how it is produced. The claims often start with Aristotle—for both poetics and rhetoric—and demonstrate how Aristotelian notions continue to be alive and well in performance theory. Shifts in knowledge production, with the Enlightenment, modernism, and postmodernism, are traced and linked to theories in each chapter. Why trace theories across centuries to explain performance theories today?

Oftentimes, we get so involved in any *one* set of ideas, or one specific performance, that we forget that all theories and performances are products of their times and larger world-shaping views. The Forest for the Trees is the analogy for starting each chapter. Even though we're standing in front of an individual tree, we're also standing in a larger forest of ideas, history, and knowledge.

This chapter attempts to demystify the word "theory" by concentrating on the kinds of questions theories ask and the assumptions these theories make about how language operates. Second, the chapter traces the relationships between communication and performance. Third, the chapter surveys definitions of performance across academic disciplines and finds three commonalities among them. Finally, the chapter makes three large claims about what performance *is* and what performance *does*. Again, welcome to the forest.

What Is Theory?

"Theory" can be an intimidating word, especially when associated with complex scientific and mathematical concepts. Most of us can link Albert Einstein, the theory of relativity, and the equation $E = mc^2$. That simple and elegant formula, however, stands for very complex relationships among space, time, mass, and energy that radically revised Newtonian physics and the accepted "laws" of gravity. One hundred years later, physicists still grapple with the implications of Einstein's work for everything from the universe's "big bang" beginning and black holes to the smallest ingredients in the universe—muons, photons, and gluons.

Brian Greene, professor of physics and mathematics at Columbia University and author of *The Elegant Universe,* is one of the world's experts on "string theory." String theory rejects the idea that the smallest building blocks of the universe are little dots—neutrons, protons, and electrons. Instead, these dots can be broken down into even smaller components: strings. Just how small is a string? If an atom were the size of our solar system, then a string within that atom would be the size of a tree. String theory maintains that these strings vibrate. Their frequencies and oscillation patterns are the fundamental music of the universe.

Neither a general theory of relativity nor string theory can be proven through direct observation. How to observe the beginning of the universe, a black hole, or the vibrations of a muon? Theory is often an invitation to imagine, to explore, and to create new knowledges and practices. This invitation goes by a variety of names: guess, speculation, supposition, conjecture, proposition, hypothesis, premise, conception, model, and explanation (Weick 1995b).

Theory Questions: What? Why? How?

Theory attempts to ask and answer three fundamental questions: what? why? and how? For Professor Greene, "We're talking about the biggest questions of all time: Why is there a universe? What is space? What is time? How is it all put together?" Greene then makes an interesting leap with the question, "If that doesn't have drama, what does?" (Evenson 1999).

While physicists are theorizing the drama of the universe, most of us are caught up in operationalizing and testing the theories that organize our daily lives. Based on experience, we *generalize* from principles to specific cases: Red is a good color for me and this shirt is great! We create *associations* between phenomena: I studied hard so I'll do well on this test. We make *predictions* about what will happen next: The traffic light will change in thirty seconds. In answering "what," "why," and "how" questions, theories serve to describe, predict, and explain the world.

We are most aware of the limitations of these theories, however, when they no longer help us understand individual lives, communities, cultures, and the physical world around us. Genres of SF (science fiction, speculative fantasy, slipstream fiction) are creative ways to question and to reimagine answers to what, why, and how questions posed by theory. "Hello Neo," the computer screen reads. Suddenly the Matrix, with new answers to the questions what, why, and how, transforms everything. If that doesn't have drama, what does?

Theorists have been contemplating performance for centuries—on the stage, in religious rites and rituals, in social and political arenas, on the page, and in the bodies of people who make these performances happen again and again. They utilize the basic questions of theory to ask, What is performance? Why do people perform? And how does performance organize, maintain, and transform lives, communities, and cultures? None of these questions can be answered "yes" or "no," nor do they have right or wrong answers. Instead, they ought to provoke observation of and reflection on performances around us (Dolan 2001, 135). Folklorist Susan Tower Hollis (1993, 3) writes, "theory is intended to pose interesting questions, not to give final, for-all-time answers."

Kinds of Theory Questions

Paul DiMaggio (1995) divides theory into three types: covering laws, enlightenment, and narrative. **Covering laws** tend to answer "what" questions. These are generalizations that describe, and most often measure, the world as we see it. The purpose of covering laws is to explain. Isaac Newton's "laws" of gravity are covering laws, answering questions about bodies in motion.

Answering the question "What is performance?" is an attempt to create covering laws that describe performance and its component parts. Most often the parts involve performers, actions, audiences, texts, contexts, and events. Such laws are difficult to set in stone, however, because what *counts* as a performance in one culture, historical period, medium, or community may not hold true for others.

Theory as **enlightenment** tends to answer "why" questions. As the word suggests, these theories can surprise us as they seek to make the familiar world around us rich, unfamiliar, and paradoxical. The purpose of enlightment theories is to explain the world in new, unexpected, and oftentimes artful ways. Karl Weick claims (1995a, 563), "A good theory explains, predicts, and delights." Einstein's theory of relativity is an enlightenment theory, as he asked physicists to conceive of gravity not as a constant but as a force that changes.

Why do people perform? Performance theorists have offered a range of answers to that question: from entertainment to efficacy, from role theory to performativity, from work to play, from rites of passage to *communitas,* from heaping sins on a community scapegoat to materializing genders, from creating political systems to overthrowing them. The most surprising answers are those that turn our taken-for-granted assumptions about our world on their heads.

Theory as **narrative** tends to answer "how" questions. Theories in this vein attempt to tell a story to account for complex and intertwined processes around us. How do these processes unfold in ways that can be observed and predicted, as well as imagined differently? Professor Greene is very much a storyteller of strings, slicing the world into smaller and smaller sections to imagine the tiniest component of the universe and asking us to listen to the music created there.

So the music of performance can also be storied. From lullabies, "Happy Birthday to You," "Pomp and Circumstance," the wedding march, and "Auld Lang Syne," to funeral dirges, the music that accompanies these transformative moments in individual lives and communities is just one story of how we mobilize performance to organize, maintain, and transform our lives. Performance theorists tell stories that account for these historical, social, political, and material processes.

A fourth strain of theory is known as **critical theory**. As its name implies, the purpose of this kind of theory is to critique. Unlike covering laws that seek to describe, critical theory recognizes that all descriptions are value-laden, political, historical, and at contest for meanings. Critical theory seeks to expose, to critique, and to change the assumptions that ground our descriptions and explanations of the world around us. Jon McKenzie (2001, 20) offers, "To theorize is to create and to critique concepts, concepts that bind together—and inevitably disseminate—diverse materialities." Della Pollock and J. Robert Cox (1991, 173) write, "Critical theory asks: What are the values girding every kind of discursive act from cereal boxes to theoretical texts? And what do we think about them? . . . From Plato through 'postfeminism,' critical theorists have argued about how to *read* the world with an eye towards *shaping* it."

Assumptions about How Language Operates in Theory

Communication processes and practices—talking, writing, reading, and interacting with others—are intimately tied to creating theory. All attempts to produce theory make unspoken assumptions about communication: What is communication? How does language operate? And how does language enable or limit the claims a theory makes?

Dennis Mumby (1997) is interested in how our understandings of language have changed across time and across theory production, complicating theory as covering laws, enlightenment, and narrative stories of processes. He argues that theory has been written in discourses of **representation, understanding,** and **suspicion.** Theories are all "games of truth" and compete for claims to authority, knowledge, and truth.

Discourses of *representation,* like covering laws, rely on the scientific method to observe and describe the world; its guiding principles are the three c's: closure, certainty, and control. This approach assumes that language is a "neutral mode of representing the observed relationships in the world" (Mumby, 1997, 4). Mumby claims that much social scientific work in Communication, using instruments like surveys and pen-and-paper questionnaires, assumes that language is an "empty conduit" for moving along already existing ideas. The boxes we are regularly asked to check—M or F—represent two genders (closed, certain, and controlled). In this instance, M or F simply "moves along" these existing ideas about gender, with a faith in language to represent the reality of those relationships of the world.

Discourses of *understanding* assume that communication is based on communities that reach a consensus about what something "means." Interpretation is central to consensual understandings of "truth" produced in and by the community. This interpretive approach in Communication Studies often relies on ethnographic studies: the researcher going into communities to explore how communication practices shape identities and communities, such as white, working-class men on factory lines. Here, language doesn't just "move along" ideas, but language and communication processes *create* ideas, identities, and organizations. In Mumby's (1997, 8) example, "talking like a man" in this community is the consensual creation of what is "'real' and meaningful."

Discourses of *suspicion* assume that surface meanings of language "obscure" deep structures of oppression. This work focuses on "power and ideologies and the processes through which certain realities are privileged over others" (9). Marxist theories are "suspicious" of capitalism; second wave feminist theories are "suspicious" of patriarchy. Critical race theories are "suspicious" of unearned white privilege. Here language can be a "mask" for covering over the operations of power.

Descriptions (like covering laws and discourses of representation), explanations (like surprises, stories, and discourses of understanding), and critiques (like critical theory and discourses of suspicion) are all attempts to explore the world around us. Judith Butler maintains that theory isn't just housed in universities or in books; theory "is an activity that takes place every time a possibility is imagined, a collective self-reflection takes place, a dispute over values, priorities, and language emerges" (2004, 176). For W. B. Worthen (1998, 1095), performance theory is "a way of exploring . . . the possibilities of performance."

This book seeks to introduce you to the world of performance as theorized—described, questioned, and reinvented—to answer fundamental what, how, and why questions through communication processes and products.

The first "Go Figure" box is an invitation to try your hand at making guesses surrounding everyday activities, describing the laws that ground these events, seeing these everyday things in new, surprising ways, telling a story of intricate processes, and critiquing the assumptions that gird them. In all the "Go Figure" boxes in this book, there are no right or wrong answers, but these are opportunities to explore possibilities—out loud, on the page, by yourself and with others.

GO FIGURE

Everyday Theorizing

Write a theory question that asks What? Why? or How? about one of the following typical activities. Put all the questions in a hat. In groups, have each group draw one of the questions to answer. Your answer should be a start in building a theory (a model, a guess, an explanation, a proposition) that explores this activity.

Write one theoretical answer in a discourse of representation (assuming language is neutral). This answer might rely heavily on the "scientific observation" of cause and effect. Write a second answer in a discourse of understanding (assuming meanings are created together). This answer might rely heavily on the jargon of "insiders" who understand the terminology. Write still a third answer in a discourse of suspicion (assuming power is obscured by language). This answer might rely heavily on politics that spell out the "have's" and the "have not's." Perform your answers for the class. How does language change across your theory answers?

Crossing the street in busy traffic

Ordering fast food

Hitting middle "C" in a song

Drawing a picture

Falling asleep

Naming a new pet

Two Models of Communication

Drama—written and staged plays in the West—has been studied, performed, and theorized for more than two thousand years. Theatre is a rich academic discipline and practice that has engendered many important theories in and of performance: from Aristotle to Augusto Boal, Shakespeare to Stanislavski, Brecht to Bakhtin. This book will necessarily cover some of their concepts, but performance theories that feature the Western stage are not the primary focus.

Instead, this book will focus on theories that have been central to the complex and dynamic relationship between performance and communication. Communication, as well as theatre, has a two-thousand-year history in the West. Aristotle, after all, wrote *The Rhetoric* and *The Poetics* to explore the many strategies for moving *audiences* in both the forum and the theatre, for making ethical *choices* in both political and aesthetic realms, for creating *action* in both oratory and poetry.

Communication theorist James Carey (1988, 4) describes the early connections between communication and democracy as intimately tied to space and bodies. In ancient Greece, citizens relied on the *spoken word* to participate in affairs of the

city-state, and men needed to be *within walking range* of the civic centers to participate. Carey concludes, "Democracies or republics were limited, then, by the range
of the foot and the power of the tongue" (4). Almost two thousand years later, the
Constitution of the United States "proposed a republic on a scale never before
imagined or thought possible." The young United States had formidable communication barriers to overcome: Communicating out loud, in person, and on foot
were impossible because of geographic barriers, across an entire continent, with a
virtually unlimited population. For the United States "to cement a union," citizens
relied on horses for transportation and the printing press to disseminate crucial
information.

These two different ways of communicating, the Greek city-states' reliance on
orality and presence and the young United States' need for print transported across
distances, gave rise to two very different conceptions of communication that are
still at odds with each other. Carey labels the emphasis on orality and presence the
Ritual Model of Communication. He labels the emphasis on transportation and
geography the Transmission Model.

SOURCE: Photo by Ed Fladung (www.edfladung.com). Copyright © 2006 by Ed Fladung.

The Transmission Model of Communication

The prevailing view of communication in the United States and in most industri-
alized cultures is the **transmission model**. In this view, communication is defined
as "a process whereby messages are transmitted and distributed in space for the
control of distance and people" (Carey 1988, 15). This definition relies on the
metaphor of geography and transportation. Carey details how roads, rivers, and
railways both determined and paralleled communication media: Telegraph,

telephone, (and now) cable lines are built next to roads, rivers, and geographic boundaries, marrying geography and transportation with communication and control. When the telegraph was invented, it was heralded as a way to spread Christianity and American democracy across vast distances and peoples. In the transmission model, several synonyms apply to communication: "imparting," "sending," "transmitting," or "giving information to others" (15). The transmission model casts communication as a vehicle for politics and trade to control people and money across vast distances. This model has limited, albeit interesting, implications for performance as a mode of communication.

The Ritual Model of Communication

The **ritual model** of communication radically departs from that commonly held notion of communication. Carey (1988) defines communication here as "a symbolic process whereby reality is produced, maintained, repaired, and transformed" (18). Its synonyms rely on the root of communication as communion, especially for the centrality of orality and presence: "sharing," "participation," "association," "fellowship," "common faith," and "community." In this view, communication is not imparting information, but representation of shared beliefs. These beliefs are expressed in community ideals and embodied in material forms: dance, plays, architecture, news stories, even strings of speech.

 Carey elaborates this ritual view of communication with the example of reading the daily newspaper:

> News reading, and writing, is a ritual act and moreover a dramatic one. What is arrayed before the reader is not pure information, but a portrayal of the contending forces in the world. . . . Under a ritual view, then, news is not information but drama. It does not describe the world but portrays an arena of dramatic forces and action; it exists solely in historical time; and it invites our participation on the basis of our assuming, often vicariously, social roles within it. (20, 21).

The ritual view of communication maintains that culture is created, maintained, repaired, and transformed in and through communication.

 This model has rich implications for performance to gather us under an umbrella called "communication" to explore talk, identities, bodies, relationships, communities, cultures, and technologies as and in performances. As we stand under this umbrella's protective cover, we're also getting wet. We are communicating when we talk about performance as a mode of communication. Carey frames the "wetness" of communication in this way:

> One of the major problems one encounters in talking about communication is that the noun refers to the most common, mundane human experience. There is truth in Marshall McLuhan's assertion that the one thing of which the fish is unaware is water, the very medium that forms its ambience and supports its existence. Similarly, communication, through language and other symbolic forms, comprises the ambience of human existence. (23–24)

Communication, the ambience we swim in every moment and the umbrella we stand under to explore that ambience, is both mundane and special. Those "special" moments are often marked as performances. Theories that pay attention to performance as one mode of communication—in everyday life, in rites and rituals, in cultural traditions and resistance, in identity creation and transformation, and in and through media—are rich accounts of individuals and groups "swimming" in the ambience of communication.

SOURCE: Photo by Ed Fladung (www.edfladung.com). Copyright © 2006 by Ed Fladung.

Performance as a Communicative Form

Folklorist Richard Bauman (1992a, xiii–xv) makes five claims about communication and the expressive—the especially meaningful—forms it can take in culture. These five claims will be touchstones throughout this book for connecting theories of performance to communication.

1. Communication is "the ways in which information, ideas, and attitudes pass among individuals, groups, nations, and generations." Communication is a construction, rooted in social relationships, and produced in the conduct of social life.

2. The expressive forms of culture, forms of art, play, display, and performance, offer an especially productive vantage point on culture, society, and communication.

3. Communicative forms constitute social resources, "equipment for living."

4. Communicative forms and practices are differently valued . . . and differently accessible to members of society.

5. Communicative forms and practices are cross-culturally and historically variable.

Bauman's (1992a) definition of communication locates social life in communication, created in and across language, order, roles, identities, and culture. He argues that the study of communication ought to explore how communicative acts "organize, produce, and reproduce" society (xiv). All the chapters in this book will explore theories that make claims about that production in and through performances.

Second, the "expressive forms of culture," created in and through communication practices, are myriad: art, play, performance, ritual, film, theatre, dance, conversation, jokes, political protests, advertising, carnivals, family stories, and so on. Bauman claims these communicative forms are *expressive* because they are specifically crafted *in performances* to accomplish three ends: to heighten experience, to comment upon experience, and to make experience available for contemplation.

How, for example, is a particularly funny joke told at the water fountain a performance that accomplishes these things? First, the telling of a great joke holds the possibility for *heightened* experience. It lifts us momentarily out of ordinary life, what Victor Turner (1988, 41) calls "boredom, ennui, and spleen," creating something *extra*ordinary. Second, the content of the joke will *comment* upon experience. The teller will craft the tiny tale in ways relevant to and illustrative of common experiences in the listeners' world. Such commentary is always a description of common ground and an evaluation of our world. And finally, the joke is an opportunity to *think* and to think *differently*—about ourselves, the joke teller, the story, the audience, and the world. Performances as modes of communication are intricately linked to opportunities for experience—as heightened, as commentary, and as reflection.

Bauman's third claim, that expressive forms are resources, draws on the work of Kenneth Burke, explored in depth in Chapter Four. Burke's famous essay, "Literature as Equipment for Living," argues that literary texts, like proverbs, are "strategies that sum up a situation." In turn, these strategies provide useful guidelines for individual and collective action. For Bauman, expressive forms of communication—like proverbs, jokes, stories, folktales, organizational stories, myths, and stage plays—are not ends in themselves, but means to social and political ends. Performance not only holds life together but can transform life. Many of the chapters in this book, but especially Chapter Eight, "Performing Resistance," will approach performance as a way to challenge the status quo of social and political life—making it anew, and hopefully, better.

Bauman's fourth claim, that all expressive, communicative forms are differently valued and differently accessible, is easily confirmed by looking at the world around us. A quick survey of the audiences and performers at a ballet, a hip-hop concert, a rodeo, a comedy club, an evangelical church service, a professional wrestling match, a cyber chat room, a quinceañera, or a college philosophy classroom makes this point. The value of and access to these performances are socially embedded, economically charged, and politically loaded. Value and access will be particularly relevant in Chapter Nine, which explores technology and mediated performance.

Finally, for Bauman, communicative forms and practices are cross-culturally and historically variable. What "counts" as a performance is embedded in a particular culture and in a particular historical time. These variations testify to the richness and dynamism of expressive forms, their cultural centeredness, and historical transformations. Chapter Five, "Performing Culture," draws on theories that explain how we perform and enact culture.

Bauman's five claims about communication—its forms, productivity, resources, variation, evaluation, and embeddedness—account for performance as a particularly rich process and product of communicative interaction. Where one stands in relation to that interaction—inside or outside of its historical, cultural, ethnic, racial, gendered, and desiring lines—is the subject of the first "Theory Meets World" box below. All of the "Theory Meets World" boxes in this book are drawn from published works by performance scholars in Communication. Through analysis of specific performances, these scholars are drawing important connections between performance theory and practice, between Communication Studies and Performance Studies, and between the always interesting ways that individuals shape and are shaped by performances.

THEORY MEETS WORLD

"Don't (SNAP!) Make (SNAP!) Me (SNAP!) Read (SNAP!) You! (SNAP!)"

E. Patrick Johnson (1995) explores multiple performances and interpretations of SNAP! as part of the communicative and expressive repertoire within African-American culture. Like many performative gestures, SNAP! is difficult to describe on the page, but Johnson writes:

> The "SNAP!" is onomatopoetic in form, in that the word sounds like the behavior. It consists of placing the thumb and the middle finger together to make a snapping sound. . . . Along with the actual snapping of the fingers, the arm makes a sweeping motion, usually from left to right, the snap coming at the end of the movement. . . . The snap is used by itself, in combination with words or with other nonverbals such as rolling the eyes. (123)

Johnson locates snapping in a variety of contexts and purposes within African-American speech communities. In "Girlfriend Culture," African-American women snap to offer compliments to other black women: "Girl, you are wearin' that dress!" (SNAP!), or to accentuate a "read," "Like if I wanna say that somebody is a tired, old, heifer wench, I might snap on each word in some kind of motion, so they'll get the point" (132). In "Queen Culture," African-American gay men "who are particularly flamboyant ('grand'), extremely effeminate ('nelly') and temperamental ('bitchy')" snap as part of a larger verbal art in African-American culture—playing the dozens, a stylized form of verbal dueling. Johnson offers this example:

> A group of gay men are standing on the sidewalk conversing when another gay male passes by. The passerby has on a pair of shoes that one of the men recognizes as coming from "Payless Shoes."

> M1: Chile. She [he] tryin' to work them shoes like she got them from a real store, knowing that she got 'em from Payless. SNAP!

> (laughter)

(Continued)

(Continued)

> M2: See. Why you tryin' to read people? The ones [shoes] you got on now came from K-Mart 'cause I was with you when you bought 'em! SNAP! SNAP! (126)
>
> Heterosexual African-American men snap differently from the above two groups: They deliberately imitate a black woman or a gay man when they snap to staunch questions about their masculinity or sexual orientation. David Alan Grier and Damon Wayans, stars of *In Living Color,* are exemplary of black heterosexual men imitating gay black men with SNAP! performances. Their characters, Blaine Edwards and Antoine Meriwether, create a new snap each week to evaluate films, books, and people. Because Grier and Wayans are such accomplished performers, they distance themselves from their created characters and reinforce their own heterosexuality. "This is not really me" is clear in their performances.
>
> Johnson points out other communities that utilize snapping in their expressive repertoires: White gay men also snap, but most use it to convey attitude. White heterosexuals may snap to parody and to stereotype. Across all of these communities, the functions, uses, contexts, and performances of snapping vary widely. "The signifiers of snapping that are recognizable to one group are foreign to another," writes Johnson. "Snapping's value, then, is contingent on the set of socially and culturally constructed value systems of a particular group of people" (Johnson 1995, 141).

Assumptions about Performance: Mimesis, Poiesis, and Kinesis

Theories that ask what, how, and why questions of performance tend to begin with different assumptions about performance, that is, about its definition, contexts, materials, processes, and purposes. Recognizing these assumptions—and their divergent claims—is important to studying theories and practices of performance.

One powerful reigning conception for performance is **mimesis**, an imitation or mirror reflection of the world. Aristotle, in the *Poetics,* maintained that the purpose of staged drama is to *imitate the action* of life. As audience members in the theatre or at a film, we understand that the action before us is an imitation. The people onstage or in the movie do not really die, and the unfolding of events is carefully planned, scripted, and choreographed. So mimesis is associated with "faking" and falsehood—the pretend world of make-believe and play. The feelings, attitudes, and values aroused in the audience, however, can be very real and lead to real consequences (Sauter 2004, 10).

This association with faking and falsehood, however, gave rise to an **antitheatrical prejudice**: Performers are not to be trusted; they easily manipulate their own emotions and those of audiences; they create falsehoods of trickery and deceit. Plato argued that the rhapsode, the oral poet who performed stories in ancient Greece, was an "imitator" with a second-order, and therefore second-rate, access to experience. The bard, rhapsode, and performer add nothing to understanding the world because such imitation is merely repetition and sham, not original knowledge or experience. While Plato's argument is a philosophical one about knowledge, we feel the tug of this prejudice when we question the sincerity, smile, and handshake of a salesperson's performance.

SOURCE: Photograph by Beth Mercer. Copyright © 2006 by Beth Mercer.

Victor Turner, a British-trained anthropologist who taught and worked in the United States, instigated a sea change in conceiving of performance not solely as mimesis, but as **poiesis,** "making not faking" (Turner 1982, 93). Turner argued that the rich corpus of performances each culture produces *makes* that culture—its traditions, communities, debates, values, and worldview. For example, at what moment and through what cultural performance are we invited to become adults? At a quinceañera? A bar mitzvah? A graduation? A driving test at the Bureau of Motor Vehicles? These performances, even though we may fake our courage and competence, are poiesis. They create a new identity, assert claims to selfhood, and are part and parcel of making us adults in the eyes of the community.

Dwight Conquergood took one more step in conceiving of performance: from faking, making, to *breaking and remaking.* Conquergood (1995) was interested in the ways that performance can transgress boundaries, break structures, and remake social and political rules. He called this process **kinesis**—"movement, motion, fluidity, fluctuation" (138). Conquergood shifts Turner's view of performance as "cultural invention" to include cultural "*inter*vention." Performance can not only sustain but subvert traditions (Conquergood 1998, 32). Adbusters is a Vancouver-based, not-for-profit organization that creates powerful advertising parodies utilizing kinesis. Their ads—for fast food, cleaning products, alcohol, and tobacco—break and remake known forms to ask us to rethink how advertising invites us to consume.

Mimesis, poiesis, and kinesis are assumptions that answer two theoretical questions: (1) What is performance? and (2) What does performance do? The answers, however, create very different claims about performance. These assumptions—about faking, making, and breaking—are alive and well in the video gaming industry. How do violent video games invite similar *imitations* in life? In what ways does the making—of characters, plots, action, and choices—through gender, race, and ethnicity *create* a worldview? And, finally, how might gamers *intervene* in performances that rework the norms?

SOURCE: Photograph by Bob Gonzalez. Copyright © 2006 by Bob Gonzalez.

What Are You this Year?

Think of the most creative Halloween costumes you've seen. Whether vampires, ghosts, M&Ms, a "Freudian slip," a "cereal killer," or "trickle down economics," all costumes draw in some measure on mimesis (imitation), poiesis (creating), and kinesis (adaptations that break from and intervene in old conceptions). Describe a costume and then make claims about what this performance does: What slice of life is recalled and presented? How does this slice produce cultural values, identities, institutions, and desires? What possibilities for breaking those structures are contained there?

Performance as a Key Term

In his book *Keywords* (1976), Raymond Williams argues that some words, like "culture," are so complicated they defy definition. Moreover, the word itself is intricately tied up in the very "thing" it tries to define. Today we could create a long list of key terms: nature, race, knowledge, sex, freedom. "Performance," across the academy and in common usage, is a key term.

All key terms are *contested*—meaning different things to different groups and people. Jon McKenzie (2001, 33) lists the academic disciplines, "from a to z," that take performance as their object and subject of study: "anthropology, art history, cultural studies (especially gender, ethnicity, class, and, of late, queer and postcolonial theory), dance history, ethnography, folklore, history, linguistics, literary criticism, media studies, philosophy, political science, psychology, sociology, speech and nonverbal communications, theatre studies, and zoology." Performance in one department, however, looks very different from performance in another. Why? These disciplines bring different intellectual histories, canons of "great works," research and production methods, and knowledge claims to the study of performance (Jackson 2004). That "performance" as a key term is contested, however, need not be a problem. This contest is part of the vibrancy of the study of performance across disciplines and across the academy (Strine, Long, and HopKins 1990).

All key terms are *slippery*—sliding across a range of meanings within one definition—and *unstable*—refusing to be pinned down to mean only one thing. Bert States (1996) describes how most dictionary definitions operate, offering as many as four different meanings of a single word. To illustrate, the word "bright" can mean (1) well lit, (2) promising, (3) cheerful, and (4) smart. How did we get from well lit to describe a level of illumination in a room to a judgment about the intelligence of a person? Each term borrows a little bit from the one before it and loses some bits along the way; by the end of the list, however, "well lit" seems to share very few qualities with "smart." The family resemblances are more and more distant. Performance, in States' example, works the same way. Performance can mean (1) theatre, (2) ritual, (3) a parade, (4) a protest, or (5) terrorism (3). We can watch the terms borrow from and build on one another, even as they lose features. At the end of the list, suddenly, performance includes both theatre and terrorism under its definitional umbrella.

All key terms are contested, slippery, and unstable. Performance theory attempts to make clear what, how, and why performance is both a "key term" and a "key" to understanding the intricate ways we participate in social and political life and create its many expressive forms.

Definitions of Performance

Arriving at a single definition that takes into account performance's contested, slippery, unstable, and discipline-bound assumptions is a difficult task. When theorists create definitions, however, they tend to feature these three interrelated concepts.

1. *Performance is both process and product.* Theorists try to account for performance as something that happens, emerges, and grows in and through a process, a set of activities or specific behaviors. This process is most often described as "emergent." According to Peggy Phelan (1993), live performance disappears even as it is happening, and it happens differently each time. In its processual unfolding, performance is also a product, an accomplishment, an event. These products are given certain statuses as performances through "framing," an invitation to the audience to perceive them as somehow "special." Here are definitions that emphasize process and product.

[Performance is] a mode of communicative behavior and a type of communication event. While the term may be employed in an aesthetically neutral sense to designate the actual conduct of communication (as opposed to the potential for communicative action), performance usually suggests an aesthetically marked and heightened mode of communication, framed in a special way and put on display for an audience. (Bauman 1992b, 41)

Performance . . . from the Old French *parfournir*—*par* ("thoroughly") plus *fournis* ("to furnish")—hence performance does not necessarily have the structuralist implication of manifesting form, but rather the processual sense of "bringing to completion" or "accomplishing." To perform is thus to complete a more or less involved process rather than to do a single deed or act. (Turner 1982, 91)

Performances mark identities, bend time, reshape and adorn the body, and tell stories. Performances—of art, rituals, or ordinary life—are made of "twice-behaved behaviors," "restored behaviors," performed actions that people train to do, that they practice and rehearse. (Schechner 2002b, 22)

Performance is a communicative process. All performances are transactional communication events between speakers and listeners. (Pelias 1992, 15)

[P]erformance is always a doing and a thing done. On the one hand, performance describes certain embodied acts, in specific sites, witnessed by others (and/or the watching self). On the other hand, it is the thing done, the completed event framed in time and space and remembered, misremembered, interpreted, and passionately revisited across a pre-existing discursive field. (Diamond 1996, 1)

2. *Performance is productive and purposeful.* Performance causes, creates, produces both itself and things outside of itself. This productivity has many purposes that are often languaged as functions, uses, or intentions. This purposeful productivity is utilized to do a number of things—for individuals, groups, and culture. Mary Strine, Beverly Long, and Mary Frances HopKins (1990, 186–89) list eight purposes for performance: aesthetic enjoyment, intellectual inquiry, affective play, cultural memory, participatory ritual, social commentary, political action, and psychological probe.

The following definitions add to, echo, and enlarge this list. Pay special attention to the infinitive verbs (they are italicized) in these definitions that emphasize productivity and purpose.

A performance may be defined as all the activity of a given participant on a given occasion which serves *to influence* in any way any of the other participants. (Goffman 1959, 15)

To perform is *to carry something into effect*—whether it be a story, an identity, an artistic artifact, a historical memory, or an ethnography. The notion of agency is implicit in performance. (Kapchan 1995, 479)

[P]erformance is dynamic and generative, enabling difficult and controversial stances and poses that ultimately help us better *to articulate* our objects (and subjects) of inquiry. (Johnson 2003, 6–7)

In all cases a performance act, interactional in nature and involving symbolic forms and live bodies, provides a way *to constitute* meaning and affirm individual and cultural values. (Stern and Henderson 1993, 3)

3. *Performance is traditional and transformative.* Performance always makes reference to former ways of doing, acting, seeing, and believing. Those references can uphold the status quo, critique the status quo, or contain the potential for changing the status quo by performing anew. The definitions below approach tradition and transformation in a variety of ways.

Performance privileges threshold-crossing, shape-shifting, and boundary-violating figures, such as shamans, tricksters, and jokers, who value the carnivalesque over the canonical, the transformative over the normative, the mobile over the monumental. (Conquergood 1995, 138)

Performance becomes a site of transformation and even a paradigm for cultural resistance. (Pollock 1995, 657)

[P]erformance is about doing, and it is about seeing; it is about image, embodiment, space, collectivity, and/or orality; it makes community and it breaks community; it repeats endlessly and it never repeats; it is intentional and unintentional, innovative and derivative, more fake and more real. (Jackson 2004, 15)

Performance is the site-specific appearance of local initiative and . . . still very much dependent on the discriminating perceptions of individual will, which may be trained to accuracy through performance. (Blau 1990, 271–72)

A performance is a specific action or set of actions—dramatic, music, athletic, and so on—which occurs on a given occasion, in a particular place. An artistic performance . . . is further defined by its status as the single occurrence of a repeatable and preexistent text or score. . . . finally, performance can be defined as an activity which generates transformations, as the reintegration of art with what is "outside" it, an "opening up" of the "field." (Sayre 1990, 91, 103)

The above definitions attempt to answer "what" questions to explain and describe performance. While a textbook ought to arrive at one definition for testing purposes, performance has too rich a heritage and too exciting a future to pin it down. Process/product, productive/purposeful, and traditional/transformative are ways to describe and explain—for the moment—the many manifestations, uses, and politics of performance.

GO FIGURE

Unpacking Definitions

Choose any one of the above definitions of performance. How does this definition answer what, why, and how questions about performance? How do specific instances or examples privilege certain kinds of performances? How do they limit, or exclude, other examples?

The first "Act Out" box below invites you to create a performance based on ideas about defining performance. Each "Act Out" box in this book is an invitation to act out, act up, act badly, act smart, and act critically. Use these as opportunities to perform your own intuitions, ideas, examples, and discoveries of theory through performing them.

ACT OUT

Contested Definitions

Divide the class into groups of two to three people. Divide the definitions among the groups and create a bumper sticker for your group's assigned definition of performance. Stage a rally with the different bumper stickers as flags. What do the different slogans enable in the rally? Who allies with whom? And who argues with whom? Why?

Claims about Performance: Constitutive, Epistemic, and Critical

The next sections introduce three large claims important to all the theories surveyed in this book: Performance is constitutive, performance is epistemic, and performance is critical. More simply, performance creates, performance is a way of knowing, and performance is a way of staking claims about that creation and knowledge.

Performance Is Constitutive

"Constituting" and "constitutive" are important terms in much contemporary theorizing about culture, identity, technology, and performance. When something is "constituted," it is established, created, given form. Kenneth Burke utilizes the example of the Constitution of the United States as a dramatic *act* that brought something *into being*—a country—that didn't exist until it was created in language by people. All constitutions of new things, for Burke, are an "*answer or rejoinder* to assertions current in the situation in which it arose" (1957, 93). The sovereignty of the king of England (the status quo for government at the time) prompted the retort "a government elected by the people" (94fn). "King" requires its opposite, "people," to bring something new into being. A constitution is a new, and arguably different, answer to something that came before.

"Constitutive" elements, then, are the components, the working parts, the gears in the machinery, of this creation. As a newly created people and country, the founding fathers spelled out the intentions of their project in the Preamble to the U.S. Constitution:

> We the People of the United States, in Order to form a more perfect Union, establish Justice, insure domestic Tranquility, provide for the common Defence, promote the general Welfare, and secure the Blessings of Liberty to ourselves and our Posterity, do ordain and establish this Constitution for the United States of America.

It is helpful to think of each of these elements' opposites—injustice, uproar, tyranny—when considering how radically new a creation this "more perfect Union" was over two hundred years ago.

Constitutions of gender (as male and female), race (as white and "other"), sexual desire (as straight or gay) and abilities (as abled and disabled) can also be fruitfully approached as acts in language that create and answer reigning assertions' demands for their opposites. And new situations call for even more new answers: The phrases "gender bending" and "gender blending" are ways of responding to and arguing with the division of the world into only two genders; studies in ethnicities work to move beyond colonial practices and policies of white and nonwhite, colonizer and native; cyber networks of new technologies offer rejoinders to old constructions of work/home, labor/management, and local/global.

Many performance theories make claims that performance *constitutes, or creates, identity*. Race, ethnicity, gender, desire, class, age, abilities, and geopolitical region are known to self and to others through performances that comply with as well as defy expectations. Social groups, whether families, organizations, communities, or even countries also are constituted through the performances they create and re-create about themselves. Family celebrations, sorority initiations, company picnics, political protests, the Pledge of Allegiance, are all means to create, maintain, and transform groups. The performances make implicit and explicit claims about what is valued in and by the group and how members ought to act.

SOURCE: Photograph by Eric Waisman. Copyright © 2006 by WickdArts Design (wickdarts-design.com).

Many performance theories will also claim that performances *constitute culture*. Ongoing, dynamic, cultural processes and structures are revealed in concrete manifestations performed by individuals: weddings, the Academy Awards, Hanukah, football games, presidential elections, step shows. The stories we tell about these events, our performances, are double-articulations: We tell stories that create ourselves, in turn creating the communities and cultures we embody; our stories are always constrained and enabled by those communities and cultures.

The challenge for any claims to performance as constitutive—for individuals, groups, and cultures—is to ask the next question. How does this process of constituting work? How are we compelled to comply with these processes? And how can we change those processes that do harm? How are processes themselves always products of history, bodies, and institutions? The "cultural moment" of adulthood available in a bar mitzvah is part of larger patterns, systems, histories, and institutions also constituted in performance.

ACT OUT

ISO Constituting Yourself

Personal ads, whether on the Internet, on video, or in the newspaper, are attempts to create yourself in language. Personal ads are concise, coded, and intended to convey the greatest amount of relevant information in the least amount of space. Successful personal ads are creative and intriguing. They make claims about who you are and create expectations in the audience about you.

Create a two-minute, live performance of your own personal ad. To guide your creation, ask, What do I want from others (friendship, job, romance)? What are the advantages and disadvantages of presenting myself in this format? How am I constituting myself—as gendered, raced, abled, classed—and as desiring in this performance?

Performance Is Epistemic

Epistemology derives from the Greek root *episteme* (meaning knowledge) and *logos* (meaning word or speech). Epistemology is a branch of philosophy that is concerned with **knowledge**: *What* is knowledge? *Where* does knowledge come from? *How* do we *know* the world and our experiences of and in it? Many performance theorists argue that performance is an epistemology, a way of knowing ourselves, others, and the world.

In Speech Communication, scholars and teachers of oral interpretation argued that oral reading is a way of *knowing a literary text.* Don Geiger was one of the first scholars in Speech to make the case that performing a text was a "particular kind of knowing." Geiger asked (1973, 313), "Do we, in knowing experience incarnated in the poem, also come to know something which lies beyond or outside the poem? What do we know? How does the poem function as a means of our knowing?"

In the next twenty years, as scholars in communication embraced other texts in and for performance—ethnographic materials, oral literatures and histories, personal narratives, performance art—many answers to Geiger's questions landed on "the other." Wallace Bacon argues (1983, 1984) that we discover and know a "sense of the other" in literature and in ethnographic materials. Bacon elaborates (1986, 19):

> The world is the other. My family are the other. My friends are the other. You are the other. The text, finally, is the other, and a particularly fruitful and sustaining other it is. It is in the matching of self and this richly human other (a matching always partial) that I find one marvelously inspiriting means of lifting myself outside the walls of my human self into realms otherwise denied to me, into the many mansions which make up the house of life.

Nor has performance of literature lost that emphasis. Thirty years after Geiger wrote of knowing, Mary S. Strine (2005, 12) claims that the poetry of Jorie Graham contains "spaces where possibilities for startlingly fresh ways of knowing self and world, self and other are rehearsed and nurtured."

How do we know all these "others"? For Ronald Pelias (1998, 16), "performance as knowing . . . is something we learn from our daily practice. We know it somatically; we know it in our bodies . . . performance is an embodied procedure that provides insights." Body knowledge, or, in Leland Roloff's (1973, 3) terminology, "somatic thinking," is a way of knowing the world through all our senses (sight, hearing, touch, taste, and smell). Somatic thinking, however, is immensely difficult to translate into words. How to describe the pain in your back to the doctor? The knowledge we gain in performance is similarly difficult to put into words; we often give up, saying, "Forget it. You just had to be there."

When we know the world in and through our bodies—delighting in the discovery of our toes with "This little piggy went to market," suffering those first halting and bruising rides on a bicycle, and risking any encounter with flying balls hurled in our direction—we are engaging in a way of knowing ourselves, others, and the world that runs counter to modern notions of knowing. Linda Park-Fuller (1998, 163) tells this story of designing an interdisciplinary college course on performance and public affairs.

> We are from theatre, performance studies, communications, sociology, social work, business management, curriculum and instruction, psychology, and nursing. While placing the final touches on the proposal, we are considering . . . the need for a large space in which to teach the class. "Yes," I agree, "we've got

to have room for twenty-two bodies moving at once." The gasps and giggles are sharp and immediate. "Oh, no," someone laughs, "that sounds like fun, and in our department, we don't have fun, we struggle." Another (only half kidding): "Please don't put that in the proposal. My department would never take it seriously." "Well," I note, "looks like we're still a long way from expecting consensus that the site of learning is the physical body." Everyone nods solemnly, and someone adds, "Only if you mean that part above the shoulders."

This **mind/body dualism**, separating our minds (heads, brains, intellect, and rationality) from our bodies (physicality, gut "feelings," intuitions, and emotionality) permeates Western approaches to how we know the world. Despite ancient traditions of learning how to perform a skill or craft through apprenticeships and hands-on training, modern Western education devalues the body and its knowledge. Not unlike the antitheatrical prejudice for its "false" contributions to knowledge, performance as knowing in and through the body risks the charge of "**anti-intellectualism**."

What we know in and through our bodies is also caught up in *how* we know. The primary *apparatus* for knowing the world is **vision**. The importance of sight to the ability to measure, to gauge, and to know the world privileges the viewer. Vision renders the other senses "second class" and detaches the knower from the object of study in much art, science, and knowledge production (Palmer 1977). The knowledge—of texts, selves, others, and the world—we gain in and through performance flies in the face of scientific methods that strive to see, measure, systematize, and verify knowledge of the world around us through vision.

Eric Dishman (2002, 238–39) works with computer software designers and uses performance "bodystorming" techniques to correct "brainstorming" strategies. Asking designers to intervene in their typical activities, "where the predominant motion is a mouse click at a computer workstation," these designers discovered that they were bringing an "impoverished inactivity" to their computer designs. Dishman also blindfolded the designers to "jar them out of their normal ways of 'seeing' the world." Dishman seeks to create "a new kind of performer-designer, one who can imagine and invent a wide range of performativities in the world" (236).

Performance as an epistemology, then, is a much different, and often maligned, way of knowing the world. The challenges for performance theory are to account for all the resources (not just our minds) that we bring to the creation, participation, and study of performances; to qualify how all our sensory equipment (and especially vision) funds and creates the knowledge claims we make; and to understand how history, institutions, and language value some ways of knowing over others. For Dwight Conquergood (1998, 26), a performance epistemology emphasizes immediacy, involvement, and intimacy. Recognizing and nurturing these ways of knowing are not always easy, nor are they readily taught in Western classrooms.

In the first "Read More About It" box below, a poet invites us to think through constitutive and epistemological claims of performance. What kind of person is created in the classroom? And how do the processes of education value some kinds of knowledge over others? In all the "Read More About It" boxes, poetry, novels, essays, and editorials are opportunities to explore the claims presented in performance theories.

READ MORE ABOUT IT

"Raising My Hand" by Antler

"Raising My Hand" is from Antler's book Selected Poems *(2000, 81).*

One of the first things we learn in school is
    if we know the answer to a question
We must raise our hand and be called on
    before we can speak.
How strange it seemed to me then,
    raising my hand to be called on,
How at first I just blurted out,
    but that was not permitted.

How often I knew the answer
And the teacher (knowing I knew)
Called on others I knew (and she knew)
    had it wrong!
How I'd stretch my arm
    as if it would break free
    and shoot through the roof
    like a rocket!
How I'd wave and groan and sigh,
Even hold up my aching arm
    with my other hand
Begging to be called on,
Please, *me,* I know the answer!
Almost leaping from my seat
    hoping to hear my name.

Twenty-nine now, alone in the wilds,
Seated on some rocky outcrop
    under all the stars,
I find myself raising my hand
    as I did in first grade
Mimicking the excitement
    and expectancy felt then,
No one calls on me
    but the wind.

SOURCE: Antler, former poet laureate of Milwaukee, is author of *Selected Poems* (Soft Skull Press), in which "Raising My Hand" appeared. Used with permission of author.

Performance Is Critical

In Krista Hirschmann's (2001) study of doctor-patient discussions of sex, she argued that approaches to performance as faking, making, and breaking also involved **staking**. Doctors framed medical advice to women and girls as cautionary tales: The stakes for sexual activity are very *dangerous* for you. Beware! These same doctors framed medical advice to men and boys as opportunities for pleasure: The stakes for sexual activity are very *important* to you. Enjoy! In both instances, the "stakes" in the performance of medical advice were very high, but very different.

Exploring the stakes in a performance—for individuals, for communities, for institutions, for language, and for culture—is a critical endeavor. Hirschmann went beyond description, predictions, and associations in studying these conversations. Instead, she engaged in **critical work** to stake claims about how underlying gender, racial, and class assumptions shaped and produced medical doctors' authority to talk about sex, its privileges, and its oppressions. All performance can be approached as faking, making, breaking, and staking: Performance holds possibilities to imitate a life world, to create a life world, to transform a life world, and to stake claims about that life world.

Whether creating, watching, critiquing, or studying performance, many of the theories in this book will help you engage in critical projects to explore the stakes in performances. D. Soyini Madison (2005, 13) offers six purposes of critical work in studying and producing performances:

1. to articulate and identify hidden forces and ambiguities that operate beneath appearances;

2. to guide judgments and evaluations emanating from our discontent;

3. to direct our attention to the critical expressions within different interpretive communities relative to their unique symbol systems, customs, and codes;

4. to demystify the ubiquity and magnitude of power;

5. to provide insight and inspire acts of justice; and

6. to name and analyze what is intuitively felt.

Madison's guidelines are important ones for understanding power as *everywhere*—expressed and resisted in language, institutions, and relationships—and for understanding the *felt realities* of those expressions and resistances—words can nurture and protect, as well as harm and violate.

In Luis Alberto Urrea's memoir *Nobody's Son: Notes from an American Life* (1998), Urrea tells the story of growing up caught between memberships in two cultures. His mother is a white American; his father is a Mexican. As a literature professor and published poet, Urrea is often asked to speak at college graduation ceremonies. At one point in his oration, he reads Wendell Berry's poem, "Do Not Be Ashamed." Urrea describes the audience's reactions to the poem:

You can almost see thought bubbles above the students' heads as they listen. *Honkies,* some are thinking. *Liberals* and *minorities,* and *commies.* And certainly *666* and the *Antichrist* bubble about up in the air: *Hispanics, Yankees, blacks, queers, Democrats. Women. Men.*

My mother thought: *Mexicans.*

My father, a Mexican, thought: *gringos.*

I, for one, think *They* are the ones with the words. You know, the Words. The ones they called my dad and me—like *wetback. Spic. Beaner. Greaser. Pepperbelly. Yellow-belly, taco-bender. Enchilada breath.* (7–8)

Urrea is engaging in all of Madison's critical points, especially "to name and analyze what is intuitively felt" as he contemplates his and others' critical expressions. When we study performance as a critical endeavor, we are interested in the operations of power that produce these names, conflicts, privileges, and oppressions in language and in the felt realities that fuel them.

The challenge for performance theory is to explore how performances are always about power, but not to assume that power is monolithic, outside of interactions, or always repressive. A critique of power in performance should also explore microprocesses, subtleties in interactions, and productively positive ways that power operates in performance to create selves and communities. Richard Bauman (1977, 45) claims that in many cultures around the world, performers are both admired and feared. We admire them "for their artistic skill and power and for the enhancement of experience they provide." We fear them because "of the potential they represent for subverting and transforming the status quo." Performance is critical when it manifests our different and shifting stakes in these moments and potentials.

READ MORE ABOUT IT

Open Wide!

Laurie Notaro is the author of six books, including The Idiot Girls' Action Adventure Club *(2002), a marvelous series of "real life" misadventures many women will find familiar. In an interview about the resonance of her works, Notaro describes herself: "A dork is a dork is a dork. . . . You can be seventeen, you can be twenty-seven or thirty-seven, you're still going to fall down and people are going to see your underwear" (Weich 2004). Notaro's (2002, 126–28) essay invites women to think critically about the gynecologist's office, body knowledge, and cultural assumptions about everyday life.*

I can almost handle going to the gynecologist because, supposedly, like every other female, I'm only supposed to go once a year.

Supposedly.

Well, as luck and my cervix would have it, I got to see a whole lot of my gynecologist this year, though she got to see a whole lot more of me.

(Continued)

(Continued)

In any case, I know better than to expect that anything connected with me would ever go smoothly or be considered routine. If things didn't happen that way, it would make me normal. The life of a freak, on the other hand, is filled with snags, bitter disappointments, and calamities, and no matter how hard I try, that's where I consistently find myself, ass-down in a puddle of freak mud.

Or legs-up on an examining table.

During my visit to my doctor last year, a vital torturing device was missing, the little toy called the Speculum. For those of you not familiar with OB-GYN lingo, I will explain. The speculum is a medieval invention with two halves that, when closed, form a conical shape. That's the part they shove into your privates. Then I guess there's some sort of handle, and behind the handle is a big crank that, when the doctor turns it, opens the conical part to an unnatural spread resembling the jaws of an infuriated crocodile. It is made out of metal, and I'm pretty sure that my doctor keeps hers in the freezer.

During my exam, my doctor didn't find out that the speculum was missing until I was naked and already had my feet up higher in the air than an adult entertainer. She searched frantically for the instrument through the cabinet below me, but to no avail. It simply wasn't there. I thought I might have been off the hook.

Instead, she raised her head through the valley of my legs.

"Barbara!" she yelled to her assistant at the front desk. "Where's the speculum?"

"It's in the cabinet!" I heard Barbara yell back, to which my doctor responded that it just wasn't there.

Then the door flew open, and there was Barbara, entering the room to join my doctor in the search for the tool.

"I don't understand it," Barbara said. "I know I saw it here."

I couldn't see what was going on. I was still on my back, with my unsheathed lower appendages up in the air, my privacy covered with nothing but an enlarged two-ply paper towel.

"It's not here," I heard them agree. "Jeanie!"

And then the door opened again, and there was Jeanie, the girl in charge of the urine samples. She also joined the party that was currently being hosted by my now-public vagina.

"Look," I expected my doctor to say to her little friends as she elbowed Barbara and Jeanie and pointed at me, giggling. "I *told* you this one has seen a lot of action."

I felt like someone who had been abducted by a UFO, and aliens were handling me very improperly. "You people aren't supposed to be down there!" the little voice in my head yelled. "This is private property! Do you see an OPEN HOUSE sign?!!"

No one even offered to cover me up. I had no recourse; I just lay there, shaking my head. So far, I had my doctor, her receptionist, and the urine girl gathered in front of my very visible biblical parts. That included two people who had no business being there in the first place, both of whom I was going to have to look in the face later when I paid for this brief visit to Magic Mortification Mountain. What's next, I thought, a knock at the door and a voice that cracked, "Did anybody order a pizza?"

"Come on in!" the three women would chorus. "We're in here!"

RETHINKING THEORY AND PERFORMANCE

This chapter is both an introduction and an invitation to rethink theory as something we operationalize every day. All theories are attempts to explain, to explore, and to imagine possibilities. Theories ask what, why, and how questions; and they ask these questions in discourses of representation, understanding, or suspicion.

No theory is apolitical or uncontested, as the "theory of evolution" debate in the public schools reveals. Some theories made claims to the world that, with time, we now recognize as inaccurate, harmful, and just plain wrong. The theory of bodily humors (blood, black and yellow bile, and phlegm) in ancient Greece gave rise to centuries of practices of bloodletting and purging to bring these humors into balance (du Pre 2005). "Deeply embedded cultural assumptions" can lead both scientists and philosophers to theorize "what they believed they saw" (Weeks 2003). Theories of performance are always political, shifting, and illustrative of deeply embedded assumptions about the world.

This chapter is also an invitation to rethink communication, not solely as the transmission of information, but as the representation of shared beliefs in material forms. In this model, communication is a rich umbrella that houses performance and its unique tensions: process/product, productivity/purpose, and tradition/transformation. All the definitions offered in this chapter featured at least one of the pairs, and all of the subsequent chapters in this book will survey performance theories that continue to do the work of describing, explaining, critiquing, and exploring those operations.

"The first rule of performance studies," according to Jill Dolan (1993, 6), is that "performance happens all around us, if you look at it that way." All theories are accounts of what "happens all around us." Inseparable from communication and as a key term across many disciplines, "performance" has been accounted for as mimesis, poiesis, and kinesis—reflecting, creating, and breaking lines around our multiple realities.

These accounts lead to even broader claims for the constitutive, epistemic, and critical power of performance, words that may be even more intimidating than "theory." They needn't be scary words: We create, we know, and we stake claims to and about ourselves, others, communities, technologies, and cultures in and through performance. Theories of what, how, and why "performance happens" are never settled. Theories are not for "all time," but are always invitations to rethink what we think we know.

CHAPTER 2

Constituting Performance

Theory in Perspective: What Makes a Performance?

Aristotle divided the constituent parts of tragedy into six elements: **plot, character, thought, spectacle, song,** and **diction.** Aristotle argued that the best plays are an artful combination of *plot* (the arrangement of the incidents), *character* (the people who carry out the action with a variety of motives), and *thought* (all the activities of the mind, including reason, emotion, and everything in between, expressed in the words of the play). The three remaining elements concern the play's production. *Spectacle* is all the visual elements—staging, costuming, props—that the audience sees. *Song* is the sound of the play—rhythm, rhyme, music—that the audience hears rendered by the actors and the chorus. *Diction* is how the actors enunciate the poetry of the verbal text. Today, we might think of diction as "the art of delivery."

Aristotle's *Poetics* is a primer, or recipe, for playwriting. Plato called the art of rhetoric—an orator persuading an audience—a "knack" and compared it to cookery. Whether plays or speeches, recipes and cooking are helpful analogies for performance theory, for they raise the questions: What makes a performance? What are a performance's ingredients and their proportions? And how are these prepared to make a performance—beautiful to look at, delicious to consume, and good for us, too. And why is it that some people—working with the same script or recipe—manage to create art, while others do not?

A good recipe ought to evidence the same characteristics as a strong theory. Organizational theorist Karl Weick (1979) argues that a strong theory is generalizable (applies across all of the examples), simple (is a basic description), and accurate (accounts for everything). We've all encountered recipes that are not generalizable, often requiring regional ingredients not available; recipes that involve many complex and difficult steps; and recipes with mistakes. Was that a 300 degree oven for one hour or a 100 degree oven for three hours? A strong theory and a good recipe are generalizable, simple, and accurate accounts of ingredients, proportions, processes, and products.

Most theorists agree on the ingredients of a performance. Ronald Pelias and James VanOosting (1987) claim that the basic concepts of any performance theory are **text, event, performer,** and **audience.** For Richard Bauman (1977), the "patterning" of performance involves **event, act, role,** and **genre.** Richard Schechner (2002b, 215) delineates the elements of the performance quadrilog: **sourcers, producers, performers,** and **partakers.**

This chapter features performance theories that move beyond naming the ingredients to explain, describe, and analyze how these parts come together to constitute, or create, a performance. In *Verbal Art as Performance* (1977), Richard Bauman postulates three constitutive elements of performance that apply to all situations "marked" as performances by their communities: performance competence, audience evaluation, and heightened experience. This marking is accomplished through framing, a concept developed by Gregory Bateson (1972) and elaborated by Erving Goffman (1974). These theories help us answer the questions: How do we know we are seeing, participating in, or passing by a performance? What does performance "feel" like for a performer? And what's expected of the audience?

The "Nature" of Performance

Consider trying to build a performance theory—an explanation or a model—that finds the commonalities in these events:

- first-graders reciting the Pledge of Allegiance
- the Kirov Ballet's production of *Swan Lake*
- a high school quarterback at third down and goal to go
- employment interviews held at a job fair
- a funeral
- a Juneteenth barbecue

Richard Bauman's (1977) theory of the "nature of performance" accounts for all of these events as performances. His three constitutive elements of performance, performance competence, audience evaluation, and heightened experience, are generalizable, simple, and accurate ingredients that apply to all communication marked as a performance.

Performance Competence: Do You Know What You're Doing?

In all performance situations, the performer should display *performance competence.* This is the "knowledge and ability to speak in socially appropriate ways" (Bauman 1977, 11). A first-grader learning to perform the Pledge of Allegiance, for example,

SOURCE: Photograph by Master Sgt. Mark A. Suban, USAF. US Department of Defense, 2002.

must learn the words of the Pledge. This is not often easy, especially when "to the republic for which it stands" becomes "to the republic for Richard Sands," or "one nation, under God, indivisible" becomes "one nation, under God, and a vegetable."

Beyond knowing and understanding the correct words, however, is the importance of knowing and displaying appropriate attitudes and postures in apt situations for the performance. Bauman explains this as "the way in which communication is carried out, above and beyond its referential content" (1977, 11). Performance competence is an accountability to the audience: The performer directly and indirectly demonstrates that "I know the rules of this particular performance."

We all know people who can't tell jokes, but these individuals often insist on telling them anyway. They flub the setup, confuse the characters, forget the punch line, have no sense of dramatic build or comedic timing, and often tell jokes at inappropriate times and places. These bad joke tellers do *not* display performance competence: They neither know, nor enact, the "rules" for good joke telling. Another nuance on performance competence is what folklorist Del Hymes calls "performance in a perfunctory key." Here the performer acts out of social obligation or cultural compliance (Bauman and Sherzer 1975). Many people perform the Pledge of Allegiance in this manner.

Anthropologist William O. Beeman (2004, 90) lists four skills common to effective performers in the West: timing, charisma (the ability to engage, hold, and direct an audience's attention), focus and concentration, and freshness and spontaneity. He also lists "universal difficulties" that hamper the effectiveness of performers: pushing ("showing obvious effort"), losing concentration, underpreparation, overpreparation, and miscalculation of context. Miscalculating the audience and context is to "present something that they already know and will be bored with or that is so esoteric that they cannot comprehend it" (90). Beeman also adds "presenting offensive material or material that is insulting to persons of importance."

Emily Yoffe, known as the Human Guinea Pig who humiliates herself "for fun and profit," writes an account of her disastrous "debut as a children's entertainer at a 3-year-old's birthday party" (2006). Yoffe watched and imitated the acts of two very successful birthday clowns, Zuccinni and Broccoli, whose antics included sucking on pacifiers, wearing diapers on their heads, and sight gags with toilet paper. Despite her careful study and preparation, Yoffe failed to display performance competence on all of Beeman's fronts, especially the ability to hold and direct the children's attention. The children never found her charismatic, and Yoffe relates that "occasionally a child would glance over at a parent plaintively, as if to ask, 'Why, Mommy, why?'"

Displaying performance competence is central to all communication marked as a performance. Those performers who display it are often considered powerful, special, even dangerous members of their communities. Those who don't, like Yoffe, have to reappraise themselves: "I had always considered myself to be 'good with kids.' But it turns out the kids saw me as one of those weird ladies who sadly thinks she's good with them and they just wish she would go away."

Audience Evaluation: How's It Going?

If the performer assumes the responsibility of displaying competence for an audience, then the audience holds a complementary responsibility. The *audience evaluates the skill and effectiveness of the performer*. Audience evaluation takes a multitude of forms—historically, culturally, and situationally—but evaluation is a constitutive part of performance.

Applause, standing ovations, and shouts of "Bravo!" are common expressions of audience evaluation in the contemporary West; booing, hissing, and vegetable throwing, too, make an audience's judgment clear. In British Parliamentary debates, the members of the House of Commons express their approval of a speaker by rapping their knuckles on their desks. If they disagree, the speaker is met with outright jeers, shouts, and raspberries. Such open *disapproval* is often a shock to Americans who expect legislative bodies to be ruled by formal and excessively polite decorum. But noise—positive or negative—need not be the only way in which audiences evaluate performers. Deaf communities, for example, applaud by rapidly fluttering their upstretched hands in the air.

Sporting events are particularly interesting manifestations of audience evaluation and run the gamut from the quiet, contained, appreciative applause at professional golf matches to the constant and rambunctious cheering and jeering at professional wrestling matches. Sharon Mazer (1990, 114) writes of World Wrestling Federation audiences: "WWF spectators are fully involved and apparently influential, ready to roar 'BORING' if the action slows or they feel ignored for too long. . . . [They] are active participants whose approval is essential to the action onstage."

Rock concerts in the 1960s and 70s were marked by audience members holding up lighted cigarette lighters to bring the featured act back for an encore. Today, concert goers hold up their cell phones, the digital screens acting as electronic flames, a much "cooler" version of audience evaluation. Musical concerts, sporting events, sacred ceremonies, poetry readings, job interviews, even funerals, are all performances in which audiences bear the responsibility of evaluation. While all have very, very different conventions for *how* an audience expresses its judgment, in all cases performers are marked as subject to audience evaluation.

SOURCE: Photograph by Mhyla Guillermo. Copyright © 2005 by Mhyla Guillermo.

Heightened Experience: Is This Special or What?

Bauman's third constitutive element of performance is that the performance itself is "marked as available for the *enhancement of experience*, through the present enjoyment of the intrinsic qualities of the act of expression itself" (1977, 11). Something special is available in and through performance for performers and audiences alike. This "specialness" is often difficult to describe, but we know it when we experience it as something qualitatively different from "ordinary" life. Peggy Phelan (2004, 571) describes this specialness available in art as a fine line: "Without a robust sense of 'life' as something other than art, the terms collapse into one another and we are left with an all-performance-all-the-time reality, a reality that risks making art nothing more than a mode of documentation." Performance competence, audience evaluation, and heightened experience are all analyzed in online journals by Kurt Lindemann (2005). He writes that "skillful online narrative performances use heightened communication and icons that transcend the mundane nature of ordinary life" (360).

Still other theorists try to describe the felt experience, or emotional, physical, and cognitive sensations in audience members, of this heightened moment. Herbert Blau (1990, 264) describes this constitutive element: "all performance moves between expectancy and observance, between attentiveness to what happens and astonishment at what appears." Blau's examples of astonishing performances are "Lynn Swann running patterns of a passing route," "Nadia Comaneci on a vaulting horse," and Muhammad Ali "dancing like a butterfly and stinging like a bee." These "marvels of performance" are "an image of perfection in the head" (265). Judith Hamera (2006, 240) puts it more simply: Scholars study performance "because they've been bowled over, or knocked flat, or knocked out by it."

The Critical Art Ensemble (CAE) describes the astonishment of audience members when they staged a "guerrilla performance" in Sheffield, UK. The CAE

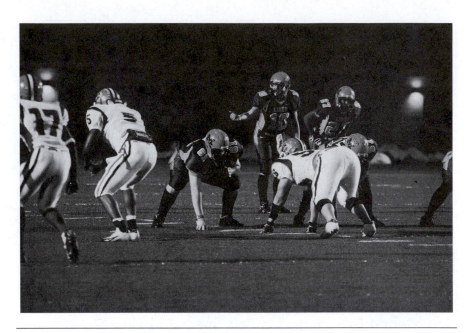

SOURCE: Compliments of *The Lion,* McKinney High School, McKinney, Texas.

sought to unveil the hidden structures of domination in everyday life—like consumption and the rules of sociality in public places. On their Web site description of this "tactical action," CAE explains that it was "designed to create a sense of what public space could be when not dominated by the commodity." They chose to give away beer and cigarettes. The first thing they noticed was that mostly men participated, revealing male privilege. CAE writes (2000, 160), "The most interesting reaction from the male participants was complete astonishment at the action. The whole context—a moment of meeting new people, having conversations, getting drunk while waiting for the tram, getting free commodities, and so on—seemed so unbelievable that as one man put it, 'It's a dream come true.'"

Performance competence, audience evaluation, and heightened experience are all constitutive elements of performance. But how do we know we're watching a performance? Marking communicative interaction as a performance involves framing.

READ MORE ABOUT IT

One Fan's Blogging Account of Astonishment

Here is sportswriter Peter Schrager's blow-by-blow of the last minutes of the January 5, 2006, Rose Bowl Game in Pasadena, California. The University of Southern California Trojans (ranked #1) played the University of Texas Longhorns (ranked #2) for the NCAA National Championship.

Vince Young's touchdown run just made Reggie Bush's touchdown run look pedestrian. Wow. It's an early Valentine's Day—I'm fully smitten for Bush, White, Leinart and Young. Gushing over here. 38–33.

- LenDale White, stopped on 4th and 2 . . . Texas ball! They hyped this up as "The Greatest Game Ever." . . . They were being modest.
- Texas driving. Love this. Commenting during this drive doesn't do this game justice. Let's just say this—Texas is marching down the field in the national title game with under a minute to go. If you're not watching yourself, you definitely aren't reading this blog at the moment.
- Funny how nobody mentioned the "URGENT NEED" for a college football playoff system this week.
- Timeout, 30 seconds left, Texas down 38–33 at the Trojans ten. Mind spinning, over here. 'Bout to throw up the Kix I didn't already spill.
- 4th and 5—this is the game . . . the season . . . the world . . . and . . . touchdown, Vince Young. Unreal.
- USC will get a chance. I wonder if Reggie Bush worked on his lateral skills since the first quarter. He may need them on this kickoff.
- Game over. Texas wins. Wow. No words do this justice. Rarely does a sportswriter have nothing to say. I have nothing to say. Just chills down my spine.

Best . . . game . . . ever. Not one unwarranted drop pass, not one poorly thrown ball, not one bad tackle, not one lazy effort, not one touchdown dance. This game was everything sports should be. What a way to spend a Wednesday night.

Now, I have to clean up some cereal.

SOURCE: Peter Schrager's Blog "Best Ever!" Copyright © 2006 by Peter Schrager. Used with permission of Fox Interactive Media.

Constituting Performance through Framing

A picture frame asks us to look at the painting inside the frame in a certain way—as art, as a masterpiece, as an aesthetic event—and to ignore the things outside the frame. A puppy may nip and lunge, but we can interpret those actions in two ways: She is playing, or she is seriously threatening to bite or to harm. Quotation marks around a word also ask us to read that word in a certain way, whether meaning something different than usual, or as somehow improper or questionable, or the marks ask us to pay attention to the word itself. Guillermo Gómez-Peña (2001, 13), for example, drops this phrase into his essay, "Technical Note: From now on, all words that appear in quotation marks are temporarily 'meaningless.'"

Gregory Bateson (1972) describes all of the above examples as **frames,** *ways of organizing, understanding, and interpreting experiences in social interaction*. Erving Goffman (1974, 8) puts the question more simply. Whenever humans engage in social interaction, they ask implicitly or explicitly, "What is it that's going on here?" Some answers to that question might be: This is play, a movie, an interview, or a job.

Once a frame is understood by participants, then the communicative interaction happening within that frame makes sense to them.

According to Bateson (1972, 187–188), frames serve to *delimit* messages ("Pay attention to the picture in the frame and not the wallpaper on the wall next to it") and offer systems to *interpret* messages ("Use a different system for evaluating the painting than you use for evaluating the wallpaper"). In this way, frames are **metacommunicative**: They carry instructions for *how* to interpret messages, events, and actions within that particular frame. The frame of a jury trial, for example, is very explicit in its instructions for how to communicate within that frame: Who talks? When and how? What is one allowed to say? What is one forbidden to say? Occasionally these instructions are spelled out by the judge; more often, these instructions are implicitly embedded in the decorum and rules of the court.

Frames are also **transformative**. An understanding of the situation may "click" for a participant who suddenly sees the interaction in a new way through a new frame. Goffman (1974, 10) writes, "while one thing may momentarily appear to be what is really going on, in fact what is actually happening is plainly a joke, or a dream, or an accident, or a mistake, or a misunderstanding, or a deception, or a theatrical performance, and so forth."

The concept of framing is central to many theories of performance and attempts to answer "what" and "how" questions: "*What* is it that's going on here?" and "*How* do we 'bracket' experience to understand, interpret, and make sense of the interaction?" According to Richard Schechner (2002a, xii), "any action can be framed, presented, highlighted, or displayed as a performance." Performance frames can be generated, broken, confused—deliberately and accidentally, and frames can slip.

GO FIGURE

Analyzing Frames

Sporting events, rehearsals, sacred and secular ceremonies, daydreams, first dates, political protests, birthday parties, and cyber chats are communicative interactions available for analysis through framing. Add to the list above and choose one to analyze. How does this frame limit the messages and interactions possible within it? How does this frame offer a system for interpretation? What instructions to the participants are implicit and explicit within this frame?

Framing Theatre, Art, Poetry, Conversation, and Media

Long before electricity and the proscenium arch stage, communities marked their festivals, rites, and popular, open-air entertainments as performances. But the modern theatrical frame is a good place to start to understand how performance conventions frame experience. In the physical space of a conventional theatre in the West, the proscenium arch of the stage frames, limits, and systematizes our experience of the action before us and around us. W. B. Worthen (1998, 1096) describes this kind of modern proscenium performance as only a century old: "a darkened auditorium, a bourgeois drama, performance conventions that confine the play behind the fourth wall of a box set onstage." These theatrical conventions "are historically grown and institutionally supported concepts of play, performance, actors, space, time and audience relationships" (Van Maanen 2004, 255).

The conventional theatrical frame asks audiences and performers to make a number of assumptions: The things we see and hear are real, but not "for real," in that they are carefully scripted, choreographed, and planned. These theatrical events are bounded by the fourth wall—the imaginary wall the audience looks through to hear and to see the events. Technical stagecraft will occur seamlessly and without drawing attention to itself. Schechner (1990, 28) argues that traditional theatre generates this frame that is acknowledged and understood by both performers and audience.

Beverly Gordon (2003) details how an ordinary women's bathroom at the University of Wisconsin was transformed into "Restroom World" through a performance frame, inviting women to experience this space in a new, heightened, and aesthetic way. Ordinary objects (magazines, stuffed animals, and plants) and "art installations" (high-heeled shoes, posters, and seasonal displays) are curated and displayed like an interactive museum. A guest book in "Restroom World" invites comments. The first comment in the guest book was "Best loo in the building," signed "The Queen Mother." Others followed suit in the guest book, commenting and signing as Madonna, Hillary Clinton, and Martha Stewart.

Visual artists have long made use of framing to ask audiences and spectators to see the creations within the frame as special. Marcel Duchamp, a French artist influenced by the Dadaists, coined the term "readymade" in 1915 to describe ordinary objects displayed as art objects. His most famous piece, "Fountain," signed with the pseudonym "R. Mutt," was a urinal submitted to a 1917 Society of Independent Artists gallery show.

Andy Warhol framed the Campbell's tomato soup can as art. Christo and Jeanne-Claude create environmental art, surrounding and adorning natural phenomena—like islands, buildings, and New York City's Central Park. These frames ask us to engage the physical world in a new way. Hargo and his cat created the Somerville Gates to parody Christo and Jeanne-Claude's "Gates" project.

"Found poetry" is still another example of framing ordinary writing as worthy of literary and critical attention. The creators of *Found Magazine* collect and publish "found stuff: love letters, birthday cards, kids' homework, to-do lists, ticket stubs, poetry on napkins, doodles—anything that gives a glimpse into someone else's life. Anything goes." The creators find poetry everywhere when framed that way.

"Overheard in New York" also relies on framing bits of overheard conversation in New York City. Publisher S. Morgan Friedman and editor Jenny Weiss collect contributions from thousands of New Yorkers who overhear bits of conversations, frame them as dialogue between characters, add a title, and post these new creations on their Web site and in their books. The winning entry for "Overheard at the Beach: Summer Special" reads:

And Can You Tuck? Says Here "Girls Get a Free Balloon."

Dad:	How old are you?
Teen boy:	Thirteen.
Dad:	How old are you?
Mom:	You know he's thirteen.
Dad:	It says here that if you're eleven or younger, you get in free . . . How old are you?
Teen:	Oh. Eleven.

—Roxy Deli
Overheard by: Kelsey
Headline by: Tom Dorey.

The years of archived texts are addictive.

Much research in communication involves the role of media in generating frames: How is a news event structured, explained, and interpreted by newspapers, television, and Internet outlets? Hard news? Human interest? An embedded journalist at the battlefront? Josh Greenberg and Graham Knight (2004) analyze newspaper accounts of Nike sweatshops on the Pacific Rim for how these stories transform social, political, and cultural issues into economic ones. This economic frame places blame on consumers of Nike products, rather than on the corporations. Television network news accounts of the Million Man March on Washington in October 1995 framed the event through the racial and political radicalism of Louis Farrakhan (Watkins 2001). The 1995 Calvin Klein jeans advertising campaign was framed as "kiddie porn" (Tucker 1998). Adbusters had a field day with this campaign.

The documentary film has received much attention as a genre framed as "true" through certain conventions: historical film footage, talking-head interviews, voice-over omniscient narrators. Bonnie Dow (2004) explores the first documentary film treatment of the women's liberation movement in the United States, aired in May of 1970. "Reality" television also frames ordinary people and events as dramas through conventions of the documentary and theatrical staging (Chvasta and Fassett 2003; Simpson 2003).

Frame Breaking, Confusion, and Slippage

If frames are generated through conventions of theatre, art, media, and film, then these same frames can be **broken**. In the theatre, when performers "break frame," they break the imaginary fourth wall—purposefully in direct address to the audience, and oftentimes accidentally, when things go wrong onstage. Autobiographies of stage performers are full of anecdotes of breaking frame onstage—either by performing too well when physical action becomes "real" or by cracking each other up in scenes. But here's an unusual frame break from the audience.

"Here's Love" at the Curran Theater, was five minutes into its second act Tues. night when a man in the third row suddenly leaped to his feet and positively hollered: "Migawd, I'm in the wrong theater!" The show stopped cold, cast convulsed, as he inched over to the aisle and ran out to "Camelot," at the next-door Geary. (quoted in Goffman 1974, 371)

Frames can also be deliberately broken for effect. Cartoonist Berkeley Breathed, creator of *Bloom County, Outland,* and a Sunday-edition *Opus,* has long complained that newspaper "frames" for cartoon strips are growing increasingly small, making the detailed work of cartoonists almost impossible to see. Jesse Jarnow (2003) writes of Breathed, "He regularly broke the fourth wall (or, in this case, the fifth panel), as when his characters threatened to strike if their space on the page was shrunk again. 'Bloom County's' absurdity meant that it seemed to melt the boundaries between the comics and the rest of the paper, broaching issues not traditionally associated with even the most experimental or political strips." Dutch artist M. C. Escher regularly breaks frame—with confusions about figure and ground in his drawings (MacLachlan and Reid 1994, 29). Aleksandra Wolska (2005, 92) describes a particularly fun frame-breaking technique in the opening sequence of the animated film *Who Framed Roger Rabbit?*

Roger participates in an absurd chain of events unleashed by Baby Herman, who reaches for a cookie jar on top of the refrigerator and manages to ignite an inferno. Roger begins his mission by rescuing the baby by tripping over a rolling pin (A), then getting baked in an oven (B), electrocuted (C), impaled by knives (D), and generally battered (E). Caught in a raging Goldbergian machine that annexes the everyday kitchen, Roger inhabits a space of near disaster. . . . The performative nature of this sequence comes into full view when we realize that all this uproar takes place on a movie set. Baby Herman, who a moment ago cooed melodiously, begins to swear and walks off the set shouting, "Until you people get it right, I will be in my trailer."

Erecting a frame through conventions of genre asks an audience to engage the performance in a particular way. Frame breaking, whether accidental or planned, is a way to call attention to the frame itself. Frame breaking as a Brechtian alienation technique will be surveyed in Chapter Eight, "Performing Resistance."

Frame **confusions** occur when some people are "in the know" about the reality of the frame, while others are not. "Candid Camera," "Punk'd," and practical jokes are typical of this kind of confusion. Ilana Harlow (1997) explores the practical joke frame at Irish wakes in which corpses are rigged to move in their coffins. Importantly, these practical jokes are not performed at wakes of people who died tragically or at children's wakes; instead, the jokes are preserved for wakes of old people who lived long lives and died of natural causes.

Orson Welles' radio drama "War of the Worlds" is probably the most famous example of frame confusion. Because some people missed the introduction to the program, they mistakenly interpreted the October 31, 1938, radio drama and its invasion of aliens from Mars as real. Scholars have explored this radio drama for how narrative can construct and frame reality, for studying the psychology of mass panic, and for Welles' "media sense" in manipulating the conventions of radio news reporting (J. Bruner 1991; Heyer 2003).

Contemporary "mockumentaries" deliberately play with frame confusion, employing the conventions of documentary film to "document" supposedly real people and events. *The Blair Witch Project* (Roscoe 2000), *Spinal Tap*, and *Bob Roberts* are films that invite discussions of the documentary frame even as they "mock" those conventions.

Still other frames can **slip**, taking deadly turns: sporting events and concerts become riots; peaceful political protests turn violent; training exercises in which people are really injured or killed are suddenly not what they appear to be. Hazing, in fraternities or in the military, often teeters dangerously on the edge of the play frame. Bateson (1972) claims that the frame for hazing is more often posed as a question, "Is this play?"

CAUGHT LOOKING

Framing Fiction as Reality and Reality as Fiction?

Choose one of the following film or television texts to analyze the framing devices employed. What conventions of narration, cinematography, and genre are employed to generate the frame? How do some of these texts engage in what Gregory Bateson (1972) calls "paradoxical framing," that is, "framing that is not really meant as this frame"?

Blair Witch Project

Spinal Tap

Bob Roberts

Nashville

The Truman Show

Team America

"Crank Yankers"

"Whose Line Is It Anyway?"

"The Colbert Report"

"The Daily Show with Jon Stewart"

"Cops"

"Survivor"

"The Apprentice"

"The Real World"

"America's Funniest Home Videos"

"The World's Funniest Animals"

"Animal Planet"

Constituting the Performance
Frame through Keying

Erving Goffman (1974) names the process by which a particular frame is invoked **keying**. He deliberately intends the musical analogy: In what "key" is a particular song played? Keys are specific codes, conventions, or language that signal or erect the frame around a communication event. Goffman (1974, 43–44) defines keying as "the set of conventions by which a given activity, one already meaningful in terms of some primary framework, is transformed into something patterned on this activity but seen by the participants to be something quite else."

Bert States (1996, 19) offers a good example of keying:

> I sometimes do an imitation of myself in the classroom to illustrate certain aspects of impersonation. I do not change my style or way of behaving, but I tell my students that I will now do an imitation of Bert States and then, after an appropriate pause (as a framing device), I go on being myself for twenty seconds or so. Then I bow and take a curtain call.

States keys the performance frame with both the direct phrase "I will now . . ." and the pause at the beginning; the bow at the end signals the end of the frame. Students complete the performance frame with their applause.

Goffman (1974) lists four major frames established through keying and some of their subsets: (1) **make-believe** (play, fantasy or daydreaming, dramatic scripting), (2) **contests** (sports and games), (3) **ceremonials** (social rituals like weddings, funerals, and investitures), and (4) **technical re-doings** (simulations and practices, demonstrations and exhibitions, rehearsals, group psychotherapy and role-playing).

While Goffman names *events* as keyings in the West, Richard Bauman enlarges the list from a range of studies by folklorists from around the world. Bauman (1977, 16) claims that

> each speech community will make use of a structured set of distinctive communicative means from among its resources of culturally conventionalized and culture-specific ways to key the performance frame, such that all communication that takes place within that frame is to be understood as a performance within that community.

Bauman lists seven common keys to the performance frame that go beyond event to include language elements and devices, delivery style and creativity, traditional ways of performing, and genre. Many of these keys overlap, and not all are evident in every performance.

1. **Special codes** are specialized language, often archaic or "old-fashioned," used only in a particular performance situation. These codes are immediately recognizable by the speech community. "Dearly beloved, we are gathered here today," for example, keys a contemporary, Christian wedding ceremony. "All rise" keys the arrival of the judge in a courtroom and the beginning of court proceedings.

2. **Figurative language** involves not just the words spoken, but the artistry and creativity of the performer. Some communities insist the figurative language of certain performances be consistent, "fixed," and accurate: "A bird in the hand is worth two in the bush" requires a fixed performance for the proverb to be both effective and understood. Other communities value new creations that demonstrate the performer's skill in manipulating figurative language. So Ice Cube changes the language to "A bird in the hand is worth more than the bush." These distinctions will be explored further in Chapter Three, "Performing Texts." Figurative language— whether fixed in words or creatively manipulated—often keys, or signals, the performance frame.

3. **Parallelism** involves systematically repeated elements of language: sounds, grammar, meaning, or structure. Poetry and speeches are often marked and signaled by parallel constructions. "I have a dream" organizes, through repetition of the phrase, Martin Luther King, Jr.'s famous speech.

4. **Special paralinguistic features** concern delivery style: *How* is the performance conventionally performed? Some performances are marked with particular styles of "rate, length, pause duration, pitch contour, tone of voice, loudness, and stress" (Bauman 1977, 20). Ghost stories told around a campfire, for example, are performed in a much different style than school announcements over an intercom system.

5. **Special formulae** announce genres of performance. Bauman lists two typical Western examples: "Once upon a time" to open a fairy tale, and "Did you hear the one about . . ." to introduce a joke.

6. **Appeal to tradition** recalls past ways of performing as a standard for evaluation by the audience. When someone says, "My grandfather told the story about . . .", that is both an appeal to conventional knowledge and wisdom and a signal that what will follow ought to be attended to as a performance.

The film *The Aristocrats* (2005) is a brilliant illustration of all of the above performance keys. One hundred stand-up comedians and comedy writers tell the *same* joke, inviting comparisons to jazz musicians' ability to "riff" on the same musical theme in very different and original ways. Please note, however, that this film is not for everyone. The language and situations depicted are extremely graphic and offensive to many, many standards of conduct. Some argue that this is precisely the goal of comedy.

7. **Disclaimer of performance** is "a surface denial" that what follows is a performance. How many speeches in classrooms begin with the phrase, "I'm not very good at giving speeches," or "I've never spoken to a group this big before"?

Bauman (1977) argues that this disclaimer does not disallow performance competence but is a "concession to standards of etiquette and decorum, where self-assertiveness is disvalued. In such situations, a disclaimer of performance serves both as a moral gesture, to counterbalance the power of performance to focus heightened attention on the performer, and a key to performance itself" (22).

Naming and delineating keys to the performance frame is an important vantage point for theories that ask, "How do we mark this as a performance?" Joseph Roach (2002, 35) claims there are "three questions that students of performance ought to be ready to pose of any event: 'When is it?' 'Where is it?' and 'What's happening?'" Keys and framing help us answer "What's happening?"

MAKE A LIST

Performance Keys

Utilizing Goffman's four categories of make-believe, contests, ceremonials, and technical re-doings, make a list of typical keys that signal the frame for each event. How do language and performance come together to mark the event as a performance in this community?

Constituting Performance through the Performer

This chapter began with a list of performers: kindergartners, ballet dancers, a quarterback, job interviewers and interviewees, Juneteenth celebrants, even the officiate and mourners at a funeral. Erving Goffman (1959, 101) claims that at a funeral, the "corpse" is the "star" of the show whose job is to "stay in character as someone who is in a deep sleep." Given that most performers are not dead, what makes a performer a performer? What does it feel like to perform, and how is this "feeling" different from ordinary experience?

One reigning conception of a performer is one who manifests **performance consciousness**. This consciousness, or *reflexive awareness of oneself as performing*, works on many levels. First, the performer is aware of the frame and pays attention to the relationships among performer, frame, and audience. For Richard Schechner (1990, 30), a key difference between "ordinary behavior" and "acting" is this reflexive awareness: "Professional actors are aware that they are acting" within the frame of the theatrical event.

A second level in performance consciousness involves a kind of inner dialogue within the performer herself. Schechner describes this consciousness as an interior distance between "me" and "not me," a tension between one's perceived sense of an ordinary self and this different self who is "on." Schechner (2002b, 28) offers these examples:

> "me behaving as if I were someone else," or "as I am told to do," or "as I have learned." Even if I feel myself wholly to be myself, acting independently, only a little investigating reveals that the units of behavior that comprise "me" were not invented by "me." Or, quite the opposite, I may experience being "beside myself," "not myself," or "taken over" as in a trance. The fact that there are multiple "me's" in every person is not a sign of derangement but the way things are.

Still a third level of performance consciousness involves how a performer "pushes" emotions, ideas, and attitudes for the sake of an audience. Michael Kirby (1995, 47) describes effective public speakers who

> energetically [project] ideas, emotions and elements of their personality, underlining and theatricalizing it for the sake of an audience. . . . This does not mean that the speakers are false or do not believe what they are saying. It merely means that they are selecting and projecting an element of character—emotion—to the audience.

Selection and projection involve both the performer's choices and the performer's reactions to audience involvement with those choices. Kristin Langellier and Eric Peterson (2004, 164–65) discuss Bateson's concepts of feedback from the audience and calibration—the performer's "continuous changes in her or his performance"—as adaptive actions in online storytelling.

Performance consciousness is not the same as performance self-consciousness, or stage fright. Yet it is often through the experience of the latter that we can create theories of the former. Ronald J. Pelias (1997, 25) writes an interior dialogue in "Confessions of Apprehensive Performer" and captures many different layers of awareness, framing, and audience involved in performance consciousness:

Voice 1:   I can do it. I'm standing here.

Voice 2:   They're watching. You're fixing your clothes! Fixing clothes is just a nervous habit.

Voice 1:   Alright, I've stopped.

Voice 2:   So what are you going to do now?

Voice 1:   Begin.

Voice 2:   Well, go ahead.

Voice 1:   But they're looking.

Voice 2:   Of course they're looking. Did you expect them to come with bags over their heads?

Voice 1:   No.

Voice 2:   Well, get started.

Voice 1:   Okay, okay. Let me fix my notes.

Voice 2:   You'll probably think you lost a page.

Voice 1:   Did I?

Voice 2:   No, but you really need to begin.

Voice 1:   Let me take a deep breath. Then I'll start.

Voice 2:   We're waiting.

Voice 1:   "Ladies and gentlemen . . . "

Voice 2:   Are you sure you wanted to use the word "ladies"?

In their analysis of the subjective experiences onstage of rock-and-roll musicians, Harris M. Berger and Giovanna P. Del Negro (2002, 72) claim that "good musicians know how to control the 'talking voice' inside their head, quieting reflexive thought and losing themselves in the flow of sound or invoking that reflexive voice to solve problems on stage." The idea of "losing" oneself in performance can be thought of as the opposite of performance consciousness, an acute awareness of that "talking voice."

Performance consciousness is not an easy idea to articulate, but all of us experience it when we are (1) aware of ourselves as "on" and work to control that "talking voice," (2) aware of the audience and its power of evaluation, (3) aware of the frame that creates that relationship, and (4) "pushing" ourselves to adapt to the situation and audience effectively and appropriately.

ACT OUT

What's Inside Your Head?

When the author described her awareness of performance consciousness, she described this voice as "the director" who constantly comments and editorializes—not unlike Pelias above—on the performance situation. One student responded to that analogy, "I don't have a director. I have a whole committee!"

Write your own interior script to capture the tensions you feel when you are experiencing performance consciousness. Can you name these different "voices" in your head? Hone this text into a two-minute performance.

READ MORE ABOUT IT

Nuit of the Living Dead

David Sedaris is a well-known writer and commentator on NPR's "This American Life." In his essay "Nuit of the Living Dead" (2004, 254–57), Sedaris is living in a beautiful, isolated old farmhouse in rural France. His partner is out of town, and Sedaris has been assembling a model of the Visible Man (a gift purchased for a nephew and then kept). He hears noises in the attic and investigates. Sedaris finds a mouse mortally injured in a mousetrap and decides to drown it "to put it out of its misery." While he is on the front porch in the middle of the night, with a bucket full of water and a broomstick to keep the mouse underwater, a van of lost tourists stops at Sedaris' house. They ask for directions. In the portion of the essay here, Sedaris details his growing performance consciousness of his house, its objects, and his own actions through the eyes of the lost tourist.

An unexpected and unknown visitor allows you to see a familiar place as if for the very first time. I'm thinking of the meter reader rooting through the kitchen at eight A.M., the Jehovah's Witness suddenly standing in your living room. "Here," they seem to say. "Use *my* eyes. The focus is much keener." I had always thought of our main room as cheerful, but walking through the door,

(Continued)

(Continued)

I saw that I was mistaken. It wasn't dirty or messy, but like being awake when all decent people are fast asleep, there was something slightly suspicious about it. I looked at the Visible Man spread out on the table. The pieces lay in the shadow of a large taxidermied chicken that seemed to be regarding them, determining which organ might be the most appetizing. The table itself was pleasant to look at—oak and hand-hewn—but the chairs surrounding it were mismatched and in various states of disrepair. On the back of one hung a towel marked with the emblem of the Los Angeles County Coroner's Office. It had been a gift, not bought personally, but still it was there, leading the eye to an adjacent daybed, upon which lay two copies of a sordid true-crime magazine I purportedly buy to help me with my French. The cover of the latest issue pictured a young Belgian woman, a camper beaten to death with a cinder block. IS THERE A SERIAL KILLER IN YOUR REGION? the headline asked. The second copy was opened to the cross-word puzzle I'd attempted earlier in the evening. One of the clues translated to "female sex organ," and in the space provided I had written the word for vagina. It was the first time I had ever answered a French crossword puzzle question, and in celebration I had marked the margins with bright exclamation points.

There seemed to be a theme developing, and everything I saw appeared to substantiate it: the almanac of guns and firearms suddenly prominent on the bookshelf, the meat cleaver lying for no apparent reason upon a photograph of our neighbor's grandchild.

"It's more of a summer home," I said, and the man nodded. He was looking now at the fireplace, which was slightly taller than he was. I tend to see only the solid stone hearth and high oak mantel, but he was examining the meat hooks hanging from the clotted black interior.

"Every other house we passed was dark," he said. "We've been driving I think for hours, just looking for someone who was awake. We saw your lights, the open door . . ." His words were familiar from innumerable horror movies, the wayward soul announcing himself to the count, the mad scientist, the were-wolf, moments before he changes.

"I hate to bother you, really."

"Oh, it's no bother, I was just drowning a mouse. Come in, please."

"So," the man said, "you say you have a map?"

I had several, and pulled the most detailed from a drawer containing, among other things, a short length of rope and a novelty pen resembling a dismem-bered finger. Where does all this stuff come from? I asked myself. There's a low cabinet beside the table, and pushing aside the delicate skull of a baby monkey, I spread the map upon the surface, identifying the road outside our house and then the village the man was looking for. It wasn't more than ten miles away. The route was fairly simple, but still I offered him the map, knowing he would feel better if he could refer to it on the road.

"Oh no," he said, "I couldn't," but I insisted, and watched from the porch as he carried it down the stairs and into the idling van. "If you have any problems, you know where I live," I said. "You and your friends can spend the night here if you like. Really, I mean it. I have plenty of beds." The man in the tracksuit waved good-bye, and then he drove down the hill disappearing behind the neighbor's pitched roof.

Constituting Performance through Audience

While entire industries—like public relations, marketing, and advertising—are dedicated to understanding audiences as consumers, performance theories have often left audiences undertheorized. Linda Park-Fuller (2003, 290) maintains that "performance scholars privilege *performers*' actions, performance *texts*, and only generalized performance *contexts*. . . ." When audience is the focus, however, most theory concentrates on audience roles and levels of participation as a group, and "personal responsiveness, somatic engagement, and cognitive analysis" as individuals (Pelias and VanOosting 1987, 222). Theory questions involving audience are "Who is the audience?" "What is expected of the audience?" and "How are these conventions enacted?"

Pelias and VanOosting (1987) characterize audience participation on a continuum, always bound by cultural and historical conventions that place the audience in relationship to performers, texts, and events (see Figure 2.1).

The **inactive receiver** audience is typical of many theatrical and musical events in the West, as well as many formal ceremonies—sacred services like funerals and weddings—in which conventions dictate that audiences remain passive receivers of the performance. Cynthia Ward (1994, 281) notes that this audience role is also typical of much film where the audience involvement is expected to be an "isolated, interiorized, silent 'reading' of the film." Kristin Langellier (1983, 34) describes audiences at this end of the spectrum as "forming a background of pure silence that allows other voices to emerge."

Respondent/active audiences are invited to complete the cues offered onstage, from the playing field, or at the alter—with laughter, applause, gasps, cheers, call and response, prayers, and so forth. When John Lennon introduced the song "Twist and Shout" at the Beatles' first royal command performance in 1963, he invited—with

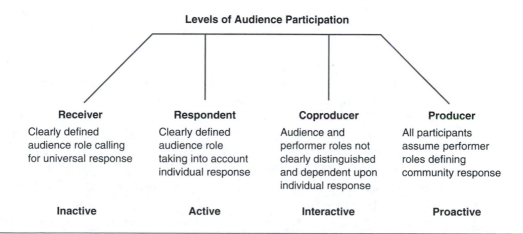

Figure 2.1   Levels of Audience Participation

SOURCE: From "A Paradigm for Performance Studies," by Ronald J. Pelias and James VanOosting. *Quarterly Journal of Speech* (1987). Reprinted by permission of Taylor & Francis Ltd., http://www.informaworld.com.

SOURCE: From the W.E.B. Dubois Collection. African American Photographs Assembled for the 1900 Paris Exposition. Library of Congress, Prints & Photographs Division [reproduction number LC-USZ62-38623].

no small degree of sarcasm—the audience to respond in class-bound ways: "For our last number, I'd like to ask your help. The people in the cheaper seats, clap your hands, and the rest of you, if you'd just rattle your jewelry" (Spitz 2005, 434).

Historians are quick to point out that theatre audiences before 1900 in the West had to be disciplined in "polite" and appropriate responses. Neil Blackadder (2000, 123) notes that "for most of theatre's history, audiences have usually talked during performances, often shouted, and quite frequently responded in an even more forthright manner, particularly if they were displeased." Tracy C. Davis details the history of the famous Peter-Pan-reviving-Tinker-Bell scene, "Clap if you believe in fairies!" in the original 1904 production of the play. Davis (2005, 65) notes that in the playscript, J. M. Barrie coached the actors, "Many clap, some don't, a few hiss. . . . But Tink is saved." For the adult, Edwardian theatre audience, Davis contends that hissing was a typical response to melodrama and a negative reaction to the sentimentality of Barrie's play.

Active responses can run the gamut from polite applause to extremely active participation. Several popular films, like *Rocky Horror Picture Show*, *Mommy Dearest*, and even *The Wizard of Oz* and *Mary Poppins*, have engendered cult followings in which audiences dress up like characters, imitate actions on the screen, and sing along.

In the third level of audience participation, both performers and audiences are seen as **interactive coproducers** in creating the performance event. Playback Theatre takes this interaction as central to its method: "Playback Theatre is an audience-interactive, improvisational performance form in which audience members tell stories from their lives and then watch those stories enacted on the spot" (Park-Fuller 2003, 291). Other "non-scripted" theatre forms of interactive coproduction include experimental theatre, educational theatre, comic-satiric theatre, populist community theatre, therapeutic theatre, and clowning (Fox 1986, 56–57). Joni Jones (1993, 246) finds improvisation central to performance work that utilizes African-based theatrical strategies based on interactive coproduction: "Improvisation creates a vitality, spontaneity, and participation not commonly found in scripted texts. Improvisation also chips away at barriers that exist among the participant observers and between the participant observers and performers."

Stacy Holman Jones' study (2007) of torch singers pays special attention to audience-performer coparticipation as **reciprocity**. Reciprocity is the idea that a performer will meet her audience halfway in creating the experience of the performance (hooks 1995, 221). Reciprocity refuses to construct an audience as a group of passive, distant observers (Elam 1997, 78). Instead, reciprocity implicates audiences in the creation of the performance. When Lena Horne performs, her road manager Ralph Harris describes the give-and-take:

> She "works on a crowd's insides, until the crowd is giving her as much as she gives the crowd. . . . She is not singing at them, and they realize they've got to give something back or its no dice. She's crystallizing something for them that needs *their* help." (quoted in Haskins 1984, 36)

Horne's audience recognizes this challenge and, through reciprocity—whether it be rapt attention, singing along, or thunderous applause—actively fulfills a responsibility to "confirm what is happening" in the performance (Elam 1997, 112).

Cynthia Ward (1994) analyzes the West African concert party—a popular form of entertainment that combines music, song, poetry, drama, and comedy—for its decidedly interactive, proactive, and inclusive conception of audience that runs counter to Western reception theories that focus on the artistic product. At concert parties, audience members wander into the performance space—an open-air bar or a neighborhood gathering area—and "the performance begins gradually" with music and comic monologues (282). Children and babies are never excluded but are welcomed as part of the community that participates actively in creating and evaluating the performances:

> Not acknowledging a "fourth wall," audience members shout admonishments and encouragements to the characters and loudly discuss their character and behavior. The audience's active response is encouraged by the actors, who are rewarded, not for "good acting," but for the virtue or suffering of their characters, when individual audience members come up to the "stage" to give them money. (282)

Nor do audience members applaud at the end, but Ward claims they "seem to take the performance with them back into the streets and real life, never having left those realms at all. Throughout the preparation and performance, the boundaries between play and real life, audience and performer, are called into question" (283).

Street performances and processional performances also depend on the interactivity of audience members who must travel with performers to see the show, in turn blurring their everyday worlds with the created performance space (Haedicke 2006). The popular children's book series *Choose Your Own Adventure* is a good example of interactive coproduction. Hypertext has also been conceptualized as interactive coproduction between computer users and screens (Fenske 2004). Much

SOURCE: Photograph by Frank Caico. Copyright © 2006 by Frank Caico.

online performance requires this interactive coproduction and will be surveyed in Chapter Nine, "Performing Technologies. "

Finally, **proactive producers** completely blur the distinctions between audience and performers as everyone comes together in time and space to create the event. Community and festival celebrants at the Juneteenth barbecue, for example, are proactive producers of the performance event. Performance scholars have studied Yoruba festivals (Jones 2002), Moroccan open-air markets (Kapchan 1995), even the Las Vegas strip (Wickstrom 2001; Wood 2005) as performances that are proactively produced by audiences and performers alike.

The divisions among these kinds of audience responses are permeable—often within the same performance. Performances in the Neo-Chautauqua movement involve all the levels of audience participation. Drawing from the nineteenth-century U.S. tradition of the Chautauqua "entertaining" lecture, today's scholar/performer creates a lecture performance of a historical personage. Richard Bello (1997) details how the performance begins with a twenty-five to forty minute monologue. Like any dramatic monologue, audiences should respond to the cues provided in actively responsive ways. Then an improvised question-and-answer period ensues with the performer still in character. This interactive coproduction relies on the performer's ability to stay in character and in history: "presuming no knowledge which that historical figure could not reasonably be expected to have known." Finally, the performer "breaks frame" to answer questions as a scholar concerning issues "such as historical research about the character, script writing, and performance techniques" (187).

An audience, whether of one or one thousand, is always bound by conventions of evaluation, activity, response, time, and space. Richard Schechner (1988a, 194) argues that all audiences "license" the performance and can "at any time, ratify or withdraw that license." Most audiences, he notes, don't know their own power.

THEORY MEETS WORLD

Audiences Are the Wild Card

Performance Studies professor Christie Logan (2005) attended three performances of Mercilee M. Jenkins' *Menopause & Desire or 452 Positions on Love*. Logan analyzes how the three performances were distinct: "I'm struck with the ways in which the intersections of performer performing, place and context, and audience generated different dynamics, different experiences, and perhaps different meanings as the text and scripted actions were articulated in each site" (282).

The first performance, in November 2002, was part of a three-day performance festival attended by college students and their teachers from around the United States. Festivals are exhilarating for their creativity and camaraderie, "where we collaborate on impulse with near strangers, and it seems possible to create anything. I think there is a special character to a festival community" (288). The festival was small enough for all participants to attend all events—workshops, discussions, performances—and all the work was conducted in the same big room with a raised platform stage. When Jenkins performed on the second night, Logan relates that

> the performance space by this point was familiar and malleable, a truly transformable space layered with ghostings of all the performance work we'd done there. . . . The performance was magical, wondrous, and thrilling for us all. This was one of those peak performance experiences, where we all rode waves of energy and emotion flowing back and forth, weaving the audience and performer into the same action. We—audience and performer—seemed in perfect concert as Lee moved us through the many emotional arcs and re-membered, re-embodied moments of this piece. (283)

The second performance of *Menopause and Desire* was in November 2003, at the National Communication Association convention. The room was huge, cavernous, and typical of hotel convention rooms. The raised platform was twice as big as the festival space. This audience was comprised of Performance Studies professors and graduate students, "a motivated and knowledgeable audience, some experienced artists—writers, performers, and directors" (284). "Here in this space," Logan writes,

> I experienced the emotional progression as more kaleidoscopic, circular or perhaps helical, and this requires a motivated and reflective audience. The convention audience was up to the task; once again, the audience was engaged and coalesced into a collective. Our responses were organic, and the energy flowed between performer and audience; there seemed to be a unity of focus and a willingness to join the performer in the space between. The chuckles, outright laughter, silences, and stillness seemed to me to become more collective as the performance progressed. (285)

The third performance, a campus venue in a small music recital hall, did not solicit magic, collectivity, or engagement, despite the fact that the acoustics were "fantastic" and the space felt "intimate and theatrical." College students

(Continued)

(Continued)

> in their twenties were dispersed throughout the space, intermixed with middle-aged women from the campus feminist network. Logan writes of this audience:

>> their participation seemed to be more intellectual and detached than either of the other venues. Though we weren't in a classroom, the zeitgeist made it one. As in a traditional lecture-style classroom, the audience was silent; this silence was occasionally broken by laughter, but it had the effect of an anomaly, perhaps even an intrusion, and faded quickly. . . . There was no fidgeting—they were clearly paying attention—but the trajectories, the arcs of this attention were plural, varied, individual. (286, 288)

> The subject matter—love, loss, aging, regret—was difficult for this young audience. After the performance, Jenkins commented, "I felt all alone out there." Logan concludes, "Indeed, it seemed she was. We could not construct the space between, we could not seem to bridge the gap between performer and audience—even audience and audience. The spaces between these disparate elements were intact and static" (286).

> Logan concludes,

>> The old theatre adage is still apt: The audience is always the wild card. We can predict but can't control what they will do. We also know there is an inherent suspense in the progressive present of performance. Once we enter that space, as performer and audience, anything can happen. We can succeed and we can fail, in any ratio or combination. We can certainly learn from successes, failure, and mixed results. But most importantly, we have to try. (288)

Rethinking Performance

As groundbreaking as Bauman's conception of performance was in 1977, he readily admits that he didn't pay sufficient attention to gender dynamics in his three-pronged theory of the "nature of performance" (Bauman 2002). Patricia E. Sawin (2002, 31) argues that performance competence and audience evaluation are especially problematic for women performers in patriarchial cultures. "Display" (Look at me! I'm on!) is a loaded term: Bauman's theory does not account for power or "explain the ways women are discouraged from or penalized for performing" (41). Sawin argues that when performance is framed without attention to gender, "something . . . is paved over, however—the personal motivation for and cost of making that commitment, as well as the political history and cultural situation that make stepping into that frame and claiming esthetic competence more or less attractive, difficult, or even imaginable" for women (36).

Bateson's concept of framing has also been critiqued by Gale MacLachlan and Ian Reid (1994, 44) for its lack of attention to power and authority: "The struggle to control the frame" is "a struggle to control meaning." MacLachlan and Reid critique Goffman's frame analysis for its attention to microprocesses among individuals, rather than macroprocesses of political frames—like gender, race, ethnicity, and class. Because of Goffman's singular attention, Goffman "helps to foster an illusion of individual autonomy" (60). Norman Denzin and Charles M. Keller (1981, 59) find Goffman's categories for frames to be "frozen" and singular, "ignor[ing] the multiple realities of the different individuals in the situation. Self-reflexive and self-aware individuals do experience more than one thing at the same time."

In his study of audience, Herbert Blau (1985a) critiques "the participation mystique" of Happenings in the 1960s, noting that audiences do not always respond as invited. Instead, implied consent (both audience and performers agreeing to be in the same place at the same time) and the potential for reciprocal, physical touch are more important foundational concepts for audience in live performance. Blau also claims that audience—as representative ideal—is a relatively new concept introduced in the eighteenth century. For theatre historians' study of audience, "That is the problem we have in trying to reimagine for performance what the drama of other periods must have been like *then*" (Blau 1985b, 205).

Studying performance through its constitutive elements is difficult—like trying to reimagine the original recipe while tasting the dish. Even if we can name all the ingredients, the experience of performance—intricately interwoven competencies, awarenesses, evaluations, and heightened experiences generated through and among frames, performers, and audiences—is always more than the sum of those parts. Elizabeth Fine (1984, 85–86) summarizes the difficulty of delineating constitutive elements of performance:

> [I]f we are to avoid the pitfall of murdering in order to dissect, that is, of reifying a dynamic process into a static form whose component parts somehow explain or equal that process, we must analyze performance as it is experienced. By analogy, although the skeletal remains of a human might help us distinguish it from non-humans, we would not claim that by understanding these structural features that we understand what it is to be human.

The challenge of describing performance is ultimately the challenge of describing human experience in its lived, embodied, participatory, and always dynamic processes. For theorists in this chapter, performance is multifaceted, demanding competence from performers and evaluation from audiences to make available a heightened, self-aware, and reflexive experience, separate from "ordinary" life. Simultaneously, constituting performance involves marking the event through framing, signaling the frame through keying, and interpreting the communication interactions that occur within these boundaries by asking and answering the question, "What is it that is happening here?"

The answer to that question, however, will be different for kindergartners, Juneteenth celebrants, high school quarterbacks, mourners, job applicants, and dancers with the Kirov Ballet. "Rethinking" constitutive elements, frames, performers, and audiences means rethinking how power always operates in performance—for gender, for "controlling the frame" and its meanings, for audience evaluation, for writing history, and for theory building itself. While a "strong" theory may be generalizable, simple, and accurate, what operations of power in performance are glossed over? Theories that account for commonalities among kindergartners, Juneteenth celebrants, high school quarterbacks, mourners, job applicants, and ballet dancers can also work to account for important and consequential differences.

CHAPTER 3

Performing Texts

Theory in Perspective: What Is a Text?

Anthropologist Clifford Geertz (1980) details three important critical orientations, or analogies for social interaction, that developed in the twentieth century: life as a game, life as drama, and life as text. The game analogy will be covered in Chapter Six, "Performing Social Roles," and life as drama anchors Chapter Four, "Performing Drama." For this chapter, the central analogy is "life as text."

How do we come to understand the world as a text? The movement in human history from orality to literacy is important to understanding (1) how we are "text-centered" in print culture, (2) how we are taught to interpret texts, and (3) how "text building" is central to the work of a number of areas of knowledge production: "literature, history, law, music, politics, psychology, trade, even war and peace" (Geertz 1980, 177).

The discipline of Speech has traditionally studied texts embodied in performances: the speeches and sermons given by powerful orators. What makes an effective oration? In antiquity and the Middle Ages, rhetoricians focused on tropes: the figures of speech, turns of phrases, and commonplaces that build effective arguments to move an audience to action. For example, the *chiasmus* is a trope that reverses the order of a phrase the second time it is said. John Kennedy, at his presidential inauguration in 1961, used this ancient form: "Ask not what your country can do for you; ask what you can do for your country."

Tropes, however, "do not walk in by themselves" (Campbell 1982, 121) but are embodied in performance by the orator. Aristotle, too, recognized the relationship between the text of a play and its embodiment onstage in performance. Plot, character, and thought concern the play, or text, itself. Spectacle, song, and diction involve getting the text on "its feet" in and through its performance. In Richard Bauman's performance keys, four of the seven (special codes, figurative language, parallelism, and special formula) are text-centered; special paralinguistic features, appeals to tradition, and disclaimers get these texts "on their feet" through embodiment in performance.

The relationship *between text and performance* is central to many academic disciplines that study performance. Text-centered theories of performance necessarily feature "what" questions: What is performed? What are the conventions of this text—on the page and in performance? And what is the relationship of the text to its uses—as canon, intertextuality, and objects? When we study texts, our engagements, understandings, and uses of texts are intricately tied to the medium that enables that text: orality, the printed page, television, radio, film, and the computer screen. Because communication scholars have been interested in texts in all these media, this chapter takes a close look at how performance theories have explored definitions, conventions, and embodiments of texts.

Humans and Symbol Use: Text Me Later. OK?

The vibration of the cell phone in your pocket is an invitation. If you're sitting in a lecture hall or driving in heavy traffic, please ignore it. If the time and place are appropriate, however, you'll most likely dig the phone out of your pocket, glance at the screen, read the text message "UR L8," and choose among a variety of ways to act. Do you then curse? Laugh? Roll your eyes?

For many people today, this is a simple and ubiquitous moment in the day, but it also involves **symbol use that is situated, mediated, learned, and enacted.** Symbol use is a uniquely human endeavor. While many ethologists argue that animals communicate in complex ways, only humans communicate in *symbols*—representations that are intricately various, generative, and infinite in their combinations. These symbol systems are always *situated in contexts* bound by history, culture, institutions, and ideologies. Symbol use is always in some way a *mediation:* sound, print, images, pixels, and digital code are all media, or tools, by which the symbols are coded and transmitted. Symbol systems are *taught and learned.* Shakespearean sonnets, musical scores, architects' blueprints, and "leet" on the pager screen are symbols that must be learned to be read and interpreted as meaningful. And, finally, symbols are *enacted by people* who use them for a variety of purposes.

SOURCE: Photograph by Todd Kravos.

James Kinneavy (1971, 39–40) compares language to a window to explore the many uses humans make of symbols:

Language is like a windowpane. I may throw bricks at it to vent my feelings about something; I may use a chunk of it to chase away an intruder; I may use it to mirror or explore reality; and I may use a stained-glass windowpane to call attention to itself. Windows can be used expressively, persuasively, referentially, and artistically.

Glancing at the screen of your phone is complex indeed. To begin to explore how the text message "UR L8" is symbol use that is situated, mediated, learned, and enacted, we need to begin thousands of years ago.

From Orality to the Page to the Screen

Long before the written word, information was stored in bodies, in cultural memories, and in oral traditions, enacted only in their performances. Walter Ong (1982) traces the ways that orality is a technology: Valuable cultural information is available *only* in sound, in bodies and performances, and in fixed, formulaic oral phrasings that aid memory. The knowledge stored in bodies was passed on, generation to generation, through performance—face-to-face, participatory, immediate, and empathetic.

Ong maintains that the way a culture stores and retrieves its important information is intricately tied to how individuals in that culture think. He details three kinds of thought, or consciousness, tied to cultural knowledge. These three kinds of thought, *mnemonic, chirographic,* and *typographic,* are important for understanding how texts have become the preeminent means and ends for understanding in the literate world.

Mnemonic Thought: Thinking Memorably

Mnemonic thought is based on *memory*. In this system, you only know what you can remember. Most cultures of the world have been (and continue to be) oral cultures. Ong (1982, 7) notes that of tens of thousands of languages spoken across the world, only 106 have written forms. Out of approximately 3,000 languages spoken today, only 78 have produced a written literature. While *Homo sapiens* has been around for 50,000 years, the earliest dated script is only from 6,000 years ago.

How do people in oral cultures manage without writing? Ong answers, they "think memorable thoughts." He offers these examples of how thought must be shaped to be memorable:

> Thought must come into being in heavily rhythmic, balanced patterns, in repetitions or antithesis, in alliterations and assonances, in epithetic and other formulary expressions, in standard thematic settings (the assembly, the meal, the duel, the hero's "helper," and so on), in proverbs which are constantly heard by everyone so that they come to mind readily and which themselves are patterned for retention and ready recall. (34)

Mnemonic thought is *nested in sound,* not in words on a page. Sound is immediate and important. Ong writes, "A hunter can see a buffalo, smell, taste, and touch a buffalo when the buffalo is completely inert, even dead, but if he hears a buffalo, he had better watch out: something is going on" (32). Words are invested with great power in oral cultures: Laws, history, and religion exist only in their repeated sayings and performances in appropriate contexts. "The spoken word is always an event," writes Ong (75).

Oral formulas for memory are never just decorative but are instrumental for remembering. Rhyme, rhythm, repetition, parallelism, word clusters, "stock" phrases, formulas, and mnemonic devices keep cultural information intact. John Kennedy's chiasmus recalled at the beginning of this chapter is an example that makes Ong's point: How many other phrases from that inaugural address do we recall so easily? The chiasmus is powerfully memorable precisely because of its formulaic phrasing.

Ong lists these familiar sayings: "Red in the morning, the sailor's warning; red in the night, the sailors delight. Divide and conquer. To err is human, to forgive is divine. . . . The clinging vine. The sturdy oak" (35). The information embedded in these sayings is crucial for a culture's work, law, ethics, and aesthetics, enacted daily in their performances.

"Rules" of Oral Expression

The experience of **primary orality**, or the *orality of a culture untouched by reading and writing,* is extremely difficult for literate people—so steeped in the page—to grasp. But we often feel the pull of oral expression when we write. English teachers critique precisely those moments in writing when we "sound" like we're talking. Ong (1982) lists four characteristics of "oral based expression" that are specifically devalued in writing.

1. **Repetition and redundancy.** How often has the exclamation "This is redundant!" appeared in the margin of your paper? There is no need to repeat on the page because a reader can reread. Yet redundancy is crucial to oral communication. Imagine an orator in ancient Greece speaking to a thousand people, long before electronic amplification carried his voice. How many times would this speaker need to repeat himself to be heard and understood by all? Moreover, this orator's ability to talk—without hesitations, without long pauses, while thinking on his feet—was highly valued. "Rhetoricians were to call this *copia*" (41), a fluency in speaking achieved in and through redundancy.

2. **Stock phrases, word clusters, and formulas.** So important in orality for keeping information intact, stock phrases are considered "clichés" in writing to be avoided, as the joke goes, "like the plague." Writing values newness, freshness, and originality. The originality in oral cultures, however, stems from new uses and applications of traditional materials: "formulas and themes are reshuffled rather than supplanted with new materials" (42).

3. **Additive connectors.** Much oral expression tends to connect thoughts additively through the use of the word "and." Listen closely to any story told out loud. You'll hear the narrator link the story elements like this: "and . . . and

then . . . and. . . ." Writing values organization that prioritizes and subordinates—like an outline's headings and subheadings. A story written down will work very hard to replace "and" with a range of other connectives: "*First* this happened. *While* that was going on. . . . Next. . . . Then. . . . Finally. . . .*"

4. **Concreteness.** Oral expression is close to the human life world. Proverbs are full of real, tangible things like birds, bushes, stitches, and cooks. Writing, however, encourages abstractions and enables analysis of those abstractions. The abstractions and analysis typical of philosophy, science, and mathematics were only possible, according to Ong, because of writing.

Learning to perform in an oral culture, however, relies on participation and apprenticeship: There are no training manuals. Isidore Okpewho (1992) details the formal and informal training of oral artists in tribes across Africa who perform hundreds of verses of praise songs, oral histories, and divination rites. "How is the poet able to retain so much text in memory and perform steadily without faltering?" Okpewho asks. For the performers of Yoruba hunters' chants,

To this question there is usually a twofold reply. First, practice makes perfect: constant repetition helps the artist to master the text so well that the chances of error are drastically reduced. Second, the chanters admit that they make use of various kinds of medicinal charms (called isoye) which aid in the retention of memory. (Okpewho 1992, 227)

Practice, repetition, memory, and retention are central to oral traditions that only exist in performance. Lee Hudson (1980, 33) writes of epic Homeric traditions, "No text existed apart from its sounding, and no epic was less than the artful performance a singer afforded it. Composition, rather than being an independent art, was the art *in* performance."

MAKE A LIST

What Can You Remember?

Much of the cultural information you store and retrieve was learned in and through performance. Make a list of examples of each of the following categories, and then analyze how these texts were taught, remembered, and performed. What oral formulas of rhyme, rhythm, repetition, alliteration, assonance, and word clusters aid your memory?

nursery rhymes

secular oaths, pledges

religious prayers

mnemonic devices

(Continued)

(Continued)

> proverbs
>
> children's songs/rhymes
>
> advertising slogans
>
> clichés
>
> tongue twisters

Chirographic Thought: Thinking Alone

Chirographic thought is based on *handwriting*. Humans began representing the world not in sound but in visual symbols thousands of years ago. The earliest writing is traced to the Sumerians in Mesopotamia around 3500 B.C.E.; Egyptian hieroglyphics date to 3000 B.C.E., Chinese script to 1500 B.C.E., and Aztec script to 1400 C.E. (Ong 1982, 84).

SOURCE: Photograph by Jonah Keegan, Mitaka, Japan. Copyright © 2005 by Jonah Keegan.

Early writing systems were often pictographic, representing things in pictures or stylistic representations. Pictographic systems are very large, requiring thousands of characters to write something down. The K'anghsi dictionary of Chinese, dated

1716 C.E., has 40,545 characters (Ong 1982, 87). With the invention of true alphabets, symbols did not represent things, but sounds. The English alphabet has 26 characters, a very elegant system compared with the thousands of characters required in a pictographic system.

The earliest manuscripts were created on papyrus, and then vellum—animal skins—and rolled. "The parchment codex (or book, as we term it today)" triumphed "over antiquity's roll format: almost always rectangular with the long axis running vertically, the book can be said to derive 'naturally' from the rectangular shape of the animal skin" (Shailor 1999, 9). These books were meticulously hand-copied by scribes and elaborately decorated in gold and paint by artists. One scribe could work for twenty years copying one book.

Ong maintains that creating words on a page, rather than out loud in speech, enabled consciousness that values analysis, visualization, and isolation. How? First, handwriting slows down thought and speech. Most people write at one tenth the speed of speech. Handwriting enables slow creation of words, pondering, mulling, trying out different ideas (their order, their exact phrasing) on the page. Oral communication, however, is immediate and irreversible.

Second, writing "locks words into a visual field." If we are native speakers of English, most of us *see* the letter "A"—perhaps in red with a shiny apple next to it—when we *hear* the sound ā. This association of sign and thing is also a reduction of sensation and experience to the visual. This reduction is especially evident in Western conceptions of time—as linear, as the face of a clock, as divisible into units. For an oral culture, words only exist in sound, not in the visual.

Third, writing "interiorizes" thought by making it private and solitary. "Oral communication," Ong maintains,

> unites people in groups. Writing and reading are solitary activities that throw the psyche back on itself. A teacher speaking to a class which he feels and which feels itself as a close-knit group, finds that if the class is asked to pick up its textbooks and read a given passage, the unity of the group vanishes as each person enters into his or her private lifeworld. (69)

Ong argues that chirographic thought was the beginning of thinking that moves consciousness from the concrete and immediate to abstract analysis, that interiorizes and visualizes thought, and that isolates people from each other.

Moving from orality to the page means that, for the first time, we conceive of a text as separate from its enactment. Betsy Bowden (1982) analyses two performances of Bob Dylan's song "Hard Rain." When Dylan was asked in an interview if he could single out any album tracks of his that were particularly good, he asked: "As songs or as performances?" This distinction is impossible in primary orality: Songs only exist in their enactments, not on the page. Studying "Hard Rain" on the page is a slow, visual, and private process. Experiencing "Hard Rain" in performance is immediate, participatory, and communal.

Typographic Thought: Thinking through the Printed Page

Typographic thought is based on *print and the production of writing through mechanical means*. The invention of moveable type and the printing press, attributed to Johann Gutenberg in Mainz, Germany, around 1453, was a "cultural and intellectual revolution" (Shailor 1999, 9). Suddenly, the printing press, not human hands creating and copying manuscripts, was central to recording, storing, and disseminating information.

Many of the traditions we now associate with books began as imitations of handwritten manuscripts. The fonts that we recognize on the printed page and on the computer screen were originally designed to imitate handwritten models. Other conventions began as conveniences for typesetters—texts spaced in even columns, "justified" margins, even pagination, word spacing, and paragraph breaks were established by typesetters laying out pages. The printing press has even been credited for the "birth of the author" when title pages were included. Most works before the seventeenth century did not include an author's name.

The invention of print was central to the Renaissance in Europe. The Protestant Reformation has been linked to the dissemination and availability of Martin Luther's German translation of the Bible. For the first time, people could read the Bible themselves rather than rely on the Catholic Church to teach it. Scientific publications, especially from publishing houses in Holland, were disseminated across Europe. Standardization of scientific knowledge and method occurred in large part because of this new availability of scientific works. While both religious and scientific treatises had been written in Latin, suddenly books were published in vernacular languages. The decline of Latin and the rise of other languages in print democratized knowledge for literate people across Europe.

Shailor (1999) summarizes the impact of the "Gutenberg revolution":

> The rapid availability of books and the uniformity of their texts meant that more people could read books, that more people could converse with one another about their contents; printing contributed to the open access to knowledge and the more broadly based discussion of ideas, whether philosophical, literary, theological, or historical. (10)

Walter Ong extends Shailor's conclusions: Only through books could we become "text" centered. Ong argues that "print culture" not only creates texts—books, history, science, philosophy, even last wills and testaments—but also creates the assumptions and values we hold about texts.

First, a "print culture" creates the impression that a text is finished, closed, final on the page. (Anyone who has ever sent copy with a "typo" to a printer knows that Ong's point is, in a way, quite accurate.) Second, only in print culture did the Romantic ideals of "originality" and "creativity" evolve as linked to an author's capacity to create new texts on the page. And, third, only in print culture can a "textbook," a repository of facts, straightforward and memorizable, hold sway over cultural knowledge formerly held only in bodies, learned through apprenticeships and hands-on participation. All of these assumptions about print will be central to "text-centered" approaches to performance.

READ MORE ABOUT IT

"Flock" by Billy Collins

Billy Collins was Poet Laureate of the United States from 2001 to 2003. "Flock" is from his collection The Trouble with Poetry and Other Poems *(2005, 35).*

> *It has been calculated that each copy of the*
> *Gutenburg Bible . . . required the skins of 300 sheep.*
>
> —from an article on printing

I can see them squeezed into the holding pen

behind the stone building

where the printing press is housed,

all of them squirming around

to find a little room

and looking so much alike

it would be nearly impossible

to count them,

and there is no telling

which one will carry the news

that the Lord is a shepherd,

one of the few things they already know.

SOURCE: From THE TROUBLE WITH POETRY AND OTHER POEMS by Billy Collins. Used by permission of Random House, Inc.

Electronic Thought: Thinking Textually through Orality

Even in 1982, Walter Ong anticipated new kinds of consciousness that he called "Post-typography: Electronics," or the *electronic transformation of verbal expression through television, radio, and sound recordings.* He calls this **secondary orality**. While these media once again put an emphasis on sound, immediacy, and oral expression, *secondary orality continues to be dependent on the page, relying on printed scripts* as their genesis. Electronic thought builds on primary orality: It has a "participation mystique," fosters a sense of community, and concentrates on the present moment.

When Collins reads "Flock" in an NPR interview, this is a wonderful example of secondary orality, for it relies on the printed poem for its enactment and immediacy.

Ong lists three ways that primary orality differs from the "new orality" of electronic communication. First, while secondary orality generates a "strong group sense," this group is much bigger than those in traditionally oral cultures. "Mass communication" puts its emphasis on numbers and distance. Millions of people across the world can experience a U.S. President's State of the Union address through television, radio, and the Internet.

Next, secondary orality encourages and values spontaneity—not because analysis through writing is unavailable, but simply because "we had decided that spontaneity is a good thing" (Ong 1982, 137). U.S. President Ronald Reagan is often called "The Great Communicator." His ability to perform manuscript speeches as if spontaneously created was at the heart of this label. President George W. Bush is notoriously bad at performing from manuscripts. His spontaneity too often creates "Bushisms," speech malapropisms that create a much different impression of him than Reagan.

Third, much of the expression in electronic forms of communication is self-consciously informal, especially compared with the "formality" we often expect of much writing and print. E-mail, instant messaging, text messaging, and leet are all new instances of orality's immediacy, participation, and community. The medium, however, is not sound, but text. This new text is a wonderfully innovative transformation of both sound and print. "L8 4 work?" the text message reads.

Research into the connections between secondary orality and performance are rich avenues to understand audiences, performers, and performance texts. Richard Bello (1997) explores Louisiana Voices, a neo-Chautauqua movement. While secondary orality emphasizes communication across large distances and "mass" audiences, these Chautauqua performances highlight immediacy of performer-audience interaction and enable local "truths" to be performed. True to Ong's sense of the spoken word, Louisiana Voices make "history come alive" (Bello 1997, 193).

Ong helps us recognize that the phrase "spoken word" in primary orality is a redundancy. There is no other kind of word. Only in a world of texts, print culture, and secondary orality do we make a distinction between "the spoken word" and "the written word."

CAUGHT LOOKING

"Turning the Pages" of Antiquity on the Computer Screen

The British Library Web site enables you to "turn the pages" of fifteen of the world's greatest books on the computer screen, to hear them read aloud, to magnify each page to study it, and to read or hear analysis of the importance of the text. Choose one of the great books to experience this way. Then explore each of Ong's categories—mnemonic, chirographic, typographic, and electronic—in relation to this book. Do Ong's claims make sense for your experience? Why or why not?

Interpreting the World as "Text"

Anthropologist Clifford Geertz (1980, 175) maintains, "When we speak, our utterances fly by as events like any other behavior; unless what we say is inscribed in writing (or some other established recording process), it is as evanescent as what we do." If we write our utterances down, however, we transform the *saying* into the *said*. The utterance becomes a text that allows "its meaning to persist in a way its actuality cannot."

Geertz argues that looking at all social phenomena *as text* allows us to focus on how we create and fix meaning in actions:

> on how the inscription of action is brought about, what its vehicles are and how they work, and on what the fixation of meaning from the flow of events—history from what happened, thought from thinking, culture from behavior—implies for sociological interpretation. To see social institutions, social customs, social changes as in some sense "readable" is to alter our whole sense of what such interpretation is toward modes of thought. . . . (175–76)

Looking at the world as a text we can "read" enables "interpretative explanation" (167). Literary criticism, or interpretative explanations of the value and meaning of texts, is an important model for exploring the world as text.

How Are We Taught to Read Texts?

Most of us were taught to read, understand, and explore literature—poems, short stories, plays, and novels—in high school English classes. And most of us can remember the central concepts for that exploration: metaphor, paradox, irony, tension, and symbolism. The school of literary criticism that introduced these concepts in literary study was called "New Criticism."

This approach to literature bloomed and thrived as the premiere way of studying literary texts from the 1930s to the 1970s in the United States. Many generations of Americans grew to love (and to hate) poetry in English classrooms because of a textbook written by two influential New Critics, Cleanth Brooks and Robert Penn Warren. *Understanding Poetry: An Anthology for College Students* was first published in 1938 and stayed in print for forty years. Robert Scholes (2001, 2) argues that "poetry anxiety" is as real and as important as "math anxiety" and was caused in large part by how the New Critics taught us to read poetry.

Kristin B. Valentine (1983, 549–50) posits that New Criticism was a reaction against the reigning critical approaches of the day. Literature was studied as biography of the writer, or history of the times, or a lens for audience analysis through Marxist, humanist, or anti-bourgeois criticism. Valentine claims that the New Critics "wanted to concentrate on the substance of literature rather than its intent or effect" (550).

How did New Criticism "concentrate on the substance of literature?" And what was "new" about this way of studying literature? First, New Criticism separated the poem from the poet, the world, and the reader, arguing that *the poem* is the autonomous object for study and interpretation. This approach maintains that a poem is a self-enclosed, organic unity—a world onto itself—available only through close reading and analysis of its arrangement, forms, and language devices. Second, New Criticism argued that poetic language is different from "ordinary" language, especially scientific language. If scientific language is denotative, then poetic language is connotative. It is densely layered, purposefully ambiguous, rife with tensions that create intrinsic pushes and pulls, and anchored in paradoxes of meaning that are dynamic yet unified. Third, the New Critics maintained that no single meaning is possible in poetry, but instead that poetic language engenders multiple meanings achieved through paradox and its reconciliation in the text.

New Criticism attempted to make textual criticism a rigorous and systematic study. While a text holds many meanings, the route to those meanings was carefully policed. Here are three critical "mistakes" readers make in the eyes of the New Critics. W. K. Wimsatt and Monroe Beardsley (1946) coined the phrase the **intentional fallacy** to argue against importing information from outside the poem. Information about the poet's life or times or personality was extraneous to the enclosed world of the poem on the page. For Wimsatt and Beardsley, the intention of the author is not a desirable standard for evaluating the success of a poem.

W. K. Wimsatt, in *The Verbal Icon* (1954), coined the phrase the **affective fallacy** to describe a different kind of importation: judging the success of a poem based on the emotional response of the reader. Wimsatt maintains that this emotional relativism—the fact that the same poem can move readers in different ways—leads to critical trouble. Instead, the critic's job is to recover the publicly accessible world contained in the poem, not his or her idiosyncratic response to it.

Cleanth Brooks argues that good poems are not paraphrasable, nor are they reducible to summaries of their themes. No other words can substitute for the words of the poem, their careful construction, their internal dynamics and tensions. Brooks calls this the **heresy of paraphrase**. Brooks (1947, 67) writes, "The poem communicates so much and communicates it so richly and with such delicate qualifications that the thing communicated is mauled and distorted if we attempt to convey it by any vehicle less subtle than that of the poem itself."

READ MORE ABOUT IT

I Need Help Fast!

Robert Scholes (2001, 23–24) surveyed online high school bulletin boards for the kinds of questions students posted regarding their assignments in English classes. Students wanted help finding the symbolism of the river in Huckleberry Finn, sexual symbols in gardens, and any symbolism in William Faulkner's "A Rose for Emily." Theme, tone, and irony were other major categories that baffled students. Here is Scholes' example of one question and his plea that we teach literature in ways other than searches for "irony."
Subject: Oedipus Rex—Irony

I need help finding Irony in Oedipus Rex! There's supposedly a lot in there, but I've been assigned Scene II and there's only so much. . . .

What a terrible thing it is to be required to find irony in *Oedipus Rex,* knowing that there's "a lot in there," and then be given a scene that got short-changed on this precious stuff. It is, one might almost say, ironic. Now this is a play about how a scandal in a ruler's private life is causing public disasters—like a plague, for instance. You might think that questions about the relation between sex and politics, between private and public life, would have a certain resonance in these times. Questions about justice, guilt, responsibility, sexual desire, and family life are raised by the play. But "irony" is a safe topic, a "literary" topic, one of those topics that seems to belong only to the artificial world of "English classes," where we English teachers feel at home. My point is that, by playing it "safe," we are losing the game. The great works of literature are worthy of our attention only if they speak to our concerns as human beings, and these must take precedence over the artificial concerns of symbol, tone, and irony. Symbol, tone, and irony, after all, are only devices, or ways of talking about technique. We need, and shall have to find, better ways of talking about what these works mean and how they connect to our lives.

The Science of Criticism and the Art of Oral Interpretation

New Criticism was extremely influential for departing from the study of literature as biography or history and for turning to the text as an object of study. New Criticism encouraged close reading by an "objective" reader and gave us a vocabulary for the work of literary analysis—taking a text apart to study its parts.

This approach may sound scientific, and, in a way, it was. Northrup Frye, in his book *The Anatomy of Criticism* (1957), argues for a true "science" of literary criticism. While both science and literature seek to name the world in accurate ways, the wisdom gained through science and literature are different. Don Geiger (1950, 513) argues that $E = mc^2$ is an accurate naming and meaningful for a wise scientist, "but this name alone does not satisfy the search for wisdom that asks, 'What does $E = mc^2$ demand of me?'"

In college speech classrooms throughout the United States from 1940 to 1970, the tenets of New Criticism dovetailed with the methods of oral interpretation of literature. Valentine (1983, 557) summarizes their convergence: The study of literature is the focus, not the performer's training in technique; an oral reading of the poem is the end product, not paraphrase or précis; and methods of analysis are intrinsic, not biographical or historical. Scholars of oral interpretation differed in their approaches to literary texts. Jill Taft-Kaufman (1985) offers three emphases in textual study through performance: the drama of the poem created through attitudes; the experience of oral performance as more "genuine" than a silent reading; and the restoration of the links between Aristotle's rhetoric and poetics.

Don Geiger (1950) maintains that literature is a complex of attitudes; the interpreter's job is discover those attitudes through close analysis and to communicate those attitudes to an audience in an oral reading. Wallace Bacon and Robert Breen (1959, 9) draw connections between literary experience and life experience: "a writer fashions a work of art which reveals his discoveries about life, and a reader tests the value of those discoveries by a kind of sympathetic and critical imitation of the actions and reactions found in the writer's work." Thomas Sloan (1967, 91) returns to Aristotelian connections between rhetoric and poetics to "negotiate a union between New Critics who see literature as aestheticians . . . and rhetoricians who see literature as transactional gesture—communicative shaping of an experience."

Unlike the literary critic whose end product is *an essay about a poem,* the oral interpreter's end product is a *performance of the poem* that returns presence, immediacy, interaction, and—most important—body to the text. Wallace Bacon (1966, v) maintained that "the *presence* of literature is the distinct task of the interpreter. . . . [Interpretation] is seen, furthermore, as carrying out the primary need of literature to be experienced, not simply analyzed." Literary analysis is part of the process, and the performance itself is a kind of "proof" of those analytical discoveries. Echoes of the science of literary criticism appear in the claim that the oral interpreter "actually tests the attitudes and actions of the work by acting them out, matching words with physical responses" (Sloan and Maclay 1972, 7).

The New Critics never were a unified group or had a single agenda (Valentine 1983), but attacks on their ways of studying literature were common. The most frequent attack, especially from students, was that this way of studying literature effectively killed any pleasure for the reader and forced painful dissection of a poem in a search for "deep" meanings. American poet Archibald MacLeish wrote a poem about this discontent, entitled "Ars Poetica," or the Art of Poetry. The famous last two lines, "A poem should not mean / but be," encapsulated this sentiment. Fortunately, oral interpretation was one effective and pleasurable method to let a poem "be."

All the World's a Text: To Infinity and Beyond

New Criticism ushered in close reading of literary texts. Structuralism, a worldwide movement across many academic disciplines, sought to engage in "close reading" of much more than literature. The basic tenet of this critical orientation is that there are fundamental, underlying structures operating in all language, culture, and society. These structures, once postulated, can be "read" and interpreted for how meaning is constructed by and for individuals and societies.

Structuralism grew out of borrowed concepts from linguistics, beginning with the concept of a deep structure, or grammar, that gives rise to particular ways of speaking. Ferdinand de Saussure (1959/1966) called these *langue* (the rules of grammar) and *parole* (the spoken manifestation of those rules). Saussure called his approach to linguistics **semiology**, or the study of signs. He approached language as a binary system composed of two concepts: the signifier (or sound image that is heard or imagined when read) and signified (the concept or meaning that we build on and through that image). So bathroom doors are marked by signifiers, iconic figures of male and female, that signify concepts of gender, imaginary constructs of male and female, and values attributed by, understood, and agreed to by the community that uses them. Many restaurants play with bathroom signifiers, asking you to guess the signified: In a seafood restaurant, are you a buoy? a gull?

SOURCE: Photograph by Jaclyn Lannon. Copyright © 2007 by Jaclyn Lannon.

French anthropologist Claude Levi-Strauss (1976) turned the "study of man" into the study of symbolic structures that organize and create meaning in social life. From the concept in structural linguistics, Levi-Strauss theorized that all cultures, like language, have a "deep structure" or grammar. Levi-Strauss (1969) argued that kinship could be studied to discover its underlying "rules" in each culture.

Kinship is a theoretical concept—whether a theory based on genetics, biology, nature, or association—that is practiced differently according to different cultural rules. Sarah Franklin and Susan McKinnon (2001, 2) note that kinship theory and practice is changing because of reproductive technologies, international adoptions, genetic screening, and "families of choice." The deep structure kinship rule for many Western cultures, "blood is thicker than water," is at question because of these changing practices.

Roland Barthes (1988), French philosopher, semiotician, and structuralist, married the concepts of structural linguistics and structural anthropology to study the "mythologies" of bourgeois culture and consumerism, treating everything—wine, food, clothing, and literature—as signifiers that become signified as cultural myths with powerful sway over bourgeois audiences. When Barthes analyzed literary texts, photographs, and advertising, he went beyond literary analysis:

> I mean by literature neither a body nor a series of works, nor even a branch of commerce or of teaching, but the complex graph of the traces of a practice, the practice of writing. Hence, it is essentially the text with which I am concerned—the fabric of signifiers which constitute the work. (1982, 462)

Susan Hayward explains Barthes' two orders of signification, denotation and connotation, which in turn produce a third: ideology. Hayward (1996, 310) uses the example of a photograph of Marilyn Monroe:

At the denotative level this is a photograph of the movie star. . . . At a connotative level we associate this photograph with Marilyn Monroe's star qualities of glamour, sexuality, beauty. . . . At a mythic level we understand this sign as activating the myth of Hollywood: the dream factory that produces glamour in the form of the stars it constructs, but also the dream machine that can crush them—all with a view to profit and expediency.

The Hollywood myth is a good example of a "fabric of signifiers" that folds into and across American culture as something to be both sought after and avoided at all costs: glamour, power, money, but also decadence, destruction, and decay.

Looking at culture through the linguistic lens of language to analyze its structures, binaries, and operations is a twentieth-century phenomenon. M. H. Abrams (1979) argues that New Criticism of the mid- twentieth century birthed "The Age of Criticism," and that structuralism of the 1960s ushered in "The Age of Reading." Abrams claims we no longer engage "a work of literature but a text, writing, *ecriture.*" As a critical orientation, structuralism was killed—for the most part—by Jacques Derrida, but text-centered approaches to the world continue on. Hazard Adams writes,

The term "text" came to include all cultural systems as if they were languages or made up of languages. The triumph of the linguistic world may be marked by the sudden ubiquity of "text" and the treatment of everything as if it were linguistic. Perhaps the phrase that most fully expresses this situation is Jacques Derrida's "Il n'y a pas de hors-texte," which is probably best translated as "There is no outside-the-text." (1990, 7)

Elinor Fuchs (1985, 173) features Derrida's pun in the phrase, "meaning both that there is nothing outside the text, but also that the text has no outside." In short, there is no way of understanding human knowledge that is not text—written, spoken, thought, created, manifested in discourse.

SOURCE: Photograph by Jon Cancelino. Copyright © 2007 by Jon Cancelino.

READ MORE ABOUT IT

Embodying Iconic Mythologies

Mimi Swartz (2007, 122–25, 284) followed Anna Nicole Smith's career for more than a decade, from tracing her upbringing in Mexia, Texas; to her famous court battle for the rights to her husband's estate; to her death in the Bahamas in 2007. Swartz captures the powerful mythologies operating in Smith's rise and fall and the nuances of denotation, connotation, and ideology in reading Smith's tabloid life as text.

When her mother emerged from obscurity to discuss her death on "Good Morning America," she shared Anna Nicole's explanation for exaggerating her small-town past. "Mom," her daughter had told her, "nobody wants to read books or see people on TV concerning, you know, 'Middle-class girl found a rich millionaire and married him.' There's not a story in that. The story is, I come from rags to riches, and so that's what I'm going to tell."

It was an easy sell. Anyone who's ever driven up Interstate 45 and passed the Mexia exit can think they know all they need to about Anna Nicole's history. . . .

Her youthful, abundant beauty from that time continues to startle. Anna Nicole could convey both purity and sophistication; she was innocence in a plunging bustier, on satin sheets, in a hay field, on the beach. Not coincidentally, her career took off at a time when the country's divide between rich and poor was widening and the price of blue jeans became an odd if critical marker. The owners of Guess, the Marciano brothers, followed a trail blazed by former socialite Gloria Vanderbilt and transformed denim from a proletarian uniform to something aspirational. Their sexy black and white ads worked a little like hip Rorschach tests—you could spend a lot of time trying to decide whether the young, hot, beautiful types pictured had just done it or were about to do it—and so created a compelling link between casual clothes, casual sex, and casual glamour. In front of the camera, Anna Nicole embodied it all effortlessly. . . .

From the moment Anna Nicole got famous, she told the world that her role model was Marilyn Monroe. It was a shrewd move, as it linked her image with one of the greatest American icons of all time, and it had a neat logic: one platinum-haired sex symbol taking after another, one poor, deprived child latching onto the success of another. But Anna Nicole couldn't keep up the act to ensure icon status of her own. Monroe had talent, but Anna Nicole's gifts were limited—she was just beautiful, and she never had any sense of how to operate in the world. She had bad manners, she was impulsive, she lied, and she was fiercely derivative. . . . Even then, Anna Nicole couldn't fathom that anyone would want her unless she was pretending to be somebody else. From the beginning, she was always trying too hard.

Monroe was probably just as needy and just as self-destructive, but all that time spent at the Actors Studio and in psychoanalysis gave her insight into herself and her culture: She saw herself as a modern-day Aphrodite, someone who could rescue the populace from the sexual constraints of the fifties and early

(Continued)

(Continued)

sixties. As James Hollis, the executive director of the C. J. Jung Educational Center, in Houston, told me, "She conceived that her role in life was to embody, represent, and channel that missing, exuberant sexual energy." Carrying that burden tends to take its toll—the authentic self has to take a backseat to perpetuating the dreams and fantasies of the public—and Anna Nicole, "an imitation of an imitation," in Hollis's words, had it a lot worse than Monroe. By the time she became a celebrity, in the early nineties, most people didn't need to be cured of their sexual inhibitions. They could watch music videos (now we have Fergie in her Girl Scout uniform), learn bedroom fashion tips from Victoria's Secret models, and enjoy 24/7 access to porn on cable and the Internet. When Anna Nicole showed up on the ubiquitous red carpets stoned, bloated, and bursting out of her clothes, she was nothing more than the embodiment of a supersexualized, celebrity-besotted culture: Aphrodite as a drunken, drug-addled slut. No wonder people turned away.

Despite suffering horribly—growing up deprived, struggling with all sorts of addictions, losing a child—she was incapable of generating sympathy. She was either too needy (even she made jokes about her appetites) or too enchanted with the surface of things (playing at being Monroe, for example), always both too near and too far from everybody else. In the end, there was nothing for the public to connect with except her slow, determined decline, and since no one much wanted to be party to that, Anna Nicole became a reliable punch line instead. She died as she had lived: as a bit of tabloid ephemera, sandwiched between a diapered, love-crazed astronaut and Britney Spears's new skinhead do. That's where Anna Nicole must have really believed she belonged; it just took her a lifetime to convince the rest of us she was right.

SOURCE: Mimi Swartz, "Punch Line," reprinted with permission of *Texas Monthly*.

When Text Meets Performance

Lynn Miller, a performance scholar in communication, claims (1998, 53), "A text is something created, something made, *text*ures are found in woven fabrics, texts are words, ideas, woven together. A family, a performance—whether of a personal narrative, a poem, a dance, a cultural ritual, or of our own bodies—all are texts that we can study, that we *do* study."

From the creation of texts in human knowledge production to the deconstruction of texts in contemporary critical theory, the study of texts is central to much performance theory. Text meets performance in different ways in different academic disciplines. For theatre practitioners and theorists, a text is a play script. For musicians, a text is a musical score. For literary critics, texts are poems, short stories, novels, and essays. For software designers, a text is a string of binary code composed in a computer language. For an architect, a text is a blueprint.

In all of these uses of the word "text," these representations on the page or screen are **enabling pre-texts** (Strine, Long, and HopKins 1990, 184). That is, a play script, a musical score, a poem, or a blueprint is a *guide or set of directions for the performer.* Paul Gray (1996, 107) summarizes well the assumptions of conceiving of texts as enabling for performance: "to start with nothing but black marks on a page and out of that silence to conjure everything—a voice, a listener, an author, a world." Even a poem is a set of directions for the reader, as she performs the poem in her head. Not all these texts are readily understandable on the page. Most of us don't know HTML code, and many of us can't "read" music or an architect's blueprint. So, every text is a set of codes or conventions that must be learned to be understood.

Still other texts can be considered **enabled post-texts** (Strine, Long, and HopKins 1990, 184), or representations of a *performance that are written down after the fact.* These post-texts are ways to capture and to store a performance in order to study it more carefully. Examples abound in many disciplines concerned with communication: Folklorists record performances of verbal art they collect in the field. Conversational analysts transcribe ordinary talk. Narrative theorists record family stories told around the dinner table. Oral historians interview people about their lives and create texts from the transcriptions.

If pre-texts go *from text to performance,* then post-texts take the opposite direction: *from performance to texts.* While this diagram (see Figure 3.1) treats the relationship between texts and performance as clear, linear, and productive, the relationship is much messier. How do performances developed through improvisational techniques fit into this diagram? Dance choreography is a good example of performance that can be based on pre-text (dance notions written down and used to guide the performance), improvisation (dance is created in the moment in and through bodies), or post-text (the performance is coded and recorded after the performance).

Strine, Long, and HopKins' characterization of pre- and post-texts is helpful for the study of performance that is text-driven and text-centered, especially in academic fields that study texts to explore their meanings, to preserve their effervescence, and to posit their worth as aesthetic, communicative, and cultural artifacts. But there are other "texts" that instigate performance in myriad cultural forms. For those, performance theorist Richard Schechner provides helpful guidelines and categories for text in performance.

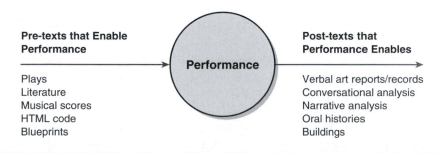

Figure 3.1   Pre-texts and Post-texts

Drama, Script, Theatre, and Performance

Richard Schechner accounts for a range of "doings," actions, gestures, and their executions—rituals, rites, stage plays, improvisations, dances, singing—across the world. Schechner conceives of this range of activities in a series of fuzzy, concentric circles that are often not discreet from each other. The innermost circle in Schechner's (1988a) schema is the **drama**. The drama does not require an expert to teach it but is independent of its production. This can be "a written text, score, scenario, instruction, plan, or map" (72). "The drama is what the writer writes" (85). "Drama is the domain of the author, composer, scenarist, shaman" (71).

Taking the Academy Awards broadcast as an example, the drama is the written outline for the show created by the producers, mapping out the order and timing of the awards, musical interludes, and prerecorded clips. Many other dramas— speeches, lists of nominees, testimonials—happen within the producer's map of the Awards.

Schechner is careful to characterize script, the next concentric circle, not as "text"—something always written—but as **script,** "something that pre-exists any given enactment, which persists from enactment to enactment" (70). Scripts are important for determining "the overall flow of events" (87). The script requires someone to teach it to others; it is *the domain of the teacher, guru, master* (71). Schechner distinguishes between tight and loose scripts. A *tight* script is carefully constructed, often written down, and followed more or less precisely.

When an award recipient pulls an acceptance speech from his tuxedo jacket pocket and reads it aloud, he is working with a tight script. When the director calls camera shots during this speech, he is working with a loose script that follows "an overall pattern consisting of accepted sequences of events" (87). Reaction shots of producers, cast members, and family are interspersed with shots of the award winner.

Theatre is the "specific set of gestures performed by the performers in any given performance" (85) and "what the performers actually do during the production" (72). Theatre is *the domain of the performers* and is "concrete and immediate." The performers at the Academy Awards ceremony make entrances and exits, give speeches, read from cue cards, sing, dance, laugh, cry, hug, and kiss, to name just a few of their concrete and immediate actions.

The outermost circle, encompassing all the others, Schechner labels **performance:** "the whole constellation of events," involving performers, audience, technicians— "anyone who is there" (85). The red-carpet interviews before the show, the jostling of paparazzi, the green-room interviews during and after the Awards, even the post-show parties are now established parts of the televised performance. Performance is *the domain of the audience,* Schechner maintains, for their arrival and departure begin and end the performance.

Schechner's categories are valuable for conceiving of performances that have no written "text" but are developed in and through improvisation, plans, action in flow, and repeated enactments. Moreover, his largest, most encompassing circle is performance with its accumulating dynamics.

GO FIGURE

Going Around in Circles

Choose one of the performances below to analyze in terms of Schechner's categories. Remember, not all of these events will include drama, scripts, or theatre; and the events will be different according to whether you are a central performer, an audience member, or a combination of both.

A telephone greeting at your workplace
A wedding reception
A quinceañera
A college class
A political rally
A church, mosque, or synagogue service
Thanksgiving dinner
YouTube
A Step Show
Dungeons & Dragons

Assumptions about Texts: Canon, Textuality, and Materiality

Basing his work on the writings of Roland Barthes, W. B. Worthen (1995, 13) lists three uses of the word "text" in performance theory: (1) a text is a canonical vehicle of authorial power and tradition; (2) a text is play in an open field of textuality; and (3) a text is a material object, the text in hand. Each use of the term has important implications for performance practices and textual interpretations.

Canonical Vehicle of Authority: You Know Why I Pulled You Over

For a text to be **canonical**, it is *recognized and accepted by experts as a worthwhile, important, and established part of a genre*, or canon of great works. Canons are established by cultural authorities (scholars, judges, church officials, scientists). Shakespeare's plays, for example, are an established part of the canon of great plays. In this use of the term "text," much scholarly debate revolves around the playwright's authority to determine meaning. This text is assumed to hold and to reveal the secrets of the author. Worthen (1995, 16) notes that it is this use of the word "text" that creates debates about specific performances. When is a production of Shakespeare not "faithful" to the original? In this use of "text," the work is "closed, fixed, single," a manifestation of one author's creative vision that is not to be tampered with.

The "canon wars" reinvent themselves every couple of decades. In the 1960s and 70s, feminists argued that the canon excluded women—as writers, artists, scientists, clergy, and political and social leaders. Tillie Olsen (1978) rightfully and accurately argued that for every twelve men in a literary anthology, only one woman appeared. "One in twelve" became a "watchword" for this exclusion across the academy. In the late 1980s, the "canon wars" involved cultural literacy: What great texts ought to be known to all members of Western culture? And how is cultural literacy about whiteness, middle-classness, and reading and writing?

If the canon wars seem particularly academic, then it is also important to note that claims to canonical authority through texts have "truth effects"—real-world implications for all of us. Your driver's license makes certain textual claims about you: your appearance, your age, your gender, your eyesight and physical abilities. If you are pulled over, then you are accountable for performing, before an officer of the law, the "truths" made in these claims. Tax codes, laws and ordinances, Supreme Court decisions are all canonical texts with truth effects: They shut down meaning in and through their "official" interpretations.

Wole Soyinka is a Nigerian playwright, poet, novelist, and director who won the Nobel prize for literature in 1986. Soyinka compares oral and written cultures for their differing attitudes toward violations of sacred textual authority:

> I know of no example in oral culture that prescribes a mandatory capital punishment for a real or imagined crime against a divine text. . . . Christianity and Islam appear to be the most vulnerable to such destructive traits. Maybe it is time we devoted some serious global attention to why, throughout the ages, the mere materialization, on perishable parchment or paper, even stone, of some immutably determined word, evokes such mortal and primitive passions. It all centers on power and domination, of course, of which the written word is mystic weapon, the magic amulet of terrestrially ambitious priesthood. (1995, 76–77)

"Canon" is a contested term and place: It is a repository and evaluation of great individual and cultural endeavors, and it holds the potential for harm and violence.

MAKE A LIST

Who's the Shakespeare in Your Canon?

Faculty members at the University of Alberta were asked to name their culture's "Shakespeare"—the canonical author in their culture. Faculty listed Matsuo Bashô, Taras Shevchenko, Miguel de Cervantes y Saavedra, Cao Xueqin, Hafiz, Johann Wolfgang von Goethe, Taha Hussein, Rabindranath Thakur, and Dante Alighieri.

Visit Geoff McMaster's (2003) article "Who's Your Shakespeare?" online to read more about these writers. Then make a list of the reasons given for the exalted status of these authors and their works.

With that list of exemplary qualities, make a case for your "Shakespeare" for the canons of popular music, television, movies, and video games. How might a canon war and "truth effects" play out in the classroom debate?

Textuality: Play, Production, and Practice

Textuality plays with the notion of writing itself—its conventions, its histories, and its interplay with other works in the canon—challenging anyone's claim to authority and enforcement. In this use, texts are open fields, a place of "play, activity, production, and practice." Painting a mustache on the image of the Mona Lisa is playful textuality: It requires our knowledge of the canon of great art, as well as a knowledge of the history of conventions of poking fun at any portrait.

All texts exist in a discursive field composed of other texts; all texts assume a relationship to those other texts. Poems, for example, are always written in light of the history and conventions of other poems. Poet Richard Howard (Rodden 1995, 237) claims of many students studying poetry in the classroom, "They enter poetry as if it were an empty, silent room. Whereas it's really an echo chamber filled with countless voices."

Examples of playful intertextuality in the media are all around us. Brian Ott and Cameron Walter (2000) detail examples of parody, appropriation, and self-reflexivity in film, music, and television and on the Internet. They explore parody in Mel Brooks' horror films; cultural critique and self-awareness in the Gangsta rap of Tupac Shakur and Notorious B.I.G.; television shows like "South Park" and "The Family Guy" that reference and re-create moments from other shows and popular culture; and texts that invite insider knowledge and commentary on Internet fan sites.

Elinor Fuchs (1985, 166–7) argues that "textuality" in the theatre "has emerged in a number of new roles, as character, as theme, as setting, and as a virtually independent theatrical constituent to be set beside Aristotle's six elements." Fuchs lists a number of ways that "texts" are coming to replace "presence" as *the* constitutive element of performance: performances made up of montages of other texts—criticism, novels, plays, theory; characters labeled as "the reader" or "the translator"; actors who "read" in monotone texts onstage; amateurs cast instead of professional actors who tend to "contaminate the performance with the enlarged personal 'presence' of the professional"; and images of writing as set pieces. Fuchs' description of two performances of Stuart Sherman's are worth detailing:

> The back wall of his 18-minute silent *Hamlet* was decorated with pages from Shakespeare's text, cut and pasted into dagger-like patterns. The character Hamlet was played by five actors carrying copies of *Hamlet*. The central design element of his 1985 *Chekhov* was a grove of two-dimensional cherry trees constructed from blow-ups of pages from Chekhov's plays. Other pieces of set furniture were covered with text as well, and two stage hands in black sat at either side of the stage reading Chekhov's plays. To a background of recorded lines from the plays, the actors performed silent gestures. One's attention flickered choicelessly from the gestures to recorded sound to the text on the stage objects. At the climactic moment of the piece, the grove of text trees toppled over and we were left for a moment to contemplate the stage, and by extension the world, stripped of text. (170–71)

Fuchs' examples put textuality—play with words, print, reading, writing, and discourse—in the middle of contemporary theatre practice that challenges canonical authority to dictate the "correct" interpretation of Shakespeare or Chekhov.

ACT OUT

When "Flock" Meets Performance

Create a solo performance of Billy Collins' poem "Flock" that features textuality—something the poem clearly comments on with great poignancy. Across the range of performances in the classroom, what features of textuality and its production are highlighted in the performance?

Materiality: Can You Hold It in Your Hand?

The **text in hand**, or the object we can hold, is a third way to conceive of text: the book, the poem on the page, the blueprint. A playscript used in rehearsal is a particularly solid example. But playscripts go through many, many versions. Worthen (1995, 18) notes these different kinds of texts of the same play: "a preproduction text, a text published in conjunction with the premiere, subsequent editions published after later productions, texts incorporating revisions which may or may not have been made directly by the author, collected editions, acting editions."

Even though we may have faith in what we can touch, see, and read, and the materiality of something we can hold, the text in hand is both invested with canonical authority and an opportunity for open, playful textuality. Playwright Richard Foreman offers an invitation to directors to play with language in his plays even as he invokes limits. He writes,

> Take a text such as any of the ones in *Unbalancing Acts*. Start by erasing all stage directions. Then erase ALL INDICATIONS OF WHO SPEAKS WHICH LINE. Re-distribute the lines among the actors, inventing additional or fewer characters than I used in my own productions. Change the sex of the actors. Feel free to combine, for instance, three lines of dialog, spoken back and forth between two performers, into one speech spoken by one actor. Or vice versa. The only thing I would insist is that lines should not be re-ordered sequentially. Aside from that—cut, repeat, do as you will. But imagine a REAL and COMPLEX world in which such a newly freed language takes place. (Foreman 1994, 39)

Not many playwrights are this generous about changing their plays.

Interestingly, when the *playwright* gives this permission, all three uses of the word "text" are implicated. Canonical vehicle assumes the author's vested power and authority to license play and to stop it. Playful textuality is evident in the author's invitation to directors to "free" the language of the play. And the text in hand—a product purchased from a publishing house—is challenged as well. Richard Schechner asked Foreman, "Why don't you offer the first ten university productions royalty free?" And he did.

The "text in hand" features materiality—not just a page of script, but the hand that holds that text. Bodies are the material that make texts happen in the doing of performance. Immediacy, presence, and embodiment constitute the text in hand.

GO FIGURE

Which Text Is This?

Choose one text from the list below. Make an argument for how this text is canonical. What is the canon? What are the canon's conventions? How is this text an authority that shuts down interpretations?

Then make a second argument for how this same text is an open, playful field. How does it reference, revise, and rework other texts?

Then make a third argument for this text in hand. What is this text made out of? How is it material? Words, fabric, digital code, images? Are these texts stable? Variable? And why?

A sampled song

A basketball uniform

A Web site

A fairy tale

Spam e-mail

A restaurant menu

An instruction manual

A board game

A Web blog

A video game

A love letter

A tattoo

Interpreting Texts

Are texts fixed in stone? Are they open to a variety of interpretations in performance? Is there a limit to "anything goes"? Beverly Whitaker Long (1977) provides a taxonomy of textual interpretation that is very helpful for understanding the elasticity and boundaries of literary texts and their multilayered meanings. Long claims that questions about textual meaning can be answered in four ways: all texts include (1) **certainties** (specific, definite, or known facts in the words on the page); (2) **probabilities** ("weighted likelihoods" given on the page); (3) **possibilities** (inferences based on hints or clues provided by the words on the page); and (4) **distortions** (deliberate negations or misrepresentations of the words on the page).

These categories are particularly revealing when applied to musical scores as texts. Marc Geelhoed (2006) writes of three different performances of the same Mozart sonata. Each pianist is true to the certainties of the notes in the musical score. The probabilities and possibilities in performing Mozart are endless; duration, stress, and tempo vary widely. Notably, none of these pianists distort the text by leaving out notes or substituting others.

Long's taxonomy is a valuable one for its vocabulary of performance choices with literary texts. The notion of certainties in texts creates a kind of obligation to the words on the page and reveals a critical faith in the existence of commonalities of meaning among all readers. Probabilities and possibilities are inferences that performers have license to make and allow for a range of differences across readers. Distortions reveal the boundaries of interpretation and the politics of the categories: One person's distortion may be another's possibility. Whether we perform texts *within* or *outside* these boundaries, however, all are commentaries on textual politics, power, and authority.

SOURCE: Photograph by Jaclyn Lannon. Copyright © 2007 by Jaclyn Lannon.

THEORY MEETS WORLD

"You Mean, We *Shouldn't* Do That"

Michael S. Bowman, in "Performing Literature in an Age of Textuality" (1996), writes of two very different performances of the same text, Kahlil Gibran's The Prophet. *Published originally in Arabic and translated into English in 1923, this book is a collection of 26 essays, or meditations, of the Lebanese-born writer. It garnered much popular attention and fame among members of the U.S. counterculture in the 1960s. Its literary worth, especially in light of New Critical tenets, is debatable. Bowman relates that one student loved the book and wanted to perform from it; a second student, who hated it, promised she was "going to do something different with it." Bowman describes the two performances.*

As it happened, both women were scheduled to give their performances of *The Prophet* on the same day of class. When I arrived that day, the first student, the one who loved the book, had everything set up for her performance. She had come to class fully costumed in a kind of harem outfit—pants, halter-top, and veil—and had taken the trouble to transcribe her text onto some old, parchment-like material in what appeared to be a form of calligraphy. She burned incense. She was on big pillows. She read the words of *The Prophet* in prophetic tones. There was not the faintest whiff of irony to perturb the performance's effluvium of earnestness. . . .

. . . the other student who was to perform *The Prophet* entered the room (she had excused herself earlier). She, too, came fully costumed: a skimpy, skin-tight, backless, red minidress; black fishnet stockings; a five-inch spiked heel on one foot, its broken mate on the other; heavy, grotesque makeup; a fifty dollar bill protruding from her cleavage; and a paper bag with a whiskey bottle in it in one hand. The first words out of her mouth were, "What a fucking night!" (in a heavy Brooklyn accent). She took off her broken heel, threw it in the trash can; grabbed the bottle out of the bag and started chugging the "whiskey." Then she began her monologue.

She told us in fairly graphic but not in the least sensational terms about her "dates" that evening; about her relationship with her "old man"; about the various men she had known in her life. Then she related that on her way home, she had passed by a street corner where a "religious nut" had set up a crate and was preaching to the passers-by. A few were gathered around listening, a few were heckling him, most were ignoring him. She stopped for a laugh, she told us, and learned that this fellow, who called himself "The Prophet," was talking about love. "What do I need this shit for?" she asked. But as she started to leave, he said something that made an impression on her. "Here, I wrote it down," she said. She picked up her paper bag and read a couple of distinctive lines from *The Prophet*. Then she began to interpret those lines for us from the perspective of the character she had created, to translate them into the character's own vernacular. She did the same with a few more passages from the text, each time becoming a little more wrapped-up in the text and its sentimentality, though she tried to hold on to her cynical, hard-bitten persona. Finally, she "caught" herself before giving in wholly to the sentiments of *The Prophet*, pulled herself together, crumpled the paper bag, and tossed it into the trashcan. End of performance.

(Continued)

(Continued)

During the discussion that followed, the class would hardly let me speak. For the most part, the students' comments sought to work through the contradictions we had just experienced: how could the "good" performance, the one that came closest to matching the speaker-in-the-text, have been "bad"; how could the "bad" performance, the one that ignored the text's dramatic speaker in favor of articulating an external point of view on the text, have been "good"? Some students felt that the first performance was the "right" one, and that the second performance was illegitimate, even though most claimed they preferred it. "We just can't do that!" I recall one student insisting. Before I could respond, another student jumped in with, "You mean, we *shouldn't* do that; obviously, it *can* be done."

SOURCE: From "Performing Literature in an Age of Textuality" by Michael S. Bowman. *Communication Education* 1996. Reprinted by permission of Taylor & Francis Ltd. http://www.informaworld.com.

ACT OUT

Your Poetic License Is Issued!

Choose a small portion of any "Read More About It" box in this book and create four one-minute group performances using Long's categories of certainties, probabilities, possibilities, and distortions. Starting with the "certainties" performance and moving to the "distortions" performance, how did the text drive each performance? How can you evaluate each performance in relation to the text, the audience, and the performers?

Text Versus Performance

The relationship between a text and its performance is often characterized as a dialectical, even antagonistic, one. Are written works of art—plays, poems, short stories—best left on the page? If not, why not? Marvin Carlson (1985) discusses the relationship between play scripts and theatrical performance in the history of Western theatre. In the Romantic period, performances were conceived as **illustrations** of texts, especially for audiences who couldn't read or write. In this relationship between performance and text, the text is clearly the superior, authoritative version; "a staging may add to the attractiveness of a play but not to its essence" (6). In the early nineteenth century, performance was conceived as a **translation** of a text, but this translation was necessarily inferior to the original written version. Also in the early nineteenth century, performances were conceived as **fulfillments** of texts. In this sense, performances are creative and artistic completions of scripts by actors, directors, and designers. And, based on the work of Jacques Derrida, performances can be conceived as **supplements** to texts. Each new performance reveals the endless possibilities of scripts in performance.

Josephine Lee (1999) characterizes the text and performance relationship as **libratory** or **embodied**. In the first sense, performance "frees" the text from the confines of textual authority. In the second sense, performance "embodies something quite analogous to the text: in some cases, the immortal spirit of the masterpiece; in others, the presence of hitherto marginalized peoples" (154).

The movement from text to performance has been justified and described in a variety of ways, always reflecting the institutional histories of disciplines that study texts. Strine, Long, and HopKins (1990, 185) note an important tension in all of these characterizations of the relationship between text and performance:

> Whatever the comparison, the performance paradoxically declares both subordination to and power over the written work: even while approximating, representing, substituting for, the performance nonetheless clarifies and illuminates to the point of resolving, for a time, the work's ambiguities.

RETHINKING TEXTS

Approaching the world as a text to be read, studied, and analyzed follows traditions of literary criticism. Clifford Geertz (1973, 452) is famous for this textual approach to the study of culture: "The culture of a people is an ensemble of texts, themselves ensembles, which the anthropologist strains to read over the shoulders of those to whom they properly belong." Text-centered approaches have been criticized for their emphasis on the printed page, for silencing or doing violence to groups without access to print, for privileging the literary critic, and for failing to pay attention to bodies in performance.

Shannon Jackson (2004, 155) argues that text-centered approaches ultimately privilege literary critics and their methods. To expand the analogy of a text to everything "position[s] the domains and objects of other fields as patiently awaiting illumination by their own methods of explication." The authority of literary study—over anthropology, history, theatre, communication, cultural studies, and sociology—is a kind of colonialism over the academy.

Dwight Conquergood (1998) labels Geertz's textual approach to culture a "visualist/textualist bias." This bias privileges writing, sight, the printed page, and literacy over orality, sound, performance, and embodied practices. This bias is especially violent to marginalized groups excluded from making knowledge about themselves in print. Any study of texts ought to include the myriad manifestations of performances as participatory and embodied ways of knowing and being.

Elizabeth Fine (1984, 92) notes that conceiving of performance as text leads to ignoring features of the performance that don't conform to the page. Building on the work of Walter Ong, Fine's list of print "preconditionings" are abstraction, linearity, disembodiment, and privileging print over the spoken word. Fine's list of performance features left out of print preconceptions include the performance's "presentational fullness, its paralinguistic and kinesic dimensions." A text lifted from its performance and written down is just a "skeleton" of its former self.

All of these critiques recall Walter Ong's claims about orality and performance as the means of creating human knowledges and practices. As human history has moved to creating *texts,* not in sound and memory but by hand, print, and now electronic and digital means, these representations are hotly contested and infinitely productive for performance theory.

Text-centered approaches to performance are evidenced in the careful study of texts as objects for performance, in the creation of texts from performances, in the assumptions we bring to and take away from the printed page, and in the multiple ways we "read" texts. When text meets performance, the politics of interpretation are always present as canon, textual play, and materiality. The criteria for our choices in performance—certainties, probabilities, possibilities, and distortions—are assumptions about texts and their relationships to politics, ways of reading, and history.

CHAPTER **4**

Performing Drama

Theory in Perspective:
How Is the World a Stage?

I f the twentieth century was *text-centered* as presented in Chapter Three, it was also *drama-centered*. In much social theory throughout this century, "life as drama" was an important orientation for theories that explore and understand human action as dramatic. In this view, humans are "actors" who play roles; human activities are conceived as "action," "acts," "scenes," and "events"; humans are driven by motives, intentions, and purposes to make moral choices; human interaction centers on conflict and moves through a particular form to its resolution. Shakespeare's claim, "All the world's a stage / And all the men and women merely players," is a frequent allusion for theorists who claim that life is dramatically realized and best understood through theatrical language.

Named "dramatism" by Kenneth Burke, the "social drama" by Victor Turner, and "dramaturgical" by Erving Goffman, dramatistic theories are an important corrective to two reigning metaphors that described and understood humans as machines and as animals. When the conception is of **humans as machines**, we are *"cogs," or working parts, in economic, social, and political systems beyond our control.* With the language of the physical sciences, gravity and entropy reign. Humans are machines that break down, wear out, always subject to physical laws.

When the conception is of **humans as animals**, we are *moved, not by physical laws, but by "natural" ones, trapped in the language of instincts, urges, and biochemistry that erases morality, ethics, and choice.* With this metaphor, humans are subject to "conditions" which coerce and control; we are reducible to cause and effect. These mechanistic, physical, and causal metaphors for human interaction in no way account for **creativity, critical thinking,** or **symbol systems that are unique to humans.** Dramatism and the social drama ask "why?" questions of human action: "Why do people act the way they do, especially when faced with conflict?" Both theories argue that humans are not animals or machines but are social actors who make moral and ethical choices.

Dramatistic theory enables three claims about the constitutive, epistemic, and critical work of performance. First, language and symbol systems are collective resources for people that constitute group life: "Language and ritual do more than reflect the experience of group life; they create it. To be a member of a community is to share in a name, a history, a mutual consciousness" (Gusfield 1989, 30). Second, as epistemology, the conventions of drama (scenes, acts, actors, motives, conflict) "are our ways of seeing and knowing, which every day we put into practice" (Williams 1958/1983, 18). Through the "dramatization of consciousness itself," Raymond Williams maintains, "we organize reality." Third, dramatistic theory provides tools and vocabulary for participating in social and political life that is constantly changing and changeable. Peter Berger (1963, 139) writes, "If social reality is dramatically created, it must also be dramatically malleable." Molding the world is always a critical endeavor.

The theories of Erving Goffman will be covered in Chapter Six; this chapter explores Kenneth Burke's dramatism and Victor Turner's social drama. This chapter begins with Aristotelian concepts of dramatic form, conflict, and action as central to Burke's critical orientations: language as symbolic action, ritual drama as hub, and analysis of human motives. The chapter then explores Turner's social drama, its four phases, and performance as integral to the social drama's unfolding. Each theory of language and social order draws life as drama as its reigning orientation to understand conflict, crisis, and its resolution. Both Burke and Turner utilize Aristotle's conception of dramatic action and the elements of tragedy as foundations to understand how individuals and groups use language and ritual to forge memberships and drive social action.

The Drama of a Roller Coaster Ride

There is no middle ground: You either love roller coasters or you hate them. As you wait in line, are you filled with excitement or paralytic fear? During the ride, do you hold your hands above your head? Or do you desperately hang on and coach yourself, "I am *not* going to die, I am *not* going to die. . . ." And, finally, when the carriage rolls back into the boarding station, do you turn to your companion and say, "Let's do it again!" or do you scream, "Don't *ever* make me do that again!"

Whether you are a joyful participant or reluctant victim, the ride takes a predictable form: the slow crawl out of the station house, the slow, steady climb upward, then the first perilous plunge downward. Larger and larger twists, turns, and loops will continue to the climax of the ride. The biggest thrill of all—whether it's the highest drop-off, the biggest loop, or the seemingly endless seconds of free fall—comes close to the end of the ride. The ride then slows, the wind stops, the screams turn to laughter, and—as at the beginning—the carriage chugs back to the boarding station. It's over.

A roller coaster ride is **dramatic**. This drama can be viewed in three interconnecting ways: (1) as a formal *arrangement* of parts that moves through beginning, middle, and end; (2) as *conflict* that must be struggled with and resolved; and (3) as a series of experiences that invite you to anticipate, participate, and *act* in certain ways. This combination of form, conflict, and action is at the heart of theories that take drama as the organizing principle for describing and understanding human activities.

SOURCE: Photo by Amazing Photos at NBC Universal, Orlando, Florida. Photo courtesy of Schuyler Long.

Reigning Metaphor: Life as Drama

Clifford Geertz (1980) argues that life as drama is not a new concept. Since Shakespeare, the idea that "all the world's a stage" has been a commonplace. Two schools of thought, however, have moved past the conception of drama as mimesis, as "faking" and as a "mere show," to emphasize the ways that drama is a fruitful analogy for understanding "the expressive devices that make collective life seem anything at all" (172). One school is dramatism and the second is ritual theory. Geertz maintains that these two approaches pull in very different directions. **Dramatism** argues for the similarities between theatre and *rhetoric* with drama *as persuasion*. In this view, the orator's platform is a stage. **Ritual theory** argues for the similarities between theatre and *religion* with drama *as communion*. Here the temple is a stage.

Raymond Williams (1983, 19) claims that we draw from drama—its conventions, its typical characters and scenes, its public participation, its fixed forms—to understand the world. A friend of Williams' claimed, "France, you know, is a bad bourgeois novel." Williams understood he was drawing a parallel between a country and the typical characters and conflicts of a bad novel, especially "struggles for property and position, for careers and careering relationships." Williams responded: "England's a bad bourgeois novel too. And New York is a bad metropolitan novel. But there's one difficulty. You can't send them back to the library. You're stuck with them. You have to read them over and over." His friend responded, yes, "but critically."

Dramatistic theory is alive and well all around us in analogies between life and something that is dramatically realized: "Life is a cabaret," the Broadway musical tells us; World War II was divided into geographic regions—the European, Pacific, and African *theatres;* the film *Wall Street* finds stock traders hollering "Show time!"

at the opening bell. More than metaphors, however, this language describes and explains human actions. James Carey's ritual model of communication, introduced in Chapter One, looks at the world through a dramatistic lens. Carey (1988, 20–21) explains the drama of reading a newspaper:

> What is arrayed before the reader is not pure information but a portrayal of the contending forces in the world. Moreover as readers make their way through the paper, they engage in a continual shift of roles or of dramatic focus. A story on the monetary crisis salutes them as American patriots fighting those ancient enemies Germany and Japan; a story on the meeting of a women's political caucus casts them into the liberation movement as supporter or opponent; a tale of violence on the campus evokes their class antagonisms and resentments. The model here is not that of information acquisition, though such acquisition occurs, but of dramatic action in which the reader joins a world of contending forces as an observer at a play. [A newspaper] is a presentation of reality that gives life an overall form, order, and tone.

Like the roller coaster and reading the newspaper, dramatistic theory maintains that life is dramatically shaped and realized through our active and critical participation in dramas—the contending forces—all around us.

READ MORE ABOUT IT

As Drama Would Like It

While most everyone knows the first two lines, here's Jaques' famous speech from Shakespeare's As You Like It, *Act 2, Scene 7, Lines 139–167.*

Jaques: All the world's a stage,
And all the men and women merely players;
They have their exits and their entrances,
And one man in his time plays many parts,
His acts being seven ages. At first, the infant,
Mewling and puking in the nurse's arms.
Then the whining schoolboy, with his satchel
And shining morning face, creeping like snail
Unwillingly to school. And then the lover,
Sighing like furnace, with a woeful ballad
Made to his mistress' eyebrow. Then a soldier,
Full of strange oaths and bearded like the pard,
Jealous in honour, sudden and quick in quarrel,

> Seeking the bubble reputation
> Even in the canon's mouth. And then the justice,
> In fair round belly with good capon lined,
> With eyes severe and beard of formal cut,
> Full of wise saws and modern instances;
> And so he plays his part. The sixth age shifts
> Into the lean and slippered pantaloon
> With spectacles on nose and pouch on side;
> His youthful hose, well saved, a world too wide
> For his shrunk shank, and his big manly voice,
> Turning again toward childish treble, pipes
> And whistles in his sound. Last scene of all,
> That ends this strange eventful history,
> Is second childishness and mere oblivion,
> Sans teeth, sans eyes, sans taste, sans everything.

What Is Aristotelian Drama?

To understand the metaphor "drama as life," it is first necessary to understand drama onstage. This section introduces Aristotelian notions of drama as realized in dramatic form, conflict, and action. For modern performance theory, the interaction of these three constitutive elements of tragedy is crucial to understanding the modern analogy "life as drama."

Dramatic Form: Arranging the Parts

When a newscaster describes the drama of a hostage situation, she uses that metaphor to account for and to describe the unfolding of events. She will narrate the story as having a beginning, a middle, and an end—even when life itself offers no such clear or tidy sequence of events. Stories—whether news accounts, fairy tales, novels, movies, soap operas, stage plays, personal narratives, urban legends, or even jokes—are purposefully and artistically shaped by what Aristotle called "dramatic principles." Aristotle's *Poetics* (XXIII) prescribes the drama: "It should have for its subject a single action, whole and complete, with a beginning, a middle, and an end. It will thus resemble a living organism in all its unity, and produce the pleasure proper to it." Going beyond "beginning, middle, and end," Gustav Freytag, a German playwright, elaborated dramatic structure in Greek and Shakespearean plays in his 1863 book *Die Technik des Dramas* (*Technique of the Drama*, 1968). He labeled five parts of drama and shaped them in a pyramid: introduction, rise, climax, return or fall, and exodus.

This rise and fall of dramatic action is typical of all conventional stories: from fairy tales to novels, urban legends to Hollywood blockbusters. In conventional narrative structure, the beginning of the action is called **exposition**. Here the storyteller sets the scene, introduces the characters, presents the conflict of the story, and offers a slice of "normal" life. The exposition ends with the **inciting incident**, the event that sets the action of the story in motion. Without this incitement, no story happens. The **rising action** is a series of complications to the conflict of the story, or a series of obstacles the protagonist faces that interfere with his or her plans. The **climax** is the turning point in the story for the protagonist: Either the situation goes from good to bad (as in a tragedy) or from bad to good (as in comedy). In the **falling action**, the conflict between the protagonist and antagonist unravels, resulting in either victory or defeat for the protagonist. The **denouement**, French for "untying," undoes all the complications, or knots, tied in the rising action of the story. The story ends with the resumption of the picture of "normal" life presented at the beginning (see Figure 4.1).

This form, or imposed structure on events, is by no means a "natural" one, despite the tendency to perceive and language certain events as happening along this curve of dramatic development. Pioneering sex researchers Masters and Johnson, for example, outlined four phases of the "human sexual response cycle" as excitement, plateau, orgasm, and resolution, mirroring Freytag's pyramid and conventional narrative structure. Indeed, many claims to the "naturalness" of this form are based on perceiving similar patterns in nature: the change of seasons through the year, the rise and fall of the moon in the sky, the development of a thunderstorm.

From nature, we also make claims about *human* nature. Narrative theorist Walter Fisher (1984) claims that this rise and fall of dramatic action is central to all stories, and "narrative probability" is the "inherent awareness of what constitutes a coherent story." Raymond Williams (1983, 13) also argues that "the slice of life, once a project of naturalist drama, is now a voluntary, habitual, internal rhythm; the flow of action and acting, of representation and performance, raised to a new convention, that of a basic need."

Whether "inherent awareness" or "basic need," the human proclivity for structuring events as a rise and fall of dramatic action is tested in everyday life. Think of

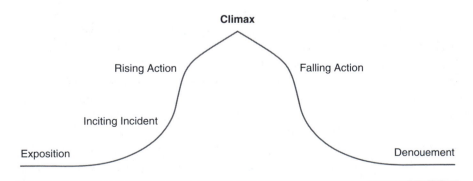

Figure 4.1   Dramatic Form

stories you've heard without a beginning, a middle, and an end. Pointless, rambling, disorganized, and seemingly endless, there is no story, no drama, there at all. Even the much acclaimed "Seinfeld," supposedly a television show "about nothing," is carefully and minutely crafted to fulfill this structure of dramatic form, even as it parodies the typical situation comedy (Morreale 2000).

ACT OUT

Shaping Drama

Everyone has a repertoire of personal experience stories. "Hey! Tell about the time you . . ." is often an invitation from friends to relate a first event (date, kiss, sex, drunkenness), an exciting episode or misadventure (broken bone, car crash, getting caught), even encounters with the supernatural. We develop these stories in and through their performances—out loud, before an audience, with often finely tuned and timed phrasing, gestures, and pauses—that develop and improve each time we create the story in performance.

Have a storytelling session in class. Then analyze the action of the stories for how well they fulfill the structural elements of Freytag's pyramid. Or, to really test Freytag's theory, have some students tell their stories out of order. What happens to form and its "naturalness" when it is subverted, inverted, changed, and left open?

Dramatic Conflict: Struggling With

Agon, the Greek root for the English word agony, is central to all drama, although its birth as a concept is much debated. In ancient Greek comedies, "agon" was the term for *a stylized debate* between the actor and the chorus, or between two actors each backed by half the chorus, in which opposing principles in the play are argued.

Sir James George Frazer, in *The Golden Bough* (1940), argues that Greek comedy and tragedy have their roots in seasonal death and rebirth rituals. In this use, agon is the name for the *ritual combat* staged in the rites between the old season (represented as aged king, hero, or god) and the new season (represented as young king).

In Western drama, agon is more generally conceived as the *struggle between opposing forces.* In literary works, conflict is realized within one character (man against himself), between a character and society (man against others), or between two characters (the protagonist against the antagonist). The centrality of conflict, as debate, as combat, as struggle, is crucial to modern conceptions of dramatic form. Teaching screenwriting to college students, Jon Stahl (2002) argues that "the core of any drama is the hero's pursuit of a goal in the face of opposition" (47).

Dramatic Action: Doing, Making, and Understanding

Intricately tied to dramatic form and conflict is dramatic action. Drama is a Greek word meaning "action," with its roots in the Greek verb *dran,* "to do." Aristotle writes in the *Poetics*, "life consists in action, and its end is a mode of action" (VI.9). Aristotle details three kinds of action: **praxis** ("to do"), **poiesis** ("to make"), and **theoria** ("to grasp and understand some truth").

Throughout the *Poetics*, Aristotle uses Sophocles' play *Oedipus Rex* as his highest example of tragedy, "the imitation of an action that is serious, complete, and of a certain magnitude." Oedipus' discovery—that he has killed his father and married his mother—organizes all the action in the plot, character, and thought of the play. Throughout the play, the tragic hero's motives revolve around action: as *praxis,* he has a job to do, to *find* the identity of the murderer of King Laius; as *poiesis,* he makes *choices and decisions* based on his growing awareness of the facts; as *theoria,* Oedipus' *discovery* that he murdered Laius and married Jocasta leads to his decision to blind himself. At the end of the play, the Chorus sees in the self-blinded Oedipus a general truth about the human condition:

> Men of Thebes: look upon Oedipus.
>
> This is the king who solved the famous riddle
>
> And towered up, most powerful of men.
>
> No mortal eyes but looked on him with envy.
>
> Yet in the end ruin swept over him.
>
> Let every man in mankind's frailty
>
> Consider his last day; and let none
>
> Presume on his good fortune until he find
>
> Life, at his death, a memory without pain.

Praxis, poiesis, and *theoria*—all forms of human action—are central to a dramatic view of both art and social interaction as process and form.

These forms are also salient ways to understand protagonists in contemporary media texts. John Stone (2000) analyzes *Platoon* and *Wall Street* for director Oliver Stone's uses of form, conflict, and dramatic action as modern morality plays of good against evil. Stone claims (2000, 85), "[Oliver] Stone's protagonists . . . [go] on journeys of vast discovery and, in so doing, learn something about themselves and the milieu of the world around them." To do, to choose, and to discover are dramatic actions in social life and artistic accounts of that life. John Osburn (1994) proposes the "tabloid" as a climactic form that raises action and resolves it in a single moment, a useful commentary on the open-endedness of some forms like soap operas and the briefness of instantaneous news.

Audience and Dramatic Form

The end of tragedy for Aristotle is pleasure; a special kind of pleasure that purges the emotions of fear and pity that have been excited in the audience by the play. Francis Fergusson (1961, 34–35) explains Aristotle's requirement of both fear and pity in appropriate measures:

Pity alone is merely sentimental, like the shameless tears of soap opera. Fear alone, such as we get from a good thriller, merely makes us shift tensely to the edge of the seat and brace ourselves for the pistol shot. But the masters of tragedy, like good cooks, mingle pity and fear in the right proportions. Having given us fear enough, they melt us with pity, purging us of our emotions, and reconciling us to our fate, because we understand it as the universal human lot.

Aristotle calls this purging of emotions **catharsis** (*Poetics* XIV): "he who hears the tale told will thrill with horror and melt to pity at what takes place. This is the impression we should receive from hearing the story of Oedipus."

Like that roller coaster with its specific arrangement of events, we also experience a very specific set of emotions on the ride: We anticipate the action, we undergo the thrills, and when we survive the ride, we experience a kind of purging of those emotions. While the comparison is perhaps a silly one, all drama creates a set of expectations in the audience, and dramatic form deliberately manipulates these expectations.

In *Counter-statement* (1931/1968), Kenneth Burke analyzes the ghost scene in *Hamlet* as Shakespeare's brilliant manipulation of audience expectations. The ghost's nightly appearance has been spoken of since the beginning of the play, and the audience anxiously awaits its appearance. But not until Act I, Scene 4, do Hamlet, Horatio, and Marcellus meet at midnight, outside on the platform, where the ghost has appeared before. Hamlet asks Horatio the time.

Horatio: I think it lacks of twelve.

Marcellus: No, it is struck.

Horatio: Indeed? I heard it not: then it draws near the season
            Wherein the spirit held his wont to walk.

Burke writes, "Hamlet's friends have established the hour at twelve. It is time for the ghost. Sounds off-stage, and of course it is not the ghost" (1931/1968, 29). Instead, they hear a blast of trumpets and a gunshot. This is the carousing of the king's men. Burke calls this "a tricky, and useful, detail. We have been waiting for a ghost, and get, startlingly, a blare of trumpets" (29). When the ghost actually does appear, some minutes later, Hamlet and his friends are deep in conversation about the drunkenness of the king's men, and the audience has taken its mind off the ghost. "This ghost, so assiduously prepared for, is yet a surprise" (30).

Dramatic structure is the creation and fulfillment of expectations *in the audience.* For Burke, the techniques of suspense and surprise are the same in classic dramatic tragedy and "the cheapest contemporary melodrama" (37). David Bordwell (1985) argues that filmmakers are limited by the typical forms that create expectations and suspense. Changing the form, however, risks altering the argumentative structure of the story.

For example, even though we know that the words "I'll be right back" signal sure death of any character in a teenage horror movie, we still participate *in the argument through the form* of these films: (1) We enjoy the creation and fulfillment of suspense; (2) we are surprised—even when we know the plot lines in advance; and

(3) we know the argument, "Teenagers who have sex in these movies die." Elizabeth C. Fine (1984, 86) offers a similar example about form and audience expectations that includes "a knowledge of *how*, as well as a knowledge of *what*."

Most Americans would not confuse the following rendition with a performance of "The Three Bears": "There were these three bears who lived in the woods. When they went for a walk, a little girl named Goldilocks came in their house and ate some porridge. She broke one of their chairs. She went to sleep in the little one's bed. They came home and woke her up. She ran away." This text, while retaining the basic plot elements, violates the norms of interaction for the performance.

What happens and *how* it is performed—on the stage, in film, in storytelling—puts audience center stage in dramatic theory.

CAUGHT LOOKING

Dramatic Scenes that Create Expectations

Horror films are particularly good at creating expectations in the audience. Bring in a clip of a scene from a horror film. Then analyze how this scene creates a series of expectations in the audience. Is the killer around the corner? What's inside the closet? Is someone is being stalked?

How are you also surprised when the expectation is *not* fulfilled—that the sound is a door banging in the wind, that inside the closet is a coat and hat, that the stalker is the family cat?

Given the surprise, how is the original expectation then fulfilled when the audience least expects it?

READ MORE ABOUT IT

Oedipus Retold

Poet Muriel Rukeyser manipulates everyone's expectations, Oedipus' included, in her poem "Myth" from her collection of poems Breaking Open *(1973, 20).*

Long afterward, Oedipus, old and blinded, walked the roads. He smelled a familiar smell. It was the Sphinx. Oedipus said, "I want to ask one question. Why didn't I recognize my mother?" "You gave the wrong answer," said the Sphinx. "But that was what made everything possible," said Oedipus. "No," she said. "When I asked, What walks on four legs in the morning, two at noon, and three in the evening, you answered, Man. You didn't say anything about woman." "When you say Men," said Oedipus, "you include women too. Everyone knows that." She said, "That's what you think."

SOURCE: Reprinted by permission of International Creative Management, Inc. Copyright © 1973 by Muriel Rukeyser.

Kenneth Burke's Dramatism: Life *Is* Drama

Kenneth Burke was a drama, music, and literary critic for the monthly magazine *The Dial* in the 1920s, but he soon turned his attention to the wide scope of human affairs. Burke called himself a "word man," "a student of strategies," and a "logologist" (Chesebro 1993, p. ix). Scott McLemee (2001, A26) writes of responses to Burke's work:

> Literary scholars who admired Burke's essays on Flaubert or Mann often found his later work bewildering. They complained that his ideas about "symbolic action" could apply just as easily to advertising campaigns as to *The Divine Comedy.* In other words, Burke may have accidentally created cultural studies.

Burke developed a system he called **dramatism** that maintains that *language is action.* Language is more than simply instrumental: It legitimates, thematizes, and performs social meanings. Even *Webster's Third International Dictionary* acknowledges Burke's definition of dramatism: "a technique of analysis of language and thought as basically modes of action rather than as means of conveying information."

Burke makes an important distinction between motion and action. **Motion** is what happens in the physical world—the growth of crops, the movement of the tides, the workings of a machine. **Action** is a thoroughly human endeavor (recall *praxis, poiesis, and theoria*) and should be "preserved for human behavior which proceeds from motives" that are revealed in choices, commitments, moral evaluations, and responsibilities (Gudas 1983a, 591).

A dramatistic approach to human interaction mandates *an awareness of ourselves as actors speaking in specific situations with specific purposes.* These motives are revealed in the ways we shape language to meet our needs, and the ways that language—in turn—shapes our identities and affiliations. David Payne and Roderick Hart (1996, 267) analyze the language of "drunk driving" for different actors and the language that reveals motives:

> [A] scientist may describe drinking-while-driving as "conditioned behavior," a phrase that downplays motive, while the libertarian and the religious cleric may highlight motives but do so oppositely (i.e., "drinking as personal freedom" vs. "drinking as sin"). For the scientist, decisions are made by the brain; for the libertarian they are made by the mind; for the preacher they are made by the conscience. . . . [For Mothers Against Drunk Driving] drinking is a social act, often a public act. . . . "Killing while drinking and driving is murder, plain and simple."

Finding the dramatic conflict, form, and action in a political speech is easy: Speakers deliberately manipulate language, create "us" and "them" versions of the situation, and appeal to the audience's loves and fears. Finding the drama in a staged play is even easier, especially when playwrights consciously and deliberately adhere to Aristotelian notions of form, conflict, and audience expectations. James Combs and Michael Mansfield (1976, xviii) explain how Burke went beyond "finding" drama in these situations to argue that life *is* drama. Action means structured behavior in terms of symbols, which implies choice, conflict and cooperation, which men communicate to each other. Society is a drama in which actions, in terms of social symbols, are the crucial events. The difference between "staged" drama and the drama of real life is the difference between human obstacles imagined by an artist and those actually experienced. The realms are homologous: Life and art both deal with the fundamental problems of human existence, and both aim at the symbolic resolution of conflict through communication.

Dramatism is a theory that accounts for human symbol use and misuse to resolve conflict through collective performances.

SOURCE: U.S. Marine Corps photo by Lance Cpl. James Green, 2006. From U.S. Department of Defense, www.defenselink.mil. Home Page photos.

THEORY MEETS WORLD

I Know a Gal in New Orleans

Jeff Parker Knight (1990) explores performances of Marine Corps "jodies," the marching chants familiar to us in films like *An Officer and a Gentleman* and *Full Metal Jacket*. Knight learned and performed the chants in the summer of 1982 at Camp Ushur, in Quantico, Virgina.

Kenneth Burke maintained that "literature is equipment for living," for it presents strategies for understanding and engaging typical situations. In "Literature as Equipment for Killing: Performance as Rhetoric in Military Training Camps,"

Knight argues that the collectively chanted rhymes are performances that serve to socialize and indoctrinate; as ritual, participatory performances, they "alter our perceptions of reality, and thus our actions" (1990, 162).

As indoctrination and socialization, the jodies perform attitudes toward Marine Corps loyalty and power:

> I had a wife and she was keen
> I traded her for my M-16

> ****

> Running through the jungle with my M-16
> I'm a mean motherfucker, I'm a U.S. Marine

> ****

> I want to be a Recon Ranger
> I want to live a life of danger

The jodies also desensitize recruits toward killing others and their own deaths:

> Flying low and feeling mean
> Fire a family by a stream
> See them burn and hear them scream
> Cause Napalm sticks to kids

> ****

> If I die in the old drop zone
> Box me up and send me home
> Pin my medals on my chest
> And tell my Mom I did my best

Many of the jodies perform attitudes toward women as sex objects, nameless and interchangeable, as a means "to demonstrate masculine dominance and prowess" (163):

> I got a gal in Kansas City
> She's got gumdrops on her titties
> When I get back to Kansas City
> Gonna suck those gumdrops off her titties

> ****

(Continued)

(Continued)

> I got a gal in New Orleans
> Kisses sailors and she blows Marines
>
> Knight writes of the last couplet, "the woman serves both as an oral recep-
> tacle and as instrument of inter-branch rivalry" (163).
> As ritual, chanted performances, jodies were one of the "few pleasures in an
> atmosphere designed to induce stress" (164), while they socialized the recruits
> into a new world. Knight writes:
>
> I am still sometimes surprised, and horrified, at the words I said and the way
> I thought during and immediately after a brief stint in a military training
> camp. The jodies were part of the change we went through. By laughing at
> the unpleasant realities of war, we no doubt were hardening ourselves to
> our own squeamishness and fear. Such hardening was to make us efficient
> soldiers, willing to kill or die on command (and, as officers, willing to give
> such commands). . . . The humorous and cathartic aspects of the songs help
> to make the training experience bearable. At the same time, they indoctri-
> nate the recruits into sharing the attitudes suggested by the songs. . . . Jody
> songs in the military, to modify Kenneth Burke, have become literature as
> equipment for killing, a tool of socializing civilians into soldiers. (166)

Ritual Drama as Hub: Two Kinds of Sacrifice

Burke argues that "symbolic resolution of conflict" is available in the form of ritual
drama, which he calls "the hub" of human activity. While the origin of Western
staged drama in ritual is a theory that is both highly contested and never provable
(Rozik 2002; Schechner 2002b), Burke was not interested in origins. He was interested in the way that ritual drama provides an Ur-form, a "test case" or "paradigm,"
for all human social interaction: "that the ritual enactment of struggle, suffering,
sacrifice, and the appearance of new light and new life, is at the root of the tragic
form" (Fergusson 1961, 39).

Burke writes in a series of "if/then" clauses that begin with Aristotelian notions
of action, drama, and tragedy to explain social interaction: "If *action* is to be our
key term, then *drama;* for drama is the culminative form of action. . . . But if
drama, then *conflict.* And if *conflict,* then *victimage.* Dramatism is always on the
edge of this vexing problem, that comes to a culmination in tragedy, the song of the
scapegoat" (1966, 54–55). Burke maintains that when humans come together—to
live, to work, to love, to war, to cooperate, and to compete—our greatest tendency
is toward sacrifice. That is, we tend to solve our conflicts in one of two ways: by sacrificing others through **victimage** or by sacrificing ourselves to a greater good
through **mortification**.

The ritual drama enacts victimage. Victimage, also called **scapegoating**, is the
symbolic heaping of sins or bestowing of guilt on an individual and destroying him

or her through sacrifice. The symbolic vessel is then purged, or cast out, from the community. In early Greek rituals of purification, this "vessel" was often a goat; hence, the "song of the goat" or scapegoat. In early Judaic rites related in the Old Testament, a priest confessed the sins of the community over the head of a goat that was then driven away into the wilderness, symbolically carrying the sins away. Fabian Gudas relates how Burke analyzed literature for this same pattern:

> Inevitably, guilt, felt as a painful attitude, must be cleansed. This is done through some cathartic means, usually involving victimage or scapegoatism. If successful, the individual or the social group is purified and redeemed, and the problematic situation has been transcended. This is the drama of human relations in its most abstract form. Literature is the symbolic expression of these relations. (1983a, 594)

So how to manipulate that guilt? Robert Adams (1983, 716) explains the many resources humans have according to Burke: "We may repress our guilt, transfer it to a scapegoat, sublimate it to an ecstasy, placate it in a ritual, seek forgiveness in prayer, mor-

SOURCE: Photograph by Cindy Mosqueda. Copyright © 2006 by Cindy Mosqueda.

tify it in an actual or symbolic suicide, or normalize it as part of a structure." In Burke's famous essay, "The Rhetoric of Hitler's Battle" (1957), he analyzed Hitler's scapegoating of European Jews for the economic ills of Germany. Today, the urge to blame through scapegoating is rampant, whether immigrants from Mexico for economic woes, people from the Middle East for terrorism, feminists for destruction of family values, or gays and lesbians for the decline of marriage.

Manipulation of guilt, however, needn't always be tragic. Comedy also operates, with a Burkean lens, through the purging of guilt. Brian Ott (2003, 72) analyzes "The Simpsons" for Homer's constant overconsumption. Ott writes:

> Homer, then, is more than a cartoon character; he is a symbol of a shared guilt and a comedic tool for coming to terms with it. Comedy teaches the fool and hence the audience, explains Brummett, "about error so that it may be corrected rather than punished. Comedy does this through dramatic irony, in which audience members are placed in a position where they see behind the facade of the sins and errors that bedevil the fool" (Brummett 1984a, 219–20). By the end of each episode, Homer is publicly embarrassed for his consumptive practices, thereby revealing the error of his ways and reintegrating him into the social hierarchy.

Blaming oneself through **mortification**, or *self-punishment,* is also a tragic urge in the dramatistic view of human action. Indeed, sacrificing oneself for others is often seen as the highest human motive: the soldier who throws himself on a hand grenade to save a group; the mother who dies rescuing her child; the one who stays behind to light the fuse. This urge to sacrifice oneself for the good of others is epitomized for Burke in the Christian tradition: Jesus Christ died on the cross for mankind so that all who believe can achieve eternal life.

While these individual actions are seen as heroic, noble, and selfless, contemporary group acts of mortification are less easy to categorize or understand. Jim Jones, in 1978, shocked the world when he and his followers in Guyana, South America, committed group suicide. Nine hundred and fourteen people, including 276 children, drank a soft drink laced with cyanide and sedatives after investigations of the People's Temple began by the U.S. Congress. In 1997, thirty-nine members of "Heaven's Gate" committed group suicide in Del Mar, California, supposedly ready to leave the Earth with aliens arriving behind Comet Hale-Bopp. A news account ("Mass Suicide" 1997) of the event relates: "The mass suicide likely took place over three days and involved three groups, proceeding in a calm, ritualistic fashion. Some members apparently assisted others and then cleaned up, then went on to take their own dose of the fatal mixture, mixed with apple sauce or pudding."

The linking of drama, tragedy, ritual, and motive is at the heart of Burke's dramatism—a perspective on human action as drama, a conception of language itself as symbolic action. Combs and Mansfield (1976, xviii) elaborate the symbolic relationship between language and action: "Humans do not simply mate, they marry; they do not simply kill for food, but for gods and country; territory is not simply defended, it is named."

Analyzing Motives: Beyond the Pentad

Most summaries of dramatism feature the dramatistic **pentad,** the five questions to ask in any study of motives in human dramas: *agent* (who), *scene* (when and where), *act* (what), *agency* (how and with what materials), and *purpose* (why). This model can be a fruitful route to *begin* asking questions. Settling for simple answers to these questions, however, "dissolves" the drama—the conflict (struggle, sacrifice, and rebirth), action (doing, choosing, and discovering), and structure (rise and fall) of the drama itself. The pentad is a "calculus," not an "algebra."

Many scholars of oral interpretation were introduced to the pentad through Don Geiger's *The Sound, Sense, and Performance of Literature* (1963, 62): "In finding answers to these questions—Who? What? How? Where? When? and Why?—we are discovering the situation-attitude relationships which comprise the piece's 'drama.'" Textbooks in performance of literature have made Burke's pentad a centerpiece (Long and HopKins 1982; Pelias 1992; Stern and Henderson 1993). When performers use the pentad to begin their analysis of a literary text, they return the drama to the words on the page. Wallace Bacon and Robert Breen (1959, 7) write, "all literature is dramatic: There is always a conflict expressed or implied, and a prevailing emotional state. Such are the conditions of drama, and such are the conditions which give all literature the semblance of life."

Burke suggests several other methods to understand and to explore human motives. In addition to the pentad, Burke utilizes perspective by incongruity, cluster agons with their God and Devil terms, and the representative anecdote. **Perspective by incongruity** asks critics to depart from traditional ways of seeing, "pieties" in Burke's term, by turning ideas on their heads. Naomi Rockler (2002) suggests looking at gender roles in media and reversing them. On "The Price is Right" for example, cast a woman in Bob Barker's role and men in the roles of "Barker's Beauties." This new perspective reveals how naturalized these gender roles are in the drama of consumerism. Elizabeth Bell (1999) uses perspective by incongruity to argue that weddings and pornography are complementary and necessary to each other, not opposites of each other, in cultural performances in the West.

Language is a grammar of motives. Words "cluster" with other words in a "what goes with what" system of usage that characterizes the conflict in particular ways. Burke calls these **cluster agons.** Related to cluster agons are **God and Devil terms**. In vocabularies of motives, certain words stand for ultimate good and ultimate evil, and we often use these terms as "shorthand" for affiliations and ideologies: pro-life and pro-choice, freedom and tyranny, Democrat and Republican, free trade and protectionism, gay rights and family values.

In 1973, members of the Speech Communication Association debated a name change for one of the association's journals. Wayne Brockriede (1973, 12) wrote:

The selection of the god-word that most accurately names what we are primarily about is something for SCA members to think about and to debate about. At one time the best word for our discipline was "rhetoric"; from about 1915 to about 1960 it was "speech"; since then we have stood at the waystation

SOURCE: Photograph by Danny Hammontree (www.digitalgrace.com). Copyright © 2006 by Danny Hammontree.

of "speech communication." Today's word is "communication" without any encumbering adjectives.

David S. Olsen (2001) analyzes the use of God and Devil terms in the polarized reactions to Martin Scorsese's controversial film *The Last Temptation of Christ.* For defenders of the film, the God-term was censorship—something to be fought at all costs. For detractors of the film, the God-term was the "American way," cast as "most Christians" in the United States and their biblical interpretation of the life of Christ. God and Devil terms organize and condense arguments.

The **representative anecdote** is a tiny story that both stands for and encompasses larger societal concerns, fears, and desires. Barry Brummett (1984b, 161) explains how the representative anecdote is a critical tool: "by examining what people are *saying*, the critic may discover what cultures are celebrating or mourning—and the critic may recommend other ways of speaking which may serve as better equipment for living." So political elections are "horse races," celebrity lives are "soap operas," famous trials are "media circuses."

Folklorist Roger Abrahams also approaches performances of verbal art through a dramatistic lens. Expressive folklore is often centered on a problem, a problem Abrahams (1968, 148) describes as

> "magically" transferred from the item to the recurrent problem when the performance operates successfully, sympathetically. Because the performer projects the conflict and resolves it, the illusion is created that it can be solved in real life; and with the addition of sympathy, of "acting with," the audience not only derives pleasure from the activity but also knowledge.

Going beyond the pentad to analyze motives means paying attention to language and its performances (1) by turning ideas or practices on their heads; (2) by isolating oppositional terms that shape and name the conflict; (3) by exploring how performance enacts the problem and its solution "magically" as a guide for action; and (4) by examining how audiences are invited to participate—with sympathy, pleasure, and knowledge.

ACT OUT

Dramatizing Competing Products

Check out advertisements for mattresses. If health is the pitch, certain medical terms will follow. If luxury is the pitch, certain economic terms follow. The conflict will be created in language and resolved in the drama of purchasing and sleeping on a new mattress.

Divide the class into groups and have each group collect numerous print advertisements for a product: homes, shampoos, internet servers, shoes, power tools, cars. Find the "God" and "Devil" terms, the agon clusters, and the representative anecdote presented in these different dramas, then stage them using the advertising copy as script.

READ MORE ABOUT IT

A Representative Anecdote

Eugene Robinson creates a representative anecdote in the 24-hour news cycle's fascination with some women. "(White) Women We Love," (2005, A2) is a potent analysis of what American culture is celebrating and mourning.

Someday historians will look back at America in the decade bracketing the turn of the 21st century and identify the era's major themes: Religious fundamentalism. Terrorism. War in Iraq. Economic dislocation. Bioengineering. Information technology. Nuclear proliferation. Globalization. The rise of superpower China. And, of course, Damsels in Distress.

Every few weeks, this stressed-out nation with more problems to worry about than hours in the day finds time to become obsessed with the saga—it's always a "saga," never just a story—of a damsel in distress. Natalee Holloway, the student who disappeared while on a class trip to the Caribbean island of Aruba, is the latest in what seems an endless series.

Holloway assumed the mantle from her predecessor, the Runaway Bride, who turned out not to have been in distress at all—not physical distress, at least, though it's obvious that the prospect of her impending 600-guest wedding caused Jennifer Wilbanks an understandable measure of mental trauma.

Before the Runaway Bride, there were too many damsels to provide a full list, but surely you remember the damsel elite: Laci Peterson. Elizabeth Smart. Lori Hacking. Chandra Levy. JonBenet Ramsey. We even found, or created, a damsel amid the chaos of war in Iraq: Jessica Lynch.

The specifics of the story line vary from damsel to damsel. In some cases, the saga begins with the discovery of a corpse. In other cases, the damsel simply vanishes into thin air. Often, there is a suspect from the beginning—an intruder, a husband, a father, a congressman, a stranger glimpsed lurking nearby.

Sometimes the tale ends well, or well enough, as in the cases of Smart and Lynch. Let's hope it ends well for Holloway. But more often, it ends badly. Once in a great while, a case like Runaway Bride comes along to provide comic relief.

But of course the damsels have much in common besides being female. You probably have some idea of where I'm headed here. A damsel must be white. This requirement is nonnegotiable. It helps if her frame is of dimensions that breathless cable television reporters can credibly describe as "petite," and it also helps if she's the kind of woman who wouldn't really mind being called "petite," a woman with a good deal of princess in her personality. She must be attractive—also nonnegotiable. Her economic status should be middle class or higher, but an exception can be made in the case of wartime (see: Lynch).

Put all this together, and you get 24-7 coverage. The disappearance of a man, or of a woman of color, can generate a brief flurry, but never the full damsel treatment. Since the Holloway story broke we've had more news reports from Aruba this past week, I'd wager, than in the preceding 10 years.

I have no idea whether the late French philosopher Jacques Derrida hung on every twist and turn of the Chandra Levy case; somehow, I doubt he did. But I doubt

(Continued)

(Continued)

> the apostle of "deconstructionism" would have analyzed the damsel-in-distress phenomenon by explaining that our society is imposing its own subconsciously chosen narrative on all these cases.
>
> It's the meta-narrative of something seen as precious and delicate being snatched away, defiled, destroyed by evil forces that lurk in the shadows, just outside the bedroom window. It's whiteness under siege. It's innocence and optimism crushed by cruel reality. It's a flower smashed by a rock.
>
> Or maybe (since Derrida believed in multiple readings of a single text) the damsel thing is just a guaranteed cure for a slow news day. The cable news channels, after all, have lots of airtime to fill.
>
> This is not to mock any one of these cases (except Runaway Bride) or to diminish the genuine tragedy experienced by family and friends. I can imagine the helplessness I'd feel if a child of mine disappeared from a remote beach in the Caribbean. But I can also be fairly confident that neither of my sons would provoke so many headlines.
>
> Whatever our ultimate reason for singling out these few unfortunate victims, among the thousands of Americans who are murdered or who vanish each year, the pattern of choosing only young, white, middle-class women for the full damsel treatment says a lot about a nation that likes to believe it has consigned race and class to irrelevance.
>
> What it says is that we haven't. What it says is that those stubborn issues are still very much alive and that they remain at the heart of the nation's deepest fears.
>
> SOURCE: "(White) Women We Love" by Eugene Robinson © 2005. The Washington Post Writers Group. Reprinted with Permission.

Performing Tragic and Comic Attitudes

For Kenneth Burke, dramatism names a critical orientation toward the world: Language and symbol systems are made by us and are in evidence everywhere humans congregate, segregate, and are urged to rise above our stations—physically, economically, socially, politically, and spiritually. Burke (1966) claims we can adopt two attitudes toward these dramas: A **tragic attitude** is one that succumbs to the inevitability of the tragic song of the scapegoat, our fatedness, and inability to change, or influence, a course of events (Lentriccia 1983, 62). A **comic attitude** does not succumb to inevitabilities, limitations, or fate, but instead appreciates the often ironic ways humans are *creative* with language, are critically *aware* of their choices, and *perform* these meanings every day of their lives.

Communication scholars have used Burke's "comic" and "tragic" attitudes to explore performances around us. Adrienne E. Christiansen and Jeremy J. Hanson (1996, 158) analyze the ACT UP activism of AIDS protests through Burke's "comic perspective," as "humans' capacity for laughter, reason, and action rather than scapegoating [of AIDS victims] and paralysis." Elizabeth Bell and Linda Forbes (1994) use Burke's comic frame to explore cartoons posted in workplaces as creative and collective responses to organizational restraints on workers. Conversational analysts use dramatism to break down the lines between life and art to argue that ordinary conversations, scripted like plays and performed anew, are valuable resources for exploring the forms, aesthetics, and drama of everyday life (Hopper 1993; Stucky 1993).

In her ethnography, *A Space on the Side of the Road: Cultural Poetics in an "Other" America* (1996), Kathleen Stewart explores one community of coal miners in the "hollers" of West Virginia. When a dog bit a child, the members of the community became very concerned about their legal responsibilities and liabilities. A "tragic" view of this incident might emphasize the community's poverty, its lack of access to the legal system, and its members' unfortunate readiness to be cast as victims in a legal system outside their control. Stewart relates the community's solution, which is a wonderfully "comic" perspective. It is creative and critically aware, and it performs an ironic reversal of legal and social meanings.

> Finally Lacy Forest announced that he had heard that "by law" if you had a NO TRESPASSING sign on your porch you couldn't be sued. So everyone went to the store in Beckley to get the official kind of sign. Neighbors brought back multiple copies and put them up for those too old or sick or poor to get out and get their own. Then everyone called everyone else to explain that the sign did not mean them. In the end, every porch and fence (except for those of the isolated shameless who didn't care) had a bright NO TRESPASSING, KEEP OFF sign, and people visited together, sitting underneath the NO TRESPASS-ING signs, looking out. (Stewart 1996, 141)

While the temptation is to approach our attitudes and performances as comic or tragic, mortification or victimage, Burke was not locked into these *either/or* approaches. Instead, he advocated a *both/and* approach. The West Virginia community performed their solution to the problem with a "both/and" comic perspective.

Dramatism is an amazingly influential and rich perspective for understanding human interaction. Fabian Gudas (1983b, 10) writes, "My own commitment to dramatism derives from the remarkable manner in which it has enabled sociology, philosophy, language study, rhetoric, and poetics to illuminate each other." Communication scholars of performance have utilized Burke's dramatistic concepts to do the work of critical analysis, pedagogy of performance, and performing texts to return the dramas of human relations to felt experience. As a theory of symbolic action and method of analysis, dramatism is a rich perspective for accounting for conflict, choice, and action in human beings' unique capacity for symbol use.

From Dramatism to Social Drama

Just as Kenneth Burke is difficult to pin down to a precise set of ideas, the theories of Victor Turner are similarly wide-ranging. A British-trained anthropologist, Turner summarizes his own work as moving "widely through geography and history, over India, Africa, Europe, China, and Meso-America, from ancient society through the medieval period to modern revolutionary times" (1974, 17). Turner's theories of liminality, communitas, and reflexivity will be explored in depth in Chapter Five, "Performing Culture," but here Turner extends Burke's notions of "dramas of living," to understand "how the living perform their lives" (Turner 1982, 68, 108).

In his fieldwork in Central Africa with the Ndembu people in the early 1950s, Turner became fascinated with the preponderance of conflict in this community. For Turner, these conflicts erupted in very public ways and followed a predictable structure. He found parallels between the Ndembu village and Greek drama "where one witnesses the helplessness of the human individual before the Fates, but in this case the Fates are the necessities of the social process" (1957, 94). Turner theorized that instead of Oedipus doing, choosing, and discovering (*praxis, poiesis,* and *theoria*) as a tragic victim of fate, the Ndembu performed these same dramatic actions; the community, not fate, become the critics of actions and arbitrators of justice.

Turner named this processual unfolding of social events the **social drama**, "a sequence of social interactions of a conflictive, competitive, or agonistic type" (1988, 33). Simply put, the social drama is Turner's label for what happens in a community when someone breaks a rule, how the community then takes sides for or against the rule breaker, and how the community works to resolve this problem. Turner utilizes Aristotelian notions of dramatic form, as well as Burkean notions of language as symbolic action, to explore how communities deal with and resolve conflict.

All social dramas are centered in **conflict**, unfold in a predictable four-stage **process**, and involve public forms of **communication**. In Turner's definition of the social drama, *conflict* is central:

> Conflict seems to bring fundamental aspects of society, normally overlaid by the customs and habits of daily intercourse, into frightening prominence. People have to take sides in terms of deeply entrenched moral imperatives and constraints, often against their own personal preferences. Choice is overborne by duty. (1974, 35)

From the eruption of conflict to its resolution, the sequence of events is *processional* in that it unfolds in predictable, observable ways. This emphasis on process is important to understanding culture and its institutions, not as "bundles of dead or cold rules," but as "dynamic processes" that become visible as the action of the social drama "heats up" (1974, 37).

This study of conflict and process necessarily involves studying *communication* and the "sources of pressures to communicate within and among groups; this leads inevitably to the study of symbols, signs, signals, and tokens, verbal and nonverbal, that people employ to attain personal and group goals" (1974, 37).

Examples of events around us can be fruitfully explored as social dramas from small scale, community affairs to national scandals that elicit media frenzies: from the opening of a neighborhood X-rated bookstore and the teaching of Annie Proulx's short story "Brokeback Mountain" in a high school English class to a hunting accident involving the vice-president of the United States, the Michael Jackson trial for child molestation, and radio commentator Don Imus calling the Rutgers women's basketball team "nappy-headed hos." These events can be explained and understood as conflictual, processual, and always centered in communication. The social drama unfolds in **four stages**, or phases, of public action. The stages are breach, crisis, redress, and resolution or schism.

Breach: Cutting the Tie that Binds

The first stage of the social drama is the **breach**, the *breaking of a rule* by a member of the community. This rule breaking is publicly visible, "the breach of a norm, the infraction of a rule of morality, law, custom or etiquette in some public arena" (Turner 1982, 70).

For this rule breaking to constitute a breach, the rule must be held by the community as "binding." That is, the rule is important to the maintenance of the group, subgroups, or relationships between people within the group. As binding, the rule can be seen as a key link to the integrity of the entire community (1988, 34). Turner offers several metaphors for this breach: cutting the knot in the rope that binds a community together; a tear in the social fabric of daily life; an eruption (think pimple or boil) on daily interaction. "Village, chiefdom, office, factory, political party or ward, church, university department" are just some of the examples Turner offers as groups that can be thrown into turmoil when someone has broken a rule central to that community's social cohesion and operations (1974, 38).

Infidelity in a marriage, for example, may be particularly egregious if the couple took their marriage vows as "binding." This interpersonal breach reached a national stage in the Bill Clinton/Monica Lewinsky affair. Laura Kipnis writes how Clinton's infidelity stood for "all broken promises, intimate and national. . . . It's about the fear that adultery puts things at risk: from the organization of daily life to the very moral fabric of the nation" (1998, 294).

Crisis: Contagion and Participation

The second stage is **crisis,** and crisis, according to Turner, is "contagious." In this stage, the members of the community participate in talk that is incessant, escalating, and divisive, as "people will be induced, seduced, cajoled, nudged, or threatened to take sides" with or against the rule breaker (1988, 34). This stage may involve physical violence, or threats of violence, and moments of danger or suspense.

The content of the talk in the crisis phase will involve members of the community debating exactly what went wrong. Again, the talk during the Clinton/Lewinsky social drama epitomizes Turner's claim. Just what "rule" did President Clinton break? Clinton lied under oath. Clinton had an extramarital affair. Clinton obstructed justice. Clinton suborned perjury. Clinton engaged in sexual relations with an employee. Clinton dishonored the office of the presidency. Pick a breach, any breach. In Turner's conception of the social drama, the *exact nature of the breach* will become one of the many debates during the crisis period.

Important to the social drama is that this talk takes place in *public forums* and "dares the representatives of order to grapple with it. It cannot be ignored or wished away" (1974, 39). In short, the crisis is a challenge to the entire community to repair the "order" that has been broken or torn by the breach.

Redress: Repairing the Social Order

The third stage is **redress**, or employing procedures to repair or remedy the breach. This machinery of repair can take a wide number of forms: from personal advice or counseling; formal, legal, judicial machinery; to the performance of public ritual. Turner (1982, 71) claims that this "ritual often involves a 'sacrifice,' literal or moral, a victim as scapegoat for the group's 'sin' of redressive violence."

No doubt thousands of couples have experienced breaches of wedding vows in their relationships. Most often the repair is informal advice given by friends and family members or marriage counseling. If this doesn't work, then redress, too, escalates: The couple moves its conflict into the court system through divorce proceedings, seeking redress through formal and judicial machinery. In the case of Bill Clinton, the breach led to an impeachment trial in the U.S. Senate, a mechanism mandated by the U.S. Constitution if a president is charged with "treasonous offenses to the nation."

Turner calls the redress stage the most **reflexive,** or self-conscious, part of the social drama. Turner defines reflexivity as "the ways in which a group tries to scrutinize, portray, understand, and then act on itself" (1981, 152). This stocktaking or plural self-scrutiny involves a community looking at itself—as a community—to measure what one member has done in relation to agreed-upon standards of behavior, and to ask if the machinery of repair is sufficient to restore peace.

The redress phase also involves moments of **liminality**, a "betwixt and between" of suspended knowledge about the outcome in the social drama. Courtroom verdicts of guilty or not guilty are exemplary of liminal moments in the redress phase of the social drama. Whether our focus was O. J. Simpson, President Clinton, or Michael Jackson, we were all "betwixt and between," in those long minutes between the jury announcing it had reached a verdict and the reading of the verdict itself.

Reintegration or Schism: Back to Normal. Or Not

Reintegration or schism is the fourth stage of the social drama. If the repair works, then the rule-breaker is reintegrated into the community. The community moves on, back to its quotidian life. Life has changed, however, because, as Turner maintains, "Every social drama alters, in however minuscule a fashion, the structure of the relevant social field" (1988, 92). New rules, laws, interpretations, and ways of seeing and relating often arise out of the old conflict. These alterations, Turner notes parenthetically, are not a "permanent ordering of social relations but merely a temporary mutual accommodation of interests."

If the machinery of redress doesn't work, then the community splits or breaks apart into factions. Turner calls this phase **schism**. "In large-scale, complex communities, continuous failure of redressive institutions may develop into a revolutionary situation, in which one of the contending parties generates a program of societal change" (1988, 35).

Turner's social drama recalls all the ways that Kenneth Burke operationalized Aristotelian drama: (1) the processual unfolding of events—breach, crisis, redress, and reintegration/schism—parallels the rise and fall of dramatic action; (2) conflict is central to the event as the community creates an antagonist and protagonist and takes sides in and through language; (3) resolution of the drama is achieved through cultural mechanisms, often involving symbolic action of sacrifice—victimization or mortification—that cleanses and reunifies the community.

GO FIGURE

Social Dramas on Your Campus

The Stanford University Marching Band is known for their playful parodies of opposing schools during their halftime shows. At the Stanford v. Brigham Young University football game on September 11, 2004, five members of the Stanford band appeared on the field dressed in wedding veils, mocking the Mormon tradition of polygamy. The incident quickly evolved through Turner's predictable stages of the social drama with all the characteristics of breach, crisis, redress, and reintegration as the Stanford band apologized formally and publicly to the Brigham Young community.

Can you name episodes on your campus, perhaps the firing of popular professors, episodes of hate speech, charges of sexual harassment, or fraternity pranks "gone awry"? How is Turner's lens valuable for understanding the conflict, processes, and communicative forms during the unfolding of the events?

Analyzing Social Dramas

While Turner studied small, homogeneous societies across the world, he also listed examples of social dramas from Western societies as well: the Boston Tea Party, the Dreyfus affair, Watergate, U.S. "urban renewal" of the 1960s, and the 1979 seizure of the U.S. embassy in Teheran and the holding of more than seventy American hostages. Turner's claims about conflict, process, and communication are particularly revelatory for understanding "drama in life" as "political processes, that is, they involve competition for scarce ends—power, dignity, prestige, honor, purity" (1982, 71).

Communication scholars utilize the social drama to explore these competitions. Thomas Farrell (1989) analyzes the broadcast of the 1984 Olympic games as the social drama threatening "America First" norms in the advertising, narration, and spectacle of the two-week media broadcast. Leah Vande Berg (1995) uses the frame of the social drama to analyze "remembrances" broadcast in and around November 22, the anniversary of the assassination of John F. Kennedy. Paul Edwards (1999, 38) writes of the "Sextext" battle within the National Communication Association as a social drama in which the organization took sides over academic "values," the proper canon for the discipline, and the future of Performance Studies in Communication.

Elizabeth C. Fine, in *Soulstepping: African American Step Shows* (2003), explores the potential for eruption of conflict among African-American college fraternities and sororities. The step shows that members learn and perform are ritual acts of membership and unity with an Afrocentric worldview. Because many of the step shows involve "cracking," "dissing," or "cutting" other groups, critiques that create the unity and camaraderie of one fraternity or sorority come at the expense of others. Fine (2003, 63) relates how Alpha Phi Alpha cracked on the Kappas with a popular refrain: "I say we're laughing at you and you don't know why . . . I say we're laughing at you cause you ain't A Phi!"

While most African-American audiences understand the playful tradition of cracking and playing the dozens, many white audiences do not. In 1990 at East Tennessee State University, Fine relates how Kappa Alpha Psi President David Harvin spoke to the mixed-race audience of the Southern Dance Traditions Conference: "I want to make it clear that while we do step and while we talk about other fraternities and they talk about us . . . that we do get along with other black Greeks, that there is unity on this campus" (2003, 141–42).

Theatre scholar Diana Taylor (2003) analyzes the "life, death, funeral, and after-life as quasi-sacred relic on display" of Princess Diana as a social drama that played out on global and local stages. Taylor ties each stage to different theatrical and per-formance frames:

> The breach—her divorce from Charles and her estrangement from the Royal family—was pure melodrama. . . . Her death—the crisis—was tragic drama. The redressive action—the funeral—was a theatrical performance. . . . The phase of reintegration, the period of reordering social norms, played itself out in multiple, less cohesive, less centralized dramas. . . . Diana's ghost became a site of intensive renegotiating among various communities. (137, 140–41)

All of these explorations of contemporary social dramas show how communi-cation and performance are resources for languaging the breach, garnering support for and against the protagonist, resolving the drama through cultural mechanisms, and returning the community to normal.

Social Drama: Raw Material for Performances

If the social drama follows a predictable unfolding of events, then it also generates performances as part and parcel of the action. The social drama is the "raw mater-ial" for performances that reflect critically on the community. Turner (1988, 41) utilizes a linguistic analogy, the "moods of culture," to characterize social life as moving between the indicative ("it is") and the subjunctive ("may be," "might be," even "should be"). For Turner, the social drama is "indicative." The breach happened. Newspapers report the facts. Heated public debates argue the facts. Courtroom performances re-create the facts of the case. The social drama *is*.

"Most cultural performances," Turner argues on the other hand, "belong to culture's 'subjunctive' mood." In the subjective, performance reframes the indicative "is" to imagine "*what if?*" For example, in the indicative social drama of the Bill Clinton/Monica Lewinsky affair, President Clinton claimed on September 26, 1998, "I did not have sex with that woman, Ms. Lewinsky." On the Internet, however, one parody imagined Clinton's State of the Union Address on September 27, 1998, as beginning, "Members of Congress, people of America, I banged her. I banged her like a cheap gong." This cultural performance imagined a very different "what if?" for the State of the Union address.

Turner argues that social dramas provide the "raw material" for aesthetic performances. These performances, "aesthetic" for their deliberate and artful shaping of conventions, include ritual, festival, Carnival, folk stories, ballet, staged drama, novels, epic poems; in short, a multitude of culturally recognized genres. Aesthetic performances also feed back into ongoing social dramas, influencing the way that politicians, orators, preachers, and opinion leaders communicate in real contexts. Turner calls this "a constant cross-looping" between the social drama and aesthetic performance genres. Richard Schechner (2002b, 68) describes this interplay as a mobius strip: The conflicts and characters in social dramas fund the content of aesthetic performances, and aesthetic performances, in turn, color and inflect the unfolding of the social drama.

The social dramas of the O. J. Simpson trial, the Clinton/Lewinsky affair, the Michael Jackson trial, Vice President Cheney's hunting accident, the Don Imus/Rutgers conflict all gave rise to aesthetic performances that critiqued, commented on, and parodied the actual events. "In Living Color," "Saturday Night Live," "The Daily Show," "The Chappell Show," "Mad TV," "The Colbert Report," even "South Park" are all forums that demonstrate Turner's claim (1988, 39): "what began as an empirical social drama may continue both as an entertainment and [as] a metasocial commentary on the lives and times of the given community." When the infamous "South Park" school mascot election pitted a *turd sandwich* against a *giant douche* as the two candidates, the creators of "South Park" were clearly commenting in entertaining ways on the 2004 presidential race between George W. Bush and John Kerry.

Kirk Fuoss, in *Striking Performances/Performing Strikes* (1997), analyzes performances that blossomed during the 1936–37 Flint, Michigan, autoworkers' strike, a social drama that pitted strikers against management, and pro-strikers against anti-strikers among the workers themselves. Strikers staged kangaroo courts acting out the parts of management, held parades, created dancing picket lines, and sang popular songs with new parodied lyrics. These performances were integral parts of the actual social drama, commenting in entertaining ways "in the subjunctive" on the "indicative" events. Elizabeth Bell (2006) analyzes performances on the Internet that critiqued, commented on, and parodied the Bill Clinton/Monica Lewinsky affair. Through jokes, parodied songs, and photoshopped pictures of Monica and Bill, the "folk" on the Internet weighed in with their own entertaining and biting performances that critiqued the social drama.

The social drama gives rise to performances; the performances themselves are integral parts of the social drama. Through these performances, communities reflect on, critique, and participate in the unfolding of actual events. Dwight Conquergood (1986, 58) describes the relationship between social dramas and their performances as both centrifugal (throwing out) and centripetal (pulling in):

> Cultural processes both pull towards a moral center as social dramas are enacted while they simultaneously express themselves outward from the depths of that symbolizing, synthesizing core. That is, cultures throw off forms of themselves—literally, "expressions" that are publicly accessible.

Turner's work is extremely important to performance theory for its characterization of life as drama. Richard Schechner (1988b, 8) claims, "Turner's gifts were many and he spent them generously. . . . He taught that there was a continuous, dynamic process linking performative behavior—art, sports, ritual, play—with social and ethical structure: the way people think about and organize their lives and specify individual and group values."

RETHINKING DRAMA

Critiques of Aristotelian conceptions of dramatic form, conflict, and action come from two overlapping camps: feminists and postmodernists. Early critiques from feminist theatre scholars centered on the absence of women in the theatre and from the *polis* of Greek citizenship. Susan Melrose (1998, 134) writes, "Aristotle institutionalized the tragic poets and projected through this institution then-prevalent attitudes to men, women and 'slaves.' Character, as Aristotle construed it, was action-based, and always performed by a man for other men. . . . Real women were simply (and politically) not there." Sue-Ellen Case (1988) argues for "a new poetics" that would "abandon the traditional patriarchal values embedded in prior notions of form, practice and audience response in order to construct new critical models and methodologies for the drama." In *Unmaking Mimesis* (1997), Elin Diamond imagines just such a new model. She argues that mimesis in performance can be a valuable place and practice for postmodern feminists, not to confirm or succumb to "truth-models" of mirror representation, but to generate many "truths" in history and time of women in performance.

Postmodern critiques and revisions of Aristotle often take mimesis as a place to explore the gap between appearance and reality, especially for notions of identity. Anne Duncan (2006) traces the historical and political routes by which actors were marginalized and stereotyped for the threats they posed to stability of the "self," government, and society. Bertolt Brecht and Augusto Boal, theatre theorists and practitioners, found new ways to intervene in the inevitability of Aristotelian action—for audiences, texts, and performers alike. Their works will be covered in detail in Chapter Eight, "Performing Resistance."

Critiques of Kenneth Burke's dramatism focus on how difficult his theory is to understand, its inaccessibility to many audiences, and his now dated and unfamiliar examples. The complexity and scope of Burke's thinking is exacerbated by the difficulty of applying Burke's "elusive" concepts (Geertz 1980, 172). Some argue that only Kenneth Burke can *really* do dramatistic analysis.

Critiques of Turner's social drama have come from many quarters in anthropology and performance studies. Geertz (1980, 173) argues that Turner's insistence on form, especially the stages of breach, crisis, redress, and reintegration, is "a form for all seasons," making cultures and performances as different as Caribbean carnivals, Icelandic sagas, and 1960s U.S. political protests "look drably homogeneous." Schechner (2002b, 67) also critiques this homogeneity to argue that Turner *imposed* "a Western aesthetic genre, the drama" on non-Western communities with no such genre in their performative repertoire. Moreover, the social drama sets beginning and ending points to action, as manageable units for analysis, even when the conflicts themselves have no closure. Schechner (2002b, 67) writes, "Perhaps today's world of terrorism, guerrilla warfare, prolonged civil wars, and economic espionage are better modeled by performance art. . . ."

Kirk Fuoss (1993) maintains that performance theorists fail to consider *how* performances can pull in different directions during the social drama. Some performances work to maintain the status quo in a community and others work to subvert it. Fuoss maintains that all performances center on contestation, *especially* those that mask their political agendas as supporting the status quo.

Life as drama is an important critical perspective for twentieth-century social theory. Utilizing Aristotelian notions of conflict, form, and action, Kenneth Burke and Victor Turner developed theories of symbolic action and dramatic form that explain, describe, and account for human social interaction. Dramatistic theories claim that (1) drama, not animal behavior or machine motion, is the best metaphor for describing, analyzing, and predicting human action; (2) language and symbol systems are collective resources for creating group life and knowing the world; and (3) through drama, we can participate ethically in decision making that molds the world of opposing forces around us.

The "danger" in dramatism is always the urge to scapegoat and to mortify—to solve our collective problems through sacrificing others or ourselves. The social drama also operates by resolving conflict through repairs that often involve sacrifice—real or symbolic. A tragic attitude succumbs to these urges; a comic attitude appreciates how humans creatively perform "both/and" choices in their lives. Dramatistic theories are lenses for exploring social interaction and models for analyzing, critiquing, and creating performances—onstage and in real life. The performances that unfold, in political and entertaining forums, are part and parcel of the drama of social relations. In this view, humans are creative, critical, and active agents of change in and through performance.

CHAPTER 5

Performing Culture

Anthropology, sociology, and even psychology in the mid-nineteenth century took "the study of man" as their central concern. The guiding method for these new academic areas was **positivism**, the belief that covering laws of human organization could be discovered through direct observation. This perspective maintains that the universe is orderly, and the job of scientific inquiry is to discover this order and classify it in systematic ways. Charles Darwin's work on **evolution** was an important model for researchers in the social sciences who searched for origins in the "evolution" of culture.

Theories of the evolution of culture are interwoven with the study of religion. Three schools of theory emerged in the nineteenth century—myth and ritual, sociological, and psychological—all asking the question, Did religion originate in myth or ritual? Mircea Eliade was interested in the phenomenology of religious experience and how **myths and rituals** are expressions of both the sacred and the profane in culture that provide unity for people. The **sociological** school, led by Emile Durkheim, maintained that religion is a social creation whose function is to preserve the welfare of a society. Sigmund Freud anchored the **psychological** approach: taboos of incest and patricide necessitate rituals that appease repressed desires.

Across these approaches, performance was studied for its window into larger cultural structures, like religion, politics, economics, language, and identity (Beeman 1993). When specific performance genres were studied (like rites, rituals, games, contests, dance, and music), performance was often seen as a fixed, static product, evidence of cross-cultural similarities, and indicative of universal needs and expressions.

This chapter traces the theories that helped transform the "study of man" into the study of performance. Arnold van Gennep's (1909/1960) rites of passage, Johan

115

Huizinga's (1938/1950) play theory, and Milton Singer's (1972) cultural performance laid the groundwork for the **performance turn** in the study of culture. This turn rejects the view of performances as fixed objects to be studied in the science of positivism and embraces performance as a paradigm for understanding how culture makes and remakes itself. Performance can be understood as "the embodied processes that produce and consume culture . . . performance makes things and does things" (Hamera 2006, 5).

The work of anthropologist Victor Turner, introduced in Chapter Four through the social drama, is credited for ushering in this performance turn in the study of culture. Turner rejects concepts of culture as static or deterministic structures that "imprint" themselves on waxlike, malleable humans. Humans push back in meaningful and efficacious ways on culture, and in turn, change it. Turner argues that a performance approach to culture (1) reflects dynamic cultural processes, (2) enables possibilities between and within cultural structures, and (3) provides opportunities for critique and transformation. Performances are *constitutive* of culture, not something added to culture; performances are *epistemic,* the way cultural members "know" and enact the possibilities in their worlds; and performances are *critical* lenses for looking at and reshaping cultural forms.

This chapter surveys theories that help us answer these questions: What is culture? How do people move in and through culture? What is ritual? How is culture performed individually and collectively, especially as a vehicle of history, public memory, and institutions? What are our ethical responsibilities toward cultures other than our own?

What Is Culture?

Dictionary definitions of "culture" have changed through time. From the Latin *cultura,* meaning "cultivation" or "tending," the growing of plants, crops, or animals is a very early meaning of the word. Most of us think of culture in two different ways based on definitions more than one hundred years old.

In 1882, British poet and social theorist Matthew Arnold proposed culture as the **refinement of tastes and sensibilities**. He maintained that culture is "the pursuit of our total perfection by means of getting to know . . . the best which has been thought and said in the world." Arnold held Western music, art, architecture, and literature as his standard for civilization and for "high culture." English anthropologist Edward Burnett Tylor (1871/1958) expanded the definition of culture as "that **complex whole** which includes knowledge, belief, art, morals, law, custom, and any other capabilities and habits acquired by man as a member of society."

Raymond Williams (1958/1983) was the first to propose that culture is **ordinary**, the "common meanings and directions" of a society. These meanings are learned, made, and remade by individuals. Culture is at once **traditional**, a whole way of life passed on through generations, and **creative**, the processes of discovery that lead to new ways of thinking and doing.

Clifford Geertz (1973) argues that culture is **semiotic**: Systems of meaning, signification, and symbol use are central to both patterned conduct and individual frames of mind. Culture is a symbolic system unique to humans in which meanings are publicly shared and the collective property of a group. Drawing from Kenneth Burke, Geertz (1973, 9–10) argues that "human behavior is symbolic action—action which, like phonation in speech, pigment in painting, line in writing, or sonance in music, signifies."

John Bodley (1994) lists three components of culture: **what people think, what they do, and the material products they produce.** Bodley summarizes the properties of culture: It is shared, learned, symbolically transmitted cross-generationally, adaptive to the physical world, and integrated with it.

Wen Shu Lee (2002) defines culture as "**the shifting tensions between the shared and the unshared,**" acknowledging that culture is contested within and across groups. She offers this example of historical and value shifts: "American *culture* has changed from master/slave, to white only/black only, to antiwar and black power, to affirmative action/multiculturalism and political correctness, to transnational capital and anti-sweatshop campaigns" (quoted in Martin and Nakayama 2004, 76).

In one hundred years, the concept of culture has developed and shifted. The tensions, however, have remained the same as theorists posit culture as between and among the individual and the group, high and low, tradition and change, symbol systems and material products, human biology and human learning, shared and unshared meanings within and between groups, systems, and power.

Approaches to Studying Culture

Robert Wuthnow (1987) outlines four contemporary approaches to studying culture that are helpful in understanding the above definitions. A **subjective** approach to culture focuses on beliefs, attitudes, and values held by individuals. Culture is conceived as *mental constructions* expressed in outlooks, anxieties, desires, and subjective states of the individual. Meaning in this approach is "the individual's interpretation of reality" (1987, 11). Social psychologists and sociologists often take this approach when they measure people's attitudes, values, and beliefs with surveys, focus groups, participant observation, and interviews.

A **structural** approach to culture seeks out the patterns and rules that hold a culture together. This approach looks for the *symbolic boundaries* evident within a culture created in language and how these *boundaries among cultural elements are maintained and changed*. A structural approach differs from a subjective approach: Culture is the object to be studied and observed, not the subjective states of individual members. Culture is characterized by its boundaries, categories, and elements that can be seen, read, recorded, and classified. Kinship systems are a good example of boundaries that maintain and change culture.

Wuthnow's third category is a **dramaturgical** approach to culture which "focuses on the expressive or communicative properties of culture. . . . Culture is approached in interaction with social structure" (1987, 13). Like structural approaches, a dramaturgical approach maintains that culture is observable, but classifies these observations as "utterances, acts, objects, and events" (13). Most important, this approach seeks to explore the dramatic ordering of social life not as information, but for the ways that rituals, ideologies, and other symbolic acts "*dramatize* the nature of *social relations*" (13). Chapter Four, "Performing Drama," featured Kenneth Burke and Victor Turner. Chapter Six features Erving Goffman. All are considered "fathers" of this approach to culture.

An **institutional** approach to culture adds the elements of culture as studied by structuralists to the moral order studied by dramaturgists to explore the organizations that constitute culture. These organizations necessarily *require resources and influence the distribution of these resources* across members of their culture. Institutional approaches most often feature the interplay between culture and state. Marxist, socialist, and systems theorists utilize this approach. "Follow the money" is a common phrase for tracking institutions (the federal, state, and local governments, education, science, even the mass media) as agents that garner and distribute resources in a culture.

How culture is conceptualized—as mental states, structures, social relations, or institutions—is intimately linked to how culture is studied across academic disciplines and methods. Moving from social scientific models of positivism to critical models of interpretation and power, Judith N. Martin and Thomas K. Nakayama (1999, 13) advocate a **dialectical** approach to studying culture *as heterogeneous, dynamic, and contested*. This approach "accepts that human nature is probably both creative and deterministic; that research goals can be to predict, describe, and change; that the relationship between culture and communication is, most likely, both reciprocal and contested."

The tensions between the individual and the group, high and low, tradition and change, symbol systems and material products, human biology and human learning, culture and communication will pull especially tight when the study of culture leaves some members out entirely.

ACT OUT

Class Culture

Think of your classroom as a culture. Divide the class into five groups to approach this culture subjectively, structurally, dramaturgically, institutionally, and dialectically. How might this class be *described,* what elements can be *studied,* and how might *change* be advocated when approached in these five different ways?

Perform your discoveries for the class. First, create a "slice of life" in this culture that seeks to highlight your approach's assumptions about culture, where it is "located," and its properties. Second, present your analysis of that performance. What are the benefits of this approach? What are its limitations?

SOURCE: Photograph by Jaclyn Lannon. Copyright © 2007 by Jaclyn Lannon.

"This Was My Life as an Undergraduate"

Donna Marie Nudd (1998, 152), Professor of Communication at Florida State University, regularly participates in teaching workshops offered at the beginning of the fall semester for new teaching assistants. She and her colleague from theatre, Frank Trezza, create and perform scenes of classrooms with the PIE (Program for Instructional Excellence) Players. The idea is to show, rather than tell, new teachers classroom dilemmas. They follow the performances with periods of discussion. The following is Nudd's description of one eight-minute scene (featuring Terry Galloway) and her analysis of the audience's reaction.

It's the third day of class, the teacher is taking role. Terry enters late and slams the door. Undergraduates mutter comments to themselves or each other: "Oooh, that's tough on a hangover," "God, her student loan must not have come through," etc. The teacher continues to call role from the desk. Terry, chatting with a student behind her, misses her name as she is actively engaged in conversation about the price of books. Class begins. The teacher tries to facilitate a discussion on affirmative action and its effect on women. She writes, "A.A." and "Women" on the chalkboard. Class discussion begins. Thinking the topic at hand is Alcoholics Anonymous, Terry at one point in the group discussion launches into a seemingly unrelated monologue about her sister who is a member of that organization and her resentment of its religious overtones. The teacher is thrown by

(Continued)

(Continued)

Terry's response, but picks up some lone thread of Terry's monologue and tries to weave it back into the topic at hand. Another member of this class makes fun of Terry and her ridiculous ideas. Terry responds in kind. As the situation becomes even more heated, the teacher unsuccessfully tries to regain control. The class degenerates into name-calling. Finally, at her wit's end, the infuriated teacher calls an end to the discussion. She tells them, "It's over!" With her back again toward Terry, she tells the class to get into their assigned small groups and adds, "You have exactly ten minutes to summarize all the key points from the textbook in regard to affirmative action's effect on women." Terry, watching the students stand up and move, and having lip-read "It's over!" thinks the class has been dismissed and leaves the classroom muttering snide comments.

That was the scene. In their small group and large group discussions, 200–250 teaching assistants analyzed this scene by noting (1) that the teacher was woefully unprepared; (2) that topics such as "affirmative action" are controversial and difficult to handle in the classroom; (3) that the rude, not-too-smart, volatile, and clearly disturbed student, Terry, should be immediately advised to go to the counseling center. After the graduate students expressed their views, the emcee of the plenary session quietly motioned to Terry. Terry said simply, "I'm deaf; this was my life as an undergraduate." Once the proverbial pin had dropped in the auditorium, Terry spoke briefly about being a deaf college student. After Terry's autobiographical follow up, the PIE Players replayed the scene. This time, the nine or ten clues to Terry's disability that were built into the scene seemed thrown into relief—her slamming the door, her missing entire sections of the teacher's lecture when the teacher was writing on the blackboard, her shifts in volume level . . . her previously viewed non-sequitur about A.A. . . .

Hundreds of graduate students were made acutely aware of how difficult it can be to pinpoint a disability even in what might seem to be the most obvious of circumstances.

SOURCE: Donna Marie Nudd, "Improvising Our Way to the Future." In *The Future of Performance Studies: Visions and Revisions,* edited by Sheron J. Dailey, 1998. Used by permission of the National Communication Association.

From Studying "Man" to Theorizing Movement and Play

D. Soyini Madison (2005, 149) writes that performance is central "to the meanings and effects of human behavior, consciousness, and culture. These days, it seems one can hardly address any subject in the arts, humanities, and social sciences without encountering the concept of performance." Performance—as central to the study of humans across academic disciplines—didn't take center stage overnight.

Two important theorists in the twentieth century asked new questions of culture to begin the shift from studying "man" as a "bearer of culture" to studying performance as constitutive of culture. Arnold van Gennep theorized rites of passage and John Huizinga theorized play as founding moments in and through culture.

Play and rites of passage are central to thinking differently and asking different questions about what people do, the movement through cultural processes, and the products they produce. Play and ritual are often conceived as opposite cultural structures:

[P]lay is understood as the force of uncertainty which counter-balances the structure provided by ritual. Where ritual depends on repetition, play stresses innovation and creativity. Where ritual is predictable, play is contingent. But all performances, even rituals, contain some element of play, some space for variation. And most forms of play involve pre-established patterns of behavior. (Bial 2004, 115)

The next two sections trace the development, central concepts, and intertwining of rites of passage and play that lay the groundwork for a performance approach to culture.

Rites of Passage: Moving through Culture

In 1909, French ethnographer and folklorist Arnold van Gennep published a book entitled *Les Rites de Passage* (*The Rites of Passage*). At the time, ethnography as an academic endeavor was thriving, but van Gennep was critical of the tendency to "extract data," the rites, ceremonies, and other practices, from the social settings and contexts in which they were performed. Van Gennep is interested not only in the "what" of religious beliefs and practices across the world, but in the "how" and "why" of those practices (Kimball 1960).

Van Gennep's central thesis is that *all individuals undergo "life crises," and that ceremonies exist to assure safe travel through those crises; hence, rites of passage.* While the forms and contents of these rites differ from group to group through time, van Gennep argues,

For groups, as well as for individuals, life itself means to separate and to be reunited, to change form and condition, to die and to be reborn. It is to act and to cease, to wait and rest, and then to begin acting again, but in a different way. And there are always new thresholds to cross: the thresholds of summer and winter, of a season or a year, of a month or a night; the thresholds of birth, adolescence, maturity, and old age; the threshold of death and that of the after-life—for those who believe in it. (1909/1960, 189–90)

While a number of ethnographers and anthropologists have studied, for example, "puberty rites" or "marriage rites" in particular cultures, van Gennep describes and explains their significance in three new ways.

1. Rites of passage are **ordered in a typical, recurring pattern**: *separation, transition, and incorporation.* All rites of passage begin by separating the individual from his or her customary environment; a period of transition is marked by

liminality—betwixt and between the two worlds; the third stage is incorporation into the new group or state and a return to the customary environment.

2. **Transition** is the stage that *orients and enables* the other two stages. If the transition period is lengthy, it will usually repeat within it the separation, transition, and incorporation phases.

3. Rites of passage are **territorial passages**. That is, they involve *physical space,* and these spaces are not just "symbols" of movement. "In fact, the spatial separation of distinct groups is an aspect of social organization. . . . In short, a change of social categories involves a change of residence, and this fact is expressed by the rites of passage in their various forms" (192).

Categories of Rites of Passage

Van Gennep categorizes six kinds of rites of passage. He begins with the often elaborate ceremonies that deal with **strangers** (greeting rituals, signs of friendship, protections, and taboos) and how to move them from separation, to transition, and to incorporation safely within the group. Rites of **pregnancy and childbirth** follow the threefold structure: The pregnant woman is separated or isolated from the group because "she is considered impure and dangerous or because her very pregnancy places her physiologically and socially in an abnormal condition" (1909/1960, 41). These may be marked by special taboos against food, sex, or places during pregnancy. Birth usually marks the beginning of "a transition period with gradual removal of barriers," and then "reintegration into ordinary life" (44) as a "social return from childbirth" for the mother.

Birth and childhood rites of passage often begin with ceremonies for the newborn child to highlight separation from mother's body. Transition rites for the newborn or the child feature moving into this new world. Incorporation involves being accepted into family, extended family, tribe, and clan through naming ceremonies, ritual nursing, or baptism. All of these serve "to introduce [the] child into the world." (54). In naming rites, especially, the child is "both individualized and incorporated into society" (62).

Initiation rites for van Gennep include a host of ceremonies "which bring about admission to age groups and secret societies" (65). Van Gennep is careful to distinguish "puberty rites," which usually involved physical or sexual maturation, from what he called "social puberty." Instead of marking the advent of sexual activity, which varies so vastly from group to group, he notes that "these are rites of separation from the asexual world, and they are followed by rites of incorporation into the world of sexuality, and, in all societies and all social groups, into a group confined to persons of one sex or the other" (67). Initiates are often cut or marked as a "a sign of union" with the new group. For clan membership or secret society, entrance is often gained through a death/rebirth dramatization. "Twice born" and "born again" are phrases that indicate a new life.

Betrothal and marriage is the fifth category of rites of passage. "Marriage is an essentially social act," according to van Gennep, and its repercussions cross groups, economics, and emotions. "To marry is to pass from the group of children or adolescents into the adult group, from a given clan to another, from one family to another, and often from one village to another" (1909/1960, 124). Marriage ceremonies, as separation from old worlds, are often denoted by acts that cut, break, or throw away something associated with the old world. The transition is sometimes marked by breaking "virginity" symbolically, bathing or annointments, veiling oneself, or changing one's name or personality. Other marriage separation rites include passing over something, whether stepping, jumping, or being carried over (131), or breaking a ritual threshold of some kind.

Marriages are essentially "rites of union," so rites of incorporation, uniting two people together, often involve exchanging gifts and food, sharing the same seat, washing or annointing each other. Van Gennep maintains that "all these rites of incorporation should be understood literally rather than symbolically: the cord which binds, the ring, the bracelet, and the garland which encircles have a real coercive effect" (134).

Finally, van Gennep details the stages of separation, initiation, and incorporation in **funeral** ceremonies. For mourners, separation involves marking

SOURCE: Photograph by Fritz Everhyi (www.memoriesbyfritz.com). Copyright © 2006 by Fritz Everhyi.

them off as a special group, often designated by special clothing and prohibitions; their specialness increases depending on their relation to the deceased. Ordinary social activity is suspended. Transition often involves the "extended stay of the corpse or coffin" in wakes or viewings. The funeral itself, for the mourners, is the transition. The meal or gathering after the funeral is a rite of incorporation, serving "to reunite all the surviving members of the group with each other, and sometimes also with the deceased, in the same way that a chain which has been broken by the disappearance of one of its links must be rejoined" (164–65).

Van Gennep sought to explain the structures that move people between life stages, groups, and social stations. "Safe travel" is always about thresholds, movement, and territory.

From Individuals to Cultural Membership

While rites of passage may seem to focus on the individual, rites of passage are crucial to culture constituted in and through its performances. Barbara Meyerhoff, Linda A. Camino, and Edith Turner (1987) argue that rites fulfill the crucial task of "inculcating a society's rules and values to those who are to become its full-fledged members" (383). Ritual participants are especially susceptible to learning during

SOURCE: Photograph by Justin B. Hankins. Copyright © 2006 by Justin B. Hankins.

rites: Old habits and ways of being are stripped away, awaiting new forms of participation and performance in culture. The crux of learning and transformation is in the performance.

While anthropologists have studied rites of passage across the world, performance studies research tends to feature historical and contemporary American rites and performances that enable group unity and personal development. Ann Larabee (1992, 53) details a rite of passage before 1914 at Wellesley College, one of the first women's colleges in the United States. First-year students had to pass under the chair of a statue of Harriet Martineau, a feminist educator, in "a brilliant and brutal parody of the transition into college life." Elizabeth Fine's 2003 *Soulstepping* explores how step shows are an integral rite of passage into full membership in the brotherhood or sisterhood of African-American fraternities and sororities. Fine (2003, 53) maintains that "joining an African American Greek-letter society involves a transition to greater social visibility as well as a fictive kinship of brotherhood or sisterhood." Tracy Stephenson (2004) investigates backpacking as a rite of passage for American youth that is a performed achievement by the individual.

Eric King Watts (2005) explores Eminem's film *8 Mile* through the real and symbolic violence of Rabbit's initiation; and Robert Westerfelhaus and Robert Brookey (2004) analyze *Fight Club* for its celebration of homosocial bonding available through initiation's liminal phase. These film analyses of rites of passage—as a tripartite structure, as transitional, and as physical movement—argue that race and heterosexual privilege are maintained at the violent expense of others. The learning that happens in these rites need not be libratory for culture.

GO FIGURE

Passage on the Web

Some argue that Northern American culture is devoid of rites of passage, giving rise to individuals without a compass or direction. The Internet is full of organizations that offer programs, retreats, and journeys for "at-risk youth," "adolescent girls," "directionless women," and even "inner-city gang members."

Choose one Web site and analyze the organization's characterization of rites of passage, its functional claims for the individuals and society, and its created ceremonies. How do these organizations enact van Gennep's three phases? How is the transition period enacted? How does the rite involve territorial movement?

Homo Ludens/Playing Man

John Huizinga was a Dutch historian well known at the time for his 1914 book, *The Waning of the Middle Ages,* but he began as a scholar of Indian literature and cultures. He brought a vast knowledge of history, literature, and cultural forms to his theory of play. Huizinga wrote *Homo Ludens: A Study of the Play-Element in Culture* in 1938; the first German edition was published in 1944; the English edition was published in 1950.

Huizinga begins his treatise on play as a cultural phenomenon with an amazing claim and description:

> Play is older than culture, for culture, however inadequately defined, always presupposes human society, and animals have not waited for man to teach them their playing. We can safely assert, even, that human civilization has added no essential feature to the general idea of play. Animals play just like men. We have only to watch young dogs to see that all the essentials of human play are present in their merry gambols. They invite one another to play by a certain ceremoniousness of attitude and gesture. They keep to the rule that you shall not bite, or not bite hard, your brother's ear. They pretend to get terribly angry. And—what is most important—in all these doings they plainly experience enjoyment. Such rompings of young dogs are only one of the simpler forms of animal play. There are other, much more highly developed forms: regular contests and beautiful performances before an admiring public. (1938/1950, 1)

Huizinga argues that play is a special and significant form of human activity, one of the main bases of civilization, a founding moment of culture.

Huizinga begins by rejecting previous theories of play that assume that play must serve some purpose: discharge of energy, need for relaxation, practice in skills, wish fulfillment, imitation, and so on. None of those explanations treat play *as play,* what it is, and what it means to the player. Nor do any of those theories account for fun. Huizinga outlines the characteristics of play as play.

Characteristics of Play

1. Play is **voluntary**. It must be freely chosen, otherwise it becomes duty or obligation. Remember when your mother *made* you play with a cousin you hated?

2. Play **steps out** of "real, ordinary life" and **into a** "temporary sphere of activity with a disposition all its own" (8). Play literally transports us into another world, and we are fully aware that this other world is "pretend." Play is not serious, but it is absorbing. The "intensity" of play is observable on the face and body of any "absorbed" video game player.

3. Play **creates its own limits** of time and place. These limits, in backyards or on front stoops, are often broken when someone hollers, "Time for dinner!" As certain forms of play are repeated, they become traditions: Repetition and alternation are integral.

The space and place for play, the play-ground, is marked off beforehand, "either materially or ideally, deliberately or as a matter of course" (10). Whether in solitary games of puzzles or skill or in gambling and athletics, play tests the player's prowess and abilities.

4. **Nothing is "produced"** by play. There are no material gains or profits, except the joy of play itself.

5. Play **creates its own rules**. These rules must be agreed to by all and adhered to by all, otherwise rule-breakers are "spoilsports." Unlike cheaters, spoilsports destroy the play world, shattering the *illusion* (which literally means "in-play") of play.

6. Play promotes both **secrecy and social groups**. Play is especially wonderful when a "secret" is made out of it, promoting and pertaining to "us" and not others. Play also creates permanent play-communities, oftentimes marked by "dressing up."

For Huizinga, these characteristics of play fund connections between play and three concepts: language, myth, and ritual. All are permeated with play. Language is always a "play on words," creating a symbolic world alongside material realities. Myth is an account of the world that plays "on the border-line between jest and earnest." In ritual, Huizinga insists, the "spirit of pure play" is "truly understood" (4–5).

Is Ritual Play Really Believed?

Ritual performances exhibit all the same formal characteristics as play: A special place is staked out, a sacred ground, creating a rule-bound world of its own. And play, as "pretend," infects poles of belief in ritual acts. Huizinga argues that all ritual involves participants who, on some level, question the "reality" of what is happening. On another level, they willingly participate and experience the moods and feelings the rite seeks to create. Huizinga writes, "Whether one is sorcerer or sorcerized one is always knower and dupe at once. But one chooses to be the dupe" (23).

Huizinga's claim is borne out by the experience of believing in and enacting traditions of Santa Claus in the West. Carl Anderson and Norman Prentice (1994) interviewed fifty-two children to ask, "When did you stop believing?" Around age seven, they claimed. The children reported they enjoyed being "in" on the Santa story. But children also "pretended" to believe for three reasons: to protect younger siblings, to avoid disappointing their parents, and to continue to garner gifts. The seriousness of "play" in the language, myth, and ritual of Santa is manifested in performances—individual, family, and culture.

READ MORE ABOUT IT

The Lion Is Real

Camara Laye, author of The Dark Child: Autobiography of an African Boy *(1954, 100–101, 106, 109), tells the story of the ceremony of the lions, prelude to his rite of passage to manhood in the Malinke tribe of French Guinea (now Mali, in northern Africa).*

Konden Diara, "the lion who eats little boys," was a constant "bogeyman" of his childhood, used by authorities to elicit his good behavior. The ceremony begins with drumming and rounding up the boys to go face the lion. Laye writes, "Here was Konden Diara leaving the dim world of hearsay, here he was taking on flesh and blood, yes, and roused by Kodoke's tom-tom was prowling around the town! This was to be the night of Konden Diara" (1954, 94–95).

Laye's description speaks to the multiple levels of experience, secrecy surrounding the rite, and the "game" played. The initiates are taken to a special place in the bush, cleared of tall grasses, near a bombax tree. They are ordered to kneel on the ground and cover their eyes, to wait for Konden Diara to appear.

We were expecting to hear this hoarse roar, we were not expecting any other sound, but it took us by surprise and shattered us, froze our hearts with its unexpectedness. And it was not only a lion, it was not only Konden Diara roaring: there were ten, twenty, perhaps thirty lions that took their lead from him, uttering their terrible roars and surrounding the hollow; ten or twenty lions separated from us by a few yards only. . . .

"You mustn't be afraid!" I said to myself. "You must master your fear! Your father has commanded you to!" . . . How was I to stave off fear when I was within range of the dread monster? If he pleased, Konden Diara could leap the fire in one bound and sink his claws in my back!

I did not doubt the presence of the monster, not for a single instant. . . .

What was it my father had said? "Konden Diara roars; but he won't do more than roar; he will not take you away." . . . Yes, something like that. But was it true, really true? . . .

And do not people also die of fright? Ah! how I wished this roaring would stop! How I wished I was far away from this clearing, back in the . . . warm security of the hut! Would this roaring never cease? . . .

Whereupon, suddenly, they stopped!

. . .

Later I got to know who Konden Diara was, and I learned these things when the time had come for me to learn them. . . . No, they were not real lions that roared in the clearing, for it was the older boys, simply the older boys. They created the roaring sound with small boards, thick at the center, sharp at the edges. . . . There was a hole on one side that permitted it to be tied to a string. The older boys swung it around like a sling, and, to increase the speed of the gyrations, they too turned with it. The board cut through the air and produced a sound like a lion's roar.

. . .

(Continued)

(Continued)

> I know that such conduct must appear strange, but it is absolutely true. If the ceremony of the lions has a character of a game, it is for the most part pure mystification, yet it has one important feature: it is a test, a training in a hardship, a rite; the prelude to a tribal rite, and for the present that is all one can say. . . . It is obvious that if the secret were to be given away, the ceremony would lose much of its power.
>
> SOURCE: Excerpts from THE DARK CHILD by Camara Laye, translated by James Kirkup, Ernest Jones, and Elaine Gottlieb. Copyright © 1954, renewed 1982 by Camara Laye. Reprinted by permission of Hill and Wang, a division of Farrar, Straus and Giroux, LLC.

Characteristics of Ritual

Ritual theorists, across academic disciplines and methods, have agreed on three characteristics of ritual activities, according to Catherine Bell (1997, 94). First, ritual action is **communal,** involving groups of people who gain social solidarity through their participation. Second, the action is **traditional** and "understood as carrying on ways of acting established in the past" (94). Third, ritual is **rooted in beliefs** in divine beings.

Ritual action is often divided into sacred and secular, but these categories are usually not distinct from each other, especially when approached as "genres of ritual action." Bell lists these genres: rites of passage, calendrical rites, rules of exchange and communication, rites of affliction; feasting, fasting, and festivals; and political rites. All of these activities are "strategic ways of acting" (7) that in turn produce and organize our knowledge of the world. These ways of acting range from the "religious to the secular, the public to the private, the routine to the improvised, the formal to the casual, and the periodic to the irregular" (138). Bell explains five characteristics of ritual-like activities, demonstrating that ritualization is a process, flexible, and strategic.

1. **Formalization** is the degree of formality in dress or speech that marks an activity as ritual-like. Ceremonial costumes, language, gestures, and movement occur on a continuum between informal and casual to highly restricted and formal. These restrictions say a great deal about hierarchy, authority, and symbolic messages. A family dinner at the kitchen table and a state dinner at the White House differ in degrees of formality.

2. **Traditionalism,** or "we have always done this" (150), appeals to cultural precedents. Bell gives the examples of using great grandmother's lace tablecloth at Thanksgiving, the British judicial system's powdered wigs and robes, and academic regalia as examples of traditional ways of acting. The Pledge of Allegiance to the U.S. flag, "invented" in 1954, testifies to the fact that "traditional" practices may be quite young.

3. **Invariance** emphasizes "precise repetition and physical control" (152). Actions are performed exactly the same each time. Military marching maneuvers and high kicks of the Radio City Rockettes are examples that speak to the rigorous

training of the body. This repetition testifies to the "timeless authority of the group, its doctrines, or its practices" (150). The structures and formulas enacted at Alcoholics Anonymous meetings, for example, are the same everywhere.

4. **Rule-governance** maintains that ritual-like activities are governed by rules that guide and direct the activities, especially by designating what is not allowed or acceptable. Sporting events and games, debates, and legal proceedings all have specific rules that "hold individuals to communally approved patterns of behavior" (155).

5. **Sacral symbolism** appeals to supernatural beings. People and objects become sacred through the ritual acts, or ritual-like acts, that create them. The Christian cross, the Star of David, the American flag, even places (war memorials, Niagara Falls, and Mt. Everest) become something special in and through ritualization.

Rituals Are Performed

All of the above characteristics are manifested in and through performance. In short, ritual or ritual-like events do not exist outside of the performances that create them. In Victor Turner's phrasing (1981, 155–56), "I like to think of ritual essentially as *performance*, as *enactment*, and not primarily as rules or rubrics. The rules frame the ritual process, and the ritual process transcends its frame. A river needs banks or it will be a dangerous flood, but banks without a river epitomize aridity."

Rituals, and ritual-like actions, abound in our daily lives as a way to give meaning and significance to experience. Memorials and tributes, for example, spring up

SOURCE: Photograph by Jack Delano. Library of Congress, Prints & Photographs Division, FSA-OWI Collection [reproduction number LC-USW3-2809-D].

spontaneously for local victims of tragic deaths or for episodes of violence that capture national attention (Jorgensen-Earp and Lanzilotti 1998). These are important moments that not only memorialize the deceased but attempt "to address larger, causative, social problems" like domestic violence, child kidnapping and abuse, massacres, and war protests (Santino 2004). September 11 tributes at baseball parks across America sought to comfort participants, but soon turned to propaganda of "belligerent patriotism" (Butterworth 2005).

Ritual events are also marked by joy, fun, and anticipation: the Olympic Games, Halloween, birthday parties, Native American powwows (Roberts 2002), the return of *Monday Night Football,* even the annual televised showing of *The Wizard of Oz* (Payne 1989). For Turner, this is the "room for play" that ritual performance enables: play with symbols, play with meanings, and play with words (1981, 162).

This room for play is evidenced in contemporary "do-it-yourself rituals." Laine Bergeson (2004, 66) writes,

> Ritual celebrations knit us into history, and even into prehistory, connecting humans to each other over geography and time. . . . Many still find connection in the rites and ceremonies passed down to them from the lives and faiths of their parents and grandparents. For others, contemporary life has grown so secular, colored by irony, or just plain different that the old ways of marking major transitions no longer resonate. As more people enter nontraditional romantic partnerships, choose not to have children, and change jobs or genders or continents, the rituals of the past feel increasingly outdated. The need for ritual is so deep, though, that people have begun creating their own.

Do-it-yourself (DIY) rituals include celebrating the arrival of menopause, births and deaths marked without religious ceremonies, divorce ceremonies, even "marry yourself" ceremonies. Remi Rubel married herself in a public ceremony, saying, "this relationship will last."

ACT OUT

DIY Rituals

Divide the class into groups. Each group should create its own ritual to mark, celebrate, mourn, or honor something in its group life. Pay special attention to levels of formality, tradition, invariance, rules, and symbols as you create the performance. How does this ritual hold possibilities for transformation for individuals? How does this ritual express, confirm, and embody cultural values?

From Great Tradition to Cultural Performance

In 1954, Milton Singer, of the Chicago School of Urban Ecology, traveled to India in search of "The Great Tradition" in Indian civilization. "The Great Tradition" claims that a civilization is assumed to have a charter for action, for organizing, a "worldview" that structures belief and calls for action. This charter is often available in sacred texts—"oral, written, inscribed, carved and painted, sung and acted" (Singer 1972, 4).

Singer quickly discovered the difficulty of the task. Across three million square miles, India is marked by twenty-three different, official languages and twenty-eight different geopolitical boundaries shaped by vastly different historical influences and religious affiliations. Where to begin putting his finger on "The Great Tradition"? Singer describes what happened:

> I discovered what I suppose every field worker knows, that the units of cogitation are not units of observation. There was nothing that could be easily labeled Little Tradition or Great Tradition, or "ethos" or "world view." Instead, I found myself confronted with a series of concrete experiences, the observation and recording of which seemed to discourage the mind from entertaining and applying the synthetic and interpretative concepts I had brought with me. (70)

Singer named these concrete experiences, observable to an outsider and recordable for study, **cultural performances.** More important, Singer claims that his Indian friends "thought of their culture as encapsulated in these discrete performances, which they could exhibit to visitors and to themselves. The performances became for [Singer] the elementary constituents of the culture and the ultimate units of observation" (71).

Elements of Cultural Performances

Singer (1972) outlined five components of cultural performances, beginning with their **formal characteristics.** Each cultural performance can be characterized by (1) a limited time span (a beginning, middle, and end), (2) an organized program of activity, (3) a set of performers, (4) an audience, and (5) a place and occasion of performance.

The **cultural stage** is the place where the performance occurs—in homes, temples, public halls, and community centers. Oftentimes the cultural training in the home, the rearing of children and passing down of traditions, is informal and casual. Traveling performances, without a fixed institutional base, are often difficult to pin down, as they create their stages in and through the performance.

Performances are created by **cultural specialists,** people who are especially recruited, trained, paid, and motivated to engage in performances. Singer lists priests, scholars, reciters, storytellers, singers, dancers, dramatic performers, and musicians. In mass mediated cultures, editors, program directors, story writers, and producers are also cultural specialists. Still other specialists assist the performers—production assistants, costumers, makeup artists, teachers, patrons, and organizers of performances. These cultural specialists often serve as arbitrators of cultural tastes, as well as make cultural policy.

SOURCE: Photograph by Beatrice Queral. Copyright © 2006 by Beatrice Queral. Courtesy of Mickee Faust Club.

Cultural media are the modes and forms of *communication* the performance utilizes: singing, dancing, acting, and recitation as well as graphic arts. Many cultural specialists are known for their mastery of one of these media. While *spoken language* is often the premiere cultural medium, nonlinguistic media are also utilized in performances. With developments in mass media, analysis of cultural performance requires considering how "cultural themes and values are communicated as well as on processes of social and cultural change" (77).

While Singer didn't discover India's "Great Tradition," he did describe a way to "trace the actual lines of communication" that create and transform cultural patterns constituted in performance, expressive of cultural beliefs and practices, and important to sociopolitical organization.

The "Performance Turn" in the Study of Culture

Van Gennep's work on rites of passage, Huizinga's characteristics of play, and Singer's characterization of cultural performance are all important developments for enabling the "performance turn" in the study of culture. This turn argues that not only are performances legitimate objects to study, but they can be the entry point for studying culture. Victor Turner sought to humanize the study of culture as performance by conceiving of humans as performers, *Homo performans*.

If man is a sapient animal, a tool-making animal, a self-making animal, a symbol-using animal, he is, no less, a performing animal, *Homo performans*, not in the sense, perhaps that a circus animal may be a performing animal, but in the sense that man is a self-performing animal—his performances are, in a way, reflexive, in performing he reveals himself to himself. (1988, 81)

A performance-centered approach enables four features of culture to be highlighted: process, play, poetics, and power. On **process**, Dwight Conquergood (1989, 83) writes, "Instead of static structures and stable systems with variables that can be measured, manipulated, and managed, culture is transacted through performance. Culture becomes an active verb, not a noun."

Huizinga's work on **play** was an important foundation for Turner's interest in Carnival, ritual reversals, tricksters, and the way cultural structures are manipulated, critiqued, and changed in and through performance genres. Carnival in Rio de Janeiro is evidence of "society in its subjunctive mood—to borrow a term from grammar—its mood of feeling, willing, and desiring, its mood of fantasizing, its playful mood" (Turner 1988, 123). Barry Ancelet (2001) and Patricia Sawin (2001) both explore play at Louisiana Mardi Gras celebrations. They argue that the serious work of group commitment and the emergence of alternative communities are enabled through play. Yoram Carmeli (2001) examines play as central to all circus performances—from its arrival in town to its departure.

Poetics emphasizes the constructedness of culture. Rites of passage, for example, are constructions—"fabricated, built, and created"—to move us through and to the stages a culture deems important (Meyerhoff et al. 1987). Chapter Four surveyed how our participation in social dramas questions and reinvents cultural values and rules as they unfold in our lives and makes them anew. But culture as "ordinary life" is also a poetic construction through cultural forms. Aleksandra Wolska (2005, 93) writes, "When we look for lost keys, burn our dinner, or crash into a garage door, our engagement with technology slips into farce, tragedy, or a combination of both. In this sense, performance remains embedded in the very fabric of cultural poesis [sic], in the ordinary process of doing things." Culture is not merely created, but it is creative (Conquergood 1989, 83).

Power is especially important in light of Turner's analysis of the social drama. "Because it is public, performance is a site of struggle where competing interests intersect, and different viewpoints and voices get articulated" (Conquergood 1989, 84). Viewpoints and voices are always embodied: "The body, within cultural and narrative performances, is of great importance as it functions as a site where politics and power are written on and through" (Holling and Calafell 2007, 61). Instead of conceiving of culture as disembodied static structures, work, rules, and top-down law, culture constituted in performance in and through embodied process, play, poetics, and power are important lenses.

Liminality: Betwixt and Between

Victor Turner built on van Gennep's liminal stage in the rite of passage to argue for a more encompassing notion of **liminality** to include categories of people and public places. *Limen,* or *the threshold between rooms,* is literally "betwixt and between." For ritual initiates, especially in rites of passage, they are "neither here nor there; they are betwixt and between the positions assigned and arrayed by law, custom, convention, and ceremonial" (Turner 1967, 98). Stripped of former markings of status, belonging, and group identification, liminal persons *have* nothing and *are* nothing: "no status, insignia, secular clothing, rank, kinship position, nothing to demarcate them structurally from their fellows" (98).

Liminality, as betwixt and between, also applies to people *between social and cultural structures:* "teenagers, students, trainees, travellers, those with new jobs, and people in times of major disaster" (E. Turner 2005, 99). Their statuses are ambiguous, and they are often perceived as dangerous to established structures. Thousands of people displaced by Hurricane Katrina in September of 2005 not only lost everything; they—mostly Black and poor—stood in an ambiguously dangerous position to the Bush administration and FEMA.

Liminality can also be experienced in *public places,* like Mardi Gras or Carnival. "Taboos are lifted, fantasies are enacted, indicative mood behavior is reversed; the low are exalted and the mighty abased. Yet there are still some controls: crime is still illicit, drunken bodies may be moved off the sidewalks" (V. Turner 1988, 102). The key features of liminality in these public spaces are heightened emotions, suspension of the rules of normal life and time, and centralization of the marginal.

Communitas: Magical Togetherness

Whether stripped of everything in formal rituals, a natural disaster, or at Mardi Gras, something is also generated among the participants who experience liminality. **Communitas** is "the sense of sharing and intimacy that develops among persons who experience liminality as a group" (E. Turner 2005, 97). Communitas is "the gift of togetherness. . . . It has something magical about it" (E. Turner 2005, 98).

Musical jam sessions among jazz musicians form a prototypic example. In these sessions, communitas is *normative:* It is characterized by "we" feelings, a loyalty to the group, and a willingness to sacrifice for it. The group is mobilized toward a goal—to make music together that no one member could make alone. Communitas is *existential:* Group differences in status are diminished, even dissolved; "the self becomes irrelevant. In the group, what is sought and what happens is unity, seamless unity" (E. Turner 2005, 98). Direct and unmediated communication takes place as musicians seem to "read each other's minds" and know the next riff or direction for the music. Finally, communitas is *spontaneous:* There is a shared "flow" of action and awareness; the structure is not governed by outside rules but by rules that emerge in the process of making music itself.

Many other groups experience communitas: religious pilgrims, parishioners of pentecostal and charismatic churches, dancers, singers, any group that "engage[s] in a collective task with full attention" (E. Turner 2005, 99). Larry Russell (2004) and Bernadette Calafell (2005) write of their own pilgrimages as ways to desire, honor, and constitute their own identities in cultural history.

Most important, communitas invites critique of established rules and structures because it arises "1) through the interstices of structure in *liminality,* times of change of status, 2) at the edges of structure, in *marginality,* and 3) from beneath structure in *inferiority*" (E. Turner 2005, 98). Liz Locke (1999, 3) explains how "inferiors" create communitas in their view from below: "The non-athletes, the readers, the musicians, the skate rats, the gamers, the geeks, the metal-heads, the ravers, the stoners, the net-heads, the writers, the outcasts, the refugees—we find a way to create communities."

Spontaneous communitas, however, is very difficult to hold on to. Victor Turner writes (1982, 47), "The great difficulty is to keep this intuition alive—regular drug-ging won't do it, repeated sexual union won't do it, constant immersion in great literature won't do it, initiation seclusion must sooner or later come to an end. We thus encounter the paradox that the *experience* of communitas becomes the mem-ory of communitas. . . . "

READ MORE ABOUT IT

Communitas on the Front Lines of Katrina

All the characteristics of communitas—as a gift, as collective, as produced between liminal, marginal, and inferior structures, are elaborated in Elizabeth Mehren's (2005, A12) story of "A Gospel and Granola Band."

Days after Hurricane Katrina hit, they began cooking together in a grocery store parking lot: evangelical Christians from Texas and Rainbow Family flower children from all over.

Soon they were serving 1,000 free meals a day at their cafe housed in a domed tent. Side by side, members of this improbable alliance worked nonstop, helping the people of what was once a scenic beach town.

Gradually, barriers melted. The evangelicals overlooked the hippies' unusual attire, outlandish humor and persistent habit of hugging total strangers. The hippies nodded politely when the church people cited Scripture. The bonds formed at Waveland Village have surprised both groups.

"We are Methodists, Episcopalians and Baptists, along with various and sundry other Christian groups," said Fay Jones, an organizer of the Bastrop (Texas) Ministerial Alliance. "Did we ever think we would have such a wonder-ful relationship with hippies? No."

Brad Stone, an emergency medical technician from the Rainbow Family, called the Christian-hippie coalition his new community. He explained: "It has been unbelievable. We are all so close. I am actually dreading leaving."

But about three months after they got here, the Rainbow Family volunteers and the Texas church delegation are preparing to head home. They will serve a grand banquet on Thanksgiving Day—turkey with all the trimmings, which at the Waveland Village Cafe includes steamed seaweed. Over the holiday week-ends they will hold a parade.

Then the church folks will hop in their pickup trucks and the hippies will climb into their psychedelic school buses. Both groups say they have been for-ever changed by the experience.

"They are as amazed as we are," said Pete Jones, who with his wife orga-nized the ministerial group. "We have all learned so much."

(Continued)

(Continued)

The Christians from about a dozen churches near Austin arrived first, four days after the hurricane hit Aug. 29, when the roads to Waveland were barely passable. Pete Jones, 67, said they were drawn by God to the asphalt in front of a demolished supermarket.

When the volunteers began cooking, famished storm victims emerged out of nowhere. Some were naked, having lost every stitch of clothing to Katrina. All were so hungry that the Texans began running out of food. They decided to pray.

"We thought we'd better be specific, so we prayed for hot dogs, because they could be cut up to feed a lot of people," Fay Jones said. "About the time we said 'Amen,' a guy drives up with a truck filled with 2,600 hot dogs. That was the beginning of the miracles around here."

The next wondrous event occurred when the Rainbow Family appeared. The ministerial group was exhausted from nonstop cooking for a crowd that multiplied with every meal. Hippies with dreadlocks and body piercings poured out of a bus painted like a Crayola box.

"We set up two 10-by-10 pop-up tents and started cooking," said 25-year-old Clovis Siemon, an organic farmer and filmmaker from Wisconsin. "We were trying to find someplace to fit in, somewhere to be useful."

Aaron Funk, an Arthur Murray dance instructor from Berkeley, also was among the first Rainbow Family volunteers here. Funk, 33, said his group was well prepared for the effort after decades of Rainbow Family gatherings on mountaintops and in national forests.

With tens of thousands of "brothers and sisters" scattered around the world, the Rainbow Family calls itself the largest "non-organization" of "nonmembers" on the planet. There are no rules, no dues and no officers—just a website (strictly unofficial, the group emphasizes) that promotes the belief that "peace and love are a great thing, and there isn't enough of that in this world."

Funk said the Katrina disaster response marked the Rainbow Family's first major volunteer effort. The call for help went out on cellphones and the Internet.

"We figured it was a social obligation," he said. "We already had the working knowledge of feeding large numbers of people. We got here, and the sense of desperation and urgency was off the charts. There was no time to talk about it. It was just service, time to do what we came here to do."

"The first week we were here," Siemon said, "we had a guy from the Pentagon sitting in a circle with us, chanting 'Om.' It was pretty cool."

Still, the organizers of Waveland Village say it is time to move on. Traditional stores and restaurants are reopening here, and though the landscape remains decimated, a shaky new normality is taking hold.

"Our purpose is not to detract from the local economy," Pete Jones said.

Siemon said he would be returning to his organic farm with far more than he brought to Waveland.

"What have I gained from this? Everything," he said. "I've gained the experience of working with other humans in a wall-less, prejudice-less environment where the sole purpose is to help other humanity.

"That's something not many people get to do."

SOURCE: "A Gospel and Granola Band" by Elizabeth Mehren © 2005, *Los Angeles Times.* Reprinted with permission.

What Do Cultural Performances Do?

Milton Singer's theory of cultural performance is a descriptive one—cataloguing the constitutive elements of performance. Victor Turner moved beyond description to posit the structures and functions of cultural performances as both reflective and reflexive.

As **reflective**, cultural performances communicate the content of culture through orchestrations of cultural media. Turner (1981, 158) argues that cultural performances are composed of "sensory codes" that enlist all of the senses: "*All* the senses of participants and performers may be engaged; they *hear* music and prayers, *see* visual symbols, *taste* consecrated foods, *smell* incense, and *touch* sacred persons and objects."

The sights, sounds, tastes, smells, and touch of Christmas, as celebrated by many North American Christians, are particularly well-orchestrated sets of sensory codes. The content of those performances—cooking seasonal foods, singing carols, exchanging gifts, decorating inside and out, attending parties—mirrors a material world. While one family may prepare a Christmas goose, others prepare Christmas tamales, but both utilize codes and materials that reflect that culture.

This reflection of the world as communicated in performances, however, is flexible and nuanced with no set "meaning" or interpretation. According to Turner (1988, 23–24), (1) cultural performances are capable of carrying many messages at once, (2) they are capable of subverting on one level what another level seems to be saying, and (3) the full "reality" of meaning and messages is only attained through the performance.

The Super Bowl, the Miss America Pageant, graduation ceremonies, and weddings are all cultural performances in the United States *reflective of ongoing social processes.* Each of these cultural performances makes an explicit or implicit claim about who is important, what is valued, how society ought to function, and why this performance demands our participation. Beauty pageants (Jones 1998; Roberts 2002), weddings and pornography (Bell 1999), lynchings (Fuoss 1999; Stephens 2000), travel on commercial airlines (Murphy 2002), and even the office Christmas party and company picnics (Pacanowsky and Trujillo 1983) have been examined as cultural performances that reflect the social processes that fund them.

Cultural performances are not just mirrors, according to Turner, but active agents of change. As **reflexive**, cultural performances provide moments to enact, comment on, critique, and evaluate the norms and values of a culture. Turner describes **performance reflexivity** (1988, 24): "a sociocultural group turns, bends, reflects back on itself, upon the relations, actions, symbols, meanings, codes, roles, statuses, social structures, ethical and legal rules, and other components that make up their public selves."

Kwanzaa celebrations, for example, resist the commodification of the Christmas season, celebrate Afrocentric roots and traditions, and offer alternative ways to engage in family and community. John MacAloon (1986, 372) describes cultural performances in ways particularly applicable to Kwanzaa celebrations as "occasions in which as a culture or society we reflect upon and define ourselves, dramatize our collective myths and history, present ourselves with alternatives, and eventually change in some ways while remaining the same in others."

MAKE A LIST

Carrying, Subverting, and Attaining Messages

Make a list of cultural performances you've participated in. Then list as many of the "messages" you can think of communicated in and through the performance. (For example, The Super Bowl privileges huge men and their physical strength and endurance.)

Now argue that that same performance communicates the opposite of each item on your list. (For example, The Super Bowl privileges team owners, their money, and business acumen.)

How do these performances create such flexible and nuanced messages in and through their sensory codes (the sights, sounds, smells, taste, and touch)?

THEORY MEETS WORLD

Roadside Shrines as Cultural Performances

Rebecca Kennerly (2002) studied roadside shrines erected by individuals to mark the death of a loved one, usually in a vehicle crash. Kennerly describes, analyzes, and writes evocatively and poetically of her encounters with over two hundred shrines across thirty states. These roadside crosses, decorated with flowers, mementos, and notes, are familiar sights to most Americans. Kennerly maintains these shrines are "performance vortices," bringing together cultural performance, ritual performance, and resistant practices.

For mourners who erect them, the shrines mark not only the death of a loved one but the last place this loved one was alive. The shrines also fall outside traditional ways to mourn and sanctioned places to grieve at funeral homes, houses of worship, and cemeteries. Builders of shrines also create them to stand as warnings to others. One mother said she built the shrine to her daughter "to catch the eyes of every passer-by [so they know] someone died there, so they think, slow down, maybe buckle up—maybe even decide not to drink and drive" (248).

For communities, these roadside shrines are contested spaces: people argue they are unsightly, appropriate community property, utilize a religious symbol on state-owned land, and, depending on state statutes, are unlawful. Still, roadside maintenance crews often mow around them, unwilling to disturb their sanctity. If they are removed by law, shrines are often replaced with stronger, studier, more permanent structures. In still other states, judges utilize the building and maintenance of roadside shrines as part of the punishment of a convicted driver responsible for the crash.

Kennerly writes, "Roadside shrines call attention to themselves, insisting on a performative engagement with them from those who mourn, those who are dead, those of us who pass by, and those who would have them removed" (252). Her conclusion, rendered in poetic form that mirrors the erect cross of many of these roadside shrines, captures the many tensions in these cultural performances:

Conclusion: Resisting Arrest
between
literacy
and
orality,
between
secular space and sacred space,
between
human nature and cultural determinations
of the
natural,
between
authentic
expression
and
performance,
between
grief
and
memory,
between
life and death,
and between research, writing, the page, and the stage

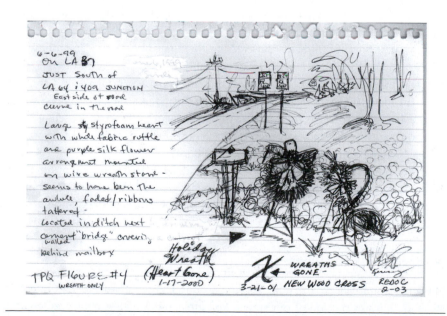

SOURCE: Sketch by Rebecca Kennerly. Copyright © 2005. Courtesy of Rebecca Kennerly.

Performing History

Performances associated with museums, tours, tourism, and historical recreations are particularly enlightening for analysis of the reflexivity available in cultural performances. In antebellum Southern mansion tours (M. Bowman 1998), living museums such as Colonial Williamsburg and Plymouth Plantation (Snow 1993), a Polynesian cultural center (Balme 1998), the LSU Rural Life Museum (R. Bowman 2006), staged slave auctions (McConachie 1998; Thompson 1996), and souvenirs purchased at tourist sites (Love and Kohn 2001), performances construct history, people, events, places, and cultural memories. They often rely on theatrical strategies of conflict, antagonists and protagonists, and dramatic build. Cajun swamp tours, in Eric Wiley's (2002) analysis, cast the tour guide as hero against the enemy alligator. The scripted and improvised speeches of tour guides are also opportunities to explore how a community languages itself in and through performance (Fine and Speer 1985).

While many of these performances are invested in historical accuracy and mimesis, they are always creations—poiesis—that

> are not neutral. They are not slice of life lifted from the everyday world and inserted into the museum gallery, though this is the rhetoric of the mimetic mode. On the contrary, those who construct the display also constitute the subject, even when they seem to do nothing more than relocate an entire house and its contents, brick by brick, board by board, chair by chair. (Kirschenblatt-Gimblett 1991, 389)

These performances *make* culture and public memory.

Phaedra Pezzullo (2003) analyzes "toxic tours" in the petrochemical belt of Louisiana along the Mississippi River where more than 125 companies manufacture fertilizers, gasoline, paint, and plastics, creating what residents call "a toxic gumbo." Residents offer tours of polluted sites, lacing their speeches with stories of cancer rates, physical ailments suffered by their neighbors, and environmental damage to the community. Such tours not only mirror the reality of ecological damage but seek to raise consciousness and mobilize action. Pezzullo's analysis relies on Victor Turner's claim that cultural performances function reflexively, as "active agencies of change, representing the eye by which culture sees itself and the drawing board on which creative actors sketch out what they believe to be more apt or interesting 'designs for living'" (Turner 1988, 24).

Performing history, public memory, and political critique are potent forms of *Homo performans,* performing humans. As reflective and reflexive, the possibilities of process, play, poetics, and power are evidenced in cultural performances.

Performing Others

Dwight Conquergood (1985) writes of the moral imperatives that saturate any study of cultures outside of one's own. For three and a half years, Conquergood conducted fieldwork among the Hmong and Lao refugees in Chicago. He created and presented performances from this fieldwork before a variety of audiences: social service agencies, educators, religious groups, and civic groups. Conquergood readily admits he was an advocate for the groups he studied.

While many of these audience members came to see the Hmong differently through Conquergood's performances of their stories, still others accused him of a number of offenses: (1) "collaborating in the work of the devil" by presenting a radically different, non Judeo-Christian religious tradition, affirming Hmong religious beliefs and stories; (2) "retarding the refugees' assimilation into mainstream America" by honoring their ancient traditions; (3) presenting the Hmong as "stupid and backward" by preserving the grammar and pronunciation of his collected texts. Conquergood also faced his own concerns about "white guilt": "What right do you, a middle-class white man, have to perform these narratives?" (4).

From these experiences, Conquergood argues that performing ethnographic materials is fraught with "complex ethical tensions, tacit political commitments, and moral ambiguities" (4). He outlines four performative stances, or ethical pitfalls, in studying and performing the "other" (see Figure 5.1).

Moral Mapping and Dialogic Performance

The poles of the box in Figure 5.1 represent the tensions among "identity" and "difference" and "detachment" and "commitment," while the center "dialogical performance" balances these poles and reconciles the extremes.

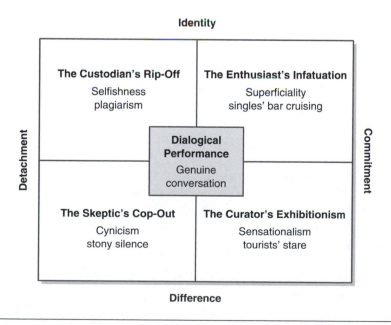

Figure 5.1   Moral Mapping of Performative Stances Toward the Other

SOURCE: From "Performing as a Moral Act," by Dwight C. Conquergood, *Literature in Performance* (1985), reprinted by permission of Taylor & Francis Ltd., http://www.informaworld.com.

The **Custodian's Rip-Off** is characterized by selfishness and the desire to take, to own, and (sometimes) to sell performances and artifacts of others, often in the guise of "preserving dying cultures" (Conquergood 1985, 5). The **Enthusiast's Infatuation** trivializes the other in superficial and often naïve performances, based on little or no fieldwork or contact. Identification with the other is too easily and quickly claimed. The **Curator's Exhibitionism** is committed to difference, but difference that is "exotic," remote, and often shaped to shock audiences. This stance denies the "other" membership in a moral, and often human, community. The **Skeptic's Cop-Out** is familiar: "I am neither black nor female: I will not perform *The Color Purple*" (8). Conquergood maintains that this detachment and difference is cynical, refusing to engage the other under a mask of arrogant imperialism. Only members of dominant groups can claim such cynical, privileged refusal. This silence forecloses dialogue with and knowledge about others.

Conquergood proposes "dialogic performance" as a way through those pitfalls. "This performative stance struggles to bring together different voices, world views, value systems, and beliefs so that they can have a conversation with one another" (9). Conquergood characterizes **Dialogical Performance** in four ways:

1. As stretched among the poles of identity, difference, detachment, and commitment, this stance falls "between competing ideologies," bringing them together even as it holds them apart.

2. As an examination of identity and difference that leads to questioning and challenging our own *a priori assumptions* about culture. Such questioning about ourselves is important to any dialogue with others.

3. As dialogue with performance, a two-way conversation with others that resists speaking to and for others.

4. As dialogue in which performance resists conclusions, but instead begins a conversation.

From Dialogue to Responsibilities

Madison (1998, 278) extends Conquergood's stances and emphasis on dialogue to argue that performances of *possibilities* are important routes for the "principles of transformation and transgression, dialogue and interrogation, as well as acceptance and imagination to build words that are *possible*." She offers three questions that help guide any performance work built on the lives of others:

1. By what definable and material means will the Subjects themselves benefit from the performance?

2. How can the performance contribute to a more enlightened and involved citizenship that will disturb systems and processes that limit freedoms and possibilities?

3. In what ways will the performers probe questions of identity, representation, and fairness that will enrich their own subjectivity, cultural politics, and art? (278)

E. Patrick Johnson (2002) utilizes Conquergood's stances and Madison's concept of "possibility" to explore the performances of "an all-white, mostly atheist, Australian gospel choir" for the contradictions among Blackness, appropriation, and authenticity. He explores the problematics of cross-cultural gospel performance as well as the mutual benefits, phrased as the transformative power available in dialogic performance, for self and other. Michelle A. Holling and Bernadette M. Calafell (2007) analyze stage performances of Richard Montoya and Guillermo Gómez-Peña through Conquergood's "dialogic performances" and Madison's "possibilities" for Chicano identities, narratives, and cultural performance.

> The body within performance, and particularly ethnographic traditions, tempers the danger of speaking for "others" through sensuous engagement, privileging dialogic performance that brings together various voices, worldviews, value systems, and beliefs in conversation that resists conclusions, remaining open to ongoing discussion between ethnographers and interlocuters. (61)

Randall Hill (1995) explores ritual performances of Native American peoples as resources for rehearsal processes; the dangers, following Conquergood, are "borrowing authority" from a ritual shaman by a director and arrogant and sacrilegious attempts at "duplication" of rituals. David Olsen (1992) details the building of a performance around Kai T. Erikson's 1978 book, *Everything in Its Path: Destruction of Community in the Buffalo Creek Flood.* The performance demanded a dialogic encounter between the victims of a devastating flood in the Appalachian mountains and the economically privileged graduate students at Northwestern University.

Kristin Valentine extends Conquergood's four pitfalls with a fifth: "some audience members, not understanding the sacredness of the ceremony, perhaps unknowingly, act in inappropriate ways" (2002, 281). She suggests guidelines for "intense spectatorship," a present-minded audiencing that assumes self-reflection at cultural performances, especially sacred ones, outside one's worldview. Valentine writes,

> Intense spectators do not pretend to understand the ceremony as they think a member of that culture might. Rather, intense spectators try to make sense of what *they* experience as audience members, basing their comments on extensive background research and careful observation of the *public* parts of the ceremonies. Knowing that ethical codes of conduct are not fixed, intense spectators necessarily live with ambiguity. (281)

Performing culture, as performer, audience, critic, insider, and outsider, is an intensely ethical act. Performance scholars have outlined pitfalls and suggested

SOURCE: Photograph by Arlene Sadcopen. Copyright © 2005. Courtesy of Arlene Sadcopen.

ways through the dilemmas of performing self and other, present and past, individual and community. Guillermo Gómez-Peña (1994, 21) offers an important watchword for performance border crossings that spreads responsibilities: "In order to dialogue we must learn each other's language, history, art, literature, and political ideas. We must travel south and east, with frequency and humility; not as cultural tourists, but as civilian ambassadors."

RETHINKING CULTURE

Positivism was a valuable way to create scientific knowledge through direct observation. But we now recognize that nineteenth-century scientists and theorists also wrote racist, sexist, and elitist assumptions on the cultures they studied: "Africa became a place of darkness, one lacking the enlightenment of the West. India has been used to model not the 'origin of man,' but the 'origin of civilization.' Both are forms of 'othering' for western symbolic operations" (Haraway 1989, 262). "Others" in cultural study in the nineteenth century were most often treated as inferior, if exotic, animals ruled by biology and emotions—especially when compared with the intellectual, rational, Western white men who studied them.

Wurtham's four approaches to studying culture (subjective, structural, dramatistic, and institutional) can be risky for studying performance. When looking for attitudes, structures and functions, dramas, or resources, performances can unwittingly be turned into second-order phenomena. Catherine Bell (2004, 93) writes that much performance theory assumes an underlying "something," a latent meaning under the performance, "that devalues the action itself, making it a second-stage representation of prior values." The challenge is to explore performance as performance, much like Huizinga's attempts to study play as play, and not to approach performance as automatically servicing other cultural goals or processes.

Jon McKenzie critiques theories of cultural performance that valorize liminality and performance's potential for cultural transformation. He calls this the "liminal norm" in performance studies research, "the transgressive or resistant potential that has come to dominate the study of cultural performance" (2001, 30). When we approach performance as a constant *challenge* to cultural structures, we obscure the many, many ways that cultural performance *upholds and strengthens* cultural traditions.

Shannon Jackson (2000, 22), following Judith Butler and Joan Scott, notes that "reading" culture, history, and performances as texts can also create "misreadings." In Jackson's *Professing Performance* (2004, 175), she offers evidence of "gendered blindspots" and racist assumptions in the history of performance. Favoring transgressive approaches to culture in this history overlooks "the implicit, domestic, everyday, life-producing performances" women and people of color have enacted to survive.

Elizabeth Bell (1995b) critiques Conquergood's moral stances as scripting the performer as prone to abusive power in the relationship with the other. Instead, Bell argues for an economy of knowledge in and through pleasure of performance. Knowledge of the "other" is impossible, but the pleasure of the "self"—as performer, creator, and owner—is a gift created in the economy of performance.

The study of culture in and through its performances has come a long way from the goal of the British structural-functionalist school of anthropology. Turner (1981, 139) describes this goal: "to exhibit the laws of structure and process which . . . determine the specific configurations of relationships and institutions detectable by trained observation." With the groundwork laid by theories of rites of passages, play, ritual, and cultural performance, Turner moved the "study of man" theorized as covering laws to an enlightenment theory of culture as performed. The study of culture as performed has moved from theories of positivism to critical theories that explore voices and viewpoints as embodiments of power. Performances are *constitutive* of culture, not something added to culture after the fact; performances are *epistemic,* in that we learn and know our worlds through our performances; and performances are *critical* lenses for looking at and pushing back on culture.

The "performance turn" generated a new lens for studying culture as process, play, poetics, and power, especially in performances that generate liminality and communitas. Cultural performances are always reflective and reflexive, offering opportunities to confirm and transform values, structures, dramas, and institutions. Whether performing, watching, critiquing, or studying performances of others, the commitments are always ethical and political. Indeed, Mary Frances HopKins (1995) extends the "performative turn" metaphor to argue for the "performance turn and toss," to suggest that a certain amount of squirming, of discomfort, of ambiguity is both necessary and inevitable in any study of performances that constitute culture.

CHAPTER 6

Performing Social Roles

Theory in Perspective: Who Am I?

Answering the question "Who am I?" has been a scientific, philosophic, and political project in the West for centuries. The **Enlightenment**, an eighteenth-century European movement epitomized in the scientific method of Francis Bacon, galvanized in the philosophical treatises of Hume and Kant, and enacted in the political works of Benjamin Franklin and Thomas Jefferson, maintained several claims about the self, knowledge, and Truth. First, the "self" exists, and it is whole, stable, and fixed. Second, reason is a route to knowing the self, and "right reasoning" leads to true knowledge. Third, such Truth is universal, natural, and eternal, and science is the right use of such knowledge (Flax 1990).

Modernity, associated first with the 1750s Industrial Revolution in Europe, takes Enlightenment ideas of self, knowledge, and Truth into the industrial age. The *pursuit of progress, the objective rationality of science,* and *consumerism* (Lyotard 1984) are characteristics of modernity that had a tremendous impact on twentieth-century thinking. New academic disciplines extended the question from "Who am I?" to include "Who am I *in relation to others?*" That is, how is the self a *product* of both others and society? New social and behavioral sciences—like social psychology, sociology, criminology, educational psychology, object relations, organizational behavior, and even a new area called interpersonal communication—took the relations among society, self, and others as their central concerns.

George Herbert Mead, in *Mind, Self, and Society* (1934), introduced the idea that the social self emerges in three intersubjective forms we create together: language, play, and the game. For Mead, all social interactions occur through shared symbol systems like words, roles, gestures, and rituals. Mead's work lays the foundation for important directions and methods in communication theory, including transactional analysis, symbolic interactionism, and ethnomethodology. At the heart of all these theories is the question "How does communication create this relationship between self and society?"

Erving Goffman, a Canadian-born sociologist, deserves special attention for answering this question by putting performance in the middle of that relationship: The social self is a performance for others. Chapter Two covered Goffman's concepts of performance keying and framing as important ways to constitute performance. Chapter Four foreshadowed that Goffman, in addition to Kenneth Burke and Victor Turner, is the third theorist who advances a dramaturgical perspective on social relations. With the publication of *The Presentation of Self in Everyday Life* (1959), Goffman adapted Burke's concept of life as drama to posit a "dramaturgical" perspective on the social. This perspective asks, *how do we present, maintain, and repair our social selves in interactions with others?* His answers, which use the language of the theatre, are immensely rich descriptions of both mundane and problematic interactions between the performed self and others.

Goffman's theories of **impression management**, **misrepresentation**, and **stigma** have influenced work in a range of academic disciplines interested in how people *are* and *are not* what they appear to be. Goffman's work marks an important moment between modernism and postmodernism, between self and society, between the social sciences and the humanities, in answering the question "Who am I in relation to others?"

Don't Play Games with Me!

Most of us are familiar with the notion of a dramatic **role**—the character named in a play script and created in performance onstage. Stewart L. Tubbs and Sylvia Moss, authors of the ninth edition of *Human Communication* (2003), explain some people's discomfort at the idea of a "role." They claim, "Actors play roles, and you might be wondering what roles have to do with human communication—especially two-person communication—in which, ideally, communication is based on mutual trust, not game-playing" (260).

Tubbs and Moss have aided the introduction to this chapter on performing social roles by invoking two powerful tropes: (1) the antitheatrical prejudice that claims that performers are not to be trusted, for they too easily manipulate others and reality, and (2) that game playing is to be avoided at all costs as not the serious stuff of adult communication. All of the chapters thus far have argued with this antitheatrical prejudice: Performance is an important way of making, not simply faking, texts, drama, and culture. Game playing is also a marvelous conception of humanity at its performing best: Ritual and play are flip sides of culture constituted in and through its performances.

When sociologist George Herbert Mead (1934) first conceptualized the notion of a "role," an emergent self, he drew from three things only humans create: language, roles, and games. All three are created in and through symbol systems that must be agreed upon to be understood. All three involve constructions of self and other only known in relationship. How does a child develop a self-concept, a consciousness, an answer to the question "Who am I?"

Mead explains that this self emerges first through language. Language is a human experience *learned through interaction* with others. Second, this self emerges through role play, specifically by taking on roles not oneself—mother, father, doctor, nurse, class clown, and so forth. This ability to stand in another's shoes through *role-playing* is central to the sense of self. And finally, game playing is evidence of understanding not a specific other—a mother, a doctor, a nurse—but a constellation of others all *playing by a set of rules* of the game. Mead (1934, 160) writes of the child, "He becomes a something which can function in the organized whole, and thus tends to determine himself in his relationship with the group to which he belongs. That process is one which is a striking stage in the development of the child's morale. It constitutes him a self-conscious member of the community to which he belongs." In short, role-playing and games are very *serious* ways we learn to enact our sense of self through communication.

From Social Psychology to Gender Roles

Mead's formulation is basic to general communication theory, focusing on the importance of symbols and communication processes as the *medium* whereby society shapes selves, and selves negotiate and manage the demands of society. Mead "birthed" the field of social psychology in the United States, recognizing that individual psychology and social processes are intimately connected. From 1940 to the 1980s in the United States, role psychology emphasized role as a *set of norms or social expectations felt by self and perceived by others.*

Transactional analysis in the 1960s grew out of role psychology with the popular works of psychiatrist Eric Berne, *Games People Play* and *I'm Okay, You're Okay.* Berne argued that people enact typical scripts for parent, child, and adult in communicative interactions. Much work in the 1970s in Interpersonal Communication was based on therapeutic movements that made use of role-playing techniques to enable productive adult-adult communicative strategies (Galvin 1979; Hutchinson et al. 1978; Langdon 1973; Roberts 1972; Glenn 1972). Role conflict, role tensions, role stereotypes, and role expectations in families, at work, and between individuals are apparent in child-parent, student-teacher, doctor-patient, husband-wife, and employer-employee relationships.

We are most aware of the importance of roles today in Communication through scholarship featuring gender roles: the social expectations for appropriate masculinity and femininity. Bonnie Dow and Julia Wood (2006) trace early questions about women's status, rights, and "sex roles" as emphasizing communicative differences between men and women, stereotypic representations in mass media, and workplace relations that assure women's helping roles and men's leadership. Performance scholarship in gender roles features the dilemmas of crossing genders in Shakespeare (Galloway 1997; Merrill 2000), gender roles in African American theatre (Stephens 2000), fashion (Waggoner and Hallstein 2001), rodeo performances of cowgirls (Shields and Coughlin 2000), and the gendered labor of flight attendants (Banks 1994; Murphy 2001).

If role model, role-playing, role conflict, and gender role are now common-place terms, then the work of Erving Goffman is enjoying a revisitation across academic disciplines interested in not just theories of roles and interactions, but in how theatrical metaphors are immensely productive for describing everyday life as performance.

"What's Wrong?"

We've all had this experience. A friend, a relative, a partner, or a child appears before us. From the expression on her face, we just *know* something bad has happened. Before any words are spoken, we ask the question, "What's wrong?" While the bad news can range from a spilled soda on the clean kitchen floor to the tragic and unexpected death of a loved one, all the elements are in place for a performance perspective on communication in daily life.

The bearer of bad news is communicating in two ways: the expressions she *gives* and the expressions she *gives off.* In this instance, with no deliberate words spoken, no verbal expressions are given. But the expressions given off—facial expression, posture, tears, eye contact (or its lack)—are performed by the individual and for the audience. In the case of spilled soda, the performance may be a **cynical** one, a "show" for the audience-parent that is self-serving and manipulative on the child's part. In the case of the death of a loved one, the performance may be **sincere**; that is, a heartfelt and honest expression of shock, grief, and sorrow while breaking the news to the audience-loved one.

All communicative interactions, according to Erving Goffman, can be approached as performances that move between cynicism and sincerity to help explain the motives of individuals and the range of resources available to create the performance. Goffman writes, "A performance may be defined as all the activity of a given participant on a given occasion which serves to influence in any way any of the other participants" (1959, 15).

Goffman's theory of performance, articulated in his 1959 book *The Presentation of Self in Everyday Life,* describes and explains the ways daily life is a series of roles we enact with and for others. Goffman's work is important for three reasons. First, these performed roles foster a *consensual reality*—the world as we know it in our interactions with others—and serve *to influence* others. Influence, especially evidenced in sales and advertising, was especially interesting to Goffman: How are we persuaded to participate and to consume in the story of modern progress?

Second, Goffman created a *vocabulary* for talking about these interactions in everyday life. Using language from the theatre, Goffman's lexicon has great descriptive power. He described and named the successful techniques used to bring off the "show"—whether that show is cynical or sincere.

Third, Goffman posited *social roles as dramatically realized;* "Life itself is a dramatically acted thing" (72). Extending Kenneth Burke's dramatistic approach to social interaction and Victor Turner's social drama, Goffman explored the ways in which reality is where and when we perform it: as *ceremony,* "an expressive rejuvenation and reaffirmation of the moral values of the community," and as *celebration.* He explains: "To stay in one's room away from the place where the party is given, or away from where the practitioner attends his client, is to stay away from where reality is being performed. The world, in truth, is a wedding" (36).

The next sections of this chapter will offer Goffman's conceptions of performance, teams, regions, impression management, and roles. His classifications and categories are rich theoretical explanations for communication as performance.

"What's Right?"

"What's wrong with you?" is a common question when we perceive another as troubled, but we rarely ask the question "What's right with you?" Sincere performances of social roles are so thoroughly internalized, seem so "natural" and unaffected, that they are rarely thought of as performances. "I am a college student," however, is a social role created in and through its performance. Goffman outlines four interlocking components of performances of social roles.

1. *Belief in the Part.* Most of us believe in—and take seriously—the social roles we enact every day. We work both directly and indirectly to create the impressions for ourselves and for others that we *are* who we claim to be (students, parents, employees, parishioners, Republicans, feminists, etc.).

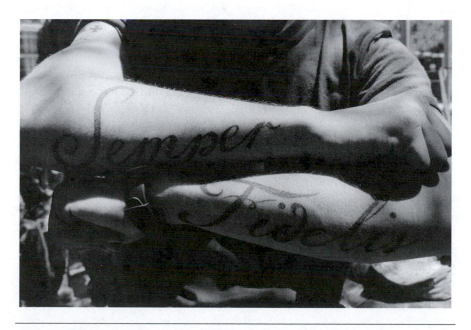

SOURCE: Photo by Sgt. Robert L. Fisher III, 2006.

2. *Social Fronts.* We perform these roles with the aid of "expressive equipment," and social fronts consist of both settings and personal fronts. The **settings** we find ourselves in—the places, décor, furniture, even props that surround us each day—help create our social fronts. The role of college student depends on attending class on a university campus, but it also spills over into student apartments, cars, and hangouts—with its attendant decor of books, papers, and paraphernalia.

Personal fronts (the "masks" we wear to create these roles) are composed of appearance and manner. **Appearance** involves dress, gender, age, size, posture, speech patterns, facial expressions, gestures—all the cues that combine to create the impression of a social role and its status. **Manner** is the enactment of attitude that accompanies these cues. A "serious" student and a "slacker" student may *appear* the same, but their *manners* will be quite different, creating different expectations for those around them.

3. *Dramatic Realization.* Social roles are produced in the moment they are performed—during the interaction. For some roles, this realization happens in a split second. Umpires at sporting events, police officers, and emergency medical technicians all make their actions visible in the moment of performance.

For other roles, this realization is often invisible, or deliberately hidden, to make the performances seem seamless and easy. Martha Stewart "hides" the intense, time-consuming labor of her products; the immense staff that accomplishes the work; and the talent, experience, and money required to achieve the results in her television show. But it is still through the performance that Stewart achieves her social role as "expert" in gracious living. Stewart's social role, as convicted felon, prisoner, then housebound parolee, required a radical revision in the dramatic realization of her social identity.

4. *Idealization.* When we perform these roles, we often try to measure up to an "ideal" that is always learned, practiced, and culturally specific. For Goffman, "a performance is 'socialized,' molded, and modified to fit into the understanding and expectations of the society in which it is presented" (1959, 35). This idealization tends to incorporate and to exemplify the officially accredited values of society. Group mottos, like *Semper fidelis* (Always loyal) for the U.S. Marines and Gloria Vanderbilt's claim, "You can never be too rich or too thin," are idealizations that affirm and maintain social values and hierarchies—often to good or to disastrous enactments.

Goffman moves from cognitive processes inside the individual (belief), to material effects (settings and fronts), to the performed action (dramatic realization), to society (idealization). Phil Manning (1991, 75) writes of Goffman's movement from individual to society, "By such means, performances are both realized and idealized as our all-too-human selves are transformed into socialized beings capable of expressive control."

SOURCE: Photo by Bob Gonzalez. Copyright © 2007 by Bob Gonzalez.

Heroes and S/Heroes

Take any superhero and her or his alter ego: Spider-Man and Peter Parker, Superman and Clark Kent, Cat Woman and Patience Phillips. Which of these social roles is the "real" identity and which is "fake"? Are "real" and "fake" even appropriate terms here? How can Goffman's vocabulary of belief, fronts, dramatic realization, and idealization help us understand their roles (and our own) as consensual reality created in performance that serves to influence others?

Teams: Performing Together

Many of our social roles depend on cooperation with others. Goffman (1959) calls this a **performance team**. Team members must trust and depend on each other to perform their roles properly in front of the audience to achieve their purpose. The doctor's office, a restaurant, a department store, even a birthday party, all involve different people performing their roles in relationship to one another.

Successful team performances are composed of two relationships: the bonds of reciprocal dependence and reciprocal familiarity. That is, any one member of a team has the power to disrupt the performance through bad or inappropriate conduct: a nurse who doesn't defer to a doctor in front of a patient; a server who sits at a table and "acts" like a patron; a man who picks a fight with his partner at a dinner party in front of guests. All performers depend and rely on each other—**reciprocal dependence**—to "maintain a given definition of the situation before their audience" (Goffman 1959, 82).

The bond of **reciprocal familiarity** is a formal relationship in which team members are "in the know." They acknowledge and protect the reality they are creating together through their familiarity with the different roles and performances required to put on this show. Disney team members at theme parks do an excellent job of protecting the impression that Disneyland is "the happiest place on earth." They also are insiders, "in the know," familiar with the labor required by each individual.

Teams depend on united action to accomplish their goals. When parents present a "united front" before their children, they are a performance team. Formal and informal rules develop to help them "maintain the line" before an audience. These rules involve dramatic "interaction," not just "action." Some of Goffman's team rules include the following:

1. Information should not be withheld from team members.

2. When mistakes are made, others need to come to the rescue of the united front.

3. Disagreement among team members should never be voiced in front of the audience.

4. Team members should be selected based on their trustworthiness (and should not include children and drunks, according to Goffman).

5. The line between team members and audience should not be crossed.

6. There is often a person in charge of "directing" the show (funerals, weddings, a picnic) with the special duty of allocating parts and bringing back into line any "bad" performance.

Team members take risks together, and the bonds that grow among them, dependence and familiarity, are acutely felt.

ACT OUT

Team Rules

Invent a performance team with a specific purpose to achieve (sales, service, entertainment, education, etc.). Improvise a scene in which all the above rules for team performance are kept. Improvise a similar scene in which all the rules are broken. What happens to the "consensual reality" created in these two scenes?

Regions: Performing Spaces

For Goffman, the swinging door between the restaurant kitchen and the restaurant dining room is a place to observe "the putting on and taking off of character" by the server. In the kitchen, the server may be in a screaming argument with the chef, but when she crosses through the swinging door, she adopts the benign good manners of an enthusiastic and attentive server.

The swinging door represents a barrier between regions in the performance. Goffman defines region as "any place bounded to some degree by barriers to perception" (1959, 106). Most restaurant patrons cannot see, hear, or experience the kitchen. Drawing from the language of the theatre, frontstage and backstage in everyday life become the "front region" and the "back region" with a boundary that separates the performers from the audience. Both regions enable and demand different expressive standards by the performers.

Front region behaviors have standards of **politeness** (how the performer treats the audience in talk) and **decorum** (how the performer acts in nonverbal ways in the presence of the audience). Team members tend to treat each other formally in front regions as well.

Back regions are places where front region performances are knowingly contradicted: Hierarchies of status may no longer be observed, and formalities will be dropped as people use these back regions to prepare for their roles, let down their hair, and do work that will later be displayed in the front region. Workrooms, break rooms, storage spaces, employee lounges, private offices, and some rooms in the home are places were teams engage in reciprocal familiarity with each other. The sanctity of back regions is often taken for granted by team members until an "outsider" or audience member enters the space. Then team members jump to repair the intrusion or accommodate the outsider.

But back regions are also maintained by rules of behavior. Team members must still create impressions that they are trustworthy, they may often help sustain each other's morale, and certain divisions among team members, like age, race, gender, class, and abilities, still abide in back regions.

Goffman's claims that team performances are intricately linked to space and power foreshadowed much theory about the relationship between geography, institutions, and knowledge in the West, like that in Michel Foucault's *Birth of the Prison* and *Discipline and Punish* (Manning 1991). Contemporary work that utilizes Goffman's region/power ideas include back regions as places of deviance (Redmon 2003), the

SOURCE: Photograph by Jaclyn Lannon. Copyright © 2007 by Jaclyn Lannon.

facework of contemporary cities (Jensen 2006), and classifications of identity produced by space (Hacking 2004). Goffman is enjoying a rebirth as theorists are looking again at his claims about space and performance.

ACT OUT

Performing Spatially

Take pictures of front and back regions in your home or workplace. With these photographs as a backdrop, create two typical performances in each region. How differently do teams act in these two regions? How are these regions divided? How do performances in each region contradict those in the other?

When Good Performances Go Bad

A coherence among belief, front, dramatic realization, and idealization is necessary to any successful performance of a social role and the impression of reality fostered in team performances. But bad things do happen that upset the performance, disrupt its careful construction, and destroy the impressions the performer seeks to create. These mishaps onstage, presented in Chapter Two as "frame breaks," are familiar: Performers crack each other up, scenery collapses, or the curtain falls on the wrong cue.

In everyday life, these same mishaps occur: We trip crossing the room, we forget the name of a longtime acquaintance, important guests drop in unannounced in the middle of painting the living room. These disruptions can be met with laughter, embarrassment, or shame and often become the fodder for personal stories of misadventure.

For theorizing performance in everyday life, these accidents reveal—in their mistakes—the underlying rules and regulations of social performances. These are often "rules" we take for granted or are unaware of, until they are broken. For Goffman, they reveal the ways that we are "blind" to the "strict test of aptness, fitness, propriety, and decorum" (1959, 55) that we apply to our own performances. These mistakes also reveal the gap between our socialized ideal selves and our actual attempts to enact them. Shame is a powerful emotion in Goffman's theory of performed interactions; shame's flip side is awe. He explains:

> The audience senses secret mysteries and powers behind the performance, and the performer senses that his chief secrets are petty ones. As countless folk tales and initiation rites show, often the real secret behind the mystery is that there really is no mystery; the real problem is to prevent the audience from learning this. (70)

Impression Management

To describe the constant negotiation between avoiding performance disruptions and possessing positive attributes, Goffman coined the term "impression management" to delineate how individuals create successful performances. He uses the term "dramaturgical" to refer to both the *drama* of enactment and the *rules* of that enactment (think "liturgy"—another "urgy" word—as a set of rules or codes spoken in church). Goffman explores five techniques of managing impressions created by a performer.

1. *Dramaturgical loyalty.* This involves team members acting as if they have accepted the moral obligations of being a team member. This results in both in-group solidarity and, oftentimes, dehumanizing the audience. Both soldiers and surgeons have moral obligations to perform correctly, and their roles are performed in relation to the audience (enemy or patient).

2. *Dramaturgical discipline.* This involves control of face and voice by an individual, the presence of mind and poise necessary to pull off the role. Films that include "bloopers" at the end of the reel provide examples of a *lack* of dramaturgical discipline.

3. *Dramaturgical circumspection.* Here a performer must show prudence, foresight, care, and honesty in the performance. A "circumspect" performer is one who is reflexive about the choices she makes. "Dressing the part" of a teacher requires careful consideration of the impressions that certain items of clothing will create.

4. *Protective practices.* These are all ways to "save" the show when things go wrong. Team members can rescue others in moments of crisis. This is especially apparent in training new employees: The trainer will step in to take over a sales transaction from a new employee. The audience can collude as well, as when a parent feeds lines to a performing child. In hospitals, nurses often save interns from dosage mistakes with patients, protecting not only the patient but the intern and the hospital.

5. *Tact.* Performers must always be alert for cues of mistaken impressions and be ready with corrections. But even the most tactful performer is sometimes at a loss when things go wrong. Here is Goffman, writing at a time when only men were doctors: "Thus, when a surgeon and his nurse both turn from the operating table and the anesthetized patient accidentally rolls off the table to his death, not only is the operation disrupted in an embarrassing way, but the reputation of the doctor, as a doctor and as a man, and also the reputation of the hospital may be weakened" (1959, 243).

Impression management is an art, not a science, according to Goffman. Moreover, the **personality** of the individuals, the **interaction** created among individuals, and the **social structure** of the context and culture all determine just how performance disruptions are managed. Much research in communication deals with precisely this management of impressions, especially when "work is talk" in particular occupations (Banks 1994). Goffman's ideas have been used to explore the roles of health care professionals for "inappropriate emotions" (Morgan and Krone 2001), motivations for medical role behaviors (Rodham 2000), at-risk doctor-patient talk (Myers 2003), and nurse status negotiations (Apker, Propp, and Zabava 2005). Impression management in the health sciences is an art that demands constant negotiation.

I Don't Have Time for This!

Katy Vine (2004, 118–19, 121, 221) writes about the Kilgore Rangerettes, the first high-kick drill team in the United States, established in 1940 at Kilgore College in Texas. Famous for their cowgirl costumes, hats, and precise routines, Rangerettes kick so high that their shins touch their hat brims. Vine goes inside the Rangerettes' weeklong tryouts, as freshmen girls at Kilgore College vie for coveted places on the sixty-member team. Dramaturgical discipline is apparent in the team rules and performances of the Rangerettes.

On Monday morning of the last week in July, Lory, Morgan, and two other hopefuls were sitting around a table in the Kilgore College cafeteria, eating bowls of Cocoa Puffs and reciting the rules they had been given the night before. They were required to wear their hair in a ponytail on top of their heads. They were not allowed to wear makeup except for red lipstick. They had to pin a gigantic name tag on their solid-colored leotards. They could not wear jewelry, needless to say. Unless given permission to speak, they had to answer all questions from their assigned advisers and other sophomore Rangerettes with only "Yes, ma'am. Thank you, Miss Jones [or whatever]." The girls eyed one another across the table, cracking up at their goofy-looking hair fountains and bright-red lip gloss. There were reasons for these rules. "Many girls need to come to a more humble place," director Dana Blair told me. "They have always been the officer and won everything and been the 'it' girl, and if we had all those egos running around, practice would be difficult.". . .

By Monday night, five days before the final results would be announced, nerves had already begun to fray. But grace under pressure is a Rangerette tradition: The group's slogan is "Beauty knows no pain." I had heard stories of girls who kept smiling even after kicking so high they bloodied their noses. I'd heard how Gussie Nell Davis, the Rangerettes' revered and beloved founder—who was never seen wearing anything but stylish suits and four-inch heels—once stomped up to a girl who had fainted on the field and yelled, "I have no time for this! Get up!" That evening, when Director Blair announced a surprise evaluation of the dance routine the hopefuls had learned on Sunday, word was out that one stressed-out girl had already packed up and left. Morgan's group of four nailed every move, while Lory's group struggled, panicking in the middle of the routine until one of them remembered a key jump. Throughout the evaluation, however, the girls' expressions remained determinedly cheerful as they strutted and leaped across the floor. Even the one who had mono. Even the one who had slipped and fallen on her behind. Even the one who had thrown up in the middle of the routine. . . .

Now it was time for the moment of truth. Blair stood before the hopefuls and began The Speech. She encouraged the ones who didn't make it to not give up on their dreams, recounting the morning's news report of a surfer who, although she'd lost an arm to a shark attack, was still surfing. The group sniffed and brushed away tears and prayed. Lory was sitting between Morgan and me, and she grabbed our hands and squeezed. . . . When the sign was lowered, the

> room fell silent as the girls searched for their numbers. Then everyone let out a high-pitched scream, as if a winning free throw and a car crash had just occurred simultaneously. Lory and Morgan had both made it.
>
> SOURCE: Katy Vine, "Alive and Kicking." Reprinted with permission of *Texas Monthly.*

Misrepresentation

Goffman was very interested in performances that deliberately misrepresent social roles and situations. Just as abnormal psychology can reveal a culture's conceptions of "normal" personalities and behaviors, we can explore performances of social roles that are misrepresentations. Cynical performances, false fronts, sham dramas, con jobs, and contrived mistakes are all ways to foster "false" impressions in audiences. For Goffman, "we can profitably study performances that are quite false in order to learn about ones that are quite honest" (1959, 66).

The commonsense question "Is this person honest?" is not much help when studying misrepresentations of social roles. Instead, Goffman proposes two other questions that help us understand the underlying social order. First, "Is this person authorized to give this performance?" When people impersonate clergy, doctors, or police officers, a "moral" authority has been violated. As audience members, we feel threatened by these impersonations.

Second, "Has this person told a lie?" leaves little room for complex answers. Instead, this question is best approached by analyzing the many communication techniques that move between lie and truth; innuendo, strategic ambiguity, and crucial omissions are ways to maintain the definition of the performance situation. Government officials, undercover police, even friends engage in small lies that hide the facts. The film *Borat: Cultural Learnings of America for Make Benefit Glorious Nation of Kazakhstan* has elicited controversy precisely because of Sacha Baron Cohen's "unauthorized" impersonation and crucial omissions in garnering the participation of others in the film.

THEORY MEETS WORLD

This Is So Not You!

Dean Schiebel spent three months observing the performances at the door of a bar near a local university. In "Faking Identity in Clubland: The Communicative Performance of 'Fake ID'" (1992), Schiebel details the "command performances" given by underage women seeking admission to the bar with their fake identification cards. These women and bouncers cocreate the performance in a context particularly salient for Goffman's dramaturgical approach. The young woman must offer a performance "designed to create impressions that influence others

(Continued)

(Continued)

on particular occasions" (Schiebel 1992, 164). The doorman has the authority to legitimate or to reject that fake identity.

In interviews, Schiebel discovered several strategies employed by the women. The performers rehearse their performances "backstage," away from the entrance. "Like in the parking lot of a bar. But you didn't want the bouncer to see you, so you didn't want to pull up, so you usually tried to park far away. And you'd sit there and memorize your ID, memorize it, you know, had to memorize social security. . . . And then your friends would like quiz you" (167–8). Part of the rehearsal process is coaching themselves not to display their nervousness, but to adopt a different attitude: "You gotta go in cocky. You gotta hand 'em your ID and start walking in the bar like you've been there a hundred times before. . . . We practice it at home. . . . You gotta practice it at home" (168).

Several strategies involve the performance team. The group of women seeking admission must do nothing to upset the reality they are creating. "I had some girl standing next to me calling me [by] my real name," one woman relates. The team also orchestrates the order of their appearances in line. They stagger "good fake IDs" with low quality, "sketchy" fake IDs in the hope that the bouncer will concentrate on the good ones. Once one member of the team has gained entrance, she may attempt to "rattle the gatekeeper" who is looking at her friend's fake ID: "He's looking at it and he's pondering and the person that's already in goes, 'Oh, Jane, what do you want to drink?' or something. Just something like, 'Oh, hurry up, Jane' or 'What's taking so long?' and say her name, and he'll be like, 'Oh, here' [and give back the ID card]" (169).

Performers must also be prepared to "save the show" with quick thinking and improvisation. One woman relates:

[M]y first ID wasn't me. It was a girl from Iowa. She had dark brown hair, she had my eye color, and my height. These were the two you had to match. 'Cause you can't, obviously, fake it. But she weighed 140, I weigh 100, and she had really pale skin, so when I went up there they said, "What! This is so not you. What a joke!" and I went, "Look, it's an Iowa license. I knew I was coming to this college. I dyed my hair, lost some weight, and got a tan." And the guy just laughed and he goes, "Okay, great." So I got in . . . 'cause it was good. . . . Everybody wants to hear a good story. (169)

Schiebel also explores the gendered power positions of underage women and male gatekeepers in the cocreated performances. Flirting and teasing often occur in these brief interactions. Bouncers may pretend to have reservations about an ID to extend the interaction. Teasing that borders on harassment, however, usually results in women having to beg, "Oh, please, *please* let me in!" (172). While flirting can be playful and egalitarian, teasing performances tend to reinforce unequal power relations between the gendered roles.

Role Distance and Discrepant Roles

Oftentimes, there is a lack of congruence among the role a person plays, the purpose of the performance, and the regions the person has access to. One lack of congruence Goffman calls **role distance**. An adult, riding a merry-go-round with a child, for example, will go to great lengths to appear bored. The discontinuity between social role and context is apparent in this performance. Teenagers at family gatherings are experts at role distance.

Tracy Stephenson (1998) played Mickey Mouse at Walt Disney World in Orlando in 1989. She writes of the cumbersome Mickey costume in ways that are important to Goffman's notion of impression management, dramaturgical loyalty, and role distance. When audience members visited Mickey in his dressing room, little did they know that three other Mickeys, in three other dressing rooms, also greeted guests. Stephenson writes tellingly of her enactment of role distance:

> Once inside [Mickey's head], the performer's face is impossible to see, and I could roll my eyes, close my eyes, stick out my tongue, crinkle my nose, or make any number of faces. For example, several of the guests were offensive, either in their appearance, hygiene, or actions, and as I would get close to them to take pictures, I often made faces expressing my displeasure. Again, even as I ceased to perform, the head continued to smile and look attentive. The Mickey head continued the performance, making absent my contradictory performance. (58–59)

Goffman spends considerable time on what he calls a **discrepant role**: A role which brings a person into a social establishment in a false guise. He outlines several of the most "spectacular" ones.

1. *The Informer.* This person pretends to be on the team, gains access to back regions, and acquires destructive information. Spies—military and industrial—are the best-known examples of informers. Linda Tripp, for example, tape-recorded conversations with Monica Lewinsky about her affair with President Bill Clinton and then turned the tapes over to the FBI and the Office of the Special Prosecutor. Her role as informer was reviled by the press and pundits.

SOURCE: Photograph by David Payne. Copyright © 1995 by David Payne.

2. *The Shill.* This person pretends to be an audience member but is really on the team, performing for the team's benefit. We are most familiar with this role in old-time medicine shows: The person in the audience pretends to be healed by the

wares. But shills can also be present in everyday interactions. A parent, for instance, who prompts his child to sing for her grandmother is acting as a shill. The father knows the routine, feeds the lines, perhaps even sings along, to further the performance for the team.

3. *The Inspector.* This person also pretends to be an audience member but is acting in the audience's interests. Quality control inspectors and secret shoppers are employed to test the thoroughness of the team's performance.

4. *The Go-Between.* This person knows the secrets of two teams and travels between them, often creating the illusion that she is loyal to both. Labor mediators, talent agents, even "middle managers" have to balance their performances carefully between the teams they purport to represent.

5. *The Non-Person.* These are people who are treated, by team members and audience alike, as if they are not there. Servants, the elderly, small children, ill persons, and people in service roles (cab drivers, court reporters, photographers) are most often ignored in team performances—especially ceremonial ones. These roles bring to light power dimensions as performed in roles: the privilege of some people to ignore others and the defenses the subordinates may use to preserve their dignity.

All of these discrepant roles speak to the powerful manipulations utilized in sales techniques in a culture of consumerism. Chapter Two argued that much performance theory has left audience undertheorized; Goffman's labeling of audience roles as enacted strategies is an exception to this tendency.

READ MORE ABOUT IT

And If You Believe That, I've Got a Bridge in Brooklyn!

In Susan Orlean's cultural history of orchids, The Orchid Thief *(1998, 119–120), she describes the massive land deals struck by Julius and Leonard Rosen's Gulf American Corporation in 1966. They bought 114 square miles of South Florida swamp, marketed it in five-acre lots at $1,250 apiece, and sold it as "the good life." Orlean's description of Florida sold by Gulf American is indicative of the narrative of progress and consumerism of modernism. Florida represented "the middle-class dream of a place you could find health and warmth and leisure. Florida wasn't grimy or industrial or hidebound or ingrown. It wasn't seared and dry like the desert—it was luscious and fruitful. . . . Florida was to Americans what America had always been to the rest of the world—a fresh, free, unspoiled start" (123).*

The Rosens' sales tactics, however, were questionable, and Goffman's vocabulary of cynical performances, shills, and informers is helpful for understanding the performed interaction. Orlean writes,

After dinner, salesmen sat down with each customer and started to work with an air of urgency. According to the salesmen, land prices were creeping upward and very soon land in Florida would be unaffordable. Gulf American pledged that anyone who bought land at the dinner would be flown to Florida for free and put up with all expenses paid in the Gulf American hotel. When a customer at one of these dinners did decide to buy, the salesman assigned to him would jump up and shout, "Lot Number Twenty-three is sold!" Or ringers hired by the company would jump up now and then and shout, "I bought one!" If a customer was interested in a parcel of land but was wavering, his salesman would offer to put the parcel on hold while the customer was considering it. A few minutes later the manager would jump up and shout, "I can't keep this on hold much longer!" and force the customer into a decision on the spot.

[In Florida,] some salesmen would drive the prospective buyer miles out in the far swamp ends of the property and then suggest that he either sign the land contract or walk back on his own. The rooms at the Gulf American hotel were bugged so salesmen could listen in on hesitant customers and adapt their sales pitch to each customer's specific concerns. Gulf American marketed its land from the mid-1950s until 1970. The cheapness of the land and the prospect of living in warm Florida and the promise of the good life to be found there turned out to be enthralling. . . . [M]ore than 470,000 acres of land were sold. The Rosens' initial investment in Florida, at Cape Coral, had been $125,000. In a few years the value of their company was $450 million.

READ MORE ABOUT IT

Recruiters Out to Get You

Veterans for Peace is an organization that tries to give an alternative vision of military life to the positive sales pitch presented by military recruiters. They sponsor speakers in public schools, provide curricular materials, and write their own poetry and prose regarding the realities of war. Veterans for Peace sponsored a contest asking young people to write their own version of "Ten Points to Consider Before You Sign a Military Enlistment Agreement." Here is Rayniel Rufino's 2006 rap version of "ten points":

1. Think about ya life, the choices you make. Recruiters out to get you, don't make a mistake.

2. Is obvious right, they target the hood. Take a home boy and write, what's wrong and what's good.

3. My words are truth, heal like medicine, don't believe me? Man, holla at a veteran.

(Continued)

(Continued)

---

4. It'll be better then, the words I write. Do you really see a cause for these wars we fight?

5. Aaight . . . if not then free your mind, focus on the prints, read between the lines.

6. Times after time, is harder than the lottery, to see one of us not become their property.

7. Probably you'll get many promises but don't leave it for later, get on your grind, get it all on paper.

8. Now Do You Wanna R.I.P., Rayniel from N.Y.C. telling you there's no guarantee . . . J.O.B.

9. You have no clue. This is for the ones who keep it real in the military, you can't be you.

10. So think, listen and see. Is a puppet to America really "all you can be." . . .

Peace . . . Rayniel

SOURCE: "Ten Points to Consider Before You Sign a Military Enlistment Agreement" by Rayniel. Used with permission of the author and Veterans for Peace New York.

CAUGHT LOOKING

Misrepresentations of Gender, Race, Occupation, and Social Class

Choose any film from the list below and discuss the multiple ways social roles are misrepresented. What expressive equipment do performers bring to misrepresentation? How are these "artful" engagements with "impression management"?

What misrepresentations are typically presented as comedy? What misrepresentations are typically presented as tragic? How do personality, interaction, and social structures collude in limiting and enabling these performances?

Catch Me If You Can

Some Like It Hot

The Birdcage

Mrs. Doubtfire

Boys Don't Cry

White Chicks

Tootsie

Goodbye Charlie

Sister Act

To Wong Foo, Thanks for Everything, Julie Newmar

Glengarry Glen Ross

Matchstick Men

Tin Men

The Sting

Six Degrees of Separation

Pretty Woman

Working Girl

Good Will Hunting

Pygmalion/My Fair Lady

House Guest

The Usual Suspects

Trading Places

Yes Men

Big Momma's House and *Big Momma's House 2*

Stigmas and "Spoiled" Identities

In his book *Stigma* (1963), Goffman explores the ways we make judgments about other people: How well or poorly does an individual fit a category of social identity and its attributes? Goffman claims that many categories of identity are *stigmatized*—certain attributes of a social role are threatening to one's sense of self, competence, and effective interactions with others. Performers must work very hard to manage these "spoiled" identities in interactions with others.

Goffman divides stigmas into three large categories: (1) *physical deformities;* (2) *negative personality characteristics* gleaned from bad, inappropriate, or criminal behavior; and (3) *tribal stigmas* based on race and ethnicity. These now questionable labels certainly reflect how society viewed individuals who were not physically able, white, employed, and economically comfortable in the middle of the twentieth century. Contemporary views of race and ethnicity are not fruitfully approached through Goffman's notion of a "tribal" stigma. At the same time, Michael Jackson's cosmetic surgeries have been criticized as his attempt to erase his "Blackness." When ethnic or racial stereotyping results in discrimination or violence toward individuals of African-American, Hispanic/Latino, Arab, or Jewish descent, however, the felt realities of a "stigmatized" identity are apparent. Most important for the concept of stigma is the centrality of performance: Stigma is "a special kind of relationship between attributes and stereotypes" (Goffman 1963, 4) best understood in *performed interaction,* not stereotypic attributes.

The performed interaction in social situations is often marked by uneasiness. Goffman describes the "shaky situation" typical of a conversation between a "stigmatized" individual and "we," in Goffman's language, the "normal":

> We will feel that the stigmatized individual is either too aggressive or too shamefaced, and in either case too ready to read unintended meanings into our actions. We ourselves may feel that if we show direct sympathetic concern for his condition, we may be overstepping ourselves; and yet if we actually forget that he has a failing we are likely to make impossible demands of him or unthinkingly slight his fellow-sufferers. Each potential source of discomfort for him when we are with him can become something we sense he is aware of, aware that we are aware of, and even aware of our state of awareness about his awareness. (1963, 18)

Awareness seems a hall of mirrors here. But as a felt reality, it echoes both the performance consciousness and self-consciousness discussed in Chapter Two.

READ MORE ABOUT IT

Pretending Not to Notice

In Lucy Grealy's Autobiography of a Face *(1994, 3–4, 10–11), she writes of her teenage years working at a horse stable and taking the ponies to children's birthday parties. Grealy had endured three years of chemotherapy for the cancer of the jaw that ravaged her face.*

Once we reached the party, there was a great rush of excitement. The children, realizing that the ponies had arrived, would come running from the back yard in their silly hats. . . . My pleasure at the sight of the children didn't last long, however. I knew what was coming. As soon as they got over the thrill of being near the ponies, they'd notice me. Half my jaw was missing, which gave my face a strange triangular shape, accentuated by the fact that I was unable to keep my mouth completely closed. When I first started doing pony parties, my hair was still short and wispy, still growing in from the chemo. But as it grew I made things worse by continuously bowing my head and hiding behind the curtain of hair, furtively peering out at the world like some nervous actor. Unlike the actor, though, I didn't secretly relish my audience, and if it were possible I would have stood behind that curtain forever, my head bent in an eternal act of deference. I was, however, dependent upon my audience. Their approval or disapproval defined everything for me, and I believed with every cell in my body that approval wasn't written into my particular script. I was fourteen years old.

****

"What's wrong with her face?"

The mothers bent down to hear this question and, still bent over, they'd look over at me, their glances refracting away as quickly and predictably as light through a prism. I couldn't always hear their response, but I knew from experience that vague pleas for politeness would hardly satisfy a child's curiosity.

While the eyes of these perfectly formed children swiftly and deftly bored into the deepest part of me, the glances from their parents provided me with an exotic sense of power as I watched them inexpertly pretend not to notice me. After I passed the swing sets and looped around to pick up the next child waiting near the picnic table littered with cake plates, juice bottles, and party favors, I'd pause confrontationally, like some Dickensian ghost, imagining that my presence served as an uneasy reminder of what might be. What had happened to me was any parent's nightmare, and I allowed myself to believe that I was dangerous to them. The parents obliged me in this: they brushed past me, around me, sometimes even smiled at me. But not once in the three years that I worked pony parties did anyone ask me directly what had happened.

SOURCE: Excerpts from AUTOBIOGRAPHY OF A FACE by Lucy Grealy. Copyright © 1994 by Lucy Grealy. Reprinted by permission of Houghton Mifflin Company. All rights reserved.

Performed Strategies of Stigma

Goffman's work on stigma has been highly influential in Disability Studies. In both *Asylums* (1961) and *Stigma* (1963), Goffman moved attention away from individual bodies as "defective biology," to account for the social structures—hospitals, institutions, doctor's offices—and communication interactions that shaped public beliefs of stigma (Snyder and Mitchell 2001). His sociological account of stigma has shaped explanations in counseling, health practices, and medical roles (Kent 2000).

Goffman was particularly interested in ways a stigma was apparent to others: A **discredited** person is one whose stigma is known or immediately apparent to others; a **discreditable** person is one whose stigma might be discovered—through either purposeful self-disclosure or accidental discovery. An individual who carries a white cane and wears dark glasses is immediately recognizable by others as blind. Other visual impairments, however, may not be apparent.

HIV status has received considerable attention as a contemporary example of stigma, especially the issue of revealing this status to health care workers and family members (Agne, Thompson, and Cusella 2000; Epstein 1992; Ingram 1999; Pittam and Gallois 2000). Dan Brouwer explores AIDS tattoos as an example of visibility politics available through "self-stigmatization," a communicative practice with many meanings. While historically tattoos have been used to punish the bearer or to warn others, some choose to tattoo themselves to indicate their HIV status; "the tattoos are worn with pride and a bit of mischief" (Brouwer 1998, 130).

Performance of personal narratives is a powerful vehicle for education and for combating the stigma of HIV/AIDS. Kristin Langellier (1993, 182) asks, "How does the performance of personal narratives produce and interpret AIDS? What speaking positions are made possible through this strategy of HIV education? How might [we] empower ourselves and our audiences to discover our stories of AIDS?" Because "stories" are a commodity in a culture that often prizes sensationalism, these same narratives may "potentially exploit and stigmatize those very persons we mean to support" (187).

Passing and Covering

Goffman discussed two performed strategies of stigmatized individuals: passing and covering. **Passing** involves an attempt to appear "normal" and to keep a stigma secret from others. This involves constant decisions on "whether to reveal, display, or lie about the stigma, and to whom, how, when, and where" (Frame 2004, 9). **Covering**, on the other hand, is a set of strategies to keep the stigma from becoming apparent to others.

Jacques Demers was promoted to general manager of the Tampa Bay Lightning NHL hockey team in 1998. No one on the Lightning staff knew that Demers could not read. Gary Shelton (2005) writes that Demers became an expert at trickery to cover his illiteracy:

> If someone asked him to read something, he would pat his chest and proclaim that he had left his glasses somewhere else. When the document was in English, he would point out that he had grown up speaking French. When the document was in French, he would say he had spent too long in the United States. He would ask one of his secretaries—"angels," he calls them—to summarize the documents. . . . At restaurants, Demers would listen closely to the specials. Or he would ask a companion what he was going to order. Or he would look for the familiar letters of "filet mignon." "If you can talk to people, it's fairly easy," he said. "You can hide. You can fool people."

Melissa Frame, author of *Blind Spots: The Communicative Performance of Visual Impairment* (2004), was diagnosed with macular degeneration at the age of seven. Her vision enables her to see shadows and movement; with computer-assisted technologies she can read typeface in 38-point fonts. Most printed material, however, is not this large. Frame jokes, "I have to hold a restaurant menu so close to my face to read it, that people ask me, 'Why are you smelling the menu?'" Her daily interactions are a constant negotiation with others, and Goffman's categories of passing and covering are valuable ways to describe her performances:

> Do persons who are visually impaired ever fake performances for their audiences? The answer to this question from my experience is yes. Especially because my visual impairment is not obvious, a fair amount of my public performance time is spent in "passing." I am never ashamed to admit my disability, but I do not walk around with a sign reading: "Attention! I am visually impaired." When I walk into McDonald's, usually with a friend, I stand and

stare at the menu board, even though I can't see it. Whenever I go to a restaurant, I have someone read the menu to me, because this is less obvious than my attempting to read it myself. In classrooms or formal lectures, I always look at the speaker and what he or she is doing or writing, even though I could sit with my eyes closed and get as much information. However, most aspects of my public life, such as walking around, interacting with others and ordering food in familiar restaurants, I accomplish with ease. Such performances serve to affirm my normal identity. (Frame 2004, 80)

Health communication, emphasizing the communication skills and strategies available to individuals in health care settings and situations, when married to performance perspectives on daily life, is a growing and important area of communication scholarship. Kristin Langellier (2001) explores the intersection of narrative and breast cancer survival through the stigma of mastectomy. Jay Baglia (2005) explores stigmatized impotence in Pfizer's advertising for Viagra.

Passing Genders and Races

Passing, in the language of Goffman's social roles, is a performance fraught with risks and dangers, with shame and awe. Historical accounts abound of stories of women who have passed as men—to fight in wars, to work in men-only occupations, and to marry women. Judith Halberstam (1998, 21) notes that passing "assumes that there is a self that masquerades as another kind of self and does so successfully; at various moments, the successful pass may cohere into something akin to identity. At such a moment, the passer has *become*." Identity, in this construction, is always a negotiation among self, society, and performance of expectations for masculinity and femininity as opposites.

Passing among genders has received much attention, especially as portrayed in the media. Daniel Lieberfeld and Judith Sanders (1998) explore the 1959 film *Some Like It Hot* for its comedic representation of cross-dressing. They argue that the comedy of gender disguise returns gender relations to the status quo. Jennifer Esposito (2003) analyzes *Boys Don't Cry* for the violent and criminal backlash that came with discovery that Brandon Teena was passing as a man. Helene Shugart (2003) explores the ways Ellen DeGeneres implicity "passed" as heterosexual in her television show that often scripted her in ambiguous ways before DeGeneres came out as a lesbian.

Bryant K. Alexander (2004b, 380) discusses passing as a cultural performance that signals membership in a group and assumes the benefits of that membership, while avoiding the stigma associated with another affiliation: "For example, gay men who pass as straight attempt to avoid the social and cultural strictures against homosexuality. Light-skinned Blacks passing for White assume the social and cultural privileges of being White and avoid the stigma that is sometimes socially associated with being Black."

What of individuals whose race and ethnic backgrounds are not easily read and coded into recognizable categories? When some individuals are mistaken for white, with no intention of passing, the interpersonal dynamics can be explosive. Danzy Senna (2005, 85) writes of witnessing everyday acts of racism, "For me not to assert myself as black in these situations was an act of betrayal against the people whom I loved the most. It was also a betrayal of myself." Performance artist Adrian Piper (1992) also explores the accusation of passing; Goffman's language of misrepresentation and shame abounds: "For this kind of shame, you don't actually need to have done anything wrong. All you need to do is care about others' image of you. . . . This was shame caused by people who conveyed to me that I was underhanded or manipulative, trying to hide something, pretending to be something I was not, by telling them I was black" (Piper 1992, 275).

The comedy and tragedy of gender and race crossing is a politically charged issue. At stake are conceptions of gender, race, and class as authentically available to self and to others. Chapter Seven, "Performing Identity," will return to authenticity as thoroughly problematic.

Performing Disability

Disability activists have turned to performance, poetry, film, and writing to refigure Goffman's language of "spoiled identities" in a culture that highly values "normalcy." This purposeful and artistic approach to body, cultural ideals, and experience runs counter to two powerful discourses: (1) the medicalization of disability with scientific jargon under the doctor's authorized gaze, and (2) cultural prohibitions against displaying disabled bodies outside those settings. Carrie Sandahl (1999, 12) writes, "No longer compliant objects of the stare, people with disabilities are staring back, claiming the body as a legitimate part of identity, a body whose metaphors and physicality belong to us." In the 1997 film *Vital Signs: Crip Culture Talks Back,* armless performance artist Mary Duffy says,

> The words you use to describe me are "congenital malformation." Those big words those doctors used—they didn't have any that fitted me properly. I felt, even in the face of such opposition, that my body was the way it was supposed to be. It was right for me, as well as being whole, complete, and functional.

She also distributes a card to onlookers who perceive her armless body as a threat to them: "This card has been coated with a noxious substance. *In twenty-four hours both of your arms will fall off.*"

Petra Kuppers' *Disability and Contemporary Performance: Bodies on Edge* (2003) is a book-length exploration of disabled performers who counter prevailing histories of disabled performance as "freak show" and "medical theatre." Kuppers analyzes the work of dozens of artists who contradict the images of disability as "frustration, tragedy, tears and struggle" (55). This performance work can develop new theories and practices of movement—in wheelchairs, on crutches, and in play with gravity. Kuppers also demonstrates how disabled performers use their bodies as weapons to embrace the discomfort, Goffman's "uneasiness," they so often experience in social interaction.

The activism of disability communities has parallels in the civil rights and gay rights movements (Sandahl 2003; Smit 2003) and in the use of performance as a political strategy to combat "freak show" discourses of bodies. The "show" of identity in the next chapter—gender, race, and disabilities—takes Goffman's early conceptions of performance, its teams, roles, management, and stigma, into the twenty-first century.

Rethinking Social Roles

Goffman's theories of self presentation have been criticized on several levels. First, many claim he is "cynical" about performance. His emphasis on negative examples—cons, shams, and misrepresentations—are instances that point to performance as "fakery" and manipulation. The audience is often a ready "dupe" in Goffman's accounts, and performers must be on constant guard to avoid shame, embarrassment, and discovery. Clifford Geertz (1980, 170) writes of Goffman's accounts of social interaction, "Goffman's is a radically unromantic vision of things, acrid and bleakly knowing, and one which sits rather poorly with traditional humanitistic pieties. But it is no less powerful for that."

Sheldon Messinger, Harold Sampson, and Robert Towne (1962) critique the "life as theatre" simile because most people do not conceive of their lives, interactions, and social selves as performances. If this is not an individual's "point of reference" for understanding the world, then the dramaturgical analyst acts much like a psychoanalyst whose job is to *interpret* and to *attribute* meanings to a patient's dreams and behaviors. They argue that we all become "mental patients" striving to project an impression of "normalcy."

A third critique involves Goffman locating the success or failure of "impression management" in others. For Alisdair MacIntyre (1984, 115), "Goffman's world is empty of objective standards of achievement." Morality is presupposed, but never made a topic, in Goffman's sociology of presentation.

Fourth, especially in Goffman's accounts of stigma and "spoiled" identities, Melissa Frame (2004) notes, disability theorists are quick to criticize (1) the breadth of Goffman's definition—leaving most everyone stigmatized on some level, (2) the difference between stigmas that are inside or outside of an individual's control and society's different reactions to those, and (3) the perpetuation of negative views of the handicapped and people of color.

These criticisms, especially with an eye to ethical and political stakes for performance, are valid ones. Still, Phil Manning (1991) argues that Goffman's early work advanced a "two selves" thesis: There is a "real" self under the mask of a social role. Manning claims that Goffman's later work emphasized not authenticity of a self, but the dramatic realization of a self only in and through social performances available for observation in everyday interactions.

Goffman's dramaturgical approach to social interaction is most interested in the micro-moments of a performed self with its strategies, dilemmas, breakdowns, and repairs as rituals of face-to-face interaction. His insistence on dramatic realization and idealization of social roles through teams, in regions, as managed, are important explanations for the pressures and requirements of individuals to manage social situations through strategic communication. Social interaction is a set of individual performances, and successful performances are the *accomplishment* of individual identity and social organization at all levels.

Goffman's theories are enjoying a rebirth across academic disciplines interested in how we engage in social interaction. The richness of his analysis, his labels, and his observations are a dramaturgical approach to everyday life that has influenced symbolic interactionists (Littlejohn 1977), conversational analysts (Pomerantz 1988), and ethnomethodologists—the research orientation in communication that maintains we ought to study "features of ordinary face-to-face interaction" (Beach 1982).

Goffman's work on discrepant roles, face work, and impression management has been fruitful for organizational theory, at-risk communication, and health communication. New directions in gender, race, and disability studies have utilized Goffman's notions of stigma, passing, and covering to expand, reject, or reconceptualize his theories with postmodern twists and corrections for power. Goffman's work stands between modernism and postmodernism, between self and society, between the social sciences and the humanities interested in the question "Who am I?"

CHAPTER 7

Performing Identity

Theory in Perspective: How Am I a Subject?

Postmodernism is a term made famous by Jean-Francois Lyotard in his 1984 book *The Postmodern Condition*. Postmodernism is a three-pronged attack on the reigning ideas of the Enlightenment that reached their height in the modern period.

First, postmodernism maintains there is no **self** that is whole, stable, and knowable to self and others. Instead, the "self" is fragmented, multiple, and shifting. Subjectivity is the way the self, or the "I," makes claims about itself as a "subject." For centuries, certain people—women, people of color, gays and lesbians, the disabled, children—were not considered subjects. They were not deemed capable of making claims about themselves, nor did they have rights to make those claims— as individuals, citizens, or groups. Donna Haraway (1992, 87) describes subjecthood in Enlightenment ideas:

> figures of coherent and masterful subjectivity, the bearers of rights, holders of property of the self, legitimate sons with access to language and the power to represent, subjects endowed with inner coherence and rational clarity, the masters of theory, founders of states, and fathers of families, bombs, and scientific theories—in short, Man as we have come to know and love him in the death of the subject critiques.

The death of the subject—in philosophy, art, literature, and theory—means that the "self" is no longer coherent, whole, stable, or fixed. Art forms that are fragmented, in pastiche, quilted together are testimony to this fluid self and a rejection of Enlightenment claims to rationality, objectivity, and Truth.

Second, postmodernism critiques "**grand**" or "**master**" **narratives** that describe, explain, and predict the world. Master narratives include rationality, universality, and "Truth." Instead, postmodernism maintains that knowledge and truth—with a

173

small "t"—is always local, contingent, historical, and political. Science, for example, finds its Truth through the detached, rational, omniscient observer who watches the world to describe and predict its operations. Postmodernism claims there is no possibility of this kind of viewpoint: Where we stand in history, with what instruments we measure, and subjectivities "in flux" determine the kinds of knowledges we can produce.

Third, postmodernism critiques the view that **language** can represent the world through direct correspondences between words and the things they stand for. Postmodern approaches to language, especially in the work of Jacques Derrida, deconstruct the one-to-one relationships between words (signifiers) and things (signified). Meaning is not anchored to either but instead is always a chain of signification—one signifier leads to another and to another, with no original and no ending point. Words also carry along "traces" of other meanings. If we think of the phrase "a head of lettuce," then we can follow its metaphorical tracings of other heads—human bodies, decapitation, figureheads, heads of state, head honcho. The chains of signification, multiple meanings, and metaphors are endless.

Postmodern rejections of "self," "grand narratives," and referential language are especially important for moving beyond social roles as an answer to "Who am I?" With the work of Judith Butler, **performativity** has come to mean that we perform multiple and shifting identities in history, language, and material embodiments. The question is not "Who am I?" but "How am 'I' a subject—in history, in language, and in material ways?" Performing gender as embodiment of history, institutions, and language is the starting point for how we perform identity.

Do Social Roles Assume a Foundational Self?

Erving Goffman's theories of self presentation, impression management, and stigma covered in Chapter Six perch on a precarious question: Is there a stable, whole "self" under the role that is performed? Is there a "real" identity under the mask one dons in daily interactions? Many postmodern critics of Goffman claim that the very "putting on" and "taking off" of character in interaction must mean a "real" self, a foundational self, lurks underneath the mask (Butler 1988).

Other critics say that Goffman always emphasized the interactional, contingent, performed character of the self (Richards 2001). At the end of *Presentation of Self in Everyday Life,* Goffman writes:

> this self—is a product of a scene that comes off and is not the cause of it. . . . The self, then, as a performed character, is not an organic thing that has a specific location, whose fundamental fate is to be born, to mature, and to die: it is a dramatic effect arising diffusely from a scene that is presented, and the characteristic issue, the crucial concern, is whether it will be credited or discredited. (1959, 252–53)

The Theory Cards is a Web site parody of baseball cards. Each card pictures a famous critical theorist and his or her main contentions. The card for Erving Goffman asks, "Accidentally invented postmodernism?"

Questioning a foundation for "self" is at the heart of postmodern theories that claim we perform identity. Foundational approaches to gender identity include biology, social construction, social psychology, and sexual difference. Each foundation makes a different claim for where we locate the "origin" of our genders.

A **biological** foundation for gender claims that biology—whether hormones, X and Y chromosomes, or the outward appearance of genitals—*determines* male and female. We are men or women based on inward biological patterns and outward appearances. This foundation is also called *biological determinism*.

Distinguished from biology, **social construction** claims that the foundation for gender is a set of culturally and socially created expectations. In this view, each culture builds its own characteristics of masculine and feminine. Many theorists rely on Gayle Rubin's (1975) distinction between sex and gender: Sex is a biological, fixed, and universal designation, and gender is socially constructed, changeable, and malleable and can be changed by society through time.

Psychological approaches locate gender identity across assumed characteristics of and behaviors associated with femininity and masculinity. Much role theory, discussed in Chapter Six, claims that social roles are the intersection of individual psychology and social pressures and obligations. In the West, women supposedly evidence nurturance, empathy, supportiveness, and noncompetitiveness; men supposedly evidence independence, autonomy, aggressiveness, and competitiveness. Research in "sex roles" often assumes that these behaviors are a combination of biology and culture through "psychosocial learning."

Sexual difference is the claim that men and women are different—and that difference is expressed in and through the meanings we attach to biology, physiology, and reproduction. Women gestate, give birth, and lactate; men do not. These are sexual differences. Sexual difference theory moves beyond these "facts" to ask how men and women enter into social and political systems that assign very different meanings and power to these sexual differences.

Each of these foundations locates a "true" identity on a different ground—in our bodies, in culture, in learning, or in difference. All of these approaches have been critiqued as "essentialist"—positing an "essence" for gender that is binary (male or female), stable (X and Y chromosomes do not change), and natural ("Boys will be boys."). Linda Nicholson (1995, 41) calls these "coatrack" theories of identity: "Here the body is viewed as a type of rack upon which differing cultural artifacts, specifically those of personality and behavior, are thrown or superimposed." The coatrack under these "clothes," however, is assumed to be stable, universal, and natural.

When we believe in gender as a binary, as natural, as universal, and as "readable" through appearances or behaviors, we are participating in the Enlightenment conception of the self. Our "self" is whole, stable, knowable, and our bodies and words outwardly "express" that inner truth. Judith Butler calls this a "fiction," and uses the example of encountering a transvestite on the bus. She writes (1988, 527), "one may want to claim, but oh, this is *really* a girl or a woman, or this is *really* a boy or a man, and further that the *appearance* contradicts the reality of the gender."

Butler argues there is no "true" gender underneath the clothes. She claims that "gender is constituted in the performance itself. . . . Indeed, the transvestite's

SOURCE: Photo by Paul Zollo. Used with permission from Zollo Photography, Los Angeles, California, USA.

gender is as fully real as anyone whose performance complies with social expectations" (1988, 527). Moving from drag performances to transgendered individuals, this faith in two discrete gender categories and in the bimorphism of male and female bodies is even more shaken. How to read a preoperative, transitional, or postoperative transexual body?

In *Crossing* (1999), the memoir of a male to female transgendered professor of economics, Deirdre McCloskey describes (in third person) her first professional experience with colleagues who had known her as Donald McCloskey.

> The debut for the professional girl economist was on the day before the convention started, a meeting at the San Francisco Hilton of the twenty-person executive committee of the Association. Dee had been elected to it as Donald, and the staff of the Association had been broad-minded about her crossing. Yet she worried as she went into the meeting room: *Will my professor colleagues be broad-minded, too? Economics is not the most progressive discipline. Will they merely laugh and dismiss me? Better a committee of anthropologists. They know "strange."* . . .
>
> The committee members used her name—"I disagree with Deirdre," "As Deirde said"—because it was hard to substitute "she" for "he" on short notice, and Dee's voice was still Donald's. She didn't talk as much as Donald would have, not because Dee had less to say but because like most other women she did not view conversation as a hockey game. Who knows? Biology or core identity or social role or socially constructed performance of a lifetime? (132–33)

McCloskey questions all the foundation approaches to gender identity. She then continues to describe the reactions of "ordinary people [who] are theoretically repelled" and morally challenged by her crossing genders: "How can you *stand* to be with him/her? Dis*gust*ing. Craaazy. But he/she walks up to you at a cocktail party and you have to decide whether to imitate Jesus" (133). Performing identity with and for others is a political, social, and ethical communication endeavor.

This chapter surveys the threefold projects of performativity as a theory of identity, a strategy of critique, and a political practice. Gender, race, class, and abilities are all constituted in and through their performances. Performativity helps us understand this constitution of self.

Performativity's Rejections and Projects

Performativity, especially as elaborated by Judith Butler, rejects these foundational approaches to identity. Performativity pays special attention to bodies, but body does not *determine* or *cause* gender as in biological determinism and sexual difference theory. Nor is the body a "blank slate" upon which culture *writes its rules* of gender as in social construction and psychosocial roles. To limit the body to either a cause or a surface shuts down possibilities for individual and cultural change.

Instead, performativity maintains that identity, especially for gender, desire, race, ethnicity, and abilities, is a *complex matrix of normative boundaries.* These boundaries are created in *language:* "Act like a man!" "You throw like a girl!" "You trying to act white?" "Shame on you!" "Hey crip!" "Disgusting." These boundaries are enacted in *institutions.* Church, state, education, medicine, science, family, and marriage all make explicit claims about what is normal and what is abnormal for gender, desire, race, ethnicity, class, and abilities. These boundaries are produced by technologies that generate certain relationships. When we encounter two bathrooms—one for women and one for men—these are public spaces that insist on dividing the world into two genders and on punishing people for crossing the boundary with the "wrong body" in the "wrong space."

These boundaries are *materially embodied* and performed by each of us: how we dress, sit, move, talk, where we live, how we live, even *if* we are allowed to live. And these boundaries are utilized in and through culture to *secure political and social ends.* In the West, who gets to marry? Who gets to adopt children? Who gets to be a Catholic priest? Who gets to play sports? Who gets to stay out late? Who avoids vans in parking lots? Who must drive a van to hold a wheelchair? Who is allowed to drive at all? Identity is not a singular constitution but is always articulated in, on, and through gender, sexuality, race, ethnicity, class, geography, age, and abilities.

To best unpack these complex ideas, performativity can be approached as three interrelated projects in performance theory. Performativity is (1) a *theory* of identity constitution, (2) a *strategy* for critiquing performances, and (3) a political *practice.* Theory, strategy, and practice are absolutely intertwined in all performances, but it is helpful to sort performativity's projects into these three approaches to discuss how performativity accounts for bodies, history, and politics in performance.

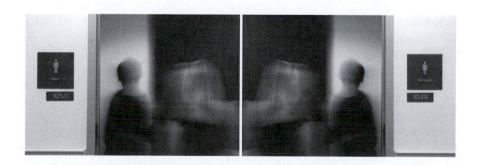

SOURCE: Photograph by Jaclyn Lannon. Copyright © 2007 by Jaclyn Lannon.

The Bathroom Problem

Judith Halberstam, author of Female Masculinity *(1998, 20–21), analyzes the boundaries and policing of gender in feminist theory, in histories of women passing as men, in film, and in drag king performances. She begins her book by noting feminist arguments with foundational approaches to gender: "that anatomy is destiny, that gender is natural, and that male and female are the only options" (21). For Halberstam, who is often mistaken for a man, her project is to explore her own performance of gender as cross-identification, that of a masculine woman. This ambiguity is not "read" as a viable alternative, but as wrong. Language, institutions, material bodies, political ends, and social relations all come together to enforce two gender lines in her "bathroom problem."*

Ambiguous gender, when and where it does appear, is inevitably transformed into deviance, thirdness, or a blurred version of either male or female. As an example, in public bathrooms for women, various bathroom users tend to fail to measure up to expectations of femininity, and those of us who present in some ambiguous way are routinely questioned and challenged about our presence in the "wrong" bathroom. For example, recently, on my way to give a talk in Minneapolis, I was making a connection in Chicago's O'Hare airport. I strode purposefully into the women's bathroom. No sooner had I entered the stall than someone was knocking at the door: "Open up, security here!" I understood immediately what had happened. I had, once again, been mistaken for a man or a boy, and some woman had called security. As soon as I spoke, the two guards at the bathroom stall realized their error, mumbled apologies, and took off. On the way home from the same trip, in the Denver airport, the same sequence of events was repeated. Needless to say, the policing of gender within the bathroom is intensified in the space of the airport, where people are literally moving through space and time in ways that cause them to want to stabilize some boundaries (gender) even as they traverse others (national). However, having one's gender challenged in the women's rest room is a frequent occurrence in the lives of many androgynous or masculine women; indeed, it is so frequent that one wonders whether the category "woman," when used to designate public functions, is completely outmoded.

It is no accident, then, that travel hubs become zones of intense scrutiny and observation. But gender policing within airport bathrooms is merely an intensified version of a larger "bathroom problem." For some gender-ambiguous women, it is relatively easy to "prove" their right to use the women's bathroom—they can reveal some decisive gender trait (a high voice, breasts), and the challenger will generally back off. For others (possibly low-voiced or hairy or breastless people), it is quite difficult to justify their presence in the women's bathroom, and these people may tend to use the men's bathroom, where scrutiny is far less intense. Obviously, in these bathroom confrontations, the gender-ambiguous person first appears as not-woman ("You are in the wrong bathroom!"), but then the person appears as something actually even more scary, not-man ("No, I am not," spoken in a voice recognized as not-male). Not-man and not-woman, the gender-ambiguous bathroom user is also not androgynous or in-between; this person is gender deviant.

SOURCE: From FEMALE MASCULINITY by Judith Halberstam. Copyright © 1998. Reprinted with permission of Duke University Press.

Performativity Project 1: Identity Constitution as Material and Historical

Judith Butler (1988) first introduced the idea of performativity by utilizing metaphors from the theatre to ask the theoretical question, "How is gender produced?" Butler answers this question by making claims about embodiment, history, and boundaries as performed onstage.

Onstage, *performers materialize characters in and through their bodies.* Butler is careful not to use the word "construction," for that would imply "social construction" of identity. Instead, materialization—the body's appearance, acting, and doing—is her important term. In a way, characters in a play do not exist until they enter the playing space or are spoken of by others. Materialization, then, is about presence (physical embodiment) and language (discourse). For Debby Thompson (2003, 132), "gender identity—or any other kind of identity—is not something that you *have,* but something that you *do*—or, at least, something that you have 'only' by doing it again and again and again."

Bodies onstage are always produced by and change through history. So actors always perform bodies within a set of historical conventions and director's cues for how the body *ought to* move, gesture, and articulate itself onstage. A quick look at a silent movie—starring Charlie Chaplin, Buster Keeton, or Clara Bow—demonstrates how differently performers approached film acting, their bodies, and their expressive equipment one hundred years ago.

Traditional theatre requires a script to be memorized, rehearsed, and enacted anew in each performance. But scripts are starting places for interpretation, not fixed repositories of meaning. Despite the time and place of any *one* performance, performers, directors, and scripts are always part of the ongoing "history" of the theatre. Butler (1988, 526) draws parallels to performance of gender: "The act that one does, the act that one performs, is, in a sense, an act that has been going on before one arrived on the scene. Hence, gender is an act which has been rehearsed, much as a script survives the particular actors who make use of it, but which requires individual actors in order to be actualized and reproduced as reality once again."

In *Undoing Gender,* Butler (2004, 1) changes her language from "act" to use a different theatrical metaphor: "[Gender] is a practice of improvisation within a scene of constraints. Moreover, one does not 'do' one's gender alone. One is always 'doing' with or for another, even if the other is only imaginary." This doing of gender is very much about the interplay between historical conventions that create room for play as well as create boundaries. We are rewarded for observing these boundaries and punished for crossing them. Butler describes this tension as "acting in concert" with others, and "acting in accord" with the conventions of gender. The metaphors of the theatre remain powerful explanations for how gender is materially and historically constituted, especially when we remember that performance is not solely mimesis (imitation), but also *poiesis* (making) and *kinesis* (breaking).

Choreographing Identity: Bodies and History

Perhaps the most illustrative and helpful example of the materiality and history of bodies in "scenes of constraint" is dance. Susan Leigh Foster (1998) argues that approaching the performance of gender as choreography is a fruitful way to concentrate on bodies, the codes and conventions for bodily movement and interaction, and the changing histories of those conventions through time.

For Foster (1998, 5), choreography is "the tradition of codes and conventions through which meaning is constructed in dance." Those traditions and their meanings have changed through time. Three hundred and fifty years ago, the now standardized, but different, movements for women and for men in classical ballet were just developing.

> Throughout the eighteenth century, male and female dancers shared a single vocabulary of positions and steps. They performed the same traveling phrases, beats, turns and jumps, with stylistic differences that signified their roles: male dancers jumped higher, multiplied the numbers of beats and turns, and exhibited a more forceful grace than female dancers, who performed smaller versions of these steps with a softer and more fluid style. By the early nineteenth century, the choreography celebrated distinct vocabularies for male and female dancers—dainty and complex footwork and extended balances for women, and high leaps, jumps with beats, and multiple pirouettes for men. . . . [By 1850] partnering included sections of sustained, slowly evolving shapes in which male and female dancers constructed intricate designs, always with the male dancer guiding and supporting the female dancer as she balanced delicately and suspensefully in fully extended shapes. (11–12)

These changing codes and conventions for gendered embodiments always "resonate with cultural values" that are structured, deeply embedded, and practiced by individuals.

If Foster's "vocabularies" for dance are foreign to you, then imagine the choreography of certain sports in the above paragraph. How do basketball, soccer, volleyball, baseball, and softball create different "vocabularies" of movement for women and for men? For race and ethnicity? For performances of class? How is partnering, or teamwork, manifested differently in these sports? How do cultural values regarding masculinity, femininity, and sexuality permeate these embodied sports practices? How have these movements changed through time?

Choreography in Performance Studies

Choreography is a rich term for performativity: bodies in movement, bodies in social relationships, bodies performing within and against historical codes and conventions are all visible in dance, sports, fashion, and their mediated representations and practices. Foster (2002) extends the dance metaphor to include "all bodily articulation, whether spoken or moved," like walking and cooking. Bodies are always positioned in space and time; what may seem "spontaneous or incidental . . . upon closer examination, signal[s] the exercise of intelligent and creative responsiveness" (127).

Much work in Performance Studies explores dance through performativity. The tango has received special attention for its carefully choreographed masculinity and femininity as both passion and violence (Roy 1995; Taylor 1998); the waltz engenders bodies, especially in Disney animated films, as asexual (Bell 1995a). Kent Drummond (2003) analyzes the Ballets Trockadero de Montecarlo dance troupe. The troupe is famous for their campy and wonderfully funny renditions of classical ballets in which men, on pointe and in tutus, perform all the women's roles. Their performance makes us think twice about what we think is "natural" and "normal" for gendered bodies in classical ballet.

Ethnographies of dance companies are important critical observations on the materialization of gender through dance. Judith Hamera (1994) studied the Pasadena Dance Theatre to discover the ways that masculinity is produced in the company. Male dancers described their work, in partnering and lifts, as "a tow truck, "a crane," "just a big set of delts," and "Here I am—upper body strength" (204–5). Yet the male body "is the show" dependent on women dancers to create their performances of masculinity, encapsulated in the phrase "can't live/lift with 'em, can't live/lift without 'em" (208).

In Marilyn Bordwell's ethnographic account of one dance production, *Where the Buffalo Roam,* staged at the University of Iowa, she describes a coming-out-as-lesbian story related in dance:

SOURCE: Photograph by Bob Gonzalez. Copyright © 1995 by Bob Gonzalez.

The section begins with LaToya slowly walking on stage carrying a straight back chair in her arms. There is a spotlight, centered on the dark stage: she places the chair in the middle, then sits, perched on the edge. . . . The chair loosely represents her shell, or the closet that both protects and stifles. She clings to the chair, and seems reluctant to leave, yet also reaches desperately out. . . . One of the spoken narratives begins, "My mother would deny me by not speaking to me for three months." . . . Each movement is urgent; LaToya's performance gives bodily voice to the stories we hear. (2000, 30)

Bordwell writes of identity as performative: "identities are negotiated on an ongoing basis. We enact who we are—or rather who we are becoming" (31).

Dance choreography—as historical conventions, as bodies in relationship, and as materialized in practice—is one vivid example of the becoming of a "self" through performativity. Performativity is a theory of how this gendered self is constituted.

MAKE A LIST

Dance Nation

Make a list of all the kinds of dances you can think of: square dances, hip-hop, clogging, break dancing, the waltz, headbanging, modern dance, tango, jazz, ballet, line dancing, and so forth. Then draw up a list of gender rules for each kind of dance: How are male and female bodies supposed to look and to move? How do typical costumes reflect and enable these movements?

How are social relations reflected in the choreography? (Solos? Couples? Groups?) How are race and ethnicity bound to these dances and social relations? Where do these dances typically take place, and how do these places reflect rules for class divisions?

How Is History a Weight?

Dance is a vivid example of bodies materializing genders within historical codes and conventions. While all of us perform identity with reference to past ways of performing, some of us feel the weight of this history of conventions more heavily than others. Elin Diamond (1996, 4–5) explains gender as "both a doing—a performance that puts conventional gender attributes into possibly disruptive play—and a thing done—a pre-existing oppressive category." For Marilyn Bordwell (1998, 375), approaching gender, race, class, and abilities as a performance "recognizes that we are born into and must operate within a network of power relations not of our own making." History is a way to describe this past and present set of power relations and categories that weigh on people to compel certain kinds of performances.

In much theatre and film, "gender trouble" is playful comedy. In the real world, however, identity issues are carefully policed, and we are punished for performing these histories incorrectly. Oriental bodies are seen as exotic, erotic, with "ineffable foreignness" in the West (Kondo 1997, 9). Some African Americans are accused of "acting white" in language and action that excludes them from community (Alexander 2004a; Lei 2003). "Acting straight" is a performance that involves a complex set of communication codes that are performed and always risk discovery (Robinson 1994). Each offstage, real-life performance brings punishment, social sanctions, and taboos that are very real.

Shame is one way to describe the felt realities of these performed identities. Eve Sedgwick describes "Shame on you!" as typical language directed at gays and lesbians by churches, government, education, the military, and families: "Indeed, like a stigma, shame is itself a form of communication. Blazons of shame, the 'fallen face' with eyes down and head averted—and, to a lesser extent, the blush—are semaphores of trouble and at the same time of a desire to reconstitute the interpersonal bridge" (2003, 36). Jim Ferris (1998), a performance scholar writing of his decision to pose in a nude photo shoot, writes, "Not only am I putting my naked body on display, but I am putting my shame on display. I am allowing people, even asking them, to think of me as a disabled man—a label I struggled against most of my life." The taboos against performing "incorrectly" are powerfully felt and embodied.

Shame is an important concept in Goffman's theory of stigma discussed in Chapter Six. While Goffman was concerned about whether this social identity would be "credited" or "discredited" by audience members, performativity is an argument for the *history* of this shame in institutions and the *felt reality* of this shame in individuals. The weight of history—for abilities, genders, and racialized selves—is felt in/on/through the body. In the body, on the body, and through the body are important ways that identity is constituted.

READ MORE ABOUT IT

Poverty's Weight of "Good" and "Bad" Poor

Dorothy Allison is the author of Bastard out of Carolina, Skin, *and* Two or Three Things I Know for Sure. *Those three titles are eloquent testimony to the power of body, history, and language in performativity as identity constitution. In her essay "A Question of Class" in* Skin *(1994, 13–36), Allison describes the weight of history on her and her family growing up poor in the Deep South.*

. . . [W]e had been encouraged to destroy ourselves, made invisible because we did not fit the myths of the noble poor generated by the middle class. . . . The poverty depicted in books and movies was romantic, a backdrop for the story of how it was escaped.

The poverty portrayed by left-wing intellectuals was just as romantic, a platform for assailing the upper and middle classes, and from their perspective, the working-class hero was invariably male, righteously indignant, and inhumanly noble. The reality of self-hatred and violence was either absent or caricatured. The poverty I knew was dreary, deadening, shameful, the women powerful in ways not generally seen as heroic by the world outside the family.

My family's lives were not on television, not in books, not even comic books. There was a myth of the poor in this country, but it did not include us, no matter how hard I tried to squeeze us in. There was the idea of the good poor—hard working, ragged but clean, and intrinsically honorable. I understood that we were the bad poor: men who drank and couldn't keep a job; women, invariably pregnant before marriage, who quickly became worn, fat, and old from working too many hours and bearing too many children; and children with runny noses, watery eyes, and the wrong attitudes. My cousins quit school, stole cars, used drugs, and took dead-end jobs pumping gas or waiting tables. We were not noble, not grateful, not even hopeful. We knew ourselves despised. My

(Continued)

(Continued)

family was ashamed of being poor, of feeling hopeless. What was there to work for, to save money for, to fight for or struggle against? We had generations before us to teach us that nothing ever changed, and that those who did try to escape failed.

* * * *

[Allison's family left South Carolina and settled in Central Florida.] We all imagine our lives are normal, and I did not know my life was not everyone's. It was in Central Florida that I began to realize just how different we were. The people we met there had not been shaped by the rigid class structure that dominated the South Carolina Piedmont. The first time I looked around my junior high classroom and realized that I did not know who those people were—not only as individuals but as categories, who their people were and how they saw themselves—I also realized that they did not know me. In Greenville, everyone knew my family, knew we were trash, and that meant we were supposed to be poor, supposed to have grim low-paid jobs, have babies in our teens, and never finish school. But Central Florida in the 1960s was full of runaways and immigrants, and our mostly white working-class suburban school sorted us out not by income and family background but by intelligence and aptitude tests. Suddenly I was boosted into the college-bound track, and while there was plenty of contempt for my inept social skills, pitiful wardrobe, and slow drawling accent, there was also something I had never experienced before: a protective anonymity, and a kind of grudging respect and curiosity about who I might become. Because they did not see poverty and hopelessness as a foregone conclusion for my life, I could begin to imagine other futures for myself.

In that new country, we were unknown. The myth of the poor settled over us and glamorized us. I saw it in the eyes of my teachers, the Lion's Club representative who paid for my new glasses, and the lady from the Junior League who told me about the scholarship I had won. Better, far better, to be one of the mythical poor than to be part of the "they" I had known before. I also experienced a new level of fear, a fear of losing what had never before been imaginable. Don't let me lose this chance, I prayed, and lived in terror that I might suddenly be seen again as what I knew myself to be.

Performativity Project 2:
A Strategy for Identity Critique

Performativity is a theory of gender constitution that rejects foundational approaches to gender and argues for gender's material and historical constitution in performance. Because identity is a performance accomplished within a "scene of constraint," this performance can be utilized to critique the boundaries, institutions, and language that produce it. Performance work that shows us identity as not fixed and finished, but always contingent and in progress, is important to counter foundational approaches to identity, especially racial and ethnic identities. Identity in progress and as process, however, must be balanced with the risk that these very performances can continue to harm people.

Identity in Progress

Anna Deavere Smith describes her performance work built on interviews with 600 people over ten years. Smith writes (1993, xxiii), "My simple introduction to anyone I interviewed was, 'If you give me an hour of your time, I'll invite you to see yourself performed.'" *Fires in the Mirror* is Smith's acclaimed one-woman performance created through interviews with residents in Crown Heights, Brooklyn: She plays men and women, young and old, African Americans, Hasidic Jews, Jamaican immigrants, even a Korean grocer and hip-hop artists. For Smith, this community was not just Black and white: "One sees motion, and one hears multiple symphonies" (xxxvi).

But there was uneasiness about Smith playing across gender, racial, and ethnic lines. She describes this as "the uneasiness we have about seeing difference displayed. Mimicry is *not* character. Character lives in the obvious gap between the real person and my *attempt* to seem like them. I try to close the gap between us, but I applaud the gap between us. I am willing to display my own unlikeness" (xxxvii–xxxviii). Here Smith is questioning mimesis: the gap between appearance and "reality."

Kay Ellen Capo describes Smith's virtuosity with the postmodern vocabulary of pastiche: "Smith stitches across the fabric of American life, stretching out the patchwork quilt of her performing body, which becomes a court where each voice has its due. Characters speak with eloquent authority, meeting the mythic demands of her 'inter-view' with a verbal beauty that emerges from the intense need to be understood" (1994, 58). Smith's work resists models of "fixed" identities, "making identities not nouns but verbs, actions, self-activations" (Thompson 2003, 133).

Performances that feature the *processes* of identities are ways to question, play, and applaud the gap between "appearances" and "reality." These processes are important for postmodern approaches to identity as performed, not solely founded in biology, culture, roles, psyche, or difference.

Identity as Product

While Smith strives to show identity in process through language, other performances seek to *exaggerate, parody, and satirize* the *products* of performance by exposing the ways the performances are accomplished. Catherine Egley Waggoner (1997) argues that Mary Kay cosmetic representatives perform femininity with great excess: elaborate makeup, stylized pink suits, high heels, and big hair are all "done" with great excess and with tremendous amounts of labor and time. Waggoner argues these exaggerations are a strategy to expose the codes and conventions of femininity.

Performance artists Peggy Shaw and Lois Weaver, of the WOW Café in New York City, are famous for their "over-the-top" performances of masculinity and femininity: "These performances were sexy and politically inflected and used parody and satire to launch . . . incisive political critiques" (Dolan 1993, 5). José Esteban Muñoz's (1999) analyses of drag queens and Judith Halberstam's (1998) analyses of drag kings are important explorations in the performativity of gender as fictions of authenticity. These drag shows turn gender into "theatre" revealing its multiple codes and conventions in everyday life.

Helene Shugart (2001) argues that Ellen DeGeneres' early television show was a parody of femininity: Ellen was quite inept at applying makeup, doing her hair, dressing in overtly sexual ways, and posing for a "glamour" shot. Each moment of her ineptness points out how carefully we enact the supposedly "natural" conventions and codes for gender.

The work of Spiderwoman Theatre, like *Winnetou's Snake-Oil Show From Wigwam City*, satirizes medicine and Wild West shows that portray Native Americans as violent, ignorant savages. A number of performance theorists have utilized the works of Spiderwoman Theatre to unpack the performativity of racial mimicry and critique. Sieg (2002, 222) notes that their performances always question the tendency to "read a social role for racial truth." Social roles, discussed in Chapter Six, were read as "truths" of identity. Postmodern performance and performativity see these performances as political strategies that critique the very notion of "Truth."

Reproducing Harmful Effects

Performances that critique the processes and products of identity always run the risk of reinforcing, rather than unsettling, those historical conventions and material bodies. Despite an *intention* to perform identity as unsettled, excessive, parodic, subversive, or transgressive, that performance can continue to produce harmful and violent effects. In her analysis of her own parody of femininity as a topless dancer, Katherine Frank (2002, 200–201) writes, "The hard truth is that I cannot predict or prescribe how my performances will be interpreted." While Frank intends a "double agent approach to womanhood" that parodies her performance as "sex object," she is still seen by many male audience members at the topless bar as a sex object:

> His interpretation does not cancel out [my] experience of agency, but the power of men to appropriate and redefine my own performances sobers me. If I am consciously performing a role, yet it is taken as truth—the truth about "women," the truth about "whores," the truth about "me"—is anything really transformed or subverted when I dance?

Much performance critique that utilizes performativity as a starting point asks similar questions. Timothy Scheie explores the community protests instigated by a 1994 production of *The Merchant of Venice* by the Shakespeare Santa Cruz company. Many community members objected to the play and its portrait of Shylock, "a stingy, cunning, and vengeful man and also a Jew" (1997, 153). How can one perform this play without reinforcing harmful, violent anti-Semitism? What happens to race when Korean adoptees, both children and adults, perform Rogers and Hammerstein's *The King and I* in Dubuque, Iowa? "To what extent are these children taught that their own 'Asianness' can be performed only through stereotype, the exaggerated style of the racial masquerade?" (Lee 2004, 104).

Performativity, as a strategy of critique, is important for asking the question "How is identity constituted?" The critiques themselves—the performances that satirize, parody, or exaggerate—always run the risk of repeating and affirming violent and painful practices. The questions enabled by the critique, however, are worth it: "As soon as performativity comes to rest on *a* performance, questions of embodiment, of social relations, of ideological interpellations, of emotional and political effects, all become discussable" (Diamond 1996, 5).

ACT OUT

Exaggerating with Intent

Take any sixty-second commercial that features people interacting. Pay special attention to how gender, sexuality, race, ethnicity, age, and class are "naturalized," made to appear "normal," through conventions and codes of dress, speech, movement, and conversation.

Perform the commercial anew by exaggerating all those conventions. Are there ways in the performance to signal your intentions to parody? At what point does exaggeration turn back on itself and risk harm through violent stereotypes?

From Philosophy to Speech Act to Laws

In 1955, philosopher J. L. Austin gave a series of lectures at Harvard University that were published in 1962 with the title *How to Do Things with Words*. In these lectures, Austin posed a class of sentences that don't describe, or report, or state something. The sentence "The room next door holds fifty people," for example, is a descriptive statement as well as a report. Instead, Austin was interested in sentences that *do* something. These sentences *perform the action they name*.

Austin gives four examples of a **performative** utterance:

"I do take this woman to be my lawful wedded wife" said in a marriage ceremony.

"I name this ship the Queen Elizabeth" said while "smashing the bottle against the stem."

"I give and bequeath my watch to my brother" written in a last will and testament.

"I bet you sixpence it will rain tomorrow." (1962/1975, 5)

Austin asks, "Can saying *make it so?*" He answers yes, if the performative is uttered within certain "conditions": in the proper circumstances, before the proper authorities, with sincere intentions, and followed by some other act—like the actual putting up of money in a bet or living together as "man and wife" after the ceremony. Austin called these performative utterances, offered in the right conditions, felicitous, or "happy."

Austin also claimed that when performatives are uttered onstage or in literature, they are not to be taken seriously; they are not felicitous. "Language in such circumstances is in special ways—intelligibly—used not seriously, but in ways *parasitic* upon its normal use—ways which fall under the doctrine of the *etiolation* of language" (1962/1975, 22).

Jacques Derrida (1988) argued with Austin's distinction between "normal" language use and language that is "cited," or "quoted" on the stage. Derrida maintains that *all language is citational:* All language can be lifted from its original context and "quoted" in a different context. All language is an *iteration,* or a repetition, with no link to an original version.

Austin's speech act theory and Derrida's critique, then, are very important to performativity: Performances of identity are iterations—repetitions of sedimented historical conventions. All performances are citations—enacted references to ways of doing gender, sexuality, ethnicity, class, and ability that are bound by constraints that are legal, medical, religious, and always political. Many of the performatives in our lives create relationships—with people and institutions—through words that bind us: "I do," "I swear to tell the truth," "I promise to do my duty," "I pledge allegiance."

The first novel in Lemony Snicket's *A Series of Unfortunate Events* offers a surprising example of the performative "I do" uttered in the wedding ceremony. In *The Bad Beginning* (1999), Violet Baudelaire is forced to marry her guardian, Count Olaf, as part of his evil plot to gain control of the Baudelaire fortune. The book climaxes in a play-within-a-play wedding ceremony in which Violet and Count Olaf, standing before a real judge and an audience of witnesses, both pronounce "I do" and sign the required legal document. Violet, however, signed the document with her left hand. Justice Strauss, presiding at the wedding, renders this on-the-spot decision about the "felicity" of the marriage:

> If Violet is indeed right-handed, and she signed the document with her left hand, then it follows that the signature does not fulfill the requirements of the nuptial laws. The law clearly states the document must be signed in the bride's *own hand.* Therefore, we can conclude that this marriage is invalid. Violet, you are *not* a countess, and Count Olaf, you are *not* in control of the Baudelaire fortune. (152)

Lemony Snicket, the narrator, addresses the reader with his own observations about the often capricious character of laws:

> Unless you are a lawyer, it will probably strike you as odd that Count Olaf's plan was defeated by Violet signing with her left hand instead of her right. But the law is an odd thing. For instance, one country in Europe has a law that requires

all its bakers to sell bread at the exact same price. A certain island has a law that forbids anyone from removing its fruit. And a town not too far from where you live has a law that bars me from coming within five miles of its borders. (152–153)

The Bad Beginning is a particularly comic portrait of laws and their citations through institutions and speech acts. Many laws and their citations, cited from the "books" of legal code, spoken out loud, in the proper circumstances, before the proper authorities, are not funny at all. These performatives render some people criminals, deviants, perverts, unreadable (think "illegible," like handwriting that can't be deciphered), and unworthy of protection in relationships, families, and culture.

GO FIGURE

Not Really Married?

In the history of American television situation comedies involving white, heterosexual married couples, many couples found themselves suddenly "not *really* married" through some glitch in the state marriage apparatus: Lucy and Desi on *I Love Lucy*, Laura and Rob Petrie on *The Dick Van Dyke Show*, The Howells on *Gilligan's Island*, even *Dharma and Greg*.

What happens to their conventional ways of being with each other when they realize the state no longer sanctions their relationship? In what ways does the law create and privilege some relationships over others?

READ MORE ABOUT IT

I Dare You, You Wuss!

Performatives require speakers, scenes, specific words, sincere intentions, and audiences. The performative utterance, when rendered "felicitously," carries a force. Andrew Parker and Eve Kosofsky Sedgwick (1995, 8–9) unpack, with delightful humor and puns, the performative utterance "I dare you." In doing so, they testify to the ways that we all are asked to "police" the "incorrect" performances of others, and they speak of how difficult it is to resist this invitation to police, to judge, and to harm others.

To begin with, while "I dare you" ostensibly involves only a singular first ["I"] and a singular second person ["you"], it effectually depends as well on the tactic requisition of a third person plural, a "they" of witness—whether or not literally present. In daring you to perform some foolhardy act (or else expose yourself as, shall we say, a wuss), "I" (hypothetically singular) necessarily invoke a consensus of the eyes of others. It is these eyes through which you risk being seen as a wuss; by the same token, it is *as* people who share with me a contempt for wussiness that these others are interpellated [referred to, located, or invited into a scene], with or without their consent, by the act I have performed in daring you.

(Continued)

(Continued)

Now, these people, supposing them real and present, may or may not in fact have any interest in sanctioning against wussiness. They might, indeed, themselves be wussy and proud of it. They may wish actively to oppose a social order based on contempt for wussitude. They may simply, for one reason or another, not identify with my contempt for wusses. Alternatively they may be skeptical of my own standing in the ongoing war on wussiness—they may be unwilling to leave the work of its arbitration to me; may wonder if I harbor wussish tendencies myself, perhaps revealed in my unresting need to test the w-quotient of others. For that matter, you yourself, the person dared, may share with them any of these skeptical attitudes on the subject; and may additionally doubt, or be uninterested in, *their* authority to classify you as wuss or better.

Thus, "I dare you" invokes the presumption, but *only* the presumption, of a consensus between speaker and witnesses, and to some extent between all of them and the addressee. The presumption is embodied in the lack of a formulaic negative response to being dared, or to being interpellated as witness to a dare. The fascinating and powerful class of negative performatives—disavowal, renunciation, repudiation, "count me out"—is marked, in almost every instance, by the assymmetrical property of being much less prone to becoming convention than the positive performatives. . . . It requires little presence of mind to find the comfortable formula "I dare you," but a good deal more for the dragooned witness to disinterpellate with, "Don't do it on my account."

Family Stories and Performativity

Many institutions, like public bathrooms, marriage, and school playgrounds (where "I dare you" is a frequent performative utterance), produce gender and its lawful relationships in very strict ways. Family is also one of these institutions. When approached through performativity, family is a set of material practices created in history, language, and institutions constituted through performances. Important work in performance studies uses performativity to explore family as political sites of gender, technology, and discourse.

Kristin Langellier and Eric Peterson's *Storytelling in Daily Life* (2004) analyzes family stories as performative accomplishments. They argue that storytelling in families "produces that which it purports to represent" (36).

In performing narrative, families are the communicative medium of storytelling—families tell stories; and families are the outcome of that ordering of information—storytelling forms families. Family is not a biological phenomenon guaranteed by nature but an ongoing performance and cultural formation. As a material expression, family storytelling is a performative struggle over personal, small group, communal, and network identities. (148)

In their analysis, Langellier and Peterson study transcripts of stories told in their family settings. They ask these questions: Whose labor enables the storytelling (at meals and gatherings)? Who tells the stories? Who listens? Whose version is the accepted one? Who is valorized in the stories themselves? Who is silenced?

"Exiles from kinship" include taboo topics not talked about and taboo people not included in family stories. Excluding gays and lesbians from some families, they argue, are ways to perpetuate boundaries for heterosexuality and procreation. Stories that exile people are manifestations of larger political power structures, expressed in "law, religion, and family itself . . . through heterosexual love, marriage, and childbearing" (49). Family stories are regulating practices. Who and what gets left out of family stories is an important answer to Judith Butler's question: "What matters for families and what families matter?" (112).

Della Pollock's *Telling Bodies Performing Birth* (1999) analyzes stories that women tell about childbirth and the selves that emerge in those stories. For the birthing mother, these stories authorize "new selves, alliances, and norms of relation, even as she reveals the deep impress of norms and expectations on herself" (8). This tension among felt experiences, embodiments, and expectations for normalcy (of bodies, babies, and birthing) is at the heart of a performative approach to birthing stories: How are some people compelled to become parents—by language, institutions, and material embodiments of history? How are others prevented from doing so? How do technologies of fertility and birthing complicate these stories?

The stories women (and men) tell of birthing do not have simple answers to these questions, but these birthing stories can be counternarratives to medical

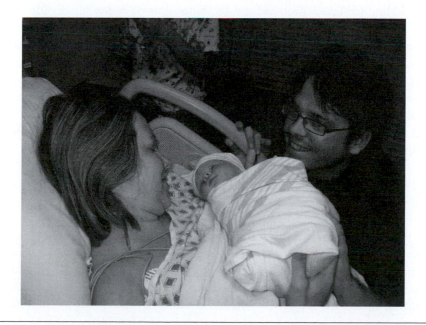

SOURCE: Photograph by Elizabeth Bell. Copyright © 2007 by Elizabeth Bell.

discourses offered by doctors and hospitals. They are also counternarratives to public politics of "abortion, sexual orientation, reproductive technologies, 'family values,' welfare and healthcare form" (8). Pollock argues that the maternal body is center stage in these stories; these bodies performed in stories are always material, social, and political. How one feels the weight of history to perform "good mother" and the felt realities of shame of "bad mother" are performative constitutions of a self, family, and relationship.

Performativity Project 3: A Political Practice of Identity

Two projects of performativity have been surveyed in this chapter: (1) performativity as a theory of identity constitution, and (2) performativity as a strategy of critique. The third project is that performativity is a political practice. While the stage is an important place to theorize the materiality and history of bodies and to engage performances that critique these normalizing practices, much theory in performativity argues that everyday practices of identity are political. These practices are evidence of agency—the ability to act to transform structures large and small.

"Disidentification" is a political, performative practice theorized by José Esteban Muñoz (1999). Disidentification is a name for survival strategies performed by minority groups that work "on and against" dominant ideologies, structures, and institutions (12). E. Patrick Johnson (2001, 12) describes these historical practices among African Americans:

> For instance, vernacular traditions that emerged among enslaved Africans—including folktales, spirituals, and the blues—provided the foundation for social and political empowerment. These discursively mediated forms, spoken and filtered through black bodies, enabled survival. . . . Although they had no institutional power, enslaved blacks refused to become helpless victims and instead enacted their agency by cultivating discursive weapons based on an identity as oppressed people. The result was the creation of folktales about the "bottom rail becoming the top riser" (i.e., a metaphor for the slave rising out of slavery) or spirituals that called folks to "Gather at the River" (i.e., to plan an escape).

Performativity as a political practice argues that people can resist and change oppressive structures and ideologies in everyday life. Johnson (2001, 13) argues:

> The stage, for instance, is not confined solely to the theatre, the dance club, or the concert hall. Streets, social services lines, picket lines, loan offices, and emergency rooms, among others, may also serve as useful staging grounds for disidentificatory performances. Theorizing the social context of performance sutures the gap between discourse and lived experience by examining how quares use performance as a strategy for survival in their day-to-day experiences.

The intersection of performance theory and political practice comes together in "queer theory." Teresa deLauretis coined the term "queer theory" in 1990 to move beyond "gay" and "lesbian" as terms differentiated by gender and its overdetermined sexual practices. She was interested in understanding multiple sexualities "in their historical, material, and discursive specificities" (1991, iii). Others use the term "queer" as a way to "make strange" the taken-for-granted assumptions about gender, sexuality, ethnicity, and abilities (Halperin 1995). For Johnson (2001, 2), "quare" was his grandmother's use of the term offered "in a thick, black, southern dialect: 'That sho'll is a quare chile.'" Queer theory is about the material consequences— violence, exclusion, even death—that performative utterances like "I am queer" have in and on real bodies.

Andrew Parker and Eve Kosofsky Sedgwick (1995) explore the performative utterance "I am queer" for producing the effects that it names, especially in the U.S. military's "Don't Ask, Don't Tell" policy of the 1990s. They draw a parallel between Austin's "conditions" of a performative utterance and that policy:

> Representative Ike Skelton, a Missouri Democrat who heads the House [Armed Services Military Forces and Personnel] subcommittee, asked [the Joint Chiefs of Staff] for reactions to four situations: a private says he is gay; a private says he thinks he is gay; an entire unit announces at 6:30 a.m. muster that they are all gay; a private frequents a gay [bar] every Friday night, reads gay magazines and marches in gay parades. He asked what would happen in each situation under the new policy. (6)

The complex relationships among speech acts, identity, and effects produced by the naming are at the heart of the performative as a political strategy.

Performing Life and Death

Performances are not a luxury in queer theory, but are politically charged by threats to life and realities of death. Works that explore the death of Matthew Shepherd, in Laramie, Wyoming, for example, explore the very real material consequences of politics that claim some bodies are not worthy of life, and some practices are not worthy of protection (Baglia and Foster 2005; Roman 2000; Tigner 2002). Still other works (Butler 2004; Sloop 2000) explore the life and death of David Reimer, an identical twin born with XY chromosomes. At the age of eight months, his penis was accidentally severed in surgery. Known as the "John/Joan Case" in medical literature, Reimer's testicles were surgically removed; he was given hormone treatments; and he was reared as a girl. At the age of fifteen, Reimer asked for surgeries to return him to a boy. Medical experts used Reimer's life and body as a case study to argue for foundations of gender identity in biology; others argued for foundations of gender in social construction. Deirdre McCloskey, quoted earlier in this chapter, asked the question, "Who knows?" concerning those foundations for identity. What we do *know* is that in June of 2004, David Reimer committed suicide at age thirty-eight.

Many movements have stakes in life-and-death issues—feminist performance, postcolonial performance, queer performance. These performance practices struggle "to bring subjugated knowledges" across borders of power (Gingrich-Philbrook 2002, 71). Performativity is a political strategy for questioning the boundaries of normalcy, these borders of power that are constituted in language, in law, and in institutions. "Perhaps it is no accident that the term 'queer performativity' grew up around acts of dying," writes Sue-Ellen Case. "Many people who died because of untreated AIDS made a political spectacle of their dying acts—a state funeral in another sense of the term" (1996, 148).

Making bodies visible is at the heart of much political activism. U.S. history is peppered with examples of political coalitions making claims for social justice through theatrical tactics: the 1960s Black Power and Black-is-beautiful marches and sit-ins (Elam and Krasner 2001); *actos,* one-act performances created and staged by organizers of migrant field workers in California (Sandoval-Sanchez 1999); Take Back the Night marches that began in the 1970s; Confront the Rapist at Work; NOW protests staged by feminist organizations (Fraser 1999; Hennessy 1995); and the contemporary performance work of the Guerrilla Girls and Radical Cheerleaders. Queer activism makes tremendous use of the visible, with the Kiss-Ins of Queer Nation, Die-Ins by ACT UP, and gay pride parades across the country (Case 1996), but the left is not the only side in the political debate to make use of visibility tactics. Peggy Phelan's (1993, 130) analysis of Operation Rescue, the anti-abortion group, takes seriously their "shrewd understanding . . . of making a spectacle *for* the sake of publicity."

For theories of identity, performativity as a political practice must deal with the postmodern self as multiple, shifting, fragmented, and contingent. The question becomes, if performativity has undermined the stable subject, how can political movements recognize this and still articulate a viable political praxis? Performativity as practical practice argues that political movement depends on understanding that identity is *not* in our bodies, our cultures, our psyches, or our differences. For centuries, those foundations have been used to exclude, to deny, and to destroy people.

Staking Identity in Performance

Chapter One argued that all performances circulate around mimesis, poiesis, and kinesis: faking, making, and breaking our notions of identity and culture. Performativity takes these claims and foregrounds the fourth stance: performance as staking. What are the political stakes of saying, "I am a subject—in history, language, and material ways"? Performativity opens up new possibilities for understanding identity as a claim to selfhood, with agency to work with and against dominant structures and ideologies.

José Esteban Muñoz explores the radically new political activism of Pedro Zamora on MTV's third season of "The Real World." Muñoz argues that Zamora

insisted on being a complicated and intersectional subject: not only gay but a sexual person; a person of color actively living with another person of color in an interracial relationship; a person living with AIDS. . . . I first encountered

Zamora before his tenure on MTV. I saw him and his father on a local Spanish-language television news program in south Florida while I was visiting my parents during college. As I sat in the living room with my parents, I marveled at the televisual spectacle of this young man and his father, both speaking a distinctly Cuban Spanish, on television, talking openly about AIDS, safe sex, and homosexuality. I was struck because this was something new; it was a new formation, a being for others. (1999, 153, 160)

Wendy Brown claims (2003, 574), "Theory's most important political offering is this opening of a breathing space between the world of common meanings and the world of alternative ones, a space of potential renewal for thought, desire, and action."

As a political practice, performativity is an important ground for grassroots organizing and micropractices of politics. Whether on the subject of gays in the military, AIDS activism, marriage entitlements, parenting, housing and employment rights, hate crime legislation, or religious doctrine, queer theory has turned common meanings of deviancy, pathology, perversion, and sin into "the world of alternative ones." Indeed, Judith Butler's *Gender Trouble* (1990/1999) was one of the works that helped the American Psychological Association to remove homosexuality from its classification of sexual disorders. The political practices of performativity do work to change the world.

THEORY MEETS WORLD

The Straight and Narrow of Nonverbal and Interpersonal Communication

Teaching Communication courses has always been a political endeavor. Through textbooks, students are invited to explore their own lives and relationships. Recent works by Karen Lovaas (2003) and Elissa Foster (2008) challenge how communication textbooks characterize people's bodies and relationships in heteronormative ways. These textbooks tend to ignore, misrepresent, or punish people for not performing nonverbal communication and committed relationships correctly.

As an undergraduate student in the late 1970s, Karen Lovaas took an undergraduate course in Nonverbal Communication. Thirty years later, she found herself teaching that course for the first time. As she prepared the course, Lovaas surveyed the seven most frequently adopted textbooks in nonverbal communication courses. "Speaking to Silence: Toward Queering Nonverbal Communication" (2003) is Lovaas' analysis of the taken-for-granted assumptions about nonverbal communication she found in the textbooks.

Lovaas found that nonverbal textbooks ground gender in genetics, modeling, and social conditioning, underscoring how powerful is the claim for biological determinism of gender. The message in these books is clear: "females and males are inherently different and deviations from this natural condition are abnormal," as illustrated by this direct quotation from a nonverbal communication textbook published in 2000.

(Continued)

(Continued)

> Some individuals . . . find these [sex role] norms to be an impediment to their full development as men or women. They see each of the stereotyped gender roles as representing only half a person. Unfortunately, the solution advanced is as bad as the problem. Females sometimes attempt to assume the behavior role of males or males that of females. All that is accomplished in such attempts is to exchange one half a person for the other half, and the new half usually does not work as well as the old one did. (Richmond and McCrosky 2000, 258)

Nonverbal communication textbooks also tend to list behaviors performed differently by men and women: "lowered eyes" vs. "stares"; "smiles" vs. "frowns"; "moves out of the way of his space/yields space" vs. "moves in on her space"; "accepts touch" vs. "initiates touch"; "bats eyelashes" vs. "initiates looks"; "cuddles" vs. "strokes"; and, "leans into" vs. "leans over" (2000, 251). For Lovaas, "each list creates a composite picture of stereotypically gendered individuals in a stereotypically heterosexualized dance" (2003, 98).

Lovaas argues that nonverbal textbooks need to "catch up" with other areas of communication "to acknowledge that not all same-sex relationships are friendships, not all cross-sex relationships are sexual, not all people identify themselves, their communities, or their practices as straight: further, that one's sexuality always 'intersects' with other social identities, every grouping based on sex is diverse rather than homogenous" (2003, 93).

Elissa Foster teaches interpersonal communication, and she surveyed the assumptions about commitment in intimate relationships in IPC textbooks in "Commitment, Communication, and Contending with Heteronormativity." Foster (2008) argues that the study of relationships in these textbooks assumes several things: (1) commitment is closely associated with marriage; (2) commitment through marriage is storied as the highest relational value, especially as evidence of stability, satisfaction, investment, dependency, and love; and (3) commitment is always offered as a hierarchical list, moving from casual dating, serious dating, and engagement to marriage. Marriage, then, becomes the epitome of the committed relationship. Interpersonal textbook accounts of commitment teach implicitly and explicitly that some relationships are worthwhile, commendable, and legitimate; others are left out.

Foster's own story dramatizes how difficult it is for heterosexual couples to "boycott marriage." She and her male partner chose a commitment ceremony over a state- and church-sanctioned marriage, but they still find themselves having to list "single" as their marital status on legal forms and to explain their non-marriage to others. They are not granted the legal privileges or the right to privacy granted married, heterosexual couples. Foster (2008) writes on privacy granted to those in heterosexual, committed relationships: "Once a (heterosexual) couple pronounces a legitimate relational classification—married, engaged, dating—then further questions are abated (unless a dating couple is together for long enough, at which time the next question arises—'When are you two planning to get married?')." Still, Foster and her partner chose this route as an opportunity for discussion, for political consciousness-raising, and for critique.

She writes, "as members of many privileged classes, [we seek] to draw attention to the inequity we perceive" in the heterosexual entitlements of marriage.

Lovaas and Foster argue that communication textbooks ought to consider who is left out, who is punished, and who is misrepresented when communication is studied across genders, sexualities, and relationships as heterosexual, as normative, and as legitimate.

ACT OUT

What's in Your Textbook?

Communication textbooks account for the processes and products of communication across a range of "areas": public speaking, intercultural communication, organizational communication, rhetoric, health communication, and media studies, to name just a few. Chose any passage from any communication textbook and create a group performance based on the passage.

How are gender, sexuality, class, race, ethnicity, age, generation, abilities, and geography created in language? What are the assumptions that ground claims about communication across these subject positions? Finally, how might you perform the silences and misrepresentations to teach us what's missing from this textbook account of communication?

RETHINKING IDENTITY

Performativity, as a theory of identity constitution, a strategy of critique, and a political practice, is not well understood. Steeped in philosophy, postmodern constructions of the self and subjectivity, as well as the politics of the real world, it crosses the academy and grassroots activism to make important claims about how identities are constituted.

Critiques of performativity, especially in Butler's early work, have featured an emphasis on the parody of drag performances. Some critics claimed that "drag" illustrates that gender can be "put on" and "taken off" at will. Butler had to defend her notion of performativity—not as a theatrical "act," or consensual "role-playing," or even mimesis, but as a way to deconstruct foundational approaches to identity.

Other critics argue with Butler's emphasis on parody as evidence of choice, access, and power, especially in "passing" for white, or abled, or straight. Jim Ferris claims that because his physical disability is visible, "I do not have available to me the choice to perform 'Ablebodied Man Realness'" (1998, 503). If *choosing* to pass raises questions of access and power, then it also raises questions about *who* can resist normalizing practices in their performances.

While performativity is a rich model for understanding gender, many critics have argued that race and ethnicity are not so easily understood, or explained, through performativity. First, if gender is commonly understood as *either* female *or* male, then race/ethnicity is no such "easy," naturalized binary. Hybrid identities, especially Gloria Anzaldúa's (1987) *new mestiza,* are important for questioning the whole, complete self of enlightenment subjectivity. Anzaldúa writes of the new mestiza: "She learns to be Indian in Mexican culture, to be Mexican from an Anglo point of view. She learns to juggle cultures" (1987, 79). Such juggling betrays notions of a "complete, whole, and unified" ethnic and racialized self.

Second, if gender exists only in its performance *through the body,* then race/ethnicity is a different kind of performative enacted *through the visual.* For Alan Hyde (1997, 223), race is about looking, "a kind of domination of the body by the eye. Race is thus not a thing or a state but a relationship, and the question is always not just what state has been constructed, but who is doing the construction and for what purpose?" The visual writes racial categories on the body, in all-too-material ways and within historical legacies of racism and violence. Indeed, for Shannon Jackson (2004, 183), racism, not race, is "the ultimate performative": Racism is created in and through institutional and legal practices; the felt realities of these practices are internalized by individuals.

Performativity is a sea change in thinking about identity and requires radical shifts in what we think we know about gender, race, sexuality, class, age, generation, and geography. As a theory of identity constitution, performativity maintains that identity is not caused by biology, but is always materially embodied, felt, and performed; identity is not determined by culture, but is always repeated within a history of conventions; identity is not an act of "self will" or volition, but is always performed with and for others in ways that elicit punishments and rewards.

As a strategy of critique, performativity exposes the processes and products by which certain performances are normalized as natural and inevitable. Performances that parody, exaggerate, and satirize are ways to denaturalize gender, race, and sexuality. These same performances risk reaffirming the supposed naturalness of these categories.

As a political practice, the micropolitics and everyday resistances, as well as grand-scale, public protests, are important projects to performativity. To echo a claim in the introductory chapter of this book, performance is always a complex interplay among faking, making, breaking, and staking. For Mary S. Strine (1998, 314), "the perspective of performativity could foreground what is fundamentally at stake but not always conscious or visible in the performance process itself."

Much work is left to do in answering the question, "How am I a subject in history, language, and material ways?" Performativity is extremely important for (1) imagining alternatives to foundational approaches to identity; (2) accounting for the weight of history, language, and institutions on material bodies; and (3) creating possibilities of critique, political resistance, and social justice.

CHAPTER **8**

Performing Resistance

By Elizabeth Bell and Stacy Holman Jones

Theory in Perspective:
How Can Performance Change the World?

Aristotle separated **rhetoric** (the art of persuasion essential to lively and effective public debate) from **poetics** (the art of fictive storytelling through dramatic and epic forms). While rhetoric is a *practical,* useful art, poetics is a *fine* art, intended to delight through imitation. Given the ancient separation of rhetoric and poetry—practical debate and aesthetics—do resistance and performance even belong in the same sentence?

A cursory look at the evening news quickly demonstrates that when citizens are actively engaged in public debates, they often take their concerns to the streets—chanting, marching, waving signs, and staging "events" for media that broadcast the sounds and images around the world. The aesthetics of these events—orchestrated as spectacle, as drama, as conflict, through media—and the political realities that prompt them demand that resistance and performance belong in the same sentence.

This chapter explores theories of performing resistance in three different sites, as real and metaphorical stages for political change: the theatrical stage, the streets as a global stage, and everyday life as a stage. These three sites pull in different theoretical directions. The first direction involves theories that *challenge Aristotelian poetics* of dramatic form, conflict, action, and resolution through catharsis. Are there better ways to represent and to intervene in real conflicts in the world through performance? Bertolt Brecht and Augusto Boal are theorists and practitioners who claim revolutionary potential of the stage to change the world through art, through critical awareness, and through active participation by audiences. Both argue that a "new poetics" of dramatic action is necessary.

The second direction involves theories that demonstrate how *Aristotelian notions and terminology are alive and well* when people take to the streets and in media accounts of political action. Carnival, dramaturgy, and spectacle are still important explanations for what happens when people *act* to change the world on global stages in the streets. This "old poetics" is mobilized to explain public events as dramaturgies available for public critique, to account for theatrical strategies and bodies in collective resistances acted out on global stages, and to understand the role of the media in resistance.

The third direction involves new conceptions of power felt and enacted in everyday life. "Where there is power, there is resistance," writes Michel Foucault (1978/1990). Any survey of theories of resistance must also account for postmodernism that has shifted the emphasis from "grand narratives" of oppressive power to the *local, the subaltern, and everyday practices as resistance* in micropolitics of contemporary life. Foucault offers a picture of new power—not solely as oppressive, but as productive. Michel de Certeau characterizes the strategies and tactics of power as everyday practices of "making do."

At the heart of resistance and performance is this theory question: How and why do people come together to instigate changes in their worlds? Roselyn Constantino (2004, 459) offers these key terms as important for answering that question: "Body. Presence. Act. Interact. Advocate. Provoke. Power. Critical. Urgent." Any survey of performance as resistance needs to account for these terms, forces, and practices.

From Aristotle to Postmodernism

Can the stage and its practices impact the real world? Philosopher Herbert Marcuse (1978, 33) writes, "Art cannot change the world, but it can contribute to changing the consciousness and drives of the men and women who could change the world." The stage is a place to imagine relationships among art and the world, plots and ideas, dramatic action and political action.

Robert W. Corrigan (1984) traces three profound shifts in notions of dramatic form that are helpful in understanding the relationship of the stage to resistance. First, Corrigan outlines the crux of **Aristotlian drama** as the predictable unfolding of **plot**—the beginning, middle, and end—as revealed in the action, the choices, and the discoveries of the protagonist. Second, in **modernist form** (outlined in the beginning of Chapter Six), this emphasis on plot and action is replaced by **consciousness**; that is, "character appears to assume primacy over plot, and the concept of action becomes increasingly interiorized" (158).

In modernist plays, action has moved into the mind, the "consciousness" of the protagonist. Plots are "subterranean and interiorized; they can only be fully known indirectly and epiphanically" (159). The epiphany—or "aha!" moment—is in the mind of the character. The film *The Sixth Sense*, for example, suddenly makes sense as a very different beginning, middle, and end and unfolding of action when the protagonist is revealed as one of the "dead people" (La Caze 2002). Modernism still practices Aristotlian form, but plot and action have gone "underground" for their unfolding in the minds of characters.

The third shift comes with **postmodernism** and its radical rejection of a "whole self" that is knowable, "Truth" as obtainable, and language as referential. Postmodernism also rejects the sureties of modernist dramatic action and form. Corrigan argues, in short, that this leaves us "with no ending." The challenge for performance as resistance onstage is threefold: to create new forms that encompass postmodern paradigms, to write new endings that express very real contemporary conflicts, and to "fix" the world in a "correspondence between our imaginative structures and the daily lives we lead" (Corrigan 1984, 163). Bertolt Brecht and Augusto Boal, two important theatre theorists and practitioners, have imagined these new forms, endings, and techniques for the stage and for stages enacted in the streets.

Bertolt Brecht on Performing Resistance

Bertolt Brecht was a political philosopher, dramatist, and theatre practitioner who honed his craft from 1921 until his death in 1956. His theories and practices were extremely influential in the twentieth century for rejecting realism in acting and Aristotelian dramatic form in playwriting. Instead, Brecht argued that theatre can be a forum for social and ideological change by creating new forms for new worlds.

According to Elin Diamond (1988), Brecht's theory of the theatre is rooted in three radical concerns: (1) attention to the dialectics and contradictions in social relations, especially class conflict; (2) commitment to staging and acting techniques that refuse to engage in mimetic representation; and (3) the production of audiences who are critical observers moved to enact social and political change.

Witnessing the fractious political times in Germany after World War I and the subsequent rise of Adolf Hitler (Motoyama 1991), Brecht was committed to Marxism as a political philosophy and sought to make the theatre a place of didactic teaching about history, power, and social conditions. Brecht drew parallels between the illusive power of the state and the illusion of reality in the theatre. Both the state and the stage should be recognized as illusions that are constructed and therefore alterable (Pollock 1988a). Rather than become emotionally and intellectually involved in the unfolding action onstage, Brecht encouraged actors and audiences to remain aware of how any performance is at once bound by historical and social contexts and changing. For Brecht, a play or performance is not here and now, but there and then—a constructed, though powerful, look at life and the world.

Brecht termed this new type of performance **epic** theatre and contrasted it with **dramatic** theatre. *Dramatic theatre* works to create a reality that unfolds before our eyes and to generate emotional identifications between audiences and performers. In contrast, *epic theatre* works to create a critical distance among the world of the performance, the performers, and the audiences. In this critical space, audiences are encouraged to evaluate the action as it relates to the world around the play. Of the distinction between dramatic and epic theatre, Brecht wrote,

> The dramatic theatre's spectator says: Yes, I have felt like that too—Just like me—It's only natural—It'll never change—The sufferings of this man appall me, because they are inescapable.

The epic theatre's spectator says: I'd never have thought it—That's not the way—That's extraordinary, hardly believable—It's got to stop—The sufferings of this man appall me, because they are unnecessary. (1964/1994, 71)

Where dramatic theatre aims primarily to entertain and to arouse emotion, epic theatre appeals to reason and teaches the audience to think in new ways. Brecht charted the distinctions (see Table 8.1) between dramatic and epic theatre.

Table 8.1   Dramatic and Epic Theatre

Dramatic Theatre Plot	Epic Theatre Narrative
Implicates the spectator in a stage situation	Turns the spectator into an observer
Wears down the spectator's capacity for action	Arouses the spectator's capacity for action
Provides the spectator with sensations	Forces the spectator to make decisions
Provides experience	Presents a picture of the world
Involves the spectator in something	Makes the spectator face something
Suggests	Argues
Preserves the spectator's instinctive feelings	Brings the spectator to the point of recognition
The spectator is in the thick of it, shares the experience. . . .	The spectator stands outside, studies. . . .

Alienation Effects of Epic Theatre

We've all gotten so involved in a film or a performance that, when a character is reunited with a loved one or boards the plane to leave forever at the end of the movie, we cry right along with the actors on the stage or screen. For Brecht, this kind of identification gets in the way of performances that critique the realities they create. In its place, Brecht proposed several techniques, breaking the fourth wall, keeping emotions in check, arresting moments, and making strange, all designed to create critical *distance* through "alienation effects" or *Verfremdungseffekt*.

Many of these techniques have worked their way into the canon of strategies enlisted in live performance, film, and television, without regard to political change or social justice agendas. In Brecht's time, however, these distancing techniques represented a radical turn away from realist dramas in which audiences were tempted and desired to get lost in a performance. Alienation techniques help create performances that "let the seams show" to question the constructions of stage characters and events as well as political realities around us.

Breaking the Fourth Wall

Like frame breaking, discussed in Chapter Two, performers "break the fourth wall" between themselves and the audience when they address the audience directly, making observers aware they are being watched and that performers, in turn, are watching their own behavior. For example, the Broadway musical *Monty Python's Spamalot,* the musical based on the film *Monty Python and the Holy Grail,* contains several moments in which the audience is directly addressed and involved in the performance. The song "Run Away!" contains the lines "we're stuck in a nasty position/why don't you take a short intermission/have a drink and a pee." At the end of Act II, the grail is found in the theatre.

Direct address is also a common feature in contemporary film and television. In the film *Kill Bill: Vol. 2,* Uma Thurman addresses the audience and makes reference to the trailer for the first *Kill Bill.* As the film ends, Thurman winks at the audience. In the television show "Saved by the Bell," the character Zack Norris pauses the action in a scene, turns to the camera, and talks directly to the viewing audience. By breaking the fourth wall of realistic drama, actors and audiences alike are asked to analyze the construction of all reality.

Keeping Emotions in Check

Performers separate themselves from the characters they play by keeping their emotions "in check" and working to stay emotionally detached in performance. This is not to say the performance is void of emotion, but rather that the performer and character do not become one. John Gassner (1952, 69) writes that Brecht "does not allow feeling to preempt the field of observation, nor does he want us to get into other people's skin, lest we fail to observe them, assess them, and draw objective conclusions." The humor in Dana Carvey's portrayal of the first President Bush emphasized and capitalized on differences between a president and his comic impersonator.

In an entertaining example of intertextuality (in which one film references and comments on another), Meg Ryan, Rosie O'Donnell, and Rita Wilson's characters in *Sleepless in Seattle* all recite the words and cry while watching the crucial scene in *An Affair to Remember.* As a commentary on a man's need to keep emotions in check (and a woman's failure to do so), Tom Hanks (Sam) and Victor Garber (Greg) reenact their own tearful version of *The Dirty Dozen.* While the women do not check their emotions, the men are clearly checking their emotional engagement in the film.

Arresting Moments

Stage setting, music, explanatory captions, reading aloud stage directions, third person address, past tense, and other technical and language effects are used to interrupt and comment on the unfolding action. For example, in the television show "CSI," we often see the pathway a bullet fired from a gun takes or the bodily effects a poisonous chemical has on an unknowing victim. In the film *Fight Club,* Jack's apartment is laid out like a page in an IKEA furniture catalog, complete with names and prices superimposed on the screen, highlighting the anti-consumerism message of the film. Arresting moments seek to break the linear flow of the narrative and identification with the story.

Making Strange

Performers give even the most mundane movements and experiences heightened emphasis, often through the juxtaposition of style, genre, and techniques. "The Daily Show," in its Great Moments in Punditry as Read by Children, makes strange by using children to read transcripts of contentious political talk shows. Baz Luhrmann's interpretation of William Shakespeare's *Romeo and Juliet* transports the story of star-crossed lovers—Elizabethan verse intact—to the fictional U.S. suburb of Verona Beach where guns stand in for swords and family rivalries turn into gang warfare.

Chris Coutt's *Tales for the Leet: Romeo and Juliet* retells the Shakespearean tragedy in leet, or leetspeak—the convention of using a cipher language and spelling among hackers, gamers, and other Internet populations. Instead of "Romeo. Romeo. Wherefore art thou, Romeo?" we read, "WTF?" making strange the language of Shakespeare, as well as star-crossed love.

ACT OUT

At the Scene

Create a scene in which several individuals are involved in a conflict situation, such as a car accident or a jury trial. Perform the scene twice, once using a dramatic approach that shows the characteristics of Brecht's dramatic theatre and again using Brecht's epic approach. How do the performances of the same situation differ? Which performance is more engaging? Convincing? Effective? Now, perform the scene a third time, introducing elements of *both* dramatic and epic performance. How does this scene compare with the others?

Brechtian Techniques as Critical Lenses

In addition to strategies for letting the seams show on the stage, a Brechtian lens can be a valuable one for looking at real events. Lee Baxandall (1969, 69) describes the October 27, 1967, march on the Pentagon in Washington, D.C., as tens of thousands of protestors lined up against National Guard troops:

Everywhere there pervaded a spirit of Epic Theatre (so many actions and performers, so much detached awareness of one's deeds even as one acted), even to the Brechtian "narrator" who stood with a bullhorn where he had a commanding view and laconically interpreted events for the majority who could not summon a whole view. The troops tried to seize the narrator; with a little help from his friends he evaded them, not once losing his cool; his ironic commentary set the context for the besiegers.

By disrupting the illusion of reality and our reliance on predictable dramatic form, Brechtian techniques invite audiences to be active, critical spectators.

Oliver Gerland (1994) explores how lawyers used the March 3, 1991, eighty-one-second videotape of Los Angeles police officers beating Rodney King. Gerland argues that defense attorneys utilized Brechtian techniques of alienation to "make strange" the beating by stopping the narrative flow of the videotape. Attorneys for the police officers "broke down the video frame by frame . . . calling police experts who separated each baton blow, kick, and stomp from the others and interpreted each of these acts as a legitimate use of force" (311). Their technique follows Brecht's claim that "breaking a story into self-contained narrative units thwarts its emotional flow, opening a space for critical judgment" (312). Instead of a "natural" narrative flow of senseless and brutal violence, the defense was able to "disrupt that momentum and to turn it in favor of the [police officer] defendants" (312).

On April 29, 1992, the jury acquitted the four white officers, sparking six days of riots in Los Angeles involving thousands of people. More than 50 people were killed, more than 2,000 injured, and more than 13,000 arrested. Storytelling, utilizing Brechtian alienation techniques in the courtroom, clearly has "truth effects"—undeniable consequences in the world.

While theatre scholars have written for over eighty years about the efficacies of Brecht as a theorist, dramaturg, and practitioner, performance studies scholars in communication have utilized Brecht to further understandings of the intersections among critical theory, political action, and rhetorical praxis (Capo 1988; Motoyama 1991; Pollock 1988a, 1988b).

CAUGHT LOOKING

Films that Make Strange

Identify the alienation techniques used in the following films. Then analyze your own critical distance—from the characters, the plots, and the realities—these techniques invite.

Alfie

The Blair Witch Project

Bridget Jones's Diary

Clueless

(Continued)

(Continued)

Dogville

Ferris Bueller's Day Off

Fight Club

Groundhog Day

Lost in Translation

Memento

Moulin Rouge

Tootsie

West Side Story

Stranger than Fiction

READ MORE ABOUT IT

Tony Kushner on Brecht

Award-winning playwright Tony Kushner, author of Angels in America, *was interviewed by Performance Studies scholar Jill Taft-Kaufman on November 26, 2002 (Taft-Kaufman 2004, 52–53). She asked how Brecht influenced Kushner's ideas about playwriting. Here's part of his answer.*

When I was a student at Columbia, I wanted to be two things: I wanted to be politically active, and I also wanted to be in the theatre. And to do both, Brecht was the answer. Also, I was trying to read Marx at that point, and Brecht taught me how to understand Marx. And Marx taught me how to understand Brecht. You use the big problem word, "distancing" the audience. I don't think that's what Brecht was writing about. I think it's the most misunderstood thing about Brecht. And what he called the *Verfremdungseffekt* is an effect of strangeness, not of distance. It's not a lack of feeling. You can't write *Mother Courage* and not expect to have people weeping in the audience. It's the most moving play of the twentieth century. It's devastating, excruciating. It's as hard to watch, in its way, as *King Lear* is. In fact, Brecht's last poem is, "If I say how things are, your heart will be torn to shreds. You'll go down if you don't stand up for yourself. Surely you see that." That's the whole poem. "Your heart will be torn to shreds." He knew exactly what he was doing. He's not about some weird pseudo-masochistic relationship with the audience, like, "I know you want to cry, but I'm going to spray vinegar in your face." And people do the most bizarre, perverted things when they're doing Brecht, because they think that's the job. But it's not. There are the early learning plays, which are extremely strange, and fascinating, and great pieces of theatre, the ones he wrote before he went into exile. Those experimental plays have a very strange relationship to the audience, not primarily emotion, a kind of theatricalization of an intellectual process.

But the great plays, the ones that we talk about when we talk about Brecht, are plays that demand genius acting. The genius of his theory is, I think, fairly simple. It's that when you look at an object on stage, it is both the thing that it seems to be, because you believe in it, and it isn't that thing at all. It's a fake thing on stage. And theatre never lets you forget that. It's why it has a unique value. It's why philosophers always turn to it as a model of human consciousness. You can't look at theatre singly. You have to look at it doubly. You have to sort of look at it with blurred vision. The body that you're seeing on stage (and the most famous example, of course, is at the end of *Hamlet*), all the dead bodies on stage, they're all breathing. And if it's been a great production of *Hamlet,* you'll weep. It doesn't make sense because you know that, of course, the actors are not dead, and yet you're moved to tears. You're made to look at the world critically.

SOURCE: From "A *TPQ* Interview: Tony Kushner on Theatre, Politics, and Culture" by Jill Taft-Kaufman. *Text and Performance Quarterly* (2004). Reprinted by permission of Taylor & Francis Ltd., http://www.informaworld.com.

From Brecht to Boal

In outlining his "innovations" for theatre, Brecht responded to the split between reason and argument (rhetoric) and entertainment and pleasure (poetics) inherited from the ancient Greeks. His solution was to bring rhetorical savvy to performance. In practice, the techniques he outlined often fell short of accomplishing the social and political goals of resistant performance. Brecht's ideas, however, have been revised and refined by other performers and directors working for social change, especially Augusto Boal.

Director, theorist, and political activist Augusto Boal was appointed director of Brazil's Arena Theatre in 1956. During his tenure there, he experimented with egalitarian forms of theatre he believed would foster democracy in an increasingly socially and politically repressive Brazil. Following military coups in 1964 and 1968, Boal worked with groups of Brazilian citizens in performances, teaching and encouraging them to enter into the action onstage as a way to "rehearse" for social change. As a result of his oppositional work, in 1971 Boal was arrested, jailed, and tortured. Following his release, he moved in exile first to Argentina and later to Europe.

During this time, he refined his ideas and techniques, which culminated in the publication of *Theatre of the Oppressed* (TO) in 1974. Boal (1985, 122) writes that the objective of Aristotle's *Poetics* is for the spectator to delegate power to the performer to think for him, which creates **catharsis.** The objective of Brecht's poetics is for the spectator to delegate power to the performer to act for her, but to reserve the right to think for herself, which creates **critical consciousness.**

In contrast, Boal's poetics of the oppressed focuses on the "**action itself.**" The objective is for the spectator to become the performer and to change the action, try out solutions, discuss plans for change, and train him- or herself for "real action." Boal's ideas in *Theatre of the Oppressed* refigured the relationship of active performers and passive spectators to one of audiences-in-action. Spect-actors can "transform" society and "engage in revolutionary action" (1985, 47). Boal developed techniques that move the theatrical stage to the streets and draw on various degrees of audience participation, including simultaneous dramaturgy, image and invisible theatre, and forum theatre.

Simultaneous Dramaturgy

Simultaneous dramaturgy is a technique designed to *involve spectators in a scene without requiring their physical presence onstage.* Performers ask spectators to propose a short scene on some topic of importance to the group. The performers develop the scene using traditional dramatic form (recall Freytag's Pyramid presented in Chapter Three), moving through the exposition, inciting incident, and rising action to the moment of climax. At this point, the performers stop the action and ask the audience to offer solutions to the problem presented. They then improvise the solutions suggested, inviting the audience to intervene to correct their actions. Audience members "write" the script that the actors perform, almost simultaneously. This type of performance begins to "demolish the wall that separates actors from spectators. Spectators feel that they can intervene in the action. The action ceases to be presented in a deterministic manner, as something inevitable, as Fate. . . . Everything is subject to criticism, to rectification" (Boal 1985, 134).

Linda Park-Fuller's work with Playback Theatre is related to simultaneous dramaturgy. In Playback Theatre, audience members do not remain seated in the audience. Instead, they are invited to the stage to tell a story "and then watch [that story] enacted on the spot" by the performers (Park-Fuller 2003, 291). The teller, having witnessed her story "played back" to her, then has an opportunity to comment and have the final say about the story. Park-Fuller has used Playback techniques in health campaigns with Mothers Against Drunk Driving and in middle schools helping adolescents deal with bullying.

Image Theatre

The second degree of participation is Image Theatre, in which *spectators become part of the performance.* Here, spectators "sculpt" as a sculptor would work with clay, manipulating the performer's postures, movements, and facial expressions so that these images make their opinions and feelings known. Participants sculpt both a "**real**" image—the image of reality, or how things are—and then an "**ideal**" image. This is a picture of how things should or could be. Finally, spectators create a "**transitional**" image to show how to get from real to ideal. Eliminating scripted dialogue at this stage also pushes participants to take action, move quickly from image to image, and attend to their senses, rather than focusing on precise language or concrete representations (Boal 1992, 3).

In working with computer software designers in London, Eric Dishman (2002, 240) utilized Image Theatre to ask designers to create their own images of telecommunications.

> One of the most striking was of a person thrown at the feet of all the other performers, who pointed accusingly down at him. During the discussion afterwards, its creator said, "I'm tired of the technology blaming us all of the time—you just feel accused all of the time. Even the teller machine tells me it's my fault when something goes awry." Another performer created a parody of AT&T's "reach out and touch someone" campaign. Her image consisted of the rest of the cast standing close, almost touching one another, but unable to really join hands and feel anything. She painted looks of horror, disgust, and pain on their faces, as they were tempted but unable to reach out and touch anyone.

Feminist performance work has utilized Image Theatre to counteract objectifying images of women's bodies as real, ideal, and transformative. Performance artist Karen Finley's "Constant State of Desire" shows the transformation of her "actual," nude body to that of an "ideal" woman as she layers on raw eggs, glitter, confetti, and garlands to form a movable evening gown. The final result is a "body that is both seductive and repellant," a constructed and "impossible object" (Hart 1994, 99). Berenice Fisher (1994) utilized Image Theatre techniques in her Women's Studies classrooms, but she noticed that women students were often reluctant to put their bodies on display. "Displaying the body was as gender-laden an activity as touching: both could give women pleasure but either might signal vulnerability and danger" (Fisher 1994, 193). Fisher adapted the Image Theatre exercises so that women performed their image sculptures in small, rather than large, groups.

Much popular work on women's body images seeks to expose the constructedness of women's ideal images in advertising and the media. In 2002, film actor Jamie Lee Curtis insisted on her own "unveiling," posing for photographs in *More* magazine without the aid of makeup artists, hair stylists, lighting technicians, and digital alterations. "True Thighs" (Wallace 2002) traces Curtis' attempt to reveal her part in the perpetuation of fraudulent, and highly constructed, images of women's bodies in the media.

Invisible Theatre

In Invisible Theatre, participants take the play to a "place which is not a theatre and [perform it] for an audience which is not an audience" (Boal 1992, 6). In Boal's workshops, for example, participants have performed scenes about sexism while riding on Paris Metro trains, an inadequate health care system while aboard Stockholm ferryboats, and prejudice against foreigners while dining at Swedish restaurants. Invisible performances blur the line between "theatre" and "reality" so thoroughly that the players, audience members who become spect-actors, and even the police arriving at the scene cannot distinguish between the play and reality, between players and spectators. Spect-actors in invisible theatre literally get swept up in the performance, moving from innocent bystander to player without ever noticing it.

The Yes Men are famous for taking their performances directly to the organizations and people they blame for oppressive practices in the world. On the Yes Men Web site, one of the FAQs about their work asks, "Would you regard what you do to be Invisible Theatre?" They answer, "Yes!" The second question asks, "Some people believe that Invisible Theatre is just trickery; others would see what you do as trickery too. Are you guys liars, or what?" The Yes Men answer: "We need to be devious in order to achieve a condition of honesty. This is very different from 'guerrilla marketing,' where companies are devious in order to achieve a condition of real criminality, sometimes. But we certainly won't stoop to actual lying, despite what you might think."

Forum Theatre

While Invisible Theatre transforms spectators into *real* protagonists even as they are unaware of a story's fictitious origin, Forum Theatre goes a step further. In Forum Theatre, audiences become *conscious* players in the action, aware of the reasons for the play and the need for their participation to intervene and change the dramatic action. One performer fulfills the role of leader or "joker" of the exercise. This person's role is to explain the rules of the game, ask for examples, invite participation, and encourage performers and spect-actors to keep playing, even as tensions mount and conflict builds (R. Bowman 1997, 147–148).

In Forum Theatre, participants tell a story containing a political or social problem that is difficult to resolve. This story might involve clearly defined roles for "oppressor" and "oppressed," or it might represent an "oppressive territory" containing a complex network of relationships (Schutzman 1994, 149). Then, a brief scene portraying the problem and a proposed solution is improvised, rehearsed, and presented as if it were a conventional play. Participants discuss whether they agree or disagree with the solution presented. Forum Theatre assumes that some participants will disagree.

The scene is performed again, exactly as in the first enactment, but spect-actors can replace any performer by shouting "Stop!" The new spect-actor takes over that performer's role, leading the action in a better or more productive direction. The spect-actor who joins the action must do just that: *act,* rather than *talk* about what the performers should be doing. The purpose of Forum exercises isn't to "win" and end the performance, but to try out tactics for dealing with difficult situations and thwarting oppressed-oppressor relationships.

Forum Theatre involves both *theory* in the analysis of complex power relationships and *therapy* in acting out how particular individuals function within these relationships (R. Bowman 1997, 145). The New York Police Academy uses Forum Theatre to help new recruits act within a complex network of identities and power relationships (Telesco 2001). Boal's techniques have been used in prisons, among refugee populations, in health care settings, and in college classrooms (Cohen-Cruz 1994; McConachie 2002). José Rodríguez, Marc Rich, Rachel Hastings, and Jennifer Page (2006) use Boal's techniques to assess the effectiveness of sexual assault intervention programs on college campuses. The authors point out that the discussion and the performance of what constitutes an effective response is heated and often difficult, forcing audiences to "see and experience the significant consequences of sexual assault" (245).

In each context, Boal's techniques offer new endings for dramatic form and action. The performer-audience relationship is adapted and revised to meet the needs of the situation and to reflect the complex, shifting, and multiple identities of the participants (Howard 2004, 231).

THEORY MEETS WORLD

Boal's Techniques in an ESL Classroom

Ross Louis teaches English as a Second Language. In "Performing English, Performing Bodies: A Case for Critical Performative Language Pedagogy" (2005), Louis describes the ESL classroom as "a delicate, ideological crossroads, where immigrant and refugee participants negotiate language competence and social identity within the imposing framework of a dominant English language ideology" (335). His fifteen students in an advanced class were natives of Afghanistan, Argentina, China, Colombia, El Salvador, Laos, Kazakhstan, Mexico, Poland, Sudan, Taiwan, Thailand, Venezuela, and Yemen.

Louis utilized TO techniques in the classroom as a particularly potent means to counter the strict and structured protocols of standard language instruction. While Louis covered basic competencies, "grammar, listening comprehension, conversation skills, pronunciation, reading comprehension, and writing," stories told by students during fifteen-minute class breaks revealed tensions between these classroom goals and the lives of his students.

They told stories about landlords who would not respond to their tenants' requests, grocery clerks who relentlessly stared at immigrant customers, and employers who belittled immigrant employees by assuming they were ignorant of basic workplace information. Unfortunately, the program's curriculum did not privilege these meaningful, embodied sites for English (342).

Louis employed Image Theatre techniques to ask students to create tableaus that illustrate typical situations they encounter. The most common obstacle for students was their failure to understand a set of instructions—whether from teachers, employers, or officials—yet they always "feigned understanding," by nodding yes. To admit they do not understand, or to ask for clarification, is to risk being seen as a "bad" student or employee. Students created this scene to illustrate the problem:

During the first sequence, the employer stood stage right, facing the employee. She crossed her arms, drew her shoulders back, and rested her weight on her heels. The employee stood stage left about fifteen feet

(Continued)

(Continued)

> away, leaned slightly forward, and nodded her head up and down in a "yes" gesture. Next, the students spoke the thoughts of their respective characters. The employer began: "I spoke to her slowly. And so I think she has understood me. . . ." The employee responded: ". . . I always say to the boss, 'I understand.' I always say one word: 'Yes.' After ten minutes . . . 'I'm sorry. I cannot understand.'" (343)

> This exercise revealed the "masks" nonnative speakers develop in their daily, "ritual gestures," especially "nodding 'yes,' while thinking 'no.'" It also connected the ESL classroom to the real world where students live and work.
> Students also employed Forum Theatre techniques to create alternatives to this common social situation. A student from Thailand and her English-speaking husband were invited to a dinner party. The Thai student spoke very little English and sat silently amid the chattering couples, but a woman sitting across from her stared at her constantly, making the Thai student so uncomfortable that she was reluctant to eat. But she never said anything to the staring woman, nor did the woman speak to her. Students offered these kinds of interventions by stopping the action, stepping in as the protagonist, and trying alternatives:

> Forum interventions mostly focused on the student asking the American guests basic questions ("How are you?" "Do you like the party?"). One intervention removed the student from the dinner table entirely to avoid the discomfort of eating while being closely watched. Another had the student respond to the intrusive staring by returning the behavior. The forum exercise concluded with discussion about how classmates had handled similar situations (347).

> Boal's TO techniques offered important ways to "bridge the gap between social critique and action" as students "openly shared their respective experiences, debated the effects of shared language obstacles, and rehearsed communicative responses" (347).

Why Do People Take to the Streets? Models of Protest

The stage, especially when characterized as underground, fringe, or alternative, has long been a place to imagine and to enact possibilities for social change. Baz Kershaw (1999, 59) lists just some of the innovative groupings that offered radical performance in the twentieth century:

community theatre, grass roots theatre, feminist theatre, women's theatre, lesbian theatre, gay theatre, queer theatre, black theatre, ethnic theatre, guerrilla theatre, theatre in education, theatre in prisons, disability theatre, reminiscence theatre, environmental theatre, performance art, physical theatre, visual theatre and so on.

SOURCE: Photo by Craig Morse (www.flickr.com/photos/culturesubculture/collection). Copyright © 2006 by Craig Morse.

But what of the cultural mainstream? When large numbers of people come together to celebrate or to protest, "theatre" takes a backseat to other theories that explain, predict, and explore how and why people are moved to take their agendas to the street.

James M. Jasper (1997) outlines a century's worth of approaches to protest movements from social psychology, sociology, and political science. Classic theories began in the nineteenth century with **crowd theory,** in which protest was conceived as "irregular and irrational." In this view, crowds are prone to violence and considered deviant and abnormal. Crowd theory reduced protest to "the release of pent-up frustration" (1997, 21).

In the mid-twentieth century, protest theorists questioned the irrational center of protest and posited a number of ways in which people who protest are indeed rational. **Rationalist theories** of collective action (not collective *behavior*), knowledgeable choices, game theory, and strategic interactions are more complex ways of looking at individual motivations within protest movements and especially in trade associations and international treaties and diplomacy.

The **mobilization** paradigm developed in the 1970s argued that "protest was a regular part of politics, that protestors were normal people pursuing reasonable goals, and that available economic resources helped determine what protestors could achieve" (Jasper 1997, 29). Mobilization theories concentrate on resources and the ways that protesters finance activities and enact successful tactics. Petitions, direct-mail campaigns, and fund-raising are all ways to garner resources for protest movements as organizations.

With the rise of civil rights and labor movements, the **political process** approach began concentrating on the strategies of groups excluded from and oppressed by political processes. Doug McAdam (1982, 25) defines social movements based on the political process approach as "those organized efforts, on the part of excluded groups, to promote or resist changes in the structure of society that involve recourse to noninstitutional forms of political participation." This approach should enable many cultural and individual factors to enter theories of protest as important political opportunities: "skills and know-how, emotional inspiration, raised expectation, shared rhetoric and images" (Jasper 1997, 39).

Jasper concludes that each of these paradigms for protest concentrates on a single, powerful metaphor: "crowd psychology, strategic rationality, material resources, and political opportunity" (1997, 39), often to the exclusion of other dimensions. Contemporary performance theorists offer an important alternative to these classic theories of protest. Brecht and Boal return to Aristotle to reject his poetics of audience catharsis as untenable for real political change. Still others return to Aristotle to embrace his poetics of dramatic form for their tremendous explanatory power for public events, carnival, spectacle, and dramaturgy.

Public Events through an Aristotelian Lens

Janelle Reinelt (2006, 71) writes that contemporary times are "aggressively theatrical." Reality television, government "spin," and social dramas like the death of Princess Diana are fruitfully explained through the "explanatory power of performance to shape ideas, question truth claims, sway public opinion, and construct an aesthetics that sometimes functions as an epistemology."

In "Toward a Poetics of Theatre and Public Events," Reinelt (2006) analyzes the death of Stephen Lawrence, a black British teenager murdered by four white youths in 1993. Reinelt argues that the murder, trial, media accounts, and public protest events unfolded like a well-constructed play, with clear protagonist and antagonists, dramatic build of the plot, and discoveries for the community. "Aristotle Rears His Head" is Reinelt's application of Aristotelian dramatic principles to the public events, revealing that "the public came to see in the Lawrence case the kind of symbolic ethical and political critique that makes it a model of the theatricalized public event."

Reinelt (2006, 74) outlines four ways that public events are theatricalized and then available for social inquiry. First, the event must be significantly grave, having consequences for the well-being and everyday life of the public/audience. Second, the event must attract significant media attention. Third, "the event must take a recognizable form, either as ceremony, game, or ritual, or else have unfolded in a form of narrative that can be apprehended in terms of protagonists and plot—in short, an old-fashioned but well-known Aristotelianism." Finally, the event must be apprehended in and by the public as symbolically staging a feature of national, everyday life. This symbolic stage is ripe for critiquing ways of living.

Reinelt is quick to point out that "endings" to and interpretations of any public event are never clear-cut, monovocal, or settled. The centrality of struggle, conflict, tragedy, and "truth," however, does not foreclose Aristotelian interpretations, but instead speaks to the value of a performance lens as "something concrete to contribute to civic life: the tools of our trade can be useful in the broader arenas of public discourse when the highly theatricalized nature of contemporary existence is examined . . ." (2006, 71). Carnival, spectacle, and "radical" dramaturgy are applications and updates of an Aristotelian lens for understanding, explaining, and theorizing resistance in performance.

Carnival and Protest

Performance theorists have long drawn from carnival for models for political action and protest. Carnival involves state- and church-sanctioned disruption of ordinary life—whether in medieval Europe, eighteenth-century Paris, contemporary Mardi Gras in New Orleans, or even Spring Break. Mikhail Bakhtin (1968) proposes that carnival disrupts the status quo of ordinary life by licensing inversions (the high become low, the low are exalted), by featuring bodily pleasures, and by creating a collectivity of people not divided by political and economic strata and statuses. Masquerading, clowning, exaggeration, and lewdness are the methods for temporarily turning the world on its head. Carnival, however, always returns to the status quo, often marked by official "closing ceremonies." For Peter Stallybrass and Allon White (1986), carnival exposes the stable hierarchies of power as "fictions" through a licensed and creative "disrespect" toward authority. In this exposure lies the potential for very real political and social change.

The carnivalesque is a valuable lens for exploring both the performance choices made by individuals and the political and social structures exposed in these choices. Raymond Schneider (1994) and Richard Schechner (1993) analyze the yearly Gasparilla Festival in Tampa, Florida, where the elite of the community dress up as pirates and invade the city. The symbolism of the already powerful invading the city as "lowly" and criminal pirates is not lost on the community. Mikita Hoy (1994) utilizes Bakhtin's carnival to explore football songs performed by crowds of British soccer fans. "Drunken, bawdy, brawling male youths violating public peace and privacy by howling out their trivial allegiances" are decidedly threatening to the status quo. At the same time, the fear associated with them addresses "social, political, racial, and sexual inequities . . . airing explicit versions of normally repressed ideas about society, its valuations and ideologies" (Hoy 1994, 289). Stephen Olbrys (2006) analyzes Chris Farley's "exotic dance" on "Saturday Night Live" for its tension between grotesque and burlesque. The lustful license of Bourbon Street in New Orleans is the topic of Ronald J. Pelias' (2006) autoethnographic account celebrating carnivalesque space.

Using concepts similar to play theory discussed in Chapter Five, Baz Kershaw (1992, 75) explores how "carnivalesque protest" or "celebratory protest" carries *ludic* (play) elements of culture into the political arena. Ordinary life and structures are temporarily suspended in playful "anti-war marches, free rock-concerts, the Greenham Common fence decorations, Rock against Racism." M. Lane Bruner (2005) explores tactics of the Solidarity Movement in 1980s Poland where protesters dressed up as elves, handing out candy and singing children's songs. When police began arresting them, the crowd chanted "Elves are real!" demonstrating how powerful a weapon "absurdity, symbolic protest, and the curious blending of the fictive and the real" can be (2005, 148).

Jill Lane (2002, 63) explores the work of "exaggerated, comic televangelist" Reverend Billy for his "ability to mobilize 'real' communities and to stage meaningful social activism."

Performance artist Bill Talen, creator of Reverend Billy, intones, "Welcome to the Church of Stop Shopping, Children! . . . In this church we gather to ask the great questions that face us. . . . Is there life after perfect teeth?"

Kathleen K. Olson (2002/2003) details carnivalesque protest events of CCNV (the Community for Creative Non-Violence) in work with and for the homeless. In 1982, members of CCNV dressed up as "fat cats" in three-piece suits, complete with whiskers and tails, and waded into a seventeen-foot apple pie. The performers shouted, "Get back! This is my share!" as they tumbled in the giant pie, drawing symbolic and real connections between corporate greed and hunger. CCNV also staged a luncheon for the U.S. Congress and reporters on Capitol Hill, serving quiche and shortcake from ingredients salvaged from dumpsters and wholesalers. On Thanksgiving Day in 1981, in an event that led to a Supreme Court case, CCNV members pitched tents across the street from the White House, creating a temporary village mimicking real living situations for many homeless people. The sign read: "Welcome to Reaganville. Population growing daily. Reaganomics at work."

While carnival is licensed by authorities, carnivalesque protest events employ strategies of carnival—masquerade, clowning, inversions, and play—to utilize humor to make very serious political statements.

Limits of Carnivalesque Protest: When Audiences Don't Get It

Not all audiences "get" the humor and critique offered in carnivalesque protest. Mickee Faust is a cabaret company founded in 1987 in Tallahassee, Florida. The company takes its name from their central character, Mickee Faust, "the scraggly, cigar-smoking evil twin of Mickey Mouse" (Schriver and Nudd, 2002, 196). In its first ten years, the company presented their work to their "own," the progressive and liberal members of the community.

In 1999, the group joined local protests around the annual Springtime Tallahassee celebration. Faust members opposed the positioning of Andrew Jackson as figurehead of the celebration and Grand Marshall of the official parade. Schriver and Nudd (2002, 198) note, "Native Americans, people of color, and other community members virulently oppose such valorization of Andrew Jackson, a known slaveholder and exterminator of native populations."

Faust created two protest performances. The first was a "celebratory protest event" that included "Dictators on Parade," featuring Jackson in parade with other bloodthirsty dictators (Genghis Khan, Imelda Marcos, and Satan). The informal parade boosted the morale of groups whose annual protests seemed to produce little change. Faust also wanted to reach the larger Tallahassee audience, so they created a float for the festival's official parade. This float also presented a motley crew of dictators, but in more subversive ways. Schriver and Nudd describe the performance:

When the streets were filled with people, when the crowd was dense, once we had passed the parade chairman [who could eject them for violating parade rules], each leader took out a placard, which referenced the discordant history of their character. One side of the placard was an innocuous, sanitized version of history. "Queen Isabella funded Christopher Columbus," one said. On the other side was another version, "Queen Isabella eliminated the Jews from Spain." (202)

This performance was met primarily with silence, which members of the troupe took as both a success—rarely are paradegoers silent participants—and a disappointment—they wondered if audience members "read" their performance in the intended way. They concluded that, when addressing audiences unfamiliar with their politics, they would be wise to revise their open-ended, playful techniques. In addition to creating pleasure and camaraderie for participants and those in the know, protest performances aimed at a general audience also require a clear and controlled message that "strategically fix[es] meaning, if only for awhile" (208). Conforming to the rules of traditional dramaturgy is one way to fix meanings.

From Traditional to Radical Dramaturgy

Dramaturgy is traditionally understood as the composition or writing of a play, attending to and shaping the rise and fall of dramatic action, the creation of characters in dialogue, and then mounting this play on the stage in spectacle (what the audience sees), voice and song (what the audience hears), and diction (how the actors perform the language). The dramaturg, in conventional theatre, is responsible for representing the playwright in rehearsals, carefully arguing for the play as written, and offering interpretations of the text to the director.

Following this lead, Lee Baxandall (1969, 62) defines traditional dramaturgy as "the art of making dramas and placing them properly on the stage; dramatic composition and representation." Baxandall argues that savvy political organizers recognize the importance of theatricalizing politics by moving dramaturgy to world stages: "This dramaturgy is realized in scenarios, which are—rather like the *improvvisa of the commedia dell'arte*—projected and agreed beforehand in part, and in part created as opportunities and fortuities arise in performance" (62).

Baxandall writes convincingly of how both conservative and liberal groups "make dramas" in staging their agendas. For the state's protection of the status quo, Baxandall notes that "the state has uncounted stages, plot-lines, and routines" through symbolic and spectacular displays of pomp and circumstance. The Nuremburg Rallies of 1936 in Nazi Germany are a potent example:

Spectacle was of the essence in Hitler's master plan: scenario activity fed into and guided by the fantastic dream of the Master race. National Socialism ("the socialism of fools" as someone well termed it) had a staggering if brief success, however, largely due to its skill in giving multitudes the illusion of participating in a dramaturgy which would realize their potential, whatever the cost, in a national destiny. (57)

Baz Kershaw (2003, 595) calls these state-sponsored events "spectacles of domination," or "rituals of the powerful," and lists as examples "spectacles of church, monarchy, state; religious rites, coronations, military parades."

Baxandall (1969) maintains that the state distills its spectacle in celebrating the drama of its central authority figure. Baxandall's point is quickly realized in considering these questions: How are leaders of state dressed, escorted, set center stage, and attended to? How are their entrances and exits choreographed, and how are their scripts embellished and accompanied? How are spectacle, song, and scenarios—mini-dramas—created around their appearances?

For political agendas without this state power and resources to orchestrate spectacle, song, and scenarios, Baxandall offers numerous examples of a dramaturgy of radical activity. A "radical" dramaturgy means "going to the roots" to invest often private issues with compelling drama through their staging. At Columbia University in 1968, student protestors of the SDS (Students for a Democratic Society) staged a disruption of the campus speech of the head of the Selective Service System for New York City.

> In the middle of the Colonel's speech a mini-demonstration appeared: fife and drum, flags, machine guns, and noise-makers. The attention of all was directed to this mocking counter-spectacle in the back of the room. Suddenly someone in the front row stood up and placed a lemon-meringue pie in the Colonel's face. The scenario accomplished, all the performers vanished at once. Aside from the old SDS leadership and the [Columbia University] administration, the entire campus seemed delighted with the way the Selective Service spokesman had "lost face." (Baxandall 1969, 59–60)

Peggy Phelan (1993, 130) notes how powerfully the anti-abortion group Operation Rescue makes use of theatrical tactics, "making a spectacle *for* the sake of publicity." Groups of men "form a wall, shoulder-to-shoulder, often screaming 'dyke' or 'whore' to any woman who walks across" the line into the abortion clinic.

> When a pregnant woman attempts to enter the clinic, a male rescuer will yell out in a strange falsetto, "Mother, please, don't murder me." Off to the side, most of the women from Operation Rescue form what is called a "Prayer Support Column": they chant hymns, stand still, try to maintain an air of "above the fray" about them, and keep their hands open and raised toward heaven. Another group of protesters carry placards with alternating images of the "innocent" and the "mutilated" fetus on them. The spatial separation between the men and the women rescuers mimics the situation often found in mainstream Western theatre: speaking men and observing women. This reinforces the idea that in any drama, including that of pregnancy, mainstream theatre will do all it can to insure that the main character remains an embryonic man. (131–132)

Photographs of fetuses are powerful spectacle, invoking sympathy as well as outrage, and function "like a flag, a banner under which protecting 'rescuers' march off to prevent the 'slaughter of the innocent'" (133).

These dramaturgies—dramas staged with abundant spectacle and clear protagonists, antagonists, and conflicts—demonstrate that Aristotelian form is alive and well, as well as effective, in creating compelling, dramatic moments. But Aristotle didn't have CNN, bullhorns, or tanks to consider 2,500 years ago. Theories of contemporary protest events as performances take all of these into consideration.

Analyzing Protest Events as Performances

Baz Kershaw (1997) proposes that the forms of popular protest today should be analyzed as synechdoche; that is, a particular protest will stand for the whole of that society. Protest events, such as marches, demonstrations, sit-ins, occupations, vigils, and peace camps, rely on and make use of spectacle—the choreographed sights, sounds, smells, touch, and arrangement of bodies in action. The particular kind of spectacle will challenge the system of authority on its own terms, using that society's forms of ceremony, ritual, and representation to expose the illusion of power held by the state. Kershaw (1997, 257) asks these questions to guide the analysis of protest events:

> How do the forms of popular protest embody their historical context through their location in identifiable traditions; and how do these same forms crack open traditions, disrupt socio-political expectations, and produce new kinds of public discourse in our increasingly mediatized and globalized world?

Kershaw finds four contemporary performance qualities that ought to guide any analysis of protest events.

First, these protests produce a "rich exchange between symbolic action and socio-political reality" (260). This exchange does not shut down possibilities for change but opens up possibilities for *constant reinterpretation* of the events and their political potential. A pie in the face has long functioned as a dramatic and comedic moment to bring down the exalted. As a symbolic act, it violates "face" without physical violence. When PETA (People for the Ethical Treatment of Animals) members spray-paint people wearing fur coats, what is the dramatic relationship between this symbolic act and political realities?

In the two-month occupation of Tiananmen Square in 1989, Chinese student leaders drew on the millennia-old Chinese tradition of petitioning, presenting Communist leaders with their requests. Kershaw maintains that "the image of three students kneeling on the steps of the Great Hall of the People would have a profound resonance for the Chinese people" (268). They also created a statue of the Goddess of Democracy and Freedom, with clear resonance in the West to the Statue of Liberty.

Second, these events are shaped by both spontaneity and set scripts or scenarios that are *other directed*. That is, contemporary protest events assume an audience—heightening the *reflexive opportunities* for everyone to think critically about the sociopolitical context that gave rise to them. Cindy Sheehan's summer campout in Crawford, Texas, in 2005 to protest the Iraq war clearly assumed an audience: at first local, then national, and finally global during August's traditional "slow news" period.

SOURCE: Photo by Danny Hammontree (www.digitalgrace.com). Copyright © 2005 by Danny Hammontree.

Third, contemporary protest events are experienced most often through their *representation in the media.* These mediations are doubly articulated: The people creating the protest may stage certain events specifically for the benefit of cameras; the media will then choose the "high points" of the drama for their cameraworthiness and render them as "news." For the West, the most salient media image from Tiananmen Square was the lone man blocking four tanks, heightening the notion of *individual* courage so valued in Western democracies. Interestingly, the photograph less broadcast was a wide shot: More than fifty tanks fill the frame, continuing to the horizon. Kershaw writes (1997, 272), "The second image displays the awful context of the heroism, and shifts it towards a different dramaturgical territory. . . . The panorama of latent violence forcefully implies many *invisible antagonists. . . .*"

Fourth, contemporary protest events rely on a great deal of planning, organizing, and scripting—especially when dealing with large numbers of people. At the same time, these events evidence much spontaneity and improvisation. This tension between *organization and the unexpected and surprising* is at the heart of a different aesthetics for the dramaturgy of protest, especially given the potential for violence. Instead of a modernist, Aristotelian development of the action, with its predictable linear form, clear protagonists and antagonists, and cathartic experience for the audience, Kershaw claims that radical dramaturgy of protest would look for and stress "multipliticity, discontinuity, abrupt eruptions of dramatic intensity, sudden shifts and changes of direction, tempo, focus" (260). Clearly, the Chinese government organized the arrival of fifty tanks. The surprising and unexpected appearance of the man in Tiananmen Square "standing down" those tanks is one such spontaneous eruption of dramatic intensity.

The Body Politic: How Do Bodies Intervene?

In histories of social movements, bodies of real people are often characterized as "mobs" whose potential for violence is characterized as a "volcano." Mob action is considered "purely spontaneous and lacking in form or technique" (Foster 2003, 397). Susan Leigh Foster argues with this too easy characterization of bodies as volatile and chaotic, "swept up in the fervor of the crowd." Instead, she asks specific questions of individual bodies in political movements and protests: "What are these bodies doing? What and how do their motions signify?" and "How have these bodies been trained?" (2003, 397).

Foster explores three important U.S. social movements: the lunch counter sit-ins of the 1960s in the American South, the ACT UP die-ins of the late 1980s protesting U.S. government unresponsiveness to AIDS, and the World Trade Organization political protests in Seattle, Washington, in 1999. All three share important similarities with regard to bodies: (1) they were grassroots movements of ordinary people acting without a single, identifiable leader; (2) they utilized public spaces and performances in strategic and symbolically significant ways; and (3) they all utilized tactics of nonviolence that were deliberately and carefully rehearsed by the participants. Each movement, however, approached media capacities to represent their agendas very differently.

Hundreds of Black Americans sat at "White Only" lunch counters throughout the southern United States. These public spaces were carefully chosen for the symbolism of bodies "not out of place," for Blacks were allowed to shop in these stores; these were bodies "of the wrong color." African-American protesters carefully planned how they would act while sitting at lunch counters:

They charged themselves with the task of remaining respectful at all times. Dressing well, they endeavored to sit upright and never talk back or laugh at those around them. If they brought books to read, they chose textbooks rather than magazines. Above all, they aspired to meet all threats and acts of violence toward them with a stoic, non-compliant non-action. (Foster 2003, 399)

Foster details one woman's account of how they trained in workshops:

We would practice things such as how to protect your head from a beating and how to protect each other. If one person was taking a severe beating, we would practice other people putting their bodies in between that person and the violence, so that the violence would be more distributed and hopefully no one would get seriously injured. We would practice not striking back if someone struck us. (400)

Media accounts, photographs, and film of the violence that ensued was instrumental in changing white Americans' attitudes when the "reality" of the color line was laid bare in the news. In the 1960s, the media were assumed to "reflect" realities.

ACT UP also chose their public spaces carefully—on Wall Street and at corporate headquarters of drug companies in Manhattan. Participants also trained for and planned their performances: "dying" in piles of bodies, creating tableaux of horrific effects; "dying" in groups of ten and forcing police to remove them with great difficulty one at a time, only to be replaced with another group of ten. They drew chalk outlines around the removed bodies, "intended to represent statistical counts of AIDS fatalities, they documented with ghostly inadequacy the effects of AIDS" (Foster 2003, 404) and government failure to deal with the disease. ACT UP organizers deliberately enlisted the media, knowing how powerful these images were in shaping public opinion, by creating press packets and news releases and contacting media outlets. From the 1960s notion that the media "reflect" reality, ACT UP organizers knew that the media "created" reality.

The WTO protests in Seattle, spread across four days, brought together incredibly diverse groups with different political agendas: environmentalists, organized labor, immigration rights activists, and nuclear proliferation protesters as well as other single-issue groups. Foster explores how each group employed its own bodily tactics, "exuberantly walking, standing, shouting, waving banners, sitting-in, holding hands, or clasping arms in differing configurations so as to create solidarity in unabashed opposition to police and in support of the people" (408). All the groups were carefully coached on nonviolent tactics.

Most important, the WTO organizers were concerned about the media—owned by global conglomerates with vested interests in world trade. Media accounts, as it turned out, featured the very few violent episodes of property destruction, just as organizers had feared. To countermand the power of the media to create only one "authorized" version of the protests, the organizers mounted a deliberate effort to create their own media accounts of the protests, with online broadcasts of protesters'

SOURCE: Photo by Hughes Léglise-Bataille. www.flickr.com/people/hughes_leglise/

multiple video and photographic accounts of their actions. The Internet now provides the means to create and to disperse "many different realities" outside the mainstream media.

Foster is careful not to homogenize the different bodies and historical contexts of these three political movements, but she does highlight agency and choice in political bodies and political movements:

> When individuals choose to participate in these kinds of political demonstration, they commit themselves to physical action, whatever form it takes. Whether they become the reflexive body sitting at the lunch counter, the campy body lying on Wall Street, or the glocal [global + local] body blockading Downtown Seattle, they choose to spend their day constructing physical interference, and this engagement with the physical imbues them with a deepened sense of personal agency. (2003, 412)

SOURCE: Photo by Craig Morse (www.flickr.com/photos/culturesubculture/collection). Copyright © 2006 by Craig Morse.

GO FIGURE

Dramatic Strategies and Performing Bodies

Choose a particular protest event and do some research through Web-based news forums (CNN, BBC, network news, and newspaper online archives). What traditions of performance are called upon and reworked in the event? How have the media represented—through images—the protesters and their agenda? How do bodies act in public spaces that are both strategic and symbolic? Some events you might research are

The Million Man March

Cindy Sheehan's occupation of Crawford, Texas

The Seattle World Trade Organization protests

Kent State Massacre

Operation Rescue and anti-abortion protesters

"A Day Without Immigrants" marches on May 3, 2006

The Birmingham bus strike

2003 Invasion of Iraq pro and con demonstrations

Resistance in Everyday Life: Foucault's Productive Power

This chapter has moved from the stage to the streets in examining performance as resistance. Brecht and Boal developed a "new poetics" of dramatic form, and street protests demonstrate that the "old poetics" of Aristotelian dramatic action are alive and well when updated for media representations and bodies. This final section considers resistance and its relationship to power in everyday life.

If Aristotelian drama assumes conflict, contemporary postmodern notions of resistance assume power. Michel Foucault, contemporary French philosopher and activist, prompted a sea change in thinking about power, its operations, and its assumptions. In Foucault's analysis (1978/1990), *traditional understandings* of power are fivefold.

1. Power is something that is acquired, seized, shared, held, or lost.

2. Power is enacted and enforced by prohibitions, laws, and taboos. Foucault calls this a "negative relation." That is, "old" power can only "say no"—by naming what one can't do. The Ten Commandments of the Old Testament, for example, outline very strict "thou shalt not's."

3. Power divides people into rulers and ruled, and it flows from the "top down" to lower groups. This is an insistence on the rule, and these rules are enforced by authorities and apply to all.

4. Power is located in specific groups, headquarters, or castes. The police, judges, kings, and tyrants are all people in locations where power is enforced through punishment and its threat.

5. Power is oppressive in a model of "power over" others, especially conceived as a "right" to control others.

Riki Wilchins (2004, 62) explains Foucault's notion of "repressive power": "the power to silence, wound, and punish. We fear this repressive power and the potential of the state to abuse the individual." Foucault turned all of these traditional notions of power on their heads by arguing for a new view of power, not as solely oppressive but as *productive*. Productive power operates not by *right* but by **technique**, not by *law* but by **normalization**, not by *punishment* but by **control**.

Foucault developed his theory of power by arguing that the West moved from public spectacles of discipline and punishment (like floggings, torture, the stocks, and hangings), through the development of the prison, to techniques of self-discipline and self-surveillance. We no longer need to be reminded through public punishment of the dangers of transgression; we already control ourselves by carefully enacting bodily techniques of normalization (for sexuality, gender, class, race, and status). In short, oppressive power threatens, like a police officer with a billy club. Productive power produces—discourses, relationships, resistances, and people. For example, the prison creates people through its practices—with the subsequent labels of criminals, deviants, and perverts—and certain kinds of resistances, like tattoos and graffiti, written on bodies and institutions (Wendt 1996, 259).

Foucault (1978/1990, 94) characterizes *productive power,* counter to oppressive power above, in these five ways:

1. Power is not seized, but "power is exercised from innumerable points of interplay" in relations that are mobile, changing, and changeable.

2. Power is produced within and among relationships, such as economic processes, knowledge relationships, and sexual relationships. Power is internal to these relations, not above or external to them.

3. Power is not oppositional—divided into the binary of ruler and ruled. Instead, power runs through the "social body as a whole," as machineries of production such as families, groups, and institutions. These relations are linked together in micropolitics of bodies.

4. Power relations are intentional, but there is no one place or person who invented them.

5. "Where there is power, there is resistance. . . . These points of resistance are present everywhere in the power network. Hence there is no single locus of great Refusal, no soul of revolt, source of all rebellions, or pure law of the revolutionary. Instead there is a plurality of resistances, each of them a special case: resistances that are possible, necessary, improbable; others that are spontaneous, savage, solitary, concerted, rampant, or violent; still others that are quick to compromise, interested, or sacrificial; by definition, they can only exist in the strategic field of power relations" (95–96).

Wilchins (2004, 66–68) explores how the techniques of discipline in the prison—where cells are arranged to keep everyone under surveillance, rigid schedules are kept, and all infractions are swiftly punished—are replicated in schools, offices, and factories, "anywhere it was desirable for a small group of people to efficiently instill norms of conduct, accountability, and self-consciousness in a large group" (68). Wilchins writes: "The organizing principle of the prison system was no longer simply punishment or public display. The prison was designed to change inmates' consciousness of themselves. Its aim was to make them, under infinite observation and control, infinitely self-conscious and self-controlling" (68).

So schools also utilize these disciplinary techniques: desks arranged so that the teacher can survey at all times, all time scheduled and allotted, "a time for arrival, for homeroom, for study, to get to the next class, or to eat. Each area has its own rules: what you can do in the classroom, the hall, or the cafeteria" (68). Disciplinary mechanisms are especially felt and enacted during tests: surveillance, identification checks, special seating arrangements, and separating students from their belongings.

Foucault's concepts of power as productive, as relational, and as strategies that traverse bodies have been extremely important lenses for critical studies in rhetoric and organizations (Wendt 1996). When performance and rhetorical scholars in

SOURCE: Photograph by Jaclyn Lannon. Copyright © 2007 by Jaclyn Lannon.

communication take up Foucault, they utilize his ideas to explore the power of confessionals to create "truth" in sexual identities (Bergman 2004; Dow 2001; LaFountain 1989), to map the production of bodies in classrooms disciplined by discourses of pedagogy (Alexander, Anderson, and Gallegos 2005), to critique creation of knowledge in the academy and in medical science (Bell 2005; Gunn 2006), and to explore how bodies are produced by scientific and medical discourses concerning the right to die, abortion, and midwifery (Lay 2003; Lay and Wahlstrom 1996; McDorman 2005).

READ MORE ABOUT IT

School Is Hell

Margaret Betz Hull, in "Postmodern Philosophy Meets Pop Cartoon" (2000, 61–64), analyzes Matt Groening cartoons in School Is Hell *and moments in the television show "The Simpsons" with a Foucauldian lens, finding disciplinary tactics operating every day to produce docile bodies in classrooms.*

The most obvious area where Foucault and Groening coincide is Groening's brilliant appropriation of the tremendous normalizing power manifested in the contemporary classroom. Cartoon after cartoon of Groening's work subtly yet comically represents how the average student is forced to conform, no matter how empty and arbitrary, to set definitions of "good," "useful," and "normal." This of course is entirely at the expense of what is artistic, spontaneous, creative, and personally meaningful. In a description of nursery school in one cartoon found in *School Is Hell,* Groening has a young child advising other children, "This is probably your last chance to be artistic—that's right! Seize the opportunity to experiment with gleeful abandon before *they show you how to do it right and ruin everything!*" [emphasis added]. Here, Groening cleverly recognizes Foucault's point that the purpose in the classroom is to normalize young bodies through years of following discreet directions, while sitting still in one place at a classroom desk. This point is made explicit in one episode of *The Simpsons* in which students complain about the torturous discomfort of new chiropractic-designed classroom chairs. The teacher responds that they should rest assured; it will only hurt until the young students' bones eventually mold to the shape of the chairs.

In another cartoon, Groening represents Foucault's understanding of the implicit relation of power and knowledge in modern power through his depiction of a teacher who barks at a cowering student, "What is important is what we say is important!". . .

Yet, what is arguably the most Foucauldian theme that appears in Groening's work is his constant nudging toward a resistance to the suffocating disciplinary control of, particularly, school. Example after example run through Groening's work: The cover of *School Is Hell* shows a student compliantly writing over and over on the board the phrase "I must remember to be cheerful and obedient." The next page depicts the same image with the same beginning, "I must remember . . . ," but now rebelliously scrawled beneath it is "School is Hell.". . . Still another cartoon offers advice in the interest of self-preservation on how not to deal with the situation of being smarter than your teachers—*not* to say the following, no matter how true: "The crime is *not* that I rebelled, the crime is that the other kids do not—that they are too bored and defeated to challenge the stultifying rules, the abuse of power and the sheer joylessness of everyday school life." Thus, like Foucault, Groening's consistent message to young people disgusted with the banality of the school system is to recognize the inanity of it all and to create fissures, to resist the normalization.

SOURCE: From "Postmodern Philosophy Meets Pop Cartoon: Michel Foucault and Matt Groening" by Margaret Betz Hull. *Journal of Popular Culture* (2000). Reprinted by permission of Blackwell.

ACT OUT

How Are You Produced by Power?

Like classrooms and prisons, the power networks mobilized in the places listed below produce certain ways of acting or being in public by heightening your own sense of self-surveillance and awareness. Create a performance in which you exaggerate the "subject" produced by these operations of power. How are Foucault's five points about productive power particularly revealing of the ways we have internalized the rules of these spaces?

(Continued)

(Continued)

> How do these same spaces produce resistances? Create a second performance in which you exaggerate the "subject" produced by resistances to these power operations. How is Foucault's list of resistances relevant to your performance choices?
>
> A public library
>
> A busy airport
>
> A locker room
>
> A medical doctor's office
>
> A high-end department store
>
> A museum
>
> A theme park
>
> A college lecture hall
>
> A hair salon

Resistance in Everyday Life: de Certeau's Strategies and Tactics

Foucault's early work on power paints a sad picture of individuals with little or no choice but to succumb to institutional discourses and mechanisms of control. Many performance theorists have turned to the work of Michel de Certeau as a better account of individual choice and agency within networks of power. In *The Practice of Everyday Life* (1984), de Certeau theorizes how people creatively and dynamically navigate cultural structures. He distinguishes between **strategies** that "produce, tabulate, and impose" the structural places of power and **tactics** that "use, manipulate, and divert those spaces" (1984, 30). In short, strategy is institutionally structured power, rules, and regulations of institutions, governments, and organizations. Tactics are bodily practices of real people that create space in between, around, and through these structures, rules, and regulations. These actual practices are often improvisational, difficult to predict in advance, and fleeting. De Certeau writes that a tactic is "always on the watch for opportunities that must be seized 'on the wing.' What it wins, it does not keep. It must constantly manipulate events in order to turn them into 'opportunities'" (xix).

De Certeau calls this "the art of making do" and details how an immigrant from North Africa lives in Paris in "a low-income housing development": "Without leaving the place where he has no choice but to live and which lays down its law for him, he establishes within it a degree of plurality and creativity. By an art of being in between, he draws unexpected results from his situation" (30). De Certeau calls this "poaching," "a practice that involves taking enough from the dominant to slip under the radar screen, using the dominant against the dominant without actually challenging the status quo" (Murphy 2002, 299).

De Certeau acknowledges power in places and the creative ways people manipulate those structures in everyday practices. This is an explanation that theorizes *local micromoments of resistance* and envisions *people as active agents who make choices.* Susan Leigh Foster (2002, 130) describes de Certeau's work as an "antidote to Foucault's mechanisms of discipline and surveillance."

Performance scholars have utilized de Certeau's "art of making do" to explain resistant, local practices within structured places of power (Conquergood 1992; Foster 2002; Hamera 2005; Schober 2003). Alexandra Murphy (2002) details how flight attendants employ "tactics" that manipulate the "strategies" of power on airline flights. When one passenger refused to stow his baggage that blocked an exit, the attendant explained to him airline regulations. When he still refused, she left the institutional "safety script," and said, "Look, if we get in a crash, your bag is going to get in the way of other passengers getting out of the plane. And I am not going to come back here and save your butt in a burning airplane" (309). Murphy also offers examples of flight attendants watering the drinks of drunken passengers (while still serving them), openly mocking the safety demonstration (while still delivering the script), and asking captains to turn on the seat belt sign and announce "rough air in the area" to force passengers to sit down. Improvisational, local, and always "poaching" on strategies of power, these tactics are choices "in the moment-to-moment communicative connections, [manipulating] the standard and stylized script" (313).

De Certeau's theory of tactics is especially important to explain the "making do" of marginalized groups and peoples. Dwight Conquergood (1998, 30) uses Zora Neal Hurston's account of how African Americans respond with survival tactics to white ethnographers and folklorists: "The theory behind our tactics: The white man is always trying to know into somebody else's business. All right, I'll set something outside the door of my mind for him to play with and handle. *He can read my writing, but he sho' can't read my mind.* I'll put this play toy in his hand, and he will seize it and go away. Then I'll say my say and sing my song." For Conquergood (1998, 31), de Certeau's works are a "powerful theory of everyday life that celebrates the restless energies and subversive powers of kinesis," the ways we all "make do" within structures of power.

RETHINKING RESISTANCE

In *Utopia in Performance,* Jill Dolan (2005, 2) argues that her book "tries to find, at the theater, a way to reinvest our energies in a different future, one full of hope and reanimated by a new, more radical humanism." Dolan readily acknowledges that her attempt risks several critiques: romanticizing resistance, a nostalgia for an imagined past, sentimentality, and even a blind, uncritical patriotism. This chapter—with its emphasis on theories of resistance on the stage, in the streets, and in everyday life—also risks these same critiques in hoping for a better, more just world.

Critiques of Brecht tend to center on rationality as a critical attitude somehow attainable and conducive to moving audiences and as Brecht's own approach to the theatre. Carl Weber (1980, 122) writes that Brecht approached his work with "the attitude of an engineer or a natural scientist." Feminist critiques feature both rationality and portraits of femininity. Elin Diamond (1988) notes, "Brecht . . . created conventionally gendered plays and too many saintly mothers (one is too many)" (83). Still, Brecht's influence in modern theatre of the West is monumental. German director Claus Peymann says, "in the hour of political extremity you'll reach for your Brecht like for the Bible" (quoted in Weber 1980, 118).

Critiques of Boal involve the difficulty of translating his techniques from his native Brazil to North America. How can one address multiple identities of people and absent oppressors, especially when oppressors are "multi-billion-dollar corporate networks" (Schutzman 1994, 145)? And what of the spect-actor who identifies with the oppressor rather than the oppressed?

The metaphor of carnival, with its inversion of social statuses and license to play, has also been critiqued on three fronts. First, carnival always ends, returning to the status quo of social and political inequities, while the risks the performers have taken may continue to have real consequences (Bruner 2005). Second, as Marcyrose Chvasta (2006, 13) points out, "while festive street performance is a display of communal strength and a means of educating the public, no policy, or law, or budget will change unless the State feels threatened." Anger, rather than celebration, is often the most effective stance for these performers. Third, women have often been real victims of "licensed" debauchery and lewdness—such as rape and physical abuse—raising the question, "*Whose* pleasure is being enabled and valorized in real practices of carnival?" (Bell and Forbes 1994, 194).

The emphasis on spectacle—the visibility of people in the streets and the media that shape and disseminate these images—too often conflates power with visibility. Peggy Phelan critiques the assumption that minority groups—the politically underrepresented—only need to gain access to the power to represent themselves in images to correct social and political inequities. To illustrate her point about conflation, Phelan (1993, 10) wrote in her now famous phrase, "If representational visibility equals power, then almost-naked young white women should be running Western culture."

Power, theorized by Foucault as productive and by de Certeau as strategies and tactics, continues to complicate the relations among performance, resistance, movements, bodies, and agency. Foucault has been critiqued by feminists for his lack of attention to gender and for foreclosing agency and choice in disciplinary knowledges and discourses (Bell 2005). Anna Schober (2003, 70) critiques the clear-cut lines de Certeau draws between structures of power and tactics of individuals: "Who and what is on the side of the law, and who or what is on the side of the threatened bodies?" She maintains these sides are already contaminated by each other, and strategies and tactics "never appear in a 'pure' way" (2003, 81).

Even as these critiques are offered, performance theorists and practitioners continue to utilize techniques of Brecht and Boal to mobilize local and global stages and streets as a revolutionary mechanism for social and artistic change and for moving audiences to political action. Public events, carnival, dramaturgy, and models of protest are important places to explore how protestors (1) plan and employ theatrical tactics (costumes, props, scripts, choreography, speeches, chanting, singing, and movement), (2) engage audiences in and through mediated representations, and (3) utilize bodies in service of political agendas through potent symbolic and real acts. These deployments and engagements do not belong to any one political ideology but are utilized by many camps in debates about war and peace, reproduction, the environment, labor, and even and especially life and death.

Two huge questions remain unanswered and are, perhaps, unanswerable in performance theory. First, if the goal of performing resistance is political effectiveness, then *how* can one measure this? While theories of the stage, the streets, and everyday life describe, explain, and explore resistant practices, performance is not reducible to variables that can be scientifically measured, predicted, and replicated anew in a laboratory. The measurements of effectiveness—legislation, court cases, political campaigns, and public opinion polling, to name a few—stand in complex social and political relations to the performances that happen in and around them.

Second, is performance a helpful lens for understanding resistance when real blood is shed and real lives are lost? And *why* do people continue to engage in symbolic acts when lives are at stake? Baz Kershaw relates the story told by Chilean director and actor Hugo Medina:

> [D]uring Pinochet's reign of terror the people would show they knew the houses of torture by silently pointing at them as they walked past; everyone knew the significance of the pointed finger, yet the dictatorship was powerless to prevent it because virtually everyone did it. Hence, the everyday act of pointing was transformed into a collective gesture that was beyond the power of control of one of the most violently oppressive post-war regimes, because to eliminate it the regime would have had to destroy the people upon whom its power ultimately rested. (1999, 26)

These how, what, and why questions of performance theories of resistance can never be answered with a simple yes or no, but instead speak to the ways that resistance and power are performances with consequences—for individuals, for groups, and for sociopolitical historical moments. Performance theory remains one way into these performances and their consequences.

CHAPTER 9

Performing Technologies

By Elizabeth Bell and Marcyrose Chvasta

Theory in Perspective: What Exists?

Despite the current fascination and dismay associated with technology, it is not new to performance or communication. Aristotle contrasted two kinds of knowledge: *episteme* (the root of our word epistemology) and *techne* (the root of our word technology). **Episteme** describes a *certain, unchangeable knowledge,* like the formulas of geometry. **Techne,** most often translated as "craft" or "art," is the *practical knowledge needed to create or produce things.* Rhetoric, for example, is a *techne,* the practical knowledge needed to compose arguments and make stylistic choices for persuading others. Navigation, in Aristotle's conception, was also a *techne*—all practical knowledge concerning the art of seafaring.

Aristotle's *techne,* however, fell victim to new kinds, methods, and purposes of human knowledge. In the Age the Enlightenment in the eighteenth century, human knowledge was grouped into three categories: the **sciences,** the **mechanical arts,** and the **fine arts.** The sciences took as their project understanding nature—the intricate workings of the natural world and human bodies—through empirical methods of observation. The mechanical arts, now known as Engineering, flowered during the Industrial Revolution, with a special emphasis on *practical solutions for industry and commerce.* American universities that take "A&M" as part of their names are legacies of the human knowledge of agriculture and mechanics.

This division of human knowledge in the Enlightenment drove a wedge between science and mechanics on one side and the fine arts on the other. The products of the mechanical arts are *"necessities" that address human needs.* The products of the fine arts—paintings, sculpture, music—are *"pleasures" that address human conveniences.* In short, "the fine arts are born from 'joy and the feelings that plenty and tranquility produce'—after needs are taken care of" (Maynard 1997, 97).

Lance Gharavi (2004, 359) notes that the Enlightenment's favorite metaphor for the cosmos was the machine. In postmodernism, the machine merges with human bodies in the phrases "building blocks of life," "genetic engineering," "natural mechanisms," and "biological clock." These metaphors "are not merely literary set dressings used to poetically describe our world, but become structural and structuring elements of our thought" (359). Technology, like performance, is constitutive, epistemic, and critical—ways of creating, knowing, and critiquing the world.

In this chapter, the most important theory question, for both technology and performance, is an **ontological** one: **What exists?** (Shields 2003, 21). Technology and performance, like the sciences and fine arts in the Enlightenment, supposedly make different and opposite claims to "what is." Jon McKenzie (1994, 92) characterizes technology as "absence, inorganicism, inauthenticity, derivativeness, and mediation." Performance, traditionally, is the opposite of each of those: "presence, organicism, authenticity, originality, and immediacy" (92). This chapter questions these traditional binaries to explore the intricate relationships between performance and technologies.

This chapter begins with a caveat about old and new technologies and demonstrates how technologies have always extended, enabled, and created access to performances. Next the chapter examines the concept of "presence" in live performance as elaborated by Peggy Phelan (1993) and Roger Copeland (1990). The chapter then explores the politics of presence in Walter Benjamin's (1936/2007) notion of "aura," Jean Baudrillard's (1983) hyperreality, and Donna Haraway's (1991) cyborg. Each conception of presence—as authentic, as image, and as hybrid of human and machine—has been a rich site for performance theory to question our faith in the liveness of performance and to explore the relationships among reality, bodies, and technologies. Finally, the chapter surveys musical recordings, interactivity, and the mediated illusion of presence in electronic and digital technologies.

The theory questions are big ones: What is technology? How do technologies of performance impact artworks, audiences, aesthetics, and bodies? How is presence "mediated" and emulated through virtual, interactive, and immersive performance environments?

Caveat Emptor: Buyer Beware of Old and New

By the time this book goes to press, anything written here about technology runs the risk of being obsolete, commonsensical, and quaint. Today's YouTube monster hit will be a vague memory, if not gone, in six months. Early work in hypertext—brandnew in 1995—now is both commonsensical and ordinary as we click through Web-based documents on Wikipedia. While the World Wide Web as "the information superhighway" was de rigueur nomenclature in 1995, today the phrase seems downright quaint. How can one provide examples of the intersection of performance and technology that will continue to be revelatory, interesting, and timely?

Media theorists in Mass Communication have been theorizing "new" media—newspapers, magazines, photography, radio, television, film—since early in the twentieth century. Comparisons with "old" media are omnipresent. Marshall McLuhan (1964, viii) argues that new media turn old media into "art forms": "When writing was new, Plato transformed the old oral dialogue into an art form. When printing was new the Middle Ages became an art form. 'The Elizabethan world view' was a view of the Middle Ages. And the industrial age turned the Renaissance into an art form."

McLuhan's claim seems especially important for today's intersection of performance and technology. "Cyberspace," according to Bonnie Marranca and Gautam Dasguta (2002, 2), "has become a performance space."

Now "characters" have given way to "agents" and "chatterbots," and "audience" yields to "participants," "browsers," "users." The notion of what is "live"—the physical body of the performer, instant feedback, and types of manipulated presence—has been called into question. And, how should we consider the performing body in comparison to the body of a mediated presence, or the no-body of a virtual performer, with regard to the condition of "action," theatre's traditional *modus operandi?* What are the differences between digital reality and theatrical reality, the varying conditions of the real, the performative, the virtual; representation and reproduction? And what of the varieties of time, real and not as real?

This chapter finds itself in the thick of theories that attempt to offer tentative answers to all these questions, despite McLuhan's claim that all histories of technologies are "views from the rearview mirror." We can only theorize backward, not forward, in time. Anticipating new forms, uses, communities, aesthetics, and impacts is difficult. In 2000, who knew that MySpace would be such a powerful site for identity, community, interaction, and performance? In 2010, will MySpace also be obsolete, commonsensical, and quaint?

What Is Technology? Extending Human Bodies and Powers

When technology is studied, many theorists tend to focus on instrumentality (technology's uses as tools or weapons) and improvement (better, faster, stronger, more efficient means) as well as sites of applications (science, industry, commerce, and the military). *Encyclopedia Britannica* defines technology as "the application of scientific knowledge to the practical aims of human life or, as it is sometimes phrased, to the change and manipulation of the human environment." In this definition, technology seems light-years away from *techne,* craft, art, aesthetics, and performance. It wasn't always this way.

Lewis Mumford, in *Art and Technics* (1952), uses the idea of *techne* as both arts and crafts to argue that it is not tools or their uses that make humankind unique in the animal kingdom, but language, art, and play. Indeed, the emphasis on tools and weaponry is decidedly phallic. In *The City in History* (1961), he writes of containers (pots, vessels, jars, bins, granaries, and houses, as well as collective containers

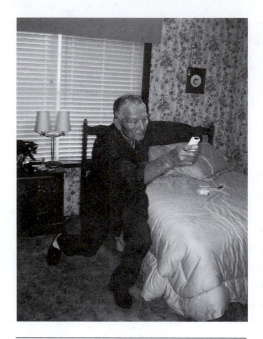

SOURCE: Photo by Michael T. Gilbert.

such as irrigation ditches and water storage) as particularly feminine technologies that "hold and enclose." These gendered images of technology always implicate human bodies. Jonathan Sterne (2006, 95) reminds us, "Techne is embodied knowledge . . . [and] requires us to rethink the relationships we posit between bodies and technologies."

Technologies, as conceived by media theorist Marshall McLuhan (1964), are **extensions of man,** *tools that extend human bodies and human capacities.* The wheel extends the foot; the hammer extends the hand; the telescope extends the eyes. McLuhan coined the terms **media** (the plural noun) and **medium** (the singular noun) to describe *all human inventions and innovations.* He considered **all technologies to be media**, including roads, housing, clothing, and money. McLuhan even considered the electric light to be a communication medium: "gay electronic signs that light up urban streets each evening, in lighted scoreboards in gymnasiums and on playing fields, in traffic signals, and everywhere else that lights convey intelligent meaning to audiences" (Marvin 1988, 158). Today we tend to associate media with communication technologies—print, radio, television, film, video, and the Internet—broadcast across large distances and across time to "mass" audiences.

McLuhan's famous dictum, "The medium is the message," changes communication theory from an emphasis on content and style (information, ideas, words rhetorically shaped) to the medium—the "how"—with which a message is conveyed. Strate writes (2004, 7): "'The medium is the message,' simply put, is the idea that the media or technologies that we use play a leading role in how and what we communicate, how we think, feel, and use our senses, and in our social organization, way of life, and world view." While McLuhan, writing in the early 1960s, is often viewed as a kind of prophetic "guru" of electronic communication, he was a professor of literature and intensely interested in the arts: "Technologies begin to perform the function of art in making us aware of the psychic and social consequences of technology" (McLuhan 1964, viii).

Patrick Maynard (1997, 98) argues that "technologies (including crafts)" are "extenders of our powers to do things . . . most fine arts are, broadly speaking, kinds of technologies: amplifiers of our powers to manifest (and thereby to develop) our conceptions and values." Walter Ong argues that handwriting and print technologies, covered in Chapter Three, extended the power of human memory. Allucquere Rosanne Stone (1995, 12) writes that computers "primarily extended the mind rather than the muscles." In Barbara Becker's (2003) analysis, digital technologies extend human skin and the possibility of touch: "every interface between person and computer is an adaptation of the ability to touch and be touched. . . . the touches of two people [across computer monitors] become a product of their own imagination."

Human speech, writing, print, books, and electronic and digital media are all technologies that extend human bodies and amplify human powers to manifest a society's conceptions and values.

ACT OUT

Google Technology

Google the word "technology" and search for definitions. Note the frequency and usage of certain words (like science, engineering, computers) and their attributes (like improvement, progress, ease, efficiency). What picture emerges around the word "technology" and its uses? Create a three-minute group performance that attempts to capture this portrait of technology.

From Deus ex Machina to Flash Mobs: Extending, Enabling, and Accessing Performance

Live performance has long utilized technologies **to extend and amplify human powers.** A Western history of these technologies might move from the built performance spaces of raised stone platforms and stairs of ancient Greece and Rome to the *deus ex machina*, a pulley system that lowered gods from the sky or allowed characters to flee by flight. The wagon stages of traveling minstrels and performers of the European Middle Ages, handcrafted musical instruments across the world, not to mention the technologies that produce textiles and cosmetics—the costumes and makeup of these performing arts—could all be included as technologies of performance.

Mechanical technologies, central to the assembly line and mass production of the Industrial Age, also found their places on modern performance stages. Petra Kuppers (2004) writes that "in traditional theater, moving metal appears as gears and levers, sustaining a machinery of make-believe, shifting props around, opening trap doors, holding lights to illuminate." Add to that the pulley systems that moved drops and scrims and opened and closed curtains, and the gas-powered (then electrical) lighting that enabled indoor performances. The "darkening" of the audience (Emeljanow 1998) and the lighting of the stage psychically separated audiences from performers for the first time. Baz Kershaw (2003, 603) claims that lighting in 1880 not only "forced the action back behind the proscenium arch" but also was "the first step toward the creation of today's docile audiences." For Kershaw, spectators (with an emphasis on seeing) became audiences (with an emphasis on careful listening); the place of performance changed from the spectatory to the auditorium.

In the Golden Age of Oratory in the United States, William Jennings Bryant, without technologies of amplification, "reportedly made himself audible to an outdoor crowd of 100,000 in 1915" (Edwards 1999, 28). Today, without Bryant's lung power, public speakers make use of many technologies of performance to extend and amplify human powers: the lectern which most public speakers stand behind and rest their notes upon, microphones and lighting, and visual aids rendered through electronic and digital means. Even the arrangement of the space—raised and raked seating to allow for improved sight lines—is a technology that extends human capacities to see.

From mechanical technologies of the Industrial Age to electronic and digital technologies of the twenty-first century, new forms of **communication technologies enable new kinds of live performances**. Digital technologies are central to staging flash mobs or "swarms." This genre, "invented" by Bill Wasik, senior editor of *Harper's Magazine,* involves the sudden yet planned congregation of large numbers of people in public places, such as department stores, fast-food restaurants, and city streets. Called together through digital and wireless technologies, e-mail, text messaging, and cell phones, the mob follows instructions on cards passed out at the performance site, then quickly disperses. Rebecca West (2006) describes how a flash mob congregated in an Irish pub, stood around the jukebox, and chirped like birds for one minute. In Auckland, New Zealand, a mob entered a Burger King restaurant, pointed at the menu, and frowned. They then smiled at the employees and finally erupted into a cheer.

Jane McGonigal (2005, 473) describes her work with supergaming, networking practices that are "both ludic, or game-like and spectacular—that is, intended to

SOURCE: Photograph by Jaclyn Lannon. Copyright © 2007 by Jaclyn Lannon.

generate an audience" through connecting massive numbers of people in real public places in gaming scenarios.

> 24 August 2004, San Francisco—Over four-thousand people, most of whom have never met in real-life, conspire to launch a twelve-week occupation of nearly one-thousand United States payphones, including a dozen phones on San Francisco's Market Street. Their regular, small-group gatherings at the far-flung payphones, which they locate using GPS devices, are part of Halo 2's *I Love Bees,* an alternate reality game with an online player base of nearly half a million and an online spectator base of over two million. (2005, 473)

Supergaming is massively scaled with millions of participants; it is embedded in and superimposed on public environments, and it involves heightened experience through participant performances as players phone other players and random strangers: "Help us save the Earth from alien invasion!" This help, however, is not simply altruistic; *I Love Bees* was also a coordinated, commercial effort by Microsoft to sell video games.

Live Pac-Man games also move on-screen gaming into real landscapes by "superimposing the virtual 3D game world on to city streets and buildings" (Sandhana 2005). GPS positioning systems, wearable computers, headsets, goggles, and Bluetooth and wi-fi technologies enable the virtual realities of Pac-Man, ghosts, and cookies to be performed by people in the "real world." YouTube examples of Pac-Man Live are both abundant and popular online.

Even if we've never participated in a flash mob, *I Love Bees,* or live Pac-Man, communication technologies **extend our access** to more public performances than ever before in history: sporting events; political rituals; dramas of real political events and fabricated dramas of radio, television, and film; musical performances as recordings, film, music videos, and iPod downloads; podcams of class lectures and television shows; not to mention digital and computer technologies that take us into blogs, chat rooms, FaceBook, World of Warcraft, Gaia Online, Second Life, and the Sims Online. Baz Kershaw (2003, 605) maintains that "mediatization is a key process for dispersing performance through culture" and offers these examples:

> The eye of the camera, the ear of the microphone, the body of the keyboard, the extra finger of the mouse, tend to reposition everything as performance for someone else and, crucially, for ourselves. When mediatization is coupled to liberal democracy, and to a late-capitalism that insinuates the market at the heart of the social, performance becomes both ubiquitous and spectacular: politicians perform, shares perform, life-styles perform for each other in the streets as well as on the screens.

Performance has always utilized technologies to extend human powers, to enable performance events, and to extend audience access, participation, and consumption. The question at the center of the relationship between performance and technology is **ontological:** *What is the essence of performance's existence?*

Performance Presence: An Ontology

Think back to a time when your teacher took roll. She called your name and you replied, "Present." When you said "Present," you meant, "I am here, now—in this space, at this time." If you've taken an online test, built into the program are ways to affirm your presence—are you really *there*? And is it really *you*? Your presence—physical, spatial, and temporal—in that classroom is a given. Your presence during an online exam is a hope.

With electronic and digital screens around almost any corner, performance theorist Peggy Phelan sought to define performance outside of the images and actions that take place on screens to claim that **presence** is the *ontology of performance*—the foundation of its very "existence." In *Unmarked* (1993, 146), Phelan writes: "Performance's only life is in the present." When Phelan uses the term "presence," she is referring to both space and time. The "here-ness" and "now-ness"—the presence—of performance are what make performance, as opposed to acting on screens, unique. The two elements that constitute performance as a live event are **immediacy** and **ephemerality**, both of which implicate presence.

Spatially, *immediacy denotes the lack of mediation, nothing in between self and other, self and event, self and action.* Temporally, *immediacy denotes instantaneous reaction to action.* Live performance is immediate: You share the same time and space with performers, and you—as audience—impact the performance itself with your attention and reactions. Producers of Elvis Presley's Las Vegas performances signaled the finality of the show and the end of presence with the now iconic statement: "Elvis has left the building." For Elvis and his audiences, the immediacy of presence in space, in time, and in interaction was really over.

Ephemerality refers to the fleeting nature of performance. Any attempt to capture the immediacy of performance—through electronic or digital documentation—is not the performance itself; therefore, claims Phelan, performance "becomes itself through disappearance" (1993, 146). Once a performance starts, it is already ending. And, it is *irreproducible.* No moment of performance—or, life, for that matter—can be replicated exactly. This precious presence keeps performance outside of the realm of mediation and reproduction by technical means. For Phelan

(1997, 149), "Performance's independence from mass production, technologically, economically, and linguistically, is its greatest strength."

Phelan's claim is borne out by any attempt to *document* performance through technologies. Craig Gingrich-Philbrook (1998, 299) claims, "The [performance of a] story punishes you for recording it by making you look stupid and small to your self later, when you watch the video." Paul Edwards (1999, 82) writes, "Writing can critique, analyze, annotate live performance, but cannot 'preserve' it." The immediacy and ephemerality of the presence of performance is unpreservable and undocumentable.

Six Types of Theatrical Presence

Roger Copeland (1990) discusses six kinds of "presence" to better understand how performance theorists often use the word.

1. **Presence as charisma.** This type is also known as "stage presence." Copeland (1990, 33) describes this presence as "the sort of charisma that enables some performers to grab us by the lapels and command 'look at me, look at me.'" This presence is also evidenced in mechanically reproduced images—on screens and in photographs. These representations also have a "mesmerizing aura," but being in the presence—first row center—of such charisma is heady indeed.

2. **Presence as authenticity.** This type of presence can come in two forms. First is a correspondence between "what the audience sees and what the performer is presumed to experience inwardly" (33). Some performers—John Wayne is often an example of this—seem to reveal an "authentic" self in performance. Second, the performance is authentic as a "certifiably nonfictional situation." When performance artist Chris Burden arranges to have himself shot in the arm with a gun as part of his performance, this is authentic.

3. **Presence as co-presence.** This type "requires nothing more than that performer and spectator share a certain amount of *time* together in the same *space*" (34, emphasis added). This is the simplest conceptualization of presence in performance, just as it is the most commonly cited requirement for a performance to have occurred. How can a performance happen if no one is there to watch the performer onstage?

4. **Presence as reciprocity.** This type of presence involves mutual reactions. "What transpires on stage" depends on "what happens in the audience" (34). The need for stage performers to wait to deliver their next lines while the audience laughs is an example of performer-audience reciprocity. If there is no laughter, there is no need to wait. Roberta Mock (2000, 6) calls this "bidirectional mutability," the potential for live performers and audiences to move or influence each other. In movies, there is no reciprocity, no mutability. Audience laughter often covers up the next lines of the film, making them impossible to hear because there is no reciprocity between performers and audience.

5. **Presence as "nowness."** If performers and audience members share the same space, they are also sharing time. Furthermore, that time spent together is experienced in the present tense. "We are here together, right now." The action and the audience's experience of the action, both on the stage and in the seats, is *live*. With liveness comes *unpredictability*—a quality that draws many performers and audiences together in the first place—and *risk*. Moreover, performance can *never be replicated* precisely; therefore, any performance you see has never been seen before and will never be seen again.

David Saltz (2001, 109) writes, "the value of live theatre, especially in a mediatized age, lies precisely in its variability. Regardless of how rigorously scripts and the rehearsal process constrain performances, each performance within those constraints is a unique event. . . . The thrill of the live is to see a performance event unfold, with all the risk that entails."

6. **Presence as the absence of representation.** If you are watching a performance about Abraham Lincoln, you know that the actor onstage who is bearded with dark hair, and is wearing a black suit and hat, is not Abraham Lincoln. You understand that the actor represents Abraham Lincoln. However, the more you can forget for the time being that the person you are watching is not Abraham Lincoln, the more you will feel present in the scenes of the play.

Copeland (1990) analyzes theatrical presence in order to critique it. He argues that there is nothing we can conceive of in this world that is *not* mediated. Even (and especially) language "mediates" between the experience of "self" and the world; "no experience (no matter how 'live') is entirely unmediated" (42). Furthermore, he accuses those who insist upon the preciousness of presence as trying to maintain an elitist separation of high and low art. Copeland writes, "the idea that the theatre's 'liveness' is—in and of itself—a virtue, a source of automatic, unearned moral superiority to film and television, is sheer bourgeois sentimentality" (42).

The idea of presence—in artworks, in media representations, and in human bodies—was a charged political topic for most of the twentieth century. The works of Walter Benjamin, Jean Baudrillard, and Donna Haraway are theories of technology with tremendous import for contemporary notions of presence in performance.

GO FIGURE

How Are You and the Performers Present?

Choose any live performance you have experienced recently and analyze it according to Copeland's six types of presence. Which kinds of presence are most important to your sense of the success, or failure, of the performance?

Losing the Aura of Presence

Walter Benjamin's famous essay, "The Work of Art in the Age of Mechanical Reproduction" (1936/2007), draws from Marxist political thought and the theatrical world of Bertolt Brecht to ask new questions of art, its production, and its reception by audiences. In an era of "mass production" with the Industrial Age, the political realm of art—like commodification and propaganda through photography and film—displaces aesthetic questions of art in painting—like creativity and genius, eternal value and mystery. Benjamin wonders what happens when photography replaces painting, and film acting replaces stage acting through mechanical reproduction.

Benjamin argues that an art object created through mechanical reproduction loses "its presence in time and space, its unique existence." It also loses its attachment to ritual and the sense of "magic" that often accompanies objects created for sacred purposes in cult worship. An original work of art has an **aura**, in Benjamin's terminology, *an authentic presence attributed to the handwork of human creation and displayed as unique.* As viewers, standing before the *Mona Lisa* in the Louvre, for example, we respond to this "aura" with awe and reverence.

Instead of an interior essence, however, Benjamin argues that this aura is really about history, ownership, and power to control, display, and authenticate originals. Mechanical reproduction diminishes the "aura" of an original. The technologies of photography can never create an "original" but rather create many copies from a negative. Nor is a film an "original" art object; it is created specifically to be reproduced and distributed to be experienced. Original works of art are carefully exhibited, controlled, and policed in museums or churches, and their technological reproduction is about historical and political conditions of distribution.

Benjamin's observations on the theatre transformed by film technologies are important ones for performance: as performers, co-present in time and space, with audiences. Benjamin writes,

> For the first time—and this is the effect of the film—man has to operate with his whole living person, yet forgoing its aura. For aura is tied to his presence; there can be no replica of it. The aura which, on the stage, emanates from MacBeth, cannot be separated for the spectators from that of the actor. However, the singularity of the shot in the studio is that the camera is substituted for the public. Consequently, the aura that envelops the actor vanishes, and with it the aura of the figure he portrays. (1240)

Philip Auslander (1999) claims that live performance, the "auratic" from Benjamin's "aura," and its ontological claims to authenticity and irreproducibility, stands in the same relation to mediated performance as painting did for photography in Benjamin's time. Auslander claims that *mediated* performance is a radical cultural shift.

> It makes little sense to ask which of the many identical productions of *Tamana* or Disney's *Beauty and the Beast* is the "authentic" one. It does not even make sense to ask which of the many iterations of that *Beauty and the Beast*—as animated film, video cassette, CD, book, or theatrical performance—is the "authentic" iteration. This situation represents the historical triumph of mechanical (and electronic) reproduction (what I am calling mediatization)

that Benjamin implies: aura, authenticity, and cult value have been definitively routed, even in live performance, the site that once seemed the last refuge of the auratic. (1999, 50–51)

Auslander is especially interested in the "incursion" of technological media in live performance. Musical concerts and sporting events, with huge screens that simultaneously *televise* the performance and *replay* the moments in sports, are better approached as the continuing history of mediated cultural production. The present moment holds television as the medium with "much greater cultural presence, prestige, and power than other forms" (1999, 62). Auslander argues that today all performance, especially live performance, aspires to include and emulate television—its production techniques and its seeming immediacy of time and intimacy in space.

Simulacra: There Is No Original

Jean Baudrillard, a contemporary French social theorist, extends Benjamin's early observations on art to all phases of contemporary life. Writing of mediation and technologies of communication, Baudrillard argues that *there is no longer any original,* there are only **simulations**—copies or representations—of originals. Baudrillard uses the example of the map to illustrate his point. If we are asked to envision Italy, we cannot do this in any kind of accurate way. If we've visited there or seen filmic representations—or even if we're natives—we may envision parts of the places we've seen. Those memories, however, are not "Italy." The best sense we have of the whole country is a map of it. To us, that bootlike figure *is* Italy. Media has affected—and continues to affect—our perception of the world around us.

Baudrillard (1983, 11–12) traces four successive phases of the image through history:

—it is the reflection of a basic reality

—it masks and perverts a basic reality

—it masks the *absence* of a basic reality

—it bears no relation to any reality whatever: it is its own pure simulacrum.

In the first case, the image is a *good* appearance—the representation is of the order of sacrament. In the second, it is an *evil* appearance—of the order of malefice. In the third, it *plays at being* an appearance—it is of the order of sorcery. In the fourth, it is no longer in the order of appearance at all, but of simulation.

Disneyland is Baudrillard's "perfect model" of all four levels of the image succession. If we think of Disneyland's Main Street, for example, this image is a *reflection* of nineteenth-century, small-town America with lovely storefronts, wide sidewalks, and colorful shop windows. At the same time, Main Street *masks and perverts* nineteenth-century realities of poor or nonexistent sewage systems, trash disposal, and water collection and runoff facilities. These two phases of the image participate in a true/false relationship between images and reality. Baudrillard claims the historical period, in which we debated truth in images, is over.

We are now in a historical period of hyperreality, the simulation. Hyperreality moves beyond true/false to claim that there is no reality to reference—let alone be true or false. Main Street *masks the absence* of a basic reality: Main Street, as represented at Disneyland, never existed; there is no original. And finally, Main Street is a simulacrum, an original with no reference in reality other than itself. Main Street only refers to and makes sense in relation to other Disneyland entertainments: Frontier Land, Future World, Pirates of the Caribbean.

In hyperreality, Disneyland serves to "secure" our faith in reality when we leave the park and drive into Anaheim. Baudrillard (1983, 25) writes, "Disneyland is presented as imaginary in order to make us believe that the rest is real, when in fact all of Los Angeles and the America surrounding it are no longer real, but of the order of the hyperreal and of simulation."

Baudrillard's claims about Disneyland apply to all media and its representations of "reality." Mark Poster (1988, 7) summarizes Baudrillard's critical stance to contemporary media representations as decidedly different from Benjamin's Marxist politics:

[T]he media generate a world of simulations which is immune to rationalist critique, whether Marxist or liberal. The media present an excess of information and they do so in a manner that precludes response by the recipient. This simulated reality has no referent, no ground, no source. It operates outside the logic of representation. But the masses have found a way of subverting it: the strategy of silence or passivity. Baudrillard thinks that by absorbing the simulations of the media, by failing to respond, the masses undermine the code.

Baudrillard's contentions of the hyperreal have been taken up by performance and cultural critics to compare him to Kenneth Burke (Carmichael 1991) and to critique mediated accounts to the 1991 Gulf War in film and onstage (Callens 2000; Colleran 2003; Jowett 1993; Klien 2005). Baudrillard's hyperreal is a valuable lens for looking at computer-generated virtual realities (Gunkel 2000; Jordan 2003; Rufo 2003).

READ MORE ABOUT IT

Does Virtual Reality Need a Sheriff?

Alan Sipress (2007, A01) writes of contemporary legal dilemmas in Second Life and World of Warcraft, when "reality" and the virtual collide in online fantasy. How can someone break the law in a "simulated reality that has no referent, no ground, no source"?

(Continued)

(Continued)

Earlier this year, one animated character in Second Life, a popular online fantasy world, allegedly raped another character.

Some Internet bloggers dismissed the simulated attack as nothing more than digital fiction. But police in Belgium, according to newspapers there, opened an investigation into whether a crime had been committed. No one has yet been charged.

Then last month, authorities in Germany announced that they were looking into a separate incident involving virtual abuse in Second Life after receiving pictures of an animated child character engaging in simulated sex with an animated adult figure. Though both characters were created by adults, the activity could run afoul of German laws against child pornography, prosecutors said.

As recent advances in Internet technology have spurred millions of users to build and explore new digital worlds, the creations have imported not only their users' dreams but also their vices. These alternative realms are testing the long-held notions of what is criminal and whether law enforcement should patrol the digital frontier.

"People have an interest in their property and the integrity of their person. But in virtual reality, these interests are not tangible but built from intangible data and software," said Greg Lastowka, a professor at the Rutgers School of Law at Camden in New Jersey.

Some virtual activities clearly violate the law, like trafficking in stolen credit card numbers, he said. Others, like virtual muggings and sex crimes, are harder to define, though they may cause real-life anguish for users.

Simulated violence and thievery have long been a part of virtual reality, especially in the computer games that pioneered online digital role-playing. At times, however, this conduct has crossed the lines of what even seasoned game players consider acceptable.

In World of Warcraft, the most popular online game, with an estimated 8 million participants worldwide, some regions of this fantasy domain have grown so lawless that players said they fear to brave them alone. Gangs of animated characters have repeatedly preyed upon lone travelers, killing them and making off with their virtual belongings.

Two years ago, Japanese authorities arrested a man for carrying out a series of virtual muggings in another popular game, Lineage II, by using software to beat up and rob characters in the game and then sell the virtual loot for real money.

Julian Dibbell, a prominent commentator on digital culture, chronicled the first known case of sexual assault in cyberspace in 1993, when virtual reality was still in its infancy. A participant in LambdaMOO, a community of users who congregated in a virtual California house, had used a computer program called a "voodoo doll" to force another player's character to act out being raped. Though this virtual world was rudimentary and the assault simulated, Dibbell recounted that the trauma was jarringly real. The woman whose character was attacked later wept—"post-traumatic tears were streaming down her face"—as she vented her outrage and demand for revenge in an online posting, he wrote.

Since then, advances in high-speed Internet, user interfaces and graphic design have rendered virtual reality more real, allowing users to endow their characters with greater humanity and identify ever more closely with their creations.

Nowhere is this truer than in Second Life, where more than 6 million people have registered to create characters called avatars, cartoon human figures that respond to keyboard commands and socialize with others' characters. The breadth of creativity and interaction in Second Life is greater than on nearly any other virtual-reality Web site because there is no game or other objective; it is just an open-ended, lifelike digital environment.

Moreover, Linden Labs, which operates Second Life, has given users the software tools to design their characters and online setting as they see fit; some avatars look like their real-life alter egos, while others are fantastical creations.

This virtual frontier has attracted a stunning array of immigrants. Former senator John Edwards of North Carolina, a candidate for the Democratic presidential nomination, has opened a virtual campaign headquarters. Reuters and other news agencies have set up virtual bureaus. IBM has developed office space for employee avatars. On May 22, Maldives became the first country to open an embassy in Second Life, with Sweden following this week.

Second Life is intended only for adults, and about 15 percent of the properties on the site—in essence, space on computer servers that appear as parcels of land—have been voluntarily flagged by their residents as having mature material. Though some is relatively innocent, in some locations avatars act out drug use, child abuse, rape and various forms of sadomasochism.

"This is the double-edged sword of the wonderful creativity in Second Life," Dibbell said in an interview.

One user found herself the unwilling neighbor of an especially sordid underage sex club. "Tons of men would drop in looking for sex with little girls and boys. I abhorred the club," wrote the user on a Second Life blog under the avatar name Anna Valeeva. She even tried to evict the club by buying their land, she wrote.

The question of what is criminal in virtual reality is complicated by disagreements among countries over what is legal even in real life. For example, virtual renderings of child abuse are not a crime in the United States but are considered illegal pornography in some European countries, including Germany.

After German authorities began their investigation, Linden Labs issued a statement on its official blog condemning the virtual depictions of child pornography. Linden Labs said it was cooperating with law enforcement and had banned two participants in the incident, a 54-year-old man and a 27-year-old woman, from Second Life.

Some Second Life users objected on the blog that Linden Labs had gone too far.

"Excuse me. You banned two residents, both mature, who did a little role-playing? No children, I repeat no children, were harmed or even involved in that act," protested another user on the Second Life blog. "Since when is fantasy against the fricking law?"

Philip Rosedale, the founder and chief executive of Linden Labs, said in an interview that Second Life activities should be governed by real-life laws for the time being. He recounted, for example, that his company has called in the FBI

(Continued)

(Continued)

several times, most recently this spring to ensure that Second Life's virtual casinos complied with U.S. law. Federal investigators created their own avatars and toured the site, he said.

In coming months, his company plans to disperse tens of thousands of computer servers from California and Texas to countries around the world in order to improve the site's performance. Also, he said, this will make activities on those servers subject to laws of the host countries.

Rosedale said he hopes participants in Second Life eventually develop their own virtual legal code and justice system.

"In the ideal case, the people who are in Second Life should think of themselves as citizens of this new place and not citizens of their countries," he said.

SOURCE: "Does Virtual Reality Need a Sheriff?" by Alan Sipress © 2007, The Washington Post Writers Group. Reprinted with Permission.

GO FIGURE

Since When Is Fantasy Against the Fricking Law of Relationships?

Quite a few online sources debate cyber-affairs with claims about the "truth" of cyber-relationships, from cyber-flirting to cyber-betrayal. If you discover your partner is engaging in an intimate, online relationship, where do you draw the line between the virtual and "reality"?

Cyborg Bodies: Human and Machine

While Benjamin centered his critique of presence on the notion of the "aura" of an original work of art and Baudrillard contends there are no longer any originals in contemporary mediated culture, postmodern feminist theorist Donna Haraway (1991) takes the cyborg as her central image. From science fiction as well as science fact, the cyborg is "a hybrid of machine and organism" and exists on the border wars of biology, technology, communication, and culture.

While science fiction has made the robot a central trope, like Philip K. Dick's *Do Androids Dream of Electric Sheep?* (the basis for the film *Blade Runner*), science fact has already turned many of us into cyborgs, blendings of machine and human, with contact lenses, hearing aids, birth control implants, breast implants, hip and knee replacements, pacemakers, wheelchairs, and dental crowns and caps, to name a few examples.

Cyborgs force us to question the division of products and uses mentioned in this chapter's Theory in Perspective: Are these "improvements" on human bodies necessities or pleasures? In an interview in *Wired* (Kunrzu 1997), Haraway goes beyond implantations.

"Think about the technology of sports footwear," [Haraway] says. "Before the Civil War, right and left feet weren't even differentiated in shoe manufacture.

Now we have a shoe for every activity." Winning the Olympics in the cyborg era isn't just about running fast. It's about "the interaction of medicine, diet, training practices, clothing and equipment manufacture, visualization and timekeeping."

In "The Cyborg Manifesto," Haraway outlines three ways the cyborg stands as the reigning image of postmodern identity and politics. First, the cyborg confuses the dividing lines between humans and animals, between culture and nature. What makes us unique and supreme in the animal kingdom? Our sense of humanness, when faced with cyborgs, exposes our own hubris in our claims to superiority. Second, the cyborg refuses our stories of origins: The cyborg is not born of nature, human bodies, family, fathers and mothers, or Gardens of Eden. The cyborg's origin is in capitalism, the state, the military, communication technologies, and technological sciences. Nor does the cyborg reproduce through or participate in an economy of biology, nature, gender, or race.

Third, the cyborg embodies contradictions: between mind and body; between genders and across races, ethnicities, and classes; between animal and machine, idealism and materialism, symbols and science; between possible destruction of the planet and pleasure in technology with new meanings. Haraway (1991, 154) writes, "A cyborg world might be about lived social and bodily realities in which people are not afraid of their joint kinship with animals and machines, not afraid of permanently partial identities and contradictory standpoints."

In "The Work of Art in the Age of Biocybernetic Reproduction," W. J. Thomas Mitchell (2003, 485) takes up Haraway's cyborg to argue that the "relation of the 'bios' and the 'cyber' is the re-writing of the traditional dialectics between nature and culture, human beings and tools, artifacts, machines and media—what we used to call the whole 'man-made world.'" Mitchell continues with examples:

> [A]nyone who has read Donna Haraway on cyborgs, or watched science fiction movies over the last twenty years cannot fail to be struck by the pervasiveness of this theme. Films such as *Blade Runner, Alien, The Matrix, Videodrome, The Fly, The Sixth Day, AI,* and *Jurassic Park* have made clear the host of fantasies and phobias clustering around biocybernetics: the spectre of the 'living machine,' the re-animation of dead matter and extinct organisms, the destabilizing of species identity and difference, the proliferation of prosthetic organs and perceptual apparatuses, and the infinite malleability of the human mind and body have become commonplaces of popular culture. (485–86)

From Benjamin's degradation of the "aura" of an original artwork, Mitchell claims that new, digital copies are improved, "scrubbed" versions of originals: Copies are no longer inferior but are *superior to originals.*

Cloning, on the science front, produces copies that are better than the original: more resistant to diseases and stripped of genetic flaws. Years of dirt on original paintings and frescoes are cleaned; the improved copy lets the viewer see what the "original" might have looked like. Computer software improves photographs through airbrushing and other digital manipulations.

Sound recordings are "remastered" and digitally enhanced. In an interview, Paul McCartney (2006) comments on the new *Love* album and remastering of Beatles' 1960s studio tapes. He says of the situation created by these technologies, "I would liken it to great people like Churchill and great writers—Tolstoy. Their original papers are in museums. They're only getting browner and more crinkly. But the Beatles stuff is getting shinier, and newer, and cleaner. It's like magic." From science to art, Mitchell (2003) claims that the watchword for the modern machine age was "things fall apart"; today's postmodern watchword is "things come alive."

MAKE A LIST

New and Improved?

Cyborg bodies, hyperreality and simulations, copies and originals are at the heart of many contemporary films—their characters, plots, conflicts, and politics. Make a list of films you've seen that engage technology as their subjects. How might the theories of Benjamin, Baudrillard, and Haraway be valuable for understanding the implicit and explicit political claims about technology in these films?

Performing Cyborgs

Digital and performance artists are participating in this revolution of human and machine: creating images of reproduction within biocybernetics, participating in new techniques and technologies to push at limits of artistic production and reproduction, and exploring both utopias and dystopias of biocybernetics. Charles R. Garoian and Yvonne M. Gaudelius (2001, 337) write, "Performance art enables us to use the cyborg metaphor to create personal narratives of identity as both a strategy of resistance and as a means through which to construct new ideas, images, and myths about ourselves living in a technological world."

Hollywood film (Cornea 2003; Hantke 2003, 2004/2005; Jordan 1999; Lavery 2001) and Japanese anime (Bolton 2002) are ripe for analysis of cyborg creations. Composer Christian Bok (2005) writes that the *Cyborg Opera* is "a kind of spoken techno that emulates the mechanical rhythms and cacophonous melodies heard in the pulse of our machines" (80).

The cyborg of disabled bodies is an important performance site for exploring difference, embodiment, prosthetic technologies, and their images (Kuppers 2001; Parker-Starbuck 2003; Sobchack 1995a). Petra Kuppers (2001) writes of physical difference represented in the media:

One form of cyborg, of metaphorised physical difference, can be found in the popular images of some disabled people. The contemporary cyborgs here include Christopher Reeve, who went from fictional "enhanced being" to a star persona in a high tech wheelchair, and the number of bionically enhanced people who parade on television channels, and who demonstrate how they can stand again due to implants and electronic impulses. Both Reeve and the men and women hoping for small wonders are part of a disability discourse of tragedy and medical redemption.

Live, multimedia works also make use of Haraway's cyborg. The cyborg is a powerful character in Lance Gharavi's digital and live performance work, staged at the University of Arizona in 2002 (2004). *IM/UR* is "a broken love story between a cyborg and a zombie. . . . They have become liminal creatures: UR is a cyborg, half machine, half man; IM is a zombie, both living and dead" (349–50). Meiling Cheng (2001) explores the multimedia artistry of the *osseus labyrint's* performance THEM, "a new species of performance that lures the audience to a specific (open) site to observe the bio-activities of rare creatures."

"El Mexterminator," created by Guillermo Gómez-Peña and Roberto Sifuentes with Sara Shelton Mann, is an "ethno-cyborg," combining stereotypically harmful portrayals of Hispanics and Latinos with playful claims to difference and identity (Kawash 1999). Their "cybervato" seeks

> to "politicize" the debate; to "brownify" virtual space; to "spanglishize the Net" to "infect" the lingua franca; to exchange a different sort of information— mythical, poetical, political, performative, imagistic; and on top of that to find grassroots applications to new technologies and hopefully to do all this with humor and intelligence. The ultimate goals are perhaps to help the Latino youth exchange their guns for computers and video cameras, and to link the community centers through the Net. (Gómez-Peña 1996, 179)

Gómez-Peña (2001, 8) has written extensively about his performance work, especially in the late 1990s, as "the virtual 'gold rush.'" Artists and performers "were trying to figure out ways to reinvent themselves and cross over with dignity into other realms: film, TV, publicity, computer design, digital arts, the new global art world."

The work of the Critical Art Ensemble (CAE 2000) is at the forefront of performance work that implicates and questions technology. As "bioartists" (Broadhurst 2005; Schneider 2000), they call their works "recombinant theatre" to recombine participation, process, pedagogy, and the experimental across everyday life, theatre, science, and analog and digital practices. Their works, *Flesh Machine, Intelligent Sperm Online,* the *Society for Reproductive Anachronisms, The Cult of the New Eve,* focus on human reproduction, genetic engineering, and the release of new organisms in the environment. *Intelligent Sperm Online* was produced "to call attention to sperm and egg donor recruitment on university campuses for use in neo-eugenic practices" (Critical Art Ensemble 2000, 159). Schneider (2000, 130) summarizes CAE's work: "They are very much manifesto-style avantgarde artists of technology. Their biggest effort is pitched toward making certain that technological development is shaped, designed, and deployed alternatively."

ACT OUT

Cyborgs R Us

Collect representations of yourself—in photographs, video, audio—stored in boxes, on videocassettes, and on your computer and phone. Add to this collection by googling your name and compiling anything interesting that pops up—despite how far it is from "you." If your name is a common one (first, middle, or last), you'll get thousands of hits, including images of people with your name. If your name is uncommon, try different search terms: your birthplace, birthdate, hobbies, and favorite things.

Now organize these collections into a performance using the medium of your choice: a live multimedia performance, a video/digital production, a PowerPoint slide show, a Web site, digital art or poetry, a sampled song. For your production concept, think about how you might combine human and machine, natural and artificial, self and its representations, presence and absence, performance and technology to create a cyborg performance of yourself.

Musical Performance:
Is it Live or Is it Memorex?

Philip Auslander (2002) argues that it was radio that first introduced the ontological crisis in liveness. When listeners first heard music on Edison's cylinder, they knew they were hearing a performance "preserved" by this brand-new technology. The recording was a complement—never a replacement—for live performance. Only with the advent of radio—broadcast live to audiences distant in space—was it necessary to rethink live and mediated as opposites, not complements.

Live performance by musicians is tremendously complicated by technology. Mark Poster (1990, 9) brings Baudrillard's observations into the music studio claiming that contemporary production practices are simulations: "no longer is there an original performance, only separate performances of tracks: The performance that the consumer hears when the recording is played is not a copy of an original but is a simulacrum, a copy that has no original . . . rock performances exist *only in their reproduction*."

Many people consider listening to recorded music an inferior aesthetic experience to "being there" to hear musicians play live. Theodore Gracyk (1997) argues with this claim. He unpacks four typical claims people make about live musical performance.

1. **Music must be performed live to be experienced**. A musical score, in this contention, "doesn't exist until it is performed." A recording, then, is not a performance but a "reproduction" brought about by technological means—sound recording and editing, cutting and pasting the "best" takes in the studio. Live concert records are also "representations" of a performance—again manipulated by technological means.

SOURCE: Library of Congress, Prints & Photographs Division, New York World-Telegram and Sun Newspaper Photograph Collection [reproduction number LC-USZ6-2068].

Instead of arguing about whether this is a performance, a representation of a performance, or a reproduction of a performance, Gracyk argues that *recordings offer access.* Most of us may never see live performances of our favorite musicians, but we can access their works through recordings. Nor is the experience of listening necessarily inferior to "being there." Indeed, listening can be a superior experience, for it enables many repeated listenings and careful attention to precise parts of the work that interest the listener.

2. **Recordings are a debased acquaintance with musical works.** Here Gracyk argues not against attending musical performances, but against the argument that listeners are "aesthetically" poorer for their loss of being witness to the virtuoso skills of the performer. Indeed, many musical performances now *depend on* the added virtuosity of sound technicians and engineers in the studios. Replicating these technical skills is impossible in live performances. Producer George Martin's innovations with the Beatles on *Revolver* is a case in point. Today's sampled songs, mixed and multitracked in the studio, are performed live against this backdrop of recorded music.

Recordings, then, are not a "debased acquaintance" with musical works but a compensation enabling a *different kind of acquaintance.* Listening to recordings enables "most people to hear a wider range of music, performed with greater skill, than they could through live performance alone." Gracyk gives some examples:

Enrico Caruso and Arturo Toscanini died before I was born, and Glenn Gould and The Beatles both retired from the stage when I was a child. I never got the chance to see Miles Davis, Charles Mingus, or Thelonious Monk in live performance, and all three died about the time I became interested in jazz. Yet I listen to their recordings, as can generations of listeners to come. Not only can we compare many interpretations of the same works made over the course of many years, but for the first time audiences can evaluate the complete scope of the career of major performers. It seems that records can both enhance and diminish our access to virtuosity in its several species. (146)

3. **With recordings, we lose the connection between sounds and gestures made by musicians.** Keyboard glissando, for example, is part of the expressivity of the performer's interpretation of the work. How do we evaluate the effectiveness of this expressivity without being there to see these gestures happen? Gracyk argues that film, television, and even music videos can provide this information to the audience member. Perhaps even better information is available through close-ups of these gestures unavailable at live performances.

4. **With records, we lose live music's "social dimension."** If live performance can create the potential for extraordinary experience and community, then recordings, the argument goes, reduce listeners "to voyeurs." Gracyk counters that there are many places of sociality created around musical recordings: "discos, Jamaican 'sound system' trucks, bars and pubs and pool halls with jukeboxes, and the British rave scene have created diverse public sites for recorded music" (147).

Gracyk wonders if this "social dimension" is really about aura and charisma—of the performer in a cult of celebrity, and of "fandom" as social bonding—rather than an aesthetic experience produced by the "co-presence" of performer and audience. Aura and charisma of the musical performer take us full circle back to presence. Debates about musical recordings and live music continue. Moving to computer-generated art, the debates center not on the aesthetics of listening for an audience member but on the creation of "interactivity" between audiences and computer screens.

Interactivity: From "Poke and See," Cyberpoetry, to Computer Art Environments

Chapter Two explored audiences as inactive, active, interactive, and proactive. Interactivity in live performance can involve high levels of improvisation and reciprocity as the audience provides content for the performances (as in Playback Theatre) or become performers themselves (as in the works of Boal). Computer screens most often invite an audience of one to engage in new kinds of interactivity with and within computer-created art. David Saltz (1997) characterizes audiences as "interactors" and describes this interactivity on a continuum.

The first level of interaction between an interactor and a computer screen is minimal: clicking on a menu item on a Web site or ATM machine. Choosing an option calls up a programmed text. "The only choice the interactor has is *which* of these presentations to view *when*" (Saltz 1997, 120). Stone (1995) calls this "poke and see what happens" technology.

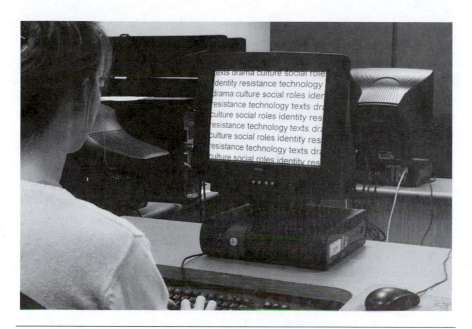

SOURCE: Photograph by Jaclyn Lannon. Copyright © 2007 by Jaclyn Lannon.

Next "on the interactive ladder" is "hypertext," followed by "hypermedia." Instead of a menu of set options, hypertext contains multiple links to more content. Most wikipedia entries, for example, are paragraphs of text with underscored "hot" words and phrases that take the interactor to more text. Hyper*media* is not limited to text, but calls up images, video, and sound files.

At this part of the continuum, the interactor chooses her own path through the content organized coherently, but not linearly with a definitive beginning, middle, and end. "Hypermedia audiences," Saltz (1997, 120) maintains, "function as explorers. They are like tourists, rushing through the areas that do not interest them, lingering when they find something that strikes their fancy. . . . All the while, the interactors keep their eyes on the road. Their object of attention is the *work*, not *themselves in the work*."

Brian Lennon (2000) explores interactors in a variety of electronic and digital poems that have been labeled cyberpoetry, hyperpoetry, infopoetry (InfoLiPo), virtual poetry, digital videopoetry, computer *Lettrisme*, experimental electronic typography, and intersign poetry. Lennon maintains (2000, 81),

It is up to the viewer to travel toward and away from and around, under, and over each word/object and subconstellation, and toward and away from and around, under, and over the entire visual-textual constellation. "Reading" hypertext poetry can take several forms, including, 1) reading the words in the conventional sense. 2) Examining the words as representations of three-dimensional objects—an operation that may involve rotating them, traveling "above," "below," "behind," "past," or even "through" them—literally, "subversion." 3) Reflecting on the nature of this simulated interaction with the simulated materiality of the words (reading one's reading). 4) Reflecting on the simulation interface itself—reading with the virtual-reality software as a work of writing or code.

Fenske (2004, 2006) explores hypertext movement as a strategy for criticism and performative writing. Technology users make meaning, discoveries, and clarity along the way through hypertext travels. Fenske (2006, 152) writes: "Things move fast and slow, and those differential speeds produce different possibilities of epiphany. The pull to surf or to move is the flow to follow, rather than a force to resist."

The third level of interaction puts audiences *in the work* by creating digital environments—whether on the screen or in art installations that utilize virtual reality software. Saltz (1997, 123) makes these distinctions between *artworks* and *performance environments*. "In nearly all Western performing art forms, and many non-Western ones, performers perform works. Actors perform plays; musicians perform music; dancers perform dances; Shamans perform rituals. The work (play, musical composition, dance, ritual) is a direct object. It is what the performer *does*."

Computer artists, however, do not create "works" but "create interactive performance *environments*. Plays, musical compositions and dances define a series of actions to be performed; interactive performance environments provide contexts within which actions are performed" (123). Using computer-art examples like walking through a virtual sculpture garden and playing music with a computer, Saltz maintains that for interactivity to be a performance, the interaction itself becomes an aesthetic object—perceived, created, enjoyed, in and for themselves *as interactions:* "You become a live performer in the work" (122).

Interactivity assumes the liveness of an audience member who becomes a performer. Timothy Binkley (1997, 114) claims that "the most dramatic new player on the cultural stage is the interactive experience found in gallery installations and home computers as well as the Internet. Interactivity epitomizes the unique contribution computers are making to our culture."

These mediated, interactive performance environments will be especially important in mediated interactions, discussed in the next section, that strive for presence *despite* the mediation.

Reach Out and Perform Someone: Five Kinds of Mediated Presence

While performance may seem to be moving away from co-presence as its essence, software designers and developers are striving, more than ever, to create media that **enhance** the perception of presence. Matthew Lombard and Theresa Ditton (1997) list a few of these technologies: "Virtual reality. Simulation rides. Home theater. 3-D IMAX films. State-of-the-art video conferencing. Computers that 'talk.'" Although these media strive to create experience that "seems truly 'natural,' 'immediate,' 'direct,' and 'real,'" what they really do is seem to make the medium itself (the movie or TV screen, the phone, the computer monitor, the joystick) disappear. We are encouraged to ignore or overlook the fact that we are *not* interacting face-to-face with other humans.

Lombard and Ditton (1997) characterize five kinds of presence we experience in mediated interactions that are especially intriguing for performance theory. Each of these notions of presence is a perceptual illusion, a willful "forgetting," that technology is a medium in the experience. Each kind of presence has been explored by performance theorists for its ability to enrich our understanding of the relationship between performance and technology.

Presence as Social Richness

This conceptualization suggests that we experience presence when "a medium is perceived as sociable, warm, sensitive, personal or intimate when it is used to interact with other people" (Lombard and Ditton 1997). The most socially rich media are those that are conducive to **intimacy** and **immediacy**—like the telephone. E-mail and snail mail, while they can certainly be *intimate*, are usually not *immediate*, as we anxiously await a response. Stone (1995, 110–11) writes of early research in computer bulletin board postings, created online to be read later: "Their participants saw them as conversations, nonetheless, as social acts. They spoke of them as real-time interchanges that occurred in physical spaces. When asked how sitting alone at a terminal was a social act, they explained that they saw the terminal as a window into a social space."

Kurt Lindemann (2005, 354) argues that "blogs," or online diaries, utilize the computer screen as a new space for the narration of a "desired self." Lindemann makes the compelling case that the presence experienced by computer users may have *more* force than the live bodies onstage and in the seats. When we read an online journal, we often yearn for the body of the author. In a seemingly paradoxical way, the absence of the fleshed body keeps the author's body in the forefront of our minds. The author, similarly, works to make his presence felt through his writing because he is acutely aware of the presence of an audience.

Because most online journals provide readers—the audiences—the opportunity to leave comments, "audiences become a part of the performance in ways similar to audiences in live performance" (359). The feedback they provide can occur almost instantly, and the author has the opportunity to adjust his performance accordingly. Lindemann argues that extended interaction between authors and readers creates the opportunity for community-building. This is an opportunity not easily nor often afforded to live performers and their audiences.

Identities created online, in chat rooms, and in fantasy games are immensely rich spaces for sociality—as immediacy and as intimacy—and as play with performed characters, plots, and conflicts. These identities are decidedly slippery, easily morphing the "stable" categories of gender, age, race, sexuality, and even species and humanness. The connections to postmodern identity constitution are obvious: "We who populate cyberspace deliberately experiment with fracturing traditional notions of identity by living as multiple simultaneous personae in different virtual neighborhoods" (Rheingold 1993, 61).

SOURCE: Image by Drew Smith. Courtesy of Drew Smith.

These virtual identities and communities are not utopias, but instead call into question our faith in intimacy and immediacy as "social virtues." Stone (1995) relates the community's sense of violation when Sanford Lewin created an entirely fictive individual on a CompuServe chat room in 1982 to explore women's ways of communicating with each other. "Julie" became an immensely popular and coveted friend and confidant in the community. When Lewin exposed the fraud, everyone—media theorists, too—had to rethink former assumptions of the term "person," the nature of "identity," and sociality in cyberspace. An account of a rape in cyberspace's LambdaMOO is not only frighteningly real; it also makes us rethink violence in terms of the "social richness" of intimacy and immediacy.

> They say he raped them that night. They say he did it with a cunning little doll, fashioned in their image and imbued with the power to make them do whatever he desired. They say that by manipulating the doll he forced them to have sex with him, and with each other, and to do horrible, brutal things to their own bodies. And though I wasn't there that night, I think I can assure you that what they say is true, because it all happened right in the living room—right there amid the well-stocked bookcases and the sofas and the fireplace—of a house I came for a time to think of as my second home. (Dibbell 1998, 1)

"Socially rich media" are conducive to intimacy and immediacy as we are encouraged to ignore the medium standing between us and others. This same richness is also conducive to violence, intimidation, and abuse—also forms of intimacy and immediacy.

Presence as Transportation

When a medium seems to create a new world, transportation happens in one of three ways: "you are there," "it is here," or "we are together." Storytelling is certainly a medium of communication that, at its best, transports. Radio shows of the 1940s, like "The Shadow," "The Lone Ranger," and "Little Orphan Annie," regularly transported listeners to aurally created worlds of suspense and danger. Film or television enables us to walk with dinosaurs and to watch a historical battle take place around us in a "you are there" experience. "It is here" transports the mediated world into ours: The noises in our houses take on new meanings when we're watching a scary movie in the living room.

"We are together" is the premise behind videoconferencing that brings far-flung people in organizations together for real-time interactions. Maria Beatriz de Medeiros (2003) details the work of Corpos Infomáticos for "telepresence"— "performances that happen at the computer World Wide Web: they are deterritorialized bodies reorganized (re-orphans) in monitors that are dispersed in the world." Marcyrose Chvasta (2005) explores the Web-based digitally mediated performance work of the Desperate Optimists, Underscore, and the Chameleon Group, all Web-based digital performance collectives. "We are together" on the Web is an important alternative to expensive travel and a way to collaborate across time and distance in the creation of artists' communities, audiences, and works.

Presence as Immersion

Immersion complicates "real" space, time, bodies, motion, and reality with virtual versions of these, creating a presence that is both physical and psychological. IMAX theatres, simulation rides at amusement parks, and flight training simulators all work to immerse the user's perceptual field in sensory experiences. If our senses are immersed *physically* (and motion sickness can be a very real result of virtual realities), then we are usually *psychologically* immersed as well. Psychological immersion, like reading a riveting novel, has been around forever, "but this book has stretched in all directions and wrapped itself around the senses of the reader" (Lombard and Ditton 1997).

Just as real books and real bodies are involved in immersion, so simulation rides *stimulate real bodies in space.* Janez Strehovec (1997) explores the induced vertigo of entertaining simulation rides. Here is Mitchell's (1995) description of a simulator at the Las Vegas Luxor hotel: "It's a scary, stomach-churning roller coaster ride through a vast virtual landscape, but we never actually move more than a few feet, and from beginning to end we don't leave the small, darkened room. The phenomenal motion is far greater than the actual motion: it's all in the cunning programming" (quoted in Strehovec 1997, 201).

Lance Gharavi (2004, 355) extends real bodies in virtual realities to *real time:* "All video games, by being interactive, also have at least some degree of liveness to them. Lara Croft may not be there in the flesh while we skulk through the catacombs of Tomb Raider, but she is present in time with us. However narrowly circum-scribed her allowable actions may be, they do not have the inevitability of film."

Jon McKenzie (1994, 85) writes of his own experiences in emerging virtual real-ity systems as "a hybrid performance in which human users perform 'real interac-tions' within continuous 'real time' and 'real space' (3-D) computer environments." McKenzie flies a hang glider through a *Blade Runner*–like cityscape, interacts with animals, birds, and insects in a virtual menagerie, and—most fun of all—flies *out-side* a jet fighter. "I trailed behind, tethered to its fuselage like some flying Barcardi beach billboard." For McKenzie (1994, 86), immersion is "the defining aspect of VR performances." Immersion also questions the traditional mind/body split: both are "immersed in electronic networks" (92).

Presence as Social Actor within the Medium

Communication theorists call this "parasocial interaction," and we've all done it. This is interacting with people on screens as if they are really present, and as if they can really hear us. We coach our favorite ballplayers ("Go left! Go left! He's open!"), swear at our least favorite politicians ("You lying bastard!"), and talk to people in commercials ("No, I don't think I'll call right now"). In many digital environments, we are encouraged to engage in parasocial interactions with humanlike and non-human avatars. Cyberpets are digital images that require food, exercise, and affec-tion to keep them "alive."

Philip Auslander (2002, 18) explores bots—short for robots—in cyberspace that are programmed to respond to our commands. "The most familiar type of bot is probably the search engine—you tell it what to look for, and it goes forth into cyberspace, seeks, and finds (you hope) what you wanted." Other bots welcome and guide you through protocols in chat rooms, like the chatterbot. Programmed to engage in humanlike conversation, a chatterbot "performs" its duties in real time, and (although programmed) its responses are based on other (real) performers whose actions are "autonomous, unpredictable, and improvisational." These char-acteristics are coming hauntingly close to Peggy Phelan's notion of presence as immediate, ephemeral, and reciprocal, just as Haraway's cyborgs confuse the lines between human and machine. Auslander (2002, 20) writes: "[chatterbots] perform live, but they are not a-live."

Presence as Medium as Social Actor

This final type of mediated presence "involves social responses of media users not to entities (people or computer characters) within a medium, but to cues provided by the medium itself" (Lombard and Ditton 1997). This involves acting as if a medium or technology is a human. Perhaps you've heard the advice, "Never tell a computer (or a printer, or an ATM machine) you're in a hurry." If you do, that's the precise moment it will freeze. This assumes reciprocity, mutuality, the ability to act to impact each other. Science fiction is full of people interacting with technology as if it were human, from the famous Hal of *2001: A Space Oddessy* to everyone's favorite android, R2D2 of *Star Wars*.

Timothy Binkley (1997, 108) describes this kind of mediated presence, or interactivity between humans and technology, as **vitality**. Digital representations "are oddly capable of reaching out to us," engaging "us in unique and personal interactive experiences." This vitality through interaction is "strangely alive," as subjects created by digital technologies "can become aware of your presence and respond to you" (108). When we import awareness to technological media, we are engaging a presence that is "related to agency, to the proximity of intentionality" (Stone 1995, 16).

Each of these kinds of mediated presence encourages us to ignore the medium that stands between us and other people; enables an otherworldly, physical, and psychological experience; promotes relationships between humans and technologies; and invites us to import agency, intention, and awareness to technologies. Live performance's notions of reciprocity, immediacy, ephemerality, and intimacy are not unique when we perceive similar qualities in mediated experience.

Performance works are exploding across digital landscapes that seek to engage in all the above kinds of mediated presence: transportation, immersion in sensory realms through interactivity and liveness in space and in time, and social richness available through social actors—whether "vitally" alive or not. Scott deLahunta (2002) calls this work "mixed realities"—the merger of physical and digital worlds. Jeffrey Shaw's *The Legible City*, Michael Benayoun's *World Skin*, and Blast Theory's *Desert Rain* all utilize video, audio, and three-dimensional computer-simulated environments to explore "open forms of audience participation and interaction; site-specific responses to space (whether virtual or actual) and the possibilities inherent in discontinuous, gaming, interactive and user/participant-led time frames" (deLahunta 2002, 105).

RETHINKING TECHNOLOGIES

Critiques of technology are omnipresent: for determinism, for human consequences, and for the digital divide. Marshall McLuhan and Walter Ong have been accused of **technological determinism**, the insistence that "technologies have a life of their own" (Silverstone 2003) and that technology drives culture, human consciousness, and human potential—instead of the other way around. Raymond Williams (1974/2003, 6) summarizes two deterministic approaches: "[technology] is either a self-acting force which creates new ways of life, or it is a self-acting force which provides materials for new ways of life." Williams accuses McLuhan of ignoring both history and human agency: "technologies may constrain," Williams argues, "but they do not determine."

While Baudrillard argues that there are no originals, only media's simulated realities, his critics point to **human consequences**. Virtuality, hyperreality, and simulations are good "theories," but there are real people, lives, deaths, and consequences to the technologies of mediated communication. Vivian Sobchack (1995a, 213) goes medieval on him: "I wish Baudrillard a little pain—maybe a lot—to bring him to his senses. Pain would remind him that he doesn't just *have* a body, but that he *is* his body, and it is in this material fact that 'affect' and anything we might call a 'moral stance' is grounded." Likewise, performance practices of virtual identities and communities are accused of trivializing real bodies and relationships. Scott Bukatman (1995, 73) calls the easy births and deaths of virtual personas "a state of terminal identity." For Vivian Sobchack (1995b, 18), "virtual identity" is an oxymoron, better described as "interactive autism."

Even Donna Haraway backed off from her early celebration of the cyborg with a warning about the limits of liberation possible through technologies. In an interview, Haraway admitted that "we really do die, that we really do wound each other, that the earth really is finite, that there aren't any other planets out there that we know of that we can live on, that escape-velocity is a deadly fantasy" (Penley and Ross 1991, 20).

The **digital divide** is "the stratification of people according to access to interactive computer-based technologies" (Hartley 2002, 70). Digital "have's" and "have not's" tend to fall along geographic, age, educational, and economic lines. The already disenfranchised—geographically, educationally, and economically—are also denied participation in and access to online technologies. A number of theorists have critiqued the gender and racial divide: White male researchers and developers overwhelm the number of women and people of color in science, engineering, and IT fields (Gajjala 2000; Kolko, Nakamura, and Rodman 2000; Sterne 2000).

Performance theorists and practitioners have weighed in on these technology debates. Indeed, this chapter might be charged with technological determinism: Is technology driving performance theory today? And how many of us are on the "have-not" side of the digital performance divide? For performance practice, the move to more and more complex technologies leaves many of us without the skills or resources to participate in the creation of mediated, virtual, and immersive performance spaces. If we do have the skills, then are we performers or programmers? (Gómez-Peña 2001). Both Gharavi (2004) and Saltz (2001) feature the irony of interactivity and virtual realities onstage: Performance work that creates imaginative characters, scenes, and plots has always been "virtual"—invitations to participate in illusions in time and space. Interactive technologies—that seek randomness through performer or audience input—are often indisguishable from planned and choreographed "magic" that happens onstage.

"Interactivity" of the computer age is open to charges of disembodiment—of both bodies and resistance. For the Critical Art Ensemble (2000, 161), "virtual theatre" has no "resistant potential; rather the virtual theatre available seems to reinforce the worst elements of the disembodiment of the technocratic class." This kind of disembodied practice—pointing and clicking—prepares us only to be better workers in capitalism, where we also spend workdays pointing and clicking with no critical thinking (Hirsch 2005). Gómez-Peña (2001, 14) critiques interactivity as an "illusion of talking back."

> We can call the TV or radio station, or email them our opinions. We can post our views in any Website we like, join a chat room, or place a classified ad in search of a quorum or accomplices. And someone will respond right away.

If we are lucky, we may be invited to a talk show to exhibit (or better said, "perform") our miseries. Students, intellectuals, and civic leaders, along with a bunch of children and housewives randomly chosen by the producer's assistant, may get invited to an electronic town meeting organized by CNN or by the President himself. Our new culture encourages everyone to have an opinion and express it (not necessarily an informed opinion, just an opinion). Not to act upon it, just to express it, as a kind of placebo or substitute for action.

Marcyrose Chvasta (2005, 167) echoes this call to action. The central question at the heart of performance and technology is not the co-presence of live bodies but the belief that "performance—whether on the stage or street—generates possibility, and by its very nature, encourages the resistance of stasis of any kind. Such is the power of performance, whether appearing in the copresence of live bodies or with the aid of technology."

Resisting stasis—standing still—and generating possibilities are the twofold projects of performance—whether the medium of performance is the voice of the storyteller, the pages of a book, the images on a screen, or the HTML code of our favorite video game or social network online. The ontological question "What exists?" is intimately linked to performance and technology as embodiments, as extenders, enablers, and dispersers, of human-created knowledge and human-felt experience.

Our fascination with presence in performance—as live, as mediated, as virtual—is matched by social theorists who turn to presence as the reigning question in postmodern politics of representation, reproduction, and materiality. Walter Benjamin's aura, Jean Baudrillard's hyperreality, and Donna Haraway's cyborg are all reminders that artworks, communication media, and human bodies are social productions whose meanings, uses, and effects are never settled, static, ahistorical, apolitical, or value-free. These social productions are about life and death.

For both Peggy Phelan and Herbert Blau, presence in live performance is about mortality. The knowledge and inevitability of death is the linchpin in the "existence" of presence in performance. Herbert Blau (1990, 267) argues that mortality is the actual subject of performance. In every performance, "Someone is dying in front of your eyes." Peggy Phelan (1997, 3) writes, "it may well be that theatre and performance respond to a psychic need to rehearse for loss, and especially for death."

If old technology, as this chapter opened, is susceptible to obsolescence, commonsense, and quaintness, new technologies perform a kind of promise of immortality as McLuhan's extensions of human bodies and powers—until, that is, they are rendered obsolete, commonsensical, and quaint by new ones. Performance and technology are very old practices with very old motivations: to hold on to life, to presence, to existence, to communication. To paraphrase Chvasta's call to action (2005), performance is the belief that we can both resist the stasis of death and generate possibilities in life.

References

Abrahams, Roger. 1968. "Introductory Remarks to a Rhetorical Theory of Folklore." *Journal of American Folklore* 81: 143–58.

Abrams, M. H. 1979. "How to Do Things with Texts." *Partisan Review* 46: 566–88.

Adams, Hazard. 1990. "Introduction." *Critical Theory Since 1965*. Ed. Hazard Adams and Leroy Searle. Tallahassee: Florida State University Press, 1–22.

Adams, Robert M. 1983, 8 July. "The Dance of Language." Rev. of *Kenneth Burke and the Drama of Human Relations* by William Rueckert. *London Times Literary Supplement*, 715–16.

Agne, Robert R., Teresa L. Thompson, and Louis P. Cusella. 2000. "Stigma in the Line of Face: Self-Disclosure of Patients' HIV Status to Health Care Providers." *Journal of Applied Communication* 28, 3: 235–62.

Alexander, Bryant K. 2004a. "Black Skin/White Masks: The Performative Sustainability of Whiteness (With Apologies to Frantz Fanon)." *Qualitative Inquiry* 10: 647–72.

Alexander, Bryant K. 2004b. "Passing, Cultural Performance, and Individual Agency: Performative Reflections on Black Masculine Identity." *Cultural Studies <=> Critical Methodologies* 4, 3: 377–404.

Alexander, Bryant K., Gary L. Anderson, and Bernardo P. Gallegos, eds. 2005. *Performance Theories in Education*. Mahwah, NJ: Lawrence Erlbaum.

Allison, Dorothy. 1994. *Skin: Talking About Sex, Class and Literature*. Ithaca, NY: Firebrand Books.

Ancelet, Barry Jean. 2001. "Falling Apart to Stay Together: Deep Play in the Grand Marais Mardi Gras." *Journal of American Folklore* 114, 452: 144–53.

Anderson, Carl J., and Norman M. Prentice. 1994. "Encounter with Reality: Children's Reactions on Discovering the Santa Claus Myth." *Child Psychiatry and Human Development* 25, 2: 67–85.

Antler. 2000. *The Selected Poems*. New York: Soft Skull Press.

Anzaldúa, Gloria. 1987. *Borderlands/La Frontera: The New Mestiza*. San Francisco: Spinsters/Aunt Lute.

Apker, Julie, Kathleen M. Propp, and Wendy S. Zabava. 2005. "Negotiating Status and Identity Tensions in Healthcare Team Interactions: An Exploration of Nurse Role Dialectics." *Journal of Applied Communication* 33, 2: 93–106.

Aristotle's Poetics. 1961. Trans. S. H. Butcher. Introduction by Francis Fergusson. New York: Hill and Wang.

Arnold, Matthew. 1882/1994. *Culture and Anarchy*. Ed. Samuel Lipman. New Haven, CT: Yale University Press.

Auslander, Philip. 1999. *Liveness: Performance in a Mediatized Culture*. New York: Routledge.

Auslander, Philip. 2002. "Live from Cyberspace: Or, I Was Sitting at My Computer this Guy Appeared He Thought I Was a Bot." *PAJ: A Journal of Performance and Art* 24, 1: 16–21.

Austin, J. L. 1962/1975. *How to Do Things with Words,* 2nd ed. Ed. J. O. Urmson and M. Sbisa. Cambridge, MA: Harvard University Press.

Bacon, Wallace. 1966. *The Art of Interpretation.* New York: Holt, Rinehart and Winston.

Bacon, Wallace. 1983. "The World Speaks." *Proceedings of the Seminar Conference on Oral Traditions.* Ed. Isabel Crouch. Las Cruces: New Mexico State University Press, 6–11.

Bacon, Wallace. 1984. "Forum: The Center that Holds." *Literature in Performance* 5, 1: 83–84.

Bacon, Wallace. 1986. "The Case for Interpretation." *Renewal and Revision: The Future of Interpretation.* Ed. Ted Colson. Denton, TX: NB Omega, 15–25.

Bacon, Wallace A., and Robert S. Breen. 1959. *Literature as Experience.* New York: McGraw-Hill.

Baglia, Jay. 2005. *The Viagra AdVenture: Masculinity, Media, and the Performance of Sexual Health.* New York: Peter Lang.

Baglia, Jay, and Elissa Foster. 2005. "Performing the 'Really' Real: Cultural Criticism, Representation, and Commodification in *The Laramie Project.*" *Journal of Dramatic Theory and Criticism* 19, 2: 127–45.

Bakhtin, Mikhail. 1968. *Rabelais and His World.* Cambridge, MA: MIT Press.

Balme, Christopher B. 1998. "Staging the Pacific: Framing Authenticity in Performances for Tourists at the Polynesian Cultural Center." *Theatre Journal* 50, 1: 53–70.

Banks, Stephen P. 1994. "Performing Public Announcements: The Case of Flight Attendants' Work Discourse." *Text and Performance Quarterly* 14, 3: 253–68.

Barthes, Roland. 1982. "Inaugural Lecture, College de France." *A Barthes Reader.* Ed. Susan Sontag. New York: Hill and Wang, 457–78.

Barthes, Roland. 1988. *Mythologies.* New York: Noonday Press.

Bateson, Gregory. 1972. *Steps to an Ecology of Mind.* Chicago: University of Chicago Press.

Baudrillard, Jean. 1983. *Simulations.* Trans. Paul Foss, Paul Patton, and Philip Beitchman. New York: Semiotext(e).

Bauman, Richard. 1977. *Verbal Art as Performance.* Prospect Heights, IL: Waveland.

Bauman, Richard, ed. 1992a. "Introduction." *Folklore, Cultural Performances, and Popular Entertainments: A Communications-Centered Handbook.* New York: Oxford University Press, xiii–xxi.

Bauman, Richard. 1992b. "Performance." *Folklore, Cultural Performances, and Popular Entertainments: A Communications-Centered Handbook.* New York: Oxford University Press, 41–49.

Bauman, Richard. 2002. "Disciplinarity, Reflexivity, and Power in *Verbal Art as Performance*: A Response." *Journal of American Folklore* 115, 455: 92–98.

Bauman, Richard, and Joel Sherzer. 1975. "The Ethnography of Speaking." *Annual Review of Anthropology* 4: 95–119.

Baxandall, Lee. 1969. "Dramaturgy of Radical Activity." *TDR: The Drama Review* 13, 4: 52–71.

Beach, Wayne A. 1982. "Everyday Interaction and Its Practical Accomplishment: Progressive Developments in Ethnomethodological Research." *Quarterly Journal of Speech* 68: 314–44.

Becker, Barbara. 2003. "Marking and Crossing Borders: Bodies, Touch, and Contact in Cyberspace." *Body, Space, Technology Journal* 3, 2. Available at http://people.brunel.ac.uk/bst/vol0302/index.html

Beeman, William O. 1993. "The Anthropology of Theater and Spectacle." *Annual Review of Anthropology* 22: 369–93.

Beeman, William O. 2004. "Performance Theory in an Anthropology Program." In *Teaching Performance Studies*. Ed. Nathan Stucky and Cynthia Wimmer. Carbondale: Southern Illinois University Press, 85–97.

Bell, Catherine M. 1997. *Ritual: Perspectives and Dimensions*. New York: Oxford University Press.

Bell, Catherine. 2004. "'Performance' and Other Analogies." *The Performance Studies Reader*. Ed. Henry Bial. New York: Routledge, 88–93.

Bell, Elizabeth. 1995a. "Somatypes at the Disney Shop: Constructing the Pentimentos of Women's Animated Bodies." *From Mouse to Mermaid: The Politics of Film, Gender, and Culture*. Ed. Elizabeth Bell, Linda Haas, and Laura Sells. Bloomington: Indiana University Press, 107–24.

Bell, Elizabeth. 1995b. "Toward a Pleasure-Centered Economy: Wondering a Feminist Aesthetics of Performance." *Text and Performance Quarterly* 15: 99–121.

Bell, Elizabeth. 1999. "Weddings and Pornography: The Cultural Performance of Sex." *Text and Performance Quarterly* 19: 173–95.

Bell, Elizabeth. 2005. "Sex Acts Beyond Boundaries and Binaries: A Feminist Challenge for Self Care in Performance Studies." *Text and Performance Quarterly* 25, 3: 187–220.

Bell, Elizabeth. 2006. "Social Dramas and Cultural Performances: All the President's Women." *Liminalities: A Journal of Performance Studies* 2, 1. Available at http://liminalities.net/

Bell, Elizabeth, and Linda C. Forbes. 1994. "Office Folklore in the Academic Paperwork Empire: The Interstitial Space of Gendered (Con)Texts." *Text and Performance Quarterly* 14, 3: 181–96.

Bello, Richard. 1997. "The Contemporary Rise of Louisiana Voices and Other Neo-Chautauquas: A Return to Oral Performance." *Text and Performance Quarterly* 17, 2: 182–96.

Benjamin, Walter. 1936/2007. "The Work of Art in the Age of Mechanical Reproduction." In *The Critical Tradition*, 3rd ed. Ed. David H. Richter. Boston: Bedford/St. Martin's, 1233–48.

Berger, Harris M., and Giovanna P. Del Negro. 2002. "Bauman's *Verbal Art* and the Social Organization of Attention: The Role of Reflexivity in the Aesthetics of Performance." *Journal of American Folklore* 115, 455: 62–91.

Berger, Peter. 1963. *Invitation to Sociology*. New York: Doubleday.

Bergeson, Laine. 2004. "Do-It-Yourself Rituals." *Utne Reader,* July/August, 66–69.

Bergman, Teresa. 2004. "Personal Narrative, Dialogism, and the Performance of 'Truth' in Complaints of a Dutiful Daughter." *Text and Performance Quarterly* 24, 1: 20–38.

Bial, Henry, ed. 2004. "Play." *The Performance Studies Reader*. London: Routledge, 115–16.

Binkley, Timothy. 1997. "The Vitality of Digital Creation." *The Journal of Aesthetics and Art Criticism* 55, 2: 107–16.

Blackadder, Neil. 2000. "Modern Theatre Scandals and the Evolution of the Theatrical Event." *Theatre History Studies* 20: 123–44.

Blau, Herbert. 1985a. *The Audience*. Baltimore: Johns Hopkins University Press.

Blau, Herbert. 1985b. "Odd, Anonymous Needs: The Audience in a Dramatized Society." *Performing Arts Journal* 9, 2/3: 199–212.

Blau, Herbert. 1990. "Universals of Performance, or Amortizing Play." *By Means of Performance: Intercultural Studies of Theatre and Ritual*. Ed. Richard Schechner and Willa Appel. Cambridge, UK: Cambridge University Press, 250–72.

Boal, Augusto. 1985. *Theatre of the Oppressed*. Trans. Charles A. Leal McBride and Maria-Odilia Leal McBride. New York: Theatre Communications Group.

Boal, Augusto. 1992. *Games for Actors and Non-actors*. Trans. Adrian Jackson. London: Routledge.

Bodley, John H. 1994. *Cultural Anthropology: Tribes, States, and the Global System*. New York: McGraw-Hill.

Bok, Christian. 2005. "Excerpt from *Mushroom Clouds* (from *The Cyborg Opera*) in Contributors' Notes." *Leonardo Music Journal* 15, 1: 80.

Bolton, Christopher. 2002. "From Wooden Cyborgs to Celluloid Souls: Bodies in Anime and Japanese Puppet Theater." *positions: east asia cultures critique* 10, 3: 729–71.

Bordwell, David. 1985. *Narration in the Fiction Film*. Madison: University of Wisconsin Press.

Bordwell, Marilyn. 1998. "Dancing with Death: Performativity and 'Undiscussable' Bodies in *Still/Here.*" *Text and Performance Quarterly, 18*, 369–79.

Bordwell, Marilyn. 2000. "Performing Culture through Embodied Rhetoric: Dancing 'Where the Buffalo Roam.'" *Theatre Annual* 53: 15–36.

Bowden, Betsy. 1982. "Performed Literature: A Case Study of Bob Dylan's 'Hard Rain.'" *Literature in Performance* 3, 1: 35–48.

Bowman, Michael S. 1996. "Performing Literature in an Age of Textuality." *Communication Education* 45: 96–101.

Bowman, Michael S. 1998. "Performing Southern History for the Tourist Gaze: Antebellum Home Tour Guide Performances." *Exceptional Spaces: Essays in Performance and History*. Ed. Della Pollock. Chapel Hill: University of North Carolina Press, 142–58.

Bowman, Ruth Laurion. 1997. "'Joking' with the Classics: Using Boal's Joker System in the Performance Classroom." *Theatre Topics* 7, 2: 139–51.

Bowman, Ruth Laurion. 2006. "Diverging Paths in Performance Genealogies." In *Opening Acts: Performance in/as Communication and Cultural Studies*." Ed. Judith Hamera. Thousand Oaks, CA: Sage, 163–94.

Brecht, Bertolt. 1964/1994. *Brecht on Theater: The Development of an Aesthetic*. Ed. and Trans. John C. Willett. New York: Hill and Wang.

Broadhurst, Sue. 2005. "Bioart: Transgenic Art and Recombinant Theater." *Body Space Technology Journal* 5. Available at http://people.brunel.ac.uk.bst.v0105/index.html

Brockriede, Wayne. 1973. "Letters." *Spectra* 9, 5: 12.

Brooks, Cleanth. 1947. *The Well-Wrought Urn: Studies in the Structure of Poetry*. New York: Harcourt, Brace.

Brouwer, Dan. 1998. "The Precarious Visibility Politics of Self-Stigmatization: The Case of HIV/AIDS Tatoos." *Text and Performance Quarterly* 18, 2: 114–36.

Brown, Wendy. 2003. "At the Edge." *Political Theory* 30, 4: 556–76.

Brummett, Barry. 1984a. "Burkean Comedy and Tragedy, Illustrated in Reactions to the Arrest of John DeLorean." *Central States Speech Journal* 35: 217–27.

Brummett, Barry. 1984b. "Burke's Representative Anecdote as a Method in Media Criticism." *Critical Studies in Mass Communication* 1: 161–76.

Bruner, Jerome. 1991. "The Narrative Construction of Reality." *Critical Inquiry* 18, 1: 1–21.

Bruner, M. Lane. 2005. "Carnivalesque Protest and the Humorless State." *Text and Performance Quarterly* 25, 2: 136–55.

Bukatman, Scott. 1995. "Gibson's Typewriter." In *Flame Wars: The Discourse of Cyberculture*. Ed. Mark Dery. Durham, NC: Duke University Press, 71–90.

Burke, Kenneth. 1931/1968. *Counter-statement*. Berkeley: University of California Press.

Burke, Kenneth. 1957. *The Philosophy of Literary Form: Studies in Symbolic Action*, Rev. ed. New York: Vintage Books.

Burke, Kenneth. 1966. *Language as Symbolic Action: Essays on Life, Literature, and Method*. Berkeley: University of California Press.

Butler, Judith. 1988. "Performative Acts and Gender Constitution: An Essay in Phenomenology and Feminist Thought." *Theatre Journal* 40: 519–31.

Butler, Judith. 1990/1999. *Gender Trouble: Feminism and the Subversion of Identity.* New York: Routledge.

Butler, Judith. 2004. *Undoing Gender.* New York: Routledge.

Butterworth, Michael L. 2005. "Ritual in the 'Church of Baseball': Suppressing the Discourse of Democracy after 9/11." *Communication & Critical/Cultural Studies* 2, 2: 107–30.

Calafell, Bernadette Marie. 2005. "Pro(re-)claiming Loss: A Performance Pilgrimage in Search of Malintzin Tenépal." *Text and Performance Quarterly* 25, 1: 43–56.

Callens, Johan. 2000. "Diverting the Integrated Spectacle of War: Sam Shepard's *States of Shock.*" *Text and Performance Quarterly* 20, 3: 290–307.

Campbell, Karlyn Kohrs. 1982. *The Rhetorical Act.* Belmont, CA: Wadsworth.

Capo, Kay Ellen. 1988. "Presence, Aura, and Memory: Implications of Walter Benjamin and the Frankfurt School for Performance Theory." *Literature in Performance* 8, 1: 28–34.

Capo, Kay Ellen. 1994. "Review/Interview: Anna Deavere Smith." *Text and Performance Quarterly* 14: 57–76.

Carey, James. 1988. *Communication as Culture: Essays on Media and Society.* Boston: Unwin Hyman.

Carlson, Marvin. 1985. "Theatrical Performance: Illustration, Translation, Fulfillment, or Supplement?" *Theatre Journal* 37, 1: 5–11.

Carmeli, Yoram. 2001. "Circus Play, Circus Talk, and the Nostalgia for a Total Order." *Journal of Popular Culture* 35, 3: 157–64.

Carmichael, Thomas. 1991. "Postmodernism, Symbolicity, and the Rhetoric of the Hyperreal: Kenneth Burke, Fredric Jameson, and Jean Baudrillard." *Text and Performance Quarterly* 11, 4: 319–24.

Case, Sue-Ellen. 1988. *Feminism and Theatre.* New York: Methuen.

Case, Sue-Ellen. 1996. *The Domain-Matrix: Performing Lesbian at the End of Print Culture.* Bloomington: Indiana University Press.

Cheng, Meiling. 2001. "Cyborgs in Mutation: Osseus Labyrint's Alien Body Art." *TDR: The Drama Review* 45, 2: 145–68.

Chesebro, James W. 1993. "Preface." *Extensions of the Burkeian System.* Tuscaloosa: University of Alabama Press, vii–xxi.

Christiansen, Adrienne E., and Jeremy J. Hanson. 1996. "Comedy as Cure for Tragedy: ACT UP and the Rhetoric of AIDS." *Quarterly Journal of Speech* 82: 157–70.

Chvasta, Marcyrose. 2005. "Remembering Praxis: Performance in the Digital Age." *Text and Performance Quarterly* 25, 2: 156–70.

Chvasta, Marcyrose. 2006. "Anger, Irony, and Protest: Confronting the Issue of Efficacy, Again." *Text and Performance Quarterly* 26, 1: 5–16.

Chvasta, Marcy R., and Deanna Fassett. 2003. "Traveling the Terrain of Screened Realities." *Survivor Lessons: Essays on Communication and Reality Television.* Ed. Matthew J. Smith and Andrew F. Wood. Jefferson, NC: McFarland Press, 213–24.

Cohen-Cruz, Jan. 1994. "Mainstream or Margin? US Activist Performance and Theatre of the Oppressed." *Playing Boal: Theatre, Therapy, Activism.* Ed. Mady Schutzman and Jan Cohen-Cruz. London: Routledge, 110–23.

Colleran, Jeanne. 2003. "Disposable Wars, Disappearing Acts: Theatrical Responses to the 1991 Gulf War." *Theatre Journal* 55, 4: 613–32.

Collins, Billy. 2005. *The Trouble with Poetry and Other Poems.* New York: Random House.

Combs, James E., and Michael W. Mansfield. 1976. "Preface." *Drama in Life: The Uses of Communication in Society.* New York: Hastings House, xiv–xxx.

Conquergood, Dwight. 1985. "Performing as a Moral Act: Ethical Dimensions of the Ethnography of Performance." *Literature in Performance* 5, 2: 1–13.

Conquergood, Dwight. 1986. "Performing Cultures: Ethnography, Epistemology, and Ethics." *Miteinander Sprechen und Handein: Festschrift fur Hellmut Geissner*. Ed. Edith Slembek. Frankfurt: Scriptor.

Conquergood, Dwight. 1989. "Poetics, Play, Process, and Power: The Performative Turn in Anthropology." *Text and Performance Quarterly* 1: 82–95.

Conquergood, Dwight. 1992. "Life in Big Red: Struggles and Accommodations in a Chicago Polyethnic Tenement." In *Structuring Diversity: Ethnographic Perspectives on the New Immigration*. Ed. Louise Lamphere. Chicago: University of Chicago Press, 95–144.

Conquergood, Dwight. 1995. "Of Caravans and Carnivals: Performance Studies in Motion." *TDR: The Drama Review* 39, 4: 137–41.

Conquergood, Dwight. 1998. "Beyond the Text: Toward a Performative Cultural Politics." *Future of Performance Studies*. Ed. Sheron J. Daily. Annandale, VA: National Communication Association, 25–36.

Constantino, Roselyn. 2004. "Latin American Performance Studies: Random Acts or Critical Moves?" *Theatre Journal* 56, 3: 459–61.

Copeland, Roger. 1990. "The Presence of Mediation." *TDR: The Drama Review* 34, 4: 28–44.

Cornea, Christine. 2003. "David Chronenberg's Crash and Performing Cyborgs." *The Velvet Light Trap* 52, 1: 4–14.

Corrigan, Robert W. 1984. "The Search for New Endings: The Theatre in Search of a Fix, Part III." *Theatre Journal* 32, 2: 153–63.

Coutt, Cris. *Tales for the Leet: Romeo and Juliet*. Available at http://uninteresting.myby.co.uk/noeffort/romjul.htm

Critical Art Ensemble (CAE). 2000. "Recombinant Theatre and Digital Resistance." *TDR: The Drama Review* 44, 4: 151–66.

Davis, Tracy C. 2005. "'Do You Believe in Fairies?' The Hiss of Dramatic License." *Theatre Journal* 57, 1: 57–81.

de Certeau, Michel. 1984. *The Practice of Everyday Life*. Trans. Steven F. Rendall. Berkeley: University of California Press.

deLahunta, Scott. 2002. "Virtual Reality and Performance." *PAJ: A Journal of Performance and Art* 24, 1: 105–14.

deLauretis, Teresa. 1991. "Queer Theory: Lesbian and Gay Sexualities, an Introduction." *differences* 3, 2: iii–xviii.

de Medeiros, Maria Beatriz. 2003. "Performance Art and Digital Bodies (Corpos Infomaticos)." *Body Space Technology Journal* 3, 2. Available at http://people.brunel.ac.uk/bst/v010302/index.html

Denzin, Norman K., and Charles M. Keller. 1981. "Frame Analysis Reconsidered." *Contemporary Sociology* 10, 1: 52–60.

Derrida, Jacques. 1988. *Limited Inc*. Evanston, IL: Northwestern University Press.

Diamond, Elin. 1988. "Brechtian Theory/Feminist Theory: Toward a Gestic Feminist Criticism." *TDR: The Drama Review* 32, 1: 82–94.

Diamond, Elin. 1996. "Introduction." *Performance and Cultural Politics*. New York: Routledge, 1–15.

Diamond, Elin. 1997. *Unmaking Mimesis*. London: Routledge.

Dibbell, Julian. 1998. *My Tiny Life: Crime and Passion in the Virtual World*. New York: Henry Holt.

DiMaggio, Paul J. 1995. "Comments on 'What Theory Is Not.'" *Administrative Science Quarterly* 40: 391–97.

Dishman, Eric. 2002. "Performative In(ter)ventions: Designing Future Technologies Through Synergetic Performance." In *Teaching Performance Studies*. Ed. Nathan Stucky and Cynthia Wimmer. Carbondale: University of Southern Illinois Press, 235–46.

Dolan, Jill. 1993. *Presence and Desire: Essays on Gender, Sexuality, Performance.* Ann Arbor: University of Michigan Press.

Dolan, Jill. 2001. *Geographies of Learning: Theory and Practice, Activism and Performance.* Middletown, CT: Wesleyan University Press.

Dolan, Jill. 2005. *Utopia in Performance: Finding Hope at the Theater.* Ann Arbor: University of Michigan Press.

Dow, Bonnie J. 2001. "Ellen, Television, and the Politics of Gay and Lesbian Visibility." *Critical Studies in Media Communication* 18, 2: 123–41.

Dow, Bonnie J. 2004. "Fixing Feminism: Women's Liberation and the Rhetoric of Television Documentary." *Quarterly Journal of Speech* 90, 1: 53–81.

Dow, Bonnie J., and Julia T. Wood, eds. 2006. "The Evolution of Gender and Communication Research: Intersections of Theory, Politics, and Scholarship." In *The Sage Handbook of Gender and Communication.* Thousand Oaks, CA: Sage, ix–xxiv.

Drummond, Kent G. 2003. "The Queering of *Swan Lake:* A New Male Gaze for the Performance of Sexual Desire." *Queer Theory and Communication: From Disciplining Queers to Queering the Discipline(s).* Ed. Gus A. Yep, Karen E. Lovaas, and J. P. Elias. New York: Harrington Park, 235–55.

Duncan, Anne. 2006. *Performance and Identity in the Classical World.* Cambridge, UK: Cambridge University Press.

du Pre, Athena. 2005. *Communicating About Health: Current Issues and Perspectives,* 2nd ed. Boston: McGraw-Hill.

Edwards, Paul. 1999. "Unstoried: Teaching Literature in the Age of Performance Studies." *Theatre Annual* 52: 1–147.

Elam, Harry J., Jr. 1997. *Taking It to the Streets: The Social Protest Theater of Luis Valdez and Amiri Baraka.* Ann Arbor: University of Michigan Press.

Elam, Harry J., Jr., and David Krasner, eds. 2001. *African American Performance and Theater History: A Critical Reader.* Oxford, UK: Oxford University Press.

Emeljanow, Victor. 1998. "Erasing the Spectator: Observations on Nineteenth Century Lighting." *Theatre History Studies* 18: 107–16.

Epstein, Julia. 1992. "AIDS, Stigma, and Narratives of Containment." *American Imago* 43, 3: 293–310.

Esposito, Jennifer. 2003. "The Performance of White Masculinity in *Boys Don't Cry:* Identity, Desire, (Mis)recognition." *Cultural Studies <=> Critical Methodologies* 3, 2: 229–41.

Evenson, Laura. 1999. "*The Elegant Universe* Author Has the World on a String." *San Francisco Chronicle,* 13 February. Available at http://www.sfgate.com/cgi-bin/article.cgi?file=/chronicle/archive/1999/02/13/DD59688.DTL

Farrell, Thomas B. 1989. "Media Rhetoric as Social Drama: The Winter Olympics of 1984." *Critical Studies in Mass Communication* 6: 158–82.

Fenske, Mindy. 2004. "The Aesthetic of the Unfinished: Ethics and Performance." *Text and Performance Quarterly* 24, 1: 1–19.

Fenske, Mindy. 2006. "The Movement of Interpretation: Conceptualizing Performative Encounters with Multimediated Performance." *Text and Performance Quarterly* 26, 2: 138–61.

Fergusson, Francis. 1961. "Introduction." *Aristotle's Poetics.* Trans. S. H. Butcher. New York: Hill and Wang.

Ferris, Jim. 1998. "Uncovery to Recovery: Reclaiming One Man's Body on a Nude Photo Shoot." *Michigan Quarterly Review* 37, 3: 502–18.

Fine, Elizabeth C. 1984. *The Folklore Text: From Performance to Print.* Bloomington: Indiana University Press.

Fine, Elizabeth C. 2003. *Soulstepping: African American Step Shows*. Urbana: University of Illinois Press.

Fine, Elizabeth C., and Jean Haskell Speer. 1985. "Tour Guide Performances as Sight Sacralization." *Annals of Tourism Research* 12: 73–95.

Fisher, Berenice. 1994. "Feminist Acts: Women, Pedagogy, and Theatre of the Oppressed." In *Playing Boal: Theatre, Therapy, Activism*. Ed. Mady Schutzman and Jan Cohen-Cruz. London: Routledge, 185–97.

Fisher, Walter. 1984. "Narration as a Human Communication Paradigm: The Case of Public Moral Argument." *Communication Monographs* 51, 1: 1–22.

Flax, Jane. 1990. "Postmodernism and Gender Relations." *Feminism/Postmodernism*. Ed. Linda J. Nicholson. New York: Routledge, 39–62.

Foreman, Richard. 1994. "Royalty Free Plays. Foreman's Invitation to Directors." *TDR: The Drama Review* 38, 1: 38–42.

Foster, Elissa. 2008. "Commitment, Communication, and Contending with Heteronormativity: An Invitation to Greater Reflexivity in Interpersonal Research." *Southern States Communication Journal* 73, 1.

Foster, Susan Leigh. 1998. "Choreographies of Gender." *Signs* 24, 1: 1–33.

Foster, Susan Leigh. 2002. "Walking and Other Choreographic Tactics: Danced Inventions of Theatricality and Performativity." *SubStance,* 31: 125–45.

Foster, Susan Leigh. 2003. "Choreographies of Protest." *Theatre Journal* 55, 3: 395–412.

Foucault, Michel. 1978/1990. *The History of Sexuality: An Introduction*. Volume 1. Trans. Robert Hurley. New York: Random House.

Found Magazine. Available at http://www.foundmagazine.com

Fox, Jonathan. 1986. *Acts of Service: Spontaneity, Commitment, Tradition in the Nonscripted Theatre*. New Paltz, NY: Tusitala.

Frame, Melissa. 2004. *Blind Spots: The Communicative Performance of Visual Impairment in Relationships and Social Interaction*. Springfield, IL: Charles C Thomas.

Frank, Katherine. 2002. "Stripping, Starving, and the Politics of Ambiguous Pleasure." *Jane Sexes It Up: True Confessions of Feminist Desire*. Ed. Merri Lisa Johnson. New York: Four Walls Eight Windows.

Franklin, Sarah, and Susan McKinnon, eds. 2001. *Relative Values: Reconfiguring Kinship Studies*. Durham, NC: Duke University Press.

Fraser, Miriam. 1999. "Classing Queer: Politics in Competition." *Theory, Culture, and Society* 16: 107–31.

Frazer, James George, Sir. 1940. *The Golden Bough: A Study in Magic and Religion,* abridged ed. New York: Macmillan.

Freytag, Gustav. 1968. *Technique of the Drama: An Exposition of Dramatic Composition and Art*. Trans. Elias J. MacEwan. New York: B. Blom.

Frye, Northrup. 1957. *The Anatomy of Criticism: Four Essays*. Princeton, NJ: Princeton University Press.

Fuchs, Elinor. 1985. "Presence and the Revenge of Writing: Re-thinking Theatre after Derrida." *Performing Arts Journal* 9, 2/3: 163–73.

Fuoss, Kirk. 1993. "Performance as Contestation: An Agonistic Perspective on the Insurgent Assembly." *Text and Performance Quarterly* 13: 331–49.

Fuoss, Kirk. 1997. *Striking Performances/Performing Strikes*. Jackson: University Press of Mississippi.

Fuoss, Kirk W. 1999. "Lynching Performances: Theatres of Violence." *Text and Performance Quarterly* 19, 1: 1–37.

Gajjala, Radhika. 2000. "Negotiating Cyberspace/Negotiating RL." *Our Voices: Essays in Culture, Ethnicity, and Communication,* 4th ed. Ed. Alberto Gonzales, Marsha Houston, and Victoria Chen. Los Angeles: Roxbury.

Galloway, Terry. 1997. "Taken: The Philosophically Sexy Transformations Engendered in a Woman by Playing Male Roles in Shakespeare." *Text and Performance Quarterly* 17, 1: 94–109.

Galvin, Kathleen M. 1979. "Social Simulation in the Family Communication Course." *Communication Education* 28, 1: 68–73.

Garoian, Charles R., and Yvonne M. Gaudelius. 2001. "Cyborg Pedagogy: Performing Resistance in the Digital Age." *Studies in Art Education* 42, 4: 333–47.

Gassner, John. 1952. "A Modern Style of Theatre." *Quarterly Journal of Speech* 38, 1: 63–74.

Geelhoed, Marc. 2006, 10 July. "Mozart Mozart Mozart! Three Pianists Tackle the Same Sonata." *Slate Magazine.* Available at http://www.slate.com/id/2145252

Geertz, Clifford. 1973. *Interpretation of Cultures.* New York: Basic Books.

Geertz, Clifford. 1980. "Blurred Genres: The Refiguration of Social Thought." *The American Scholar* 29: 165–82.

Geiger, Don. 1950. "Oral Interpretation and the 'New Criticism.'" *Quarterly Journal of Speech* 36, 4: 508–13.

Geiger, Don. 1963. *The Sound, Sense, and Performance of Literature.* Glenview, IL: Scott-Foresman.

Geiger, Don. 1973. "Poetic Realizing as Knowing." *Quarterly Journal of Speech* 59, 3: 311–19.

Gerland, Oliver. 1994. "Brecht and the Courtroom: Alienating Evidence in the 'Rodney King' Trials." *Text and Performance Quarterly* 14: 305–18.

Gharavi, Lance. 2004. "Dancing on the Emerald Table: (Mis)adventures in Performance and Esoterica." *Text and Performance Quarterly* 24, 3/4: 348–63.

Gingrich-Philbrook, Craig. 1998. "What I 'Know' about the Story (for Those about to Tell Personal Narratives on Stage)." *The Future of Performance Studies: Visions and Revisions.* Ed. Sheron J. Dailey. Annandale, VA: National Communication Association, 298–300.

Gingrich-Philbrook, Craig. 2002. "The Queer Performance that Will Have Been." In *Teaching Performance Studies.* Ed. Nathan Stucky and Cynthia Wimmer. Carbondale: University of Southern Illinois Press, 69–84.

Glenn, Ethel C. 1972. "Role-Playing in Fundamentals of Speech Course." *Speech Teacher* 21, 4: 321–26.

Goffman, Erving. 1959. *Presentation of Self in Everyday Life.* Garden City, NY: Doubleday.

Goffman, Erving. 1961. *Asylums: Essays on the Social Situation of Mental Patients and Other Inmates.* New York: Doubleday.

Goffman, Erving. 1963. *Stigma: Notes on the Management of Spoiled Identity.* Englewood Cliffs, NJ: Prentice Hall.

Goffman, Erving. 1974. *Frame Analysis: An Essay on the Organization of Experience.* New York: Harper and Row.

Gómez-Peña, Guillermo. 1994. "The Multicultural Paradigm: An Open Letter to the National Arts Community." *Negotiating Performance: Gender, Sexuality, and Theatricality in Latin/o America.* Ed. Diana Taylor and Juan Villegas. Durham, NC: Duke University Press, 17–29.

Gómez-Peña, Guillermo. 1996. "The Virtual Barrio @ the Other Frontier (or the Chicano Interneta). *Clicking In: Hot Links to a Digital Culture.* Ed. L. Hershman Leeson. Seattle, WA: Bay, 173–79.

Gómez-Peña, Guillermo. 2001. "The New Global Culture: Somewhere between Corporate Multiculturalism and the Mainstream Bizarre (a Border Perspective)." *TDR: The Drama Review* 45, 1: 7–30.

Gordon, Beverly. 2003. "Embodiment, Community Building, and Aesthetic Saturation in 'Restroom World,' A Backstage Women's Space." *Journal of American Folklore* 116, 462: 444–64.

Gracyk, Theodore. 1997. "Listening to Music: Performances and Recordings." *The Journal of Aesthetics and Art Criticism* 55, 2: 139–50.

Gray, Paul H. 1996. "The Thoroughbred and the Four-Wheeled Cab: Performance Beyond Literature." *Communication Education* 45: 102–7.

Grealy, Lucy. 1994. *Autobiography of a Face.* Boston: Houghton Mifflin.

Greenberg, Josh, and Graham Knight. 2004. "Framing Sweatshops: Nike, Global Production, and the American News Media." *Communication and Critical/Cultural Studies* 1, 2: 151–76.

Gudas, Fabian. 1983a. "Dramatism and Modern Theories of Oral Interpretation." *Performance of Literature in Historical Perspectives.* Ed. David W. Thompson. Lantham, NY: University Press of America, 589–627.

Gudas, Fabian. 1983b. "The Vitality of Dramatism." *Literature in Performance* 3, 2: 1–12.

Gunkel, David. 2000. "Rethinking Virtual Reality: Simulation and the Deconstruction of the Image." *Critical Studies in Media Communication* 17, 1: 45–62.

Gunn, Joshua. 2006. "ShitText: Toward a New Coprophilic Style." *Text and Performance Quarterly* 26, 1: 79–98.

Gusfield, Joseph R. 1989. "Introduction." *Kenneth Burke: On Symbols and Society.* Chicago: University of Chicago Press, 1–49.

Hacking, Ian. 2004. "Between Michel Foucault and Erving Goffman: Between Discourse in the Abstract and Face-to-Face Interaction." *Economy and Society* 33, 3: 277–302.

Haedicke, Susan C. 2006. "Discomfort at the Intersection of the Imaginary and Everyday Worlds in Friches Theatre Urbain's *Macbeth* for the Street." *Text and Performance Quarterly* 26, 3: 253–73.

Halberstam, Judith. 1998. *Female Masculinity.* Durham, NC: Duke University Press.

Halperin, David M. 1995. *Saint Foucault: Towards a Gay Hagiography.* New York: Oxford University Press.

Hamera, Judith. 1994. "The Ambivalent, Knowing Male Body in the Pasadena Dance Theatre." *Text and Performance Quarterly* 14: 197–209.

Hamera, Judith. 2005. "All the (Dis)Comforts of Home: Place, Gendered Self-Fashioning, and Solidarity in a Ballet Studio." *Text and Performance Quarterly* 25, 2: 93–112.

Hamera, Judith, ed. 2006. "Introduction." *Opening Acts: Performance in/as Communication and Cultural Studies.* Thousand Oaks, CA: Sage.

Hantke, Steffen. 2003. "In the Belly of the Mechanical Beast: Technological Environments in the 'Alien' Films." *Journal of Popular Culture* 36, 3: 518–46.

Hantke, Steffen. 2004/2005. "Spectacular Optics: The Deployment of Special Effects in David Cronenberg's Films." *Film Criticism* 29, 2: 34–52.

Haraway, Donna. 1989. *Primate Visions: Gender, Race and Nature in the World of Modern Science.* New York: Routledge.

Haraway, Donna J. 1991. "A Cyborg Manifesto." *Simians, Cyborgs, and Women: The Reinvention of Nature.* New York: Routledge, 149–82.

Haraway, Donna. 1992. "Ecce Homo, Ain't (Ar'n't) I Am Woman, and Inappropriate/d Others: The Human in a Post-Humanist Landscape." *Feminists Theorize the Political.* Ed. Judith Butler and Joan W. Scott. New York: Routledge, 86–100.

Harlow, Ilana. 1997. "Creating Situations: Practical Jokes and the Revival of the Dead in Irish Tradition." *Journal of American Folklore* 110, 436: 140–68.

Hart, Lynda. 1994. *Fatal Women: Lesbian Sexuality and the Mark of Aggression.* Princeton, NJ: Princeton University Press.

Hartley, John. 2002. "Digital Divide." *Communication, Cultural and Media Studies: The Key Concepts.* London: Routledge.

Haskins, James. 1984. *Lena: A Personal and Professional Biography of Lena Horne.* With K. Benson. New York: Stein.

Hayward, Susan. 1996. *Key Concepts in Cinema Studies.* London: Routledge.

Hennessy, Rosemary. 1995. "Queer Visibility in Commodity Culture." *Social Postmodernism: Beyond Identity Politics.* Ed. Linda Nicholson and Steven Seidman. Cambridge, UK: Cambridge University Press, 142–83.

Heyer, P. 2003, 1 January. "America Under Attack 1: The War of the Worlds, Orson Welles, and 'Media Sense.'" *Canadian Journal of Communication,* 28(2). Available at http://www.cjc-online.ca/viewarticle.php?id=779

Hill, Randall T. 1995. "The Nakwa Powamu Ceremony as Rehearsal: Authority, Ethics and Ritual Appropriation." *Text and Performance Quarterly* 15, 4: 301–20.

Hirsch, Robert. 2005. "The Strange Case of Steve Kurtz: Critical Art Ensemble and the Price of Freedom." *Afterimage* 32, 6: 22–25, 28–32.

Hirschmann, Krista. 2001. "Fidelity and Fecundity: A Study of Sex Communication as Performance in Parent-Child and Physician-Patient Relationships." Unpublished dissertation, University of South Florida.

Holling, Michelle A., and Bernadette Marie Calafell. 2007. "Identities on Stage and Staging Identities: ChicanoBrujo Performances as Emancipatory Practices." *Text and Performance Quarterly* 27, 1: 58–83.

Hollis, Susan Tower. 1993. "Preface." *Feminist Theory and the Study of Folklore.* Ed. S. T. Hollis, L. Pershing, and M. J. Young. Chicago: University of Illinois Press.

hooks, bell. 1995. "Performance Practice as a Site of Opposition." *Let's Get It On: The Politics of Black Performance.* Ed. C. Ugwu. Seattle, WA: Bay, 210–21.

HopKins, Mary Frances. 1995. "The Performance Turn and Toss." *Quarterly Journal of Speech* 81, 2: 228–36.

Hopper, Robert. 1993. "Conversational Dramatism and Everyday Life Performance." *Text and Performance Quarterly* 13, 2: 181–83.

Howard, Leigh Anne. 2004. "Speaking Theatre/Doing Pedagogy: Re-visiting Theatre of the Oppressed." *Communication Education* 53, 3: 217–33.

Hoy, Mikita. 1994. "Joyful Mayhem: Bakhtin, Football Songs, and the Carnivalesque." *Text and Performance Quarterly* 14, 4: 289–304.

Hudson, Lee. 1980. "Between Singer and Rhapsode." *Literature in Performance* 1, 1: 33–45.

Huizinga, Johan. 1938/1950. *Homo Ludens: A Study of the Play-Element in Culture.* Boston: Beacon Press.

Hull, Margaret Betz. 2000. "Postmodern Philosophy Meets Pop Cartoon: Michel Foucault and Matt Groening." *Journal of Popular Culture* 34, 2: 57–67.

Hutchinson, Atman, Kenneth N. Leone Cissna, Mary Elizabeth Hall, Philip E. Backlund, and James H. Tolhuizen. 1978. "Video Self-Confrontation as a Technique to Enhance Interpersonal Communication Effectiveness." *Communication Education* 27, 3: 245–51.

Hyde, Alan. 1997. *Bodies of Law.* Princeton, NJ: Princeton University Press.

Ingram, Deborah. 1999. "HIV-Positive Mothers and Stigma." *Health Care for Women International* 20, 1: 93–103.

Jackson, Shannon. 2000. *Lines of Activity: Performance, Historiography, Hull-House Domesticity.* Ann Arbor: University of Michigan Press.

Jackson, Shannon. 2004. *Professing Performance: Theatre in the Academy from Philology to Performativity.* Cambridge, UK: Cambridge University Press.

Jarnow, Jesse. 2003, 20 November. "The Penguin Is Mightier than the Sword." *Salon*. Available at http://dir.salon.com/story/ent/feature/2003/11/20/breathed/index.html?pn=1

Jasper, James M. 1997. *The Art of Moral Protest*. Chicago: University of Chicago Press.

Jensen, Ole B. 2006. "'Facework,' Flow and the City: Simmel, Goffman, and Mobility in the Contemporary City." *Mobilities* 1, 2: 143–65.

Johnson, E. Patrick. 1995. "SNAP! Culture: A Different Kind of 'Reading.'" *Text and Performance Quarterly* 15: 122–42.

Johnson, E. Patrick. 2001. "'Quare Studies, or (Almost) Everything I Know About Queer Studies I Learned from My Grandmother." *Text and Performance Quarterly* 21, 1: 1–25.

Johnson, E. Patrick. 2002. "Performing Blackness Down Under: The Café of the Gate of Salvation." *Text and Performance Quarterly* 22, 2: 99–119.

Johnson, E. Patrick. 2003. *Appropriating Blackness: Performance and Politics of Authenticity*. Durham, NC: Duke University Press.

Jones, Jennifer. 1998. "The Beauty Queen as Deified Sacrificial Victim." *Theatre History Studies* 18: 99–106.

Jones, Joni L. 1993. "Improvisation as a Performance Strategy for African-based Theatre." *Text and Performance Quarterly* 13, 3: 233–51.

Jones, Joni L. 2002. "Performance Ethnography: The Role of Embodiment in Cultural Authenticity." *Theater Topics* 12, 1: 1–15.

Jones, Stacy Holman. 2007. *Torch Singing: Performing Resistance and Desire from Billie Holiday to Edith Piaf*. Lanham, MD: AltaMira Press.

Jordan, John W. 1999. "Vampire Cyborgs and Scientific Imperialism: A Reading of the Science-Mysticism Polemic in 'Blade.'" *Journal of Popular Film and Television* 27, 2: 4–15.

Jordan, John W. 2003. "(Ad)Dressing the Body on Online Shopping Sites." *Critical Studies in Media Communication* 20, 3: 248–69.

Jorgensen-Earp, Cheryl R., and Lori A. Lanzilotti. 1998. "Public Memory and Private Grief: The Construction of Shrines at the Sites of Public Tragedy." *Quarterly Journal of Speech* 84, 2: 150–71.

Jowett, Garth S. 1993. "Propaganda and the Gulf War." *Critical Studies in Mass Communication* 10, 3: 287–301.

Kapchan, Deborah A. 1995. "Performance." *The Journal of American Folklore* 108, 430: 479–508.

Kawash, Samira. 1999. "Interactivity and Vulnerability." *PAJ: A Journal of Performance and Art* 21, 1: 46–52.

Kennerly, Rebecca M. 2002. "Getting Messy: In the Field and at the Crossroads with Roadside Shrines." *Text and Performance Quarterly* 22, 4: 229–60.

Kent, G. 2000. "Understanding the Experiences of People With Disfigurements: An Integration of Four Models of Social and Psychological Functioning." *Psychology, Health and Medicine* 5, 2: 117–29.

Kershaw, Baz. 1992. *The Politics of Performance: Radical Theatre as Cultural Intervention*. London: Routledge.

Kershaw, Baz. 1997. "Fighting in the Streets: Dramaturgies of Popular Protest, 1968–1989." *New Theatre Quarterly* 13, 3: 255–76.

Kershaw, Baz. 1999. *The Radical in Performance: Between Brecht and Baudrillard*. London: Routledge.

Kershaw, Baz. 2003. "Curiosity or Contempt: On Spectacle, the Human, and Activism." *Theatre Journal* 55, 4: 591–611.

Kimball, Solon T. 1960. "Introduction." *The Rites of Passage*. By Arnold van Gennep. Chicago: University of Chicago Press, v–xix.

Kinneavy, James. 1971. *A Theory of Discourse*. Englewood Cliffs, NJ: Prentice Hall.

Kipnis, Laura. 1998. "Adultery." *Critical Inquiry* 24 (Winter): 289–327.

Kirby, Michael. 1995. "On Acting and Non-acting." In *Acting (Re)Considered*. Ed. Phillip B. Zarrilli. New York: Routledge, 43–58.

Kirschenblatt-Gimblett, Barbara. 1991. "Objects of Ethnography." In *The Poetics and Politics of Museum Display*. Ed. Ivan Karp and Steven D. Lavine. Washington, DC: Smithsonian Institution Press, 386–443.

Klien, Stephen. 2005. "Patriot and Citizen Agency in *Black Hawk Down*." *Critical Studies in Mass Communication* 22, 5: 427–50.

Knight, Jeff Parker. 1990. "Literature as Equipment for Killing: Performance as Rhetoric in Military Training Camps." *Text and Performance Quarterly* 10, 2: 157–68.

Kolko, Beth E., Lisa Nakamura, and Gilbert B. Rodman, eds. 2000. "Race in Cyberspace: An Introduction." *Race in Cyberspace*. New York: Routledge, 1–14.

Kondo, Dorinne. 1997. *About Face: Performing Race in Fashion and Theater. New York: Routledge*.

Kunrzu, Hari. 1997. "You Are Cyborg." *Wired* 5, 2. Available at http://www.wired.com/wired/archive/5.02/ffharaway_pr.html

Kuppers, Petra. 2001. "Addenda? Contemporary Cyborgs and the Mediation of Embodiment." *Body Space Technology Journal* 1. Available at http://people.brunel.ac.uk/bst/v010101/index.html

Kuppers, Petra. 2003. *Disability and Contemporary Performance: Bodies on Edge*. New York: Routledge.

Kuppers, Petra. 2004. "Space Rules: Techno-Nomad Theatre." *Body Space Technology Journal* 4. Available at http://people.brunel.ac.uk/bst/v0104/index.html

La Caze, Marguerite. 2002. "The Mourning of Loss in 'The Sixth Sense.'" *Post Script: Essays in Film and the Humanities* 21, 3: 111–21.

LaFountain, Marc J. 1989. "Foucault and Dr. Ruth." *Critical Studies in Mass Communication* 6, 2: 123–38.

Lane, Jill. 2002. "Reverend Billy: Preaching, Protest, and Postindustrial Flanerie." *TDR: The Drama Review* 46, 1: 60–84.

Langdon, Harry N. 1973. "Role-Playing in the Speech Fundamentals Class." *Speech Teacher* 22, 1: 78–81.

Langellier, Kristin M. 1983. "A Phenomenological Approach to Audience." *Literature in Performance* 3, 2: 34–39.

Langellier, Kristin M. 1993. "Personal Narrative as Performance Practice in HIV Education." *HIV Education: Performing Personal Narratives*. Ed. Frederick C. Corey. Tempe: Arizona State University, 181–93.

Langellier, Kristin M. 2001. "You're Marked: Breast Cancer, Tattoo, and the Narrative Performance of Identity." *Narrative and Identity: Studies in Autobiography, Self, and Culture*. Ed. J. Brockmeier and D. Carbaugh. Philadelphia: John Benjamins, 145–84.

Langellier, Kristin M., and Eric E. Peterson. 2004. *Storytelling in Daily Life: Performing Narrative*. Philadelphia: Temple University Press.

Larabee, Ann. 1992. "Going through Harriet: Ritual and Theatre in the Women's Colleges." *New England Theatre Journal* 3: 39–59.

Lavery, David. 2001. "From Cinespace to Cyberspace: Zionists and Agents, Realists and Gamers in 'The Matrix' and 'eXistenZ.'" *Journal of Popular Film and Television* 28, 4: 150–57.

Lay, Mary M. 2003. "Midwifery on Trial: Balancing Privacy Rights and Health Concerns after Roe v. Wade." *Quarterly Journal of Speech* 89, 1: 60–78.

Lay, Mary M., and Billie J. Wahlstrom. 1996. "The Rhetoric of Midwifery: Conflicts and Conversations in the Minnesota Home Birth Community in the 1990s." *Quarterly Journal of Speech* 82, 4: 383–402.

Laye, Camara. 1954. *The Dark Child: Autobiography of an African Boy.* New York: Farrar, Straus and Giroux.

Lee, Josephine. 1999. "Disciplining Theater and Drama in the English Department: Some Reflections on 'Performance' and Institutional History." *Text and Performance Quarterly* 19, 2: 145–58.

Lee, Josephine. 2004. "Asian America Is in the Heartland: Performing Korean Adoptee Experience." *Asian North American Identities: Beyond the Hyphen.* Ed. Eleanor Ty and Donald C. Goellnicht. Bloomington: Indiana University Press.

Lee, Wen Shu. 2002. "Dialogue on the Edge: Ferment in Communication and Culture." *Transforming Communication About Culture.* Ed. M. J. Collier et al. Thousand Oaks, CA: Sage, 219–80.

Lei, Joy L. 2003. "'(Un)necessary Toughness': Those 'Loud Black Girls' and Those 'Quiet Asian Boys.'" *Anthropology and Education Quarterly* 32: 158–81.

Lennon, Brian. 2000. "Screening a Digital Visual Poetics." *Configurations* 8, 1: 63–85.

Lentriccia, Frank. 1983. *Criticism and Social Change.* Chicago: University of Chicago Press.

Levi-Strauss, Claude. 1969. *The Elementary Structures of Kinship.* Boston: Beacon Press.

Levi-Strauss, Claude. 1976. *Structural Anthropology.* New York: Basic Books.

Lieberfeld, Daniel, and Judith Sanders. 1998. "Comedy and Identity in 'Some Like It Hot': Keeping the Characters Straight." *Journal of Popular Film and Television* 26, 3: 128–35.

Lindemann, Kurt. 2005. "Live(s) Online: Narrative Performance, Presence, and Community in LiveJournal.com." *Text and Performance Quarterly* 25, 4: 354–72.

Littlejohn, Stephen W. 1977. "Symbolic Interactionism as an Approach to the Study of Human Communication." *Quarterly Journal of Speech* 63: 84–91.

Locke, Liz. 1999. "Don't Dream It, Be It." *New Directions in Folklore* 3: 1–3.

Logan, Christie. 2005. "The Space Between: Phenomenologies of Audience, Performer, and Place for Three Performances of *Menopause and Desire.*" *Text and Performance Quarterly* 25, 3: 282–89.

Lombard, Matthew, and Theresa Ditton. 1997. "At the Heart of It All: The Concept of Presence." *Journal of Computer-Mediated Communication* 3, 2. Available online at http://jcmc.indiana.edu/v013/issue2/lombard.html

Long, Beverly Whitaker. 1977. "Evaluating Performed Literature." In *Studies in Interpretation II.* Ed. Esther M. Doyle and Virginia Hastings Floyd. The Netherlands: Rodopi.

Long, Beverly, and Mary Frances HopKins. 1982. *Performing Literature: An Introduction to Oral Interpretation.* Englewood Cliffs, NJ: Prentice Hall.

Louis, Ross. 2005. "Performing English, Performing Bodies: A Case for Critical Performative Language Pedagogy." *Text and Performance Quarterly* 25, 4: 334–54.

Lovaas, Karen E. 2003. "Speaking to Silence: Toward Queering Nonverbal Communication." *Queer Theory and Communication: From Disciplining Queers to Queering the Discipline(s).* Ed. Gus A. Yep, Karen E. Lovaas, and Jon P. Elias. New York: Harrington Park, 87–107.

Love, Lisa L., and Nathaniel Kohn. 2001. "This, That, and the Other: Fraught Possibilities of the Souvenir." *Text and Performance Quarterly* 21: 47–63.

Lyotard, Jean-Francois. 1984. *The Postmodern Condition: A Report on Knowledge.* Trans. G. Bennington and B. Masumi. Minneapolis: University of Minnesota Press.

MacAloon, John. 1986. "Toward a Definition of Performance Studies, Part I." *Theatre Journal* 38, 3: 372–76.

MacIntyre, Alasdair. 1984. *After Virtue: A Study in Moral Theory,* 2nd ed. Notre Dame, IN: University of Notre Dame Press.

MacLachlan, Gale, and Ian Reid. 1994. *Framing and Interpretation.* Melbourne: Melbourne University Press.

Madison, D. Soyini. 1998. "Performance, Personal Narratives, and Politics of Possibility." *The Future of Performance Studies: The Next Millennium.* Ed. Sheron J. Dailey. Annandale, VA: National Communication Association, 276–86.

Madison, D. Soyini. 2005. *Critical Ethnography.* Thousand Oaks, CA: Sage.

Manning, Phil. 1991. "Drama as Life: The Significance of Goffman's Changing Use of the Theatrical Metaphor." *Sociological Theory* 9, 1: 70–86.

Marcuse, Herbert. 1978. *The Aesthetic Dimension: Toward a Critique of Marxist Aesthetics.* Boston: Beacon Press.

Marranca, Bonnie, and Gautam Dasguta. 2002. "Editorial: A New PAJ Platform." *PAJ: A Journal of Performance and Arts* 24, 1: 1–4.

Martin, Judith N., and Thomas K. Nakayama. 1999. "Thinking Dialectically About Culture and Communication." *Communication Theory* 9: 1–25.

Martin, Judith N., and Thomas K. Nakayama. 2004. *Intercultural Communication in Contexts,* 3rd ed. Boston: McGraw-Hill.

Marvin, Carolyn. 1988. *When Old Technologies Were New: Thinking About Electric Communication in the Late Nineteenth Century.* New York: Oxford University Press.

"Mass Suicide Involved Sedatives, Vodka, and Careful Planning." 1997, 27 March. *U.S. News* Story Page. CNN Interactive. Available at http://www.cnn.com/us/9703/27/suicide/index.html

Maynard, Patrick. 1997. "Introduction to Perspectives on the Arts and Technology." *The Journal of Aesthetics and Art Criticism* 55, 2: 95–106.

Mazer, Sharon. 1990. "The Doggie Doggie World of Professional Wrestling." *TDR: The Drama Review* 34, 4: 96–122.

McAdam, Doug. 1982. *Political Process and the Development of Black Insurgency, 1930–1970.* Chicago: University of Chicago Press.

McCartney, Paul. 2006. "Question #4: Interview about Love Album." Available at http://www.thebeatles.com/hub/love/site/?sec=listen

McCloskey, Deirdre. 1999. *Crossing: A Memoir.* Chicago: University of Chicago Press.

McConachie, Bruce. 1998. "Slavery and Authenticity: Performing a Slave Auction at Colonial Williamsburg." *Theatre Annual* 51: 71–81.

McConachie, Bruce. 2002. "Theatre of the Oppressed with Students of Privilege: Practicing Boal in the American College Classroom." In *Teaching Performance Studies.* Ed. Nathan Stucky and Cynthia Wimmer. Carbondale: University of Southern Illinois Press, 247–60.

McDorman, Todd F. 2005. "Controlling Death: Bio-Power and the Right-to-Die Controversy." *Communication and Critical/Cultural Studies* 2, 3: 257–80.

McGonigal, Jane. 2005. "SuperGaming: Ubiquitous Play and Performance for Massively Scaled Community." *Modern Drama* 48, 3: 471–91.

McKenzie, Jon. 1994. "Virtual Reality: Performance, Immersion, and the Thaw." *TDR: The Drama Review* 38, 4: 83–106.

McKenzie, Jon. 2001. *Perform or Else: From Discipline to Performance.* New York: Routledge.

McLemee, Scott. 2001, 20 April. "A Puzzling Figure in Literary Criticism Is Suddenly Central." *Chronicle of Higher Education* 46, 32: A26.

McLuhan, Marshall. 1964. *Understanding Media: The Extensions of Man.* New York: McGraw-Hill.

McMaster, Geoff. 2003, 27 October. "Who's Your Shakespeare?" *Express News,* University of Alberta. Available at http://www.expressnews.ualberta.ca/article.cfm?id=5189

Mead, George Herbert. 1934. *Mind, Self, and Society.* Chicago: University of Chicago Press.

Mehren, Elizabeth. 2005. "A Gospel and Granola Band." *Los Angeles Times,* 23 November.

Melrose, Susan. 1998. "Introduction to Part Four: Feminist Approaches to Gender in Performance." In *The Routledge Reader in Gender and Performance.* Ed. Lizbeth Goodman and Jane de Gay. London: Routledge, 131–35.

Merrill, Lisa. 2000. *When Romeo Was a Woman: Charlotte Cushman and Her Circle of Female Spectators.* Ann Arbor: University of Michigan Press.

Messinger, Sheldon L., with Harold Sampson and Robert D. Towne. 1962. "Life as Theater: Some Notes on the Dramaturgic Approach to Social Reality." *Sociometry,* 25. Reprinted in *Drama in Life: The Uses of Communication in Society.* Ed. James E. Combs and Michael W. Mansfield. New York: Hastings, 1976, 73–83.

Meyerhoff, Barbara G., Linda A. Camino, and Edith Turner. 1987. "Rites of Passage: An Overview." *Encyclopedia of Religion.* Volume 12. Ed. Mircea Eliade. New York: Macmillan, 380–87.

Miller, Lynn C. 1998. "The Study of Literature in Performance: A Future?" *The Future of Performance Studies.* Ed. Sheron J. Daily. Annandale, VA: National Communication Association, 51–55.

Mitchell, William J. 1995. *City of Bits.* Cambridge, MA: MIT Press.

Mitchell, W. J. Thomas. 2003. "The Work of Art in the Age of Biocybernetic Reproduction." *Modernism/Modernity* 10, 3: 481–500.

Mock, Roberta. 2000. *Performing Processes: Creating Live Performance.* Bristol, UK: Intellect Books.

Morgan, Jayne M., and Kathleen J. Krone. 2001. "Bending the Rules of 'Professional' Display: Emotional Improvisation in Caregiver Performances." *Journal of Applied Communication* 29, 4: 317–40.

Morreale, Joanne. 2000. "Sitcoms Say Goodbye: The Cultural Spectacle of 'Seinfeld's' Last Episode." *Journal of Popular Film and Television* 28, 3: 108–15.

Motoyama, Kate T. 1991. "Mauser: A Critique of *Measures Taken.*" *Text and Performance Quarterly* 11: 46–55.

Mumby, Dennis K. 1997. "Modernism, Postmodernism, and Communication Studies: A Rereading of an Ongoing Debate." *Communication Theory* 7, 1: 1–28.

Mumford, Lewis. 1952. *Art and Technics.* New York: Columbia University Press.

Mumford, Lewis. 1961. *The City in History: Its Origins, Its Transformations, and Its Prospects.* New York: Harcourt Brace and World.

Muñoz, José Esteban. 1999. *Disidentifications: Queers of Color and the Performance of Politics.* Minneapolis: University of Minnesota Press.

Murphy, Alexandra G. 2001. "The Flight Attendant Dilemma: An Analysis of Communication and Sensemaking during In-Flight Emergencies." *Journal of Applied Communication Research* 29, 1: 30–53.

Murphy, Alexandra G. 2002. "Organizational Politics of Place and Space: The Perpetual Liminoid Performance of Commercial Flight." *Text and Performance Quarterly* 22, 4: 297–316.

Myers, Greg. 2003. "Risk and Face: A Review of the Six Studies." *Health, Risk and Society* 5, 2: 215–20.

Nicholson, Linda. 1995. "Interpreting Gender." *Social Postmodernism: Beyond Identity Politics.* Ed. Linda Nicholson and Steven Seidman. Cambridge, UK: Cambridge University Press, 39–67.

Notaro, Laurie. 2002. *The Idiot Girls' Action Adventure Club.* New York: Villard.

Nudd, Donna Marie. 1998. "Improvising Our Way to the Future." *The Future of Performance Studies.* Ed. Sheron J. Dailey. Annandale, VA: National Communication Association, 150–55.

Okpewho, Isidore. 1992. "The Oral Artist: Training and Preparation." *African Oral Literature.* Bloomington: Indiana University Press, 21–25. Reprinted in *The Performance Studies Reader,* 2004. Ed. Henry Bial. New York: Routledge, 226–30.

Olbrys, Stephen Gencarella. 2006. "Disciplining the Carnivalesque: Chris Farley's Exotic Dance." *Communication and Critical/Cultural Studies* 3, 3: 240–60.

Olsen, David. 1992. "Floods and Church Secretaries, Buffalo Creek and Northwestern: Struggling with the Seams Between." *Text and Performance Quarterly* 12: 329–48.

Olsen, David S. 2001. "The New Religious Right Versus Media Wrongs: AFA Fights 'Temptation.'" *Journal of Film and Video* 53, 2–3: 3–22.

Olsen, Tillie. 1978. *Silences.* New York: Delacorte Press/Seymour Lawrence.

Olson, Kathleen K. 2002/2003. "Homelessness as Political Theater: The Community for Creative Non-violence and Symbolic Speech." *Free Speech Yearbook* 40: 115–28.

Ong, Walter. 1982. *Orality and Literacy. The Technologizing of the Word.* New York: Methuen.

Orlean, Susan. 1998. *The Orchid Thief.* New York: Random House.

Osburn, John. 1994. "The Dramaturgy of the Tabloid: Climax and Novelty in a Theory of Condensed Forms." *Theatre Journal* 46: 507–22.

Ott, Brian L. 2003. 'I'm Bart Simpson, Who the Hell Are You?' A Study in Postmodern Identity (Re)Construction." *Journal of Popular Culture* 37, 1: 56–81

Ott, Brian, and Cameron Walter. 2000. "Intertextuality: Interpretive Practice and Textual Strategy." *Critical Studies in Media Communication* 17, 4: 429–46.

Overheard in New York. Available at http://www.overheardinnewyork.com

Pacanowsky, Michael E., and Nick O'Donnell Trujillo. 1983. "Organizational Communication as Cultural Performance." *Communication Monographs* 50, 3: 127–47.

Palmer, Richard. 1977. "Toward a Postmodern Hermeneutics of Performance." *Performance in Postmodern Culture.* Ed. Michel Benamou and Charles Caramello. Milwaukee, WI: Coda Press, 19–32.

Parker, Andrew, and Eve Kosofsky Sedgwick. 1995. "Introduction: Performativity and Performance." *Performativity and Performance.* Ed. Andrew Parker and Eve Kosofsky Sedgwick. New York: Routledge, 1–18.

Parker-Starbuck, Jennifer. 2003. "The Body Electric: Cathy Weis at Dance Theatre Workshop." *PAJ: A Journal of Performance and Art* 25, 2: 93–98.

Park-Fuller, Linda M. 1998. "Towards an Interdisciplinary Performance Course: Process and Poetics." In *The Future of Performance Studies: Visions and Revisions.* Ed. Sheron J. Dailey. Annandale, VA: National Communication Association, 163–69.

Park-Fuller, Linda M. 2003. "Audiencing the Audience: Playback Theatre, Performative Writing, and Social Activism." *Text and Performance Quarterly* 23, 3: 288–310.

Payne, A. David. 1989. "*The Wizard of Oz:* Therapeutic Rhetoric in a Contemporary Media Ritual." *Quarterly Journal of Speech* 75, 1: 25–40.

Payne, David, with Roderick Hart. 1996. "Dramatistic Criticism." In *Modern Rhetorical Criticism,* 2nd ed. Boston: Allyn and Bacon, 259–84.

Pelias, Ronald J. 1992. *Performance Studies: The Interpretation of Aesthetic Texts.* New York: St. Martin's Press.

Pelias, Ronald J. 1997. "Confessions of an Apprehensive Performer." *Text and Performance Quarterly* 17, 1: 25–32.

Pelias, Ronald J. 1998. "Meditations and Mediations." In *The Future of Performance Studies: Visions and Revisions.* Ed. Sheron J. Dailey. Annandale, VA: National Communication Association, 14–22.

Pelias, Ronald J. 2006. "A Personal History of Lust on Bourbon Street." *Text and Performance Quarterly* 26, 1: 47–57.

Pelias, Ronald J., and James VanOosting. 1987. "A Paradigm for Performance Studies." *Quarterly Journal of Speech* 73: 219–31.

Penley, Constance, and Andrew Ross. 1991. "Cyborgs at Large: Interview with Donna Haraway." *Social Text* 25/26: 8–23.

Pezzullo, Phaedra C. 2003. "Touring 'Cancer Alley,' Louisiana: Performances of Community and Memory for Environmental Justice." *Text and Performance Quarterly* 23, 3: 226–52.

Phelan, Peggy. 1993. *Unmarked: The Politics of Performance.* New York: Routledge.

Phelan, Peggy. 1997. *Mourning Sex: Performing Public Memories.* New York: Routledge.

Phelan, Peggy. 2004. "Marina Abramovic: Witnessing Shadows." *Theatre Journal* 56: 569–77.

Piper, Adrian. 1992. "Passing for White, Passing for Black." *Out of Order, Out of Sight, Volume 1: Selected Writings in Meta-Art, 1968–1992.* Cambridge, MA: MIT Press, 275–307.

Pittam, Jeffery, and Cynthia Gallois. 2000. "Malevolence, Stigma, and Social Distance: Maximizing Intergroup Differences in HIV/AIDS Discourse." *Journal of Applied Communication Research* 21, 1: 24–44.

Pollock, Della. 1988a. "Aesthetic Negation after WWII: Mediating Bertolt Brecht and Theodor Adorno." *Literature in Performance* 8, 1: 12–20.

Pollock, Della. 1988b. "The Play as Novel: Reappropriating Brecht's *Drums in the Night.*" *Quarterly Journal of Speech* 74: 296–309.

Pollock, Della. 1995. "Performativity." *The Oxford Companion to Women's Writing in the United States.* Ed. Cathy N. Davidson and Linda Wagner-Martin. Oxford: Oxford University Press, 657–58.

Pollock, Della. 1999. *Telling Bodies Performing Birth: Everyday Narratives of Childbirth.* New York: Columbia University Press.

Pollock, Della, and J. Robert Cox. 1991. "Historicizing 'Reason': Critical Theory, Practice, and Postmodernity." *Communication Monographs* 58: 170–78.

Pomerantz, Anita. 1988. "Offering a Candidate Answer: An Information Seeking Strategy." *Communication Monographs* 55: 360–73.

Poster, Mark. 1988. "Introduction." *Jean Baudrillard: Selected Writings.* Stanford, CA: Stanford University Press, 1–9.

Poster, Mark. 1990. *The Mode of Information: Poststructuralism and Social Context.* Cambridge, UK: Polity Press.

Redmon, David. 2003. "Playful Deviance as an Urban Leisure Activity: Secret Selves, Self-Validation, and Entertaining Performances." *Deviant Behavior* 24, 1: 27–51.

Reinelt, Janelle. 2006. "Toward a Poetics of Theatre and Public Events." *TDR: The Drama Review* 50, 3: 69–87.

Rheingold, Howard. 1993. "A Slice of Life in My Virtual Community." *Global Networks: Computers and International Communication.* Ed. Linda M. Harasim. Cambridge, MA: MIT Press, 57–80.

Richards, Alison. 2001. "Shaking the Frame: Erving Goffman and Performance Studies." *Australasian Drama Studies* 39: 58–75.

Richmond, Virginia P., and James C. McCrosky. 2000. *Nonverbal Behavior in Interpersonal Relations.* Boston: Allyn and Bacon.

Roach, Joseph. 2002. "Theatre Studies/Cultural Studies/Performance Studies: The Three Unities." In *Teaching Performance Studies.* Ed. Nathan Stucky and Cynthia Wimmer. Carbondale: Southern Illinois University Press, 33–40.

Roberts, Churchill. 1972. "The Effects of Self-Confrontation, Role Playing, and Response Feedback on the Level of Self-Esteem." *Speech Teacher* 21, 1: 22–39.

Roberts, Kathleen Glenister. 2002. "Speech, Gender, and the Performance of Culture: Native American 'Princesses.'" *Text and Performance Quarterly* 22, 4: 261–79.

Robinson, Amy. 1994. "It Takes One to Know One: Passing and Communities of Common Interest." *Critical Inquiry* 20: 715–36.

Robinson, Eugene. 2005. "(White) Women We Love." *Washington Post,* 10 June, A2.

Rockler, Naomi R. 2002. "Overcoming 'It's Just Entertainment': Perspective by Incongruity as a Strategy for Media Literacy." *Journal of Popular Film and Television* 30, 1: 16–22.

Rodden, John. 1995. "A TPQ Interview with Howard's End (and Means)." *Text and Performance Quarterly* 15, 3: 229–44.

Rodham, Karen. 2000. "Role Theory and the Analysis of Managerial Work: The Case of Occupational Health Professionals." *Journal of Applied Management Studies* 9, 1: 71–81.

Rodríguez, José, Marc D. Rich, Rachel Hastings, and Jennifer L. Page. 2006. "Assessing the Impact of Augusto Boal's 'Proactive Performance': An Embodied Approach for Cultivating Prosocial Responses to Sexual Assault." *Text and Performance Quarterly* 26, 3: 229–53.

Roloff, Leland. 1973. *The Perception and Evocation of Literature.* Glenview, IL: Scott, Foresman.

Roman, David. 2000. "Comment: The Details of Difference." *Theatre Journal* 52, 3: 302–4.

Roscoe, Jane. 2000. "Mock-Documentary Goes Mainstream: 'The Blair Witch Project.'" *Jump Cut* 43: 3–8.

Roy, Parama. 1995. "Tango and the Postmodern Uses of Passion." *Cruising the Performative: Interventions into the Representation of Ethnicity, Nationality, and Sexuality.* Ed. Sue-Ellen Case, Philip Brett, and Susan Leigh Foster. Bloomington: Indiana University Press.

Rozik, Eli. 2002. *The Roots of Theatre: Rethinking Ritual and Other Theories of Origin.* Iowa City: University of Iowa Press.

Rubin, Gayle. 1975. "The Traffic in Women: Notes on the 'Political Economy' of Sex." *Toward an Anthropology of Women.* Ed. Rayna R. Reiter. New York: Monthly Review Press, 157–210.

Rufino, Rayniel. 2006. "Ten Points to Consider Before You Sign a Military Enlistment Agreement." Available at www.veteransforpeaceny.org/vfpnyvsorayniel.htm

Rufo, Kenneth. 2003. "The Mirror in *The Matrix* of Media Ecology." *Critical Studies in Media Communication* 20, 2: 117–40.

Rukeyser, Muriel. 1973. "Myth." *Breaking Open.* New York: Random House.

Russell, Larry. 2004. "A Long Way Toward Compassion." *Text and Performance Quarterly* 24, 3/4: 233–54.

Saltz, David. 1997. "The Art of Interaction: Interactivity, Performativity, and Computers." *The Journal of Aesthetics and Art Criticism* 5, 2: 117–27.

Saltz, David. 2001. "Live Media: Interactive Technology and Theatre." *Theatre Topics* 11, 2: 107–30.

Sandahl, Carrie. 1999. "Ahhh Freak Out: Metaphors of Disability and Femaleness in Performance." *Theatre Topics* 9, 1: 11–30.

Sandahl, Carrie. 2003. "Queering The Crip or Cripping The Queer? Intersections of Queer and Crip Identities in Solo Autobiographical Performance." *GLQ: A Journal of Lesbian and Gay Studies* 9, 1–2: 25–56.

Sandhana, Lakshmi. 2005, 6 June. "Pacman Comes to Life Virtually." BBC News. Available at http://news.bbc.co.uk/go/pr/fr/-/2/hi/technology/4607449.stm

Sandoval-Sanchez, Alberto. 1999. *Jose, Can You See? Latinos On and Off Broadway.* Madison: University of Wisconsin Press.

Santino, Jack. 2004. "Performative Commemoratives, the Person, and the Public: Spontaneous Shrines, Emergent Ritual, and the Field of Folklore." *Journal of American Folklore* 117, 466: 363–72.

Saussure, Ferdinand de. 1959/1966. *Course in General Linguistics.* New York: McGraw-Hill.

Sauter, Willmar. 2004. "Introducing the Theatrical Event." *Theatrical Events: Borders, Dynamics, Frames.* Ed. Vicky Ann Cremona, Peter Eversmann, Hans van Maanen, Willmar Sauter, and John Tulloch. Amsterdam: Rodopi, 3–14.

Sawin, Patricia E. 2001. "Transparent Masks: The Ideology and Practice of Disguise in Contemporary Cajun Mardi Gras." *Journal of American Folklore* 114, 452: 173–201.

Sawin, Patricia E. 2002. "Performance at the Nexus of Gender, Power, and Desire: Reconsidering Bauman's *Verbal Art* from the Perspective of Gendered Subjectivity as Performance." *Journal of American Folklore* 115, 455: 28–61.

Sayre, Henry. 1990. "Performance." *Critical Terms for Literary Study.* Ed. Frank Lentricchia and Thomas McLaughlin. Chicago: University of Chicago Press, 91–104.

Schechner, Richard. 1988a. *Performance Theory,* Rev. ed. New York: Routledge.

Schechner, Richard. 1988b. "Victor Turner's Last Adventure." *Anthropology of Performance.* By Victor Turner. New York: PAJ, 7–20.

Schechner, Richard. 1990. "Magnitudes of Performance." *By Means of Performance: Intercultural Studies of Theatre and Ritual.* Ed. Richard Schechner and Willa Appel. Cambridge, UK: Cambridge University Press, 19–49.

Schechner, Richard. 1993. *The Future of Ritual: Writing on Culture and Performance.* New York: Routledge.

Schechner, Richard. 2002a. "Fundamentals of Performance Studies." In *Teaching Performance Studies.* Ed. Nathan Stucky and Cynthia Wimmer. Carbondale: Southern Illinois University Press, ix–xii.

Schechner, Richard. 2002b. *Performance Studies: An Introduction.* London: Routledge.

Scheie, Timothy. 1997. "'Questionable Terms': Shylock, Celine's *L'Eglise,* and the Performative." *Text and Performance Quarterly* 17: 153–69.

Schiebel, Dean. 1992. "Faking Identity in Clubland: The Communicative Performance of 'Fake ID.'" *Text and Performance Quarterly* 12, 2: 160–76.

Schneider, Raymond J. 1994. "Tampa: Tales of Two Cities." *Text and Performance Quarterly* 14, 4: 334–42.

Schneider, Rebecca. 2000. "Nomamedia: On Critical Art Ensemble." *TDR: The Drama Review* 44, 4: 120–31.

Schober, Anna. 2003. "The Desire for Bodily Subversions: Episodes, Interplays, and Monsters." *Performance Research* 8, 1: 69–81.

Scholes, Robert. 2001. *The Crafty Reader.* New Haven, CT: Yale University Press.

Schriver, Kristina, and Donna Marie Nudd. 2002. "Mickee Faust Club's Performative Protest Events." *Text and Performance Quarterly* 22, 3: 196–216.

Schutzman, Mady. 1994. "Brechtian Shamanism: The Political Therapy of Augusto Boal." In *Playing Boal: Theatre, Therapy, Activism.* Ed. Mady Schutzman and Jan Cohen-Cruz. London: Routledge, 137–56.

Sedaris, David. 2004. "Nuit of the Living Dead." *Dress Your Family in Corduroy and Denim.* New York: Back Bay Books, 254–57.

Sedgwick, Eve K. 2003. *Touching Feeling: Affect, Pedagogy, Performativity.* Durham, NC: Duke University Press.

Senna, Danzy. 2005. "Passing and the Problematic of Multiracial Pride (or, Why One Mixed Girl Still Answers to Black)." *Black Cultural Traffic: Crossroads in Global Performance and Popular Culture.* Ed. Harry J. Elam Jr. and Kennell Jackson. Ann Arbor: University of Michigan Press, 83–87.

Shailor, Barbara A. 1999. "Adventure and Art." In *Adventure and Art: The First One Hundred Years of Printing.* Ed. Paul Needham and Michael Joseph. New Brunswick, NJ: Rutgers University Libraries.

Shelton, Gary. 2005. "Free from Fear." *St. Petersburg Times,* 11 November, 1C.

Shields, Rob. 2003. *The Virtual*. London: Routledge.

Shields, Vickie Rutledge, and Colleen Coughlin. 2000. "Performing Rodeo Queen Culture: Athleticism and Excessive Feminine Masquerade." *Text and Performance Quarterly* 20, 2: 182–203.

Shugart, Helene A. 2001. "Parody as Subversive Performance: Denaturalising Gender and Reconstituting Desire in *Ellen*." *Text and Performance Quarterly* 21: 95–113.

Shugart, Helene A. 2003. "Performing Ambiguity: The Passing of Ellen DeGeneres." *Text and Performance Quarterly* 23, 1: 30–54.

Sieg, Katrin. 2002. *Ethnic Drag: Performing Race, Nation, Sexuality in West Germany*. Ann Arbor: University of Michigan Press.

Silverstone, Roger. 2003. "Preface." *Television: Technology and Cultural Form*. Raymond Williams. London: Taylor and Francis, vii–xiii.

Simpson, Philip L. 2003. "America's Scariest Home Videos: Serial Killers and Reality Television." *Post Script: Essays in Film and the Humanities* 22, 2: 103–23.

Singer, Milton. 1972. *When a Great Tradition Modernizes: An Anthropological Approach to Indian Civilization*. New York: Praeger.

Sipress, Alan. 2007, 2 June. "Does Virtual Reality Need a Sheriff?" *Washington Post*, A01

Sloan, Thomas O. 1967. "Restoration of Rhetoric to Literary Study." *Speech Teacher* 16: 91–97.

Sloan, Thomas O., and Joanna H. Maclay. 1972. *Interpretation: An Approach to the Study of Literature*. New York: Random House.

Sloop, John M. 2000. "A Van with a Bar and a Bed: Ritualized Gender Norms in the John/Joan Case." *Text and Performance Quarterly* 20, 2: 130–49.

Smit, Christopher R. 2003. "'Please Call Now, Before It's Too Late': Spectacle Discourse in the Jerry Lewis Muscular Dystrophy Telethon." *Journal of Popular Culture* 36, 4: 687–703.

Smith, Anna Deavere. 1993. *Fires in the Mirror*. New York: Anchor.

Snicket, Lemony. 1999. *The Bad Beginning*. New York: Scholastic Press.

Snow, Stephen Eddy. 1993. *Performing the Pilgrims: A Study of Ethnohistorical Role-Playing at Plimoth Plantation*. Jackson: University Press of Mississippi.

Snyder, Sharon L., and David T. Mitchell. 2001. "Re-engaging the Body: Disability Studies and the Resistance to Embodiment." *Public Culture* 13, 3: 367–89.

Sobchack, Vivian. 1995a. "Beating the Meat/Surviving the Text, or How to Get Out of this Century Alive." *Body and Society* 1, 3: 205–14.

Sobchack, Vivian. 1995b. "New Age Mutant Ninja Hackers: Reading *Mondo 2000*." In *Flame Wars: The Discourse of Cyberculture*. Ed. Mark Dery. Durham, NC: Duke University Press, 11–28.

Soyinka, Wole. 1995. "Unholy Words and Terminal Censorship." *The Dissident Word: The Oxford Amnesty Lectures 1995*. Ed. Chris Miller. New York: Basic Books, 62–92.

Spitz, Bob. 2005. *The Beatles: The Biography*. New York: Little, Brown.

Stahl, Jon. 2002. "Guiding the Creation of the Short, Narrative Script: A Pedagogical Model." *Journal of Film and Video* 54, 4: 47–53.

Stallybrass, Peter, and Allon White. 1986. *The Politics and Poetics of Transgression*. Ithaca, NY: Cornell University Press.

States, Bert O. 1996. "Performance as Metaphor." *Theatre Journal* 48, 1: 1–26.

Stephens, Judith L. 2000. "Politics and Aesthetics, Race and Gender: Georgia Douglas Johnson's Lynching Dramas as Black Feminist Cultural Performance." *Text and Performance Quarterly* 20, 3: 251–67.

Stephenson, Tracy. 1998. "My Silence Speaks Volumes: Mickey Mouse and the Ideology of an Icon." *Theatre Annual* 51: 54–70.

Stephenson, Tracy. 2004. "Performing Backpacking: Constructing 'Authenticity' Every Step of the Way." *Text and Performance Quarterly* 24, 2: 139–61.

Stern, Carol Simpson, and Bruce Henderson. 1993. *Performance: Texts and Contexts.* New York: Longman.

Sterne, Jonathan. 2000. "The Computer Race Goes to Class: How Computers in Schools Helped Shape the Racial Topography of the Internet." In *Race in Cyberspace.* Ed. Beth E. Kolko, Lisa Nakamura, and Gilbert G. Rodman. New York: Routledge, 191–212.

Sterne, Jonathan. 2006. "Communication as Techne." In *Communication as . . . Perspectives on Theory.* Ed. Gregory J. Shepherd, Jeffrey St. John, and Ted Striphas. Thousand Oaks, CA: Sage, 91–98.

Stewart, Kathleen. 1996. *A Space on the Side of the Road: Cultural Poetics in an "Other" America.* Princeton, NJ: Princeton University Press.

Stone, Allucquere Rosanne. 1995. *The War of Desire and Technology at the Close of the Mechanical Age.* Cambridge, MA: MIT Press.

Stone, John. 2000. "Evil in the Early Cinema of Oliver Stone: 'Platoon' and 'Wall Street' as Modern Morality Plays." *Journal of Popular Film and Television* 28, 2: 80–87.

Strate, Lance. 2004. "A Media Ecology Review." *A Quarterly Review of Communication Research* 23, 2: 1–48.

Strehovec, Janez. 1997. "Vertigo—on Purpose: Entertainment in Simulators." *Journal of Popular Culture* 31, 1: 199–210.

Strine, Mary S. 1998. "Articulating Performance/Performativity: Disciplinary Tasks and the Contingencies of Practice." *Communication: Views from the Helm for the 21st Century.* Ed. Judith S. Trent. Boston: Allyn and Bacon, 312–17.

Strine, Mary S. 2005. "Jorie Graham's Subversive Poetics: Appetites of Mind, Empire-building, and the Spaces of Lyric Performativity." *Text and Performance Quarterly* 25, 1: 3–13.

Strine, Mary C., Beverly Whitaker Long, and Mary Frances HopKins. 1990. "Research in Interpretation and Performance Studies: Trends, Issues, Priorities." *Speech Communication: Essays to Commemorate the 75th Anniversary of The Speech Communication Association.* Ed. Gerald M. Phillips and Julia T. Wood. Carbondale: Southern Illinois University Press, 181–204.

Stucky, Nathan. 1993. "Toward an Aesthetics of Natural Performance." *Text and Performance Quarterly* 13, 2: 168–80.

Swartz, Mimi. 2007, April. "Punch Line." *Texas Monthly,* 122–25, 284.

Taft-Kaufman, Jill. 1985. "Oral Interpretation: Twentieth-Century Theory and Practice." In *Speech Communication in the 20th Century.* Ed. Thomas W. Benson. Carbondale: Southern Illinois University Press, 157–83.

Taft-Kaufman, Jill. 2004. "A *TPQ* Interview: Tony Kushner on Theatre, Politics, and Culture." *Text and Performance Quarterly* 24, 1: 38–54.

Taylor, Diana. 2003. *The Archive and the Repertoire: Performing Cultural Memory in the Americas.* Durham, NC: Duke University Press.

Taylor, Julie. 1998. *Paper Tangos.* Durham, NC: Duke University Press.

Telesco, Grace. 2001. "Theatre of the Recruits." *Theatre* 31, 3: 55–61.

Theory Cards. Available at http://www.theorycards.org.uk/card06.htm

Thompson, Debbie. 2003. "'Is Race a Trope?' Anna Deavere Smith and the Question of Racial Performativity." *African American Review* 37: 127–38.

Thompson, Deborah. 1996. "Blackface, Rape, and Beyond: Rehearsing Interracial Dialogue in *Sally's Rape.*" *Theatre Journal* 48, 2: 123–39.

Tigner, Amy L. 2002. "'*The Laramie Project*': Western Pastoral." *Modern Drama* 45, 1: 138–56.

Tubbs, Stewart L., and Sylvia Moss. 2003. *Human Communication: Principles and Contexts,* 9th ed. Boston: McGraw-Hill.

Tucker, Lauren R. 1998. "The Framing of Calvin Klein: A Frame Analysis of Media and Discourse about the August 1995 Calvin Klein Jeans Advertising Campaign." *Critical Studies in Mass Communication* 15, 2: 141–58.

Turner, Edith. 2005. "Rites of Communitas." *Encyclopedia of Religious Rites, Rituals, and Festivals.* Ed. Frank A. Salamone. New York: Routledge, 97–101.

Turner, Victor. 1957. *Schism and Continuity in an African Society: A Study of Ndembu Village Life.* Manchester: Berg.

Turner, Victor. 1967. *The Forest of Symbols: Aspects of Ndembu Ritual.* Ithaca, NY: Cornell University Press.

Turner, Victor. 1974. *Dramas, Fields, and Metaphors: Symbolic Action in Human Society.* Ithaca, NY: Cornell University Press.

Turner, Victor. 1981. "Social Dramas and Stories about Them." *On Narrative.* Ed. W. J. T. Mitchell. Chicago: University of Chicago Press, 137–64.

Turner, Victor. 1982. *From Ritual to Theater: The Human Seriousness of Play.* New York: PAJ.

Turner, Victor. 1988. *The Anthropology of Performance.* New York: PAJ.

Tylor, Edward Burnett. 1871/1958. *Primitive Culture.* New York: Harper.

Urrea, Luis Alberto. 1998. *Nobody's Son: Notes from an American Life.* Tucson: University of Arizona Press.

Valentine, Kristine B. 1983. "'New Criticism' and the Emphasis on Literature in Interpretation." *Performance of Literature in Historical Perspectives.* Ed. David W. Thompson. Lanham, MD: University Press of America, 549–66.

Valentine, Kristin Bervig. 2002. "Yaqui Easter Ceremonies and the Ethics of Intense Spectatorship." *Text and Performance Quarterly* 22, 4: 280–96.

Vande Berg, Leah. 1995. "Living Room Pilgrimages: Television's Cyclical Commemoration of the Assassination Anniversary of John F. Kennedy." *Communication Monographs* 62: 47–65.

van Gennep, Arnold. 1909/1960. *The Rites of Passage.* Trans. Monika B. Vizedom and Gabrielle L. Caffee. Intro. Solon T. Kimball. Chicago: University of Chicago Press.

Van Maanen, Hans. 2004. "How Contexts Frame Theatrical Events." *Theatrical Events: Borders, Dynamics, Frames.* Ed. Vicky Ann Cremona, Peter Eversmann, Hans van Maanen, Willmar Sauter, and John Tulloch. Amsterdam: Rodopi, 243–75.

Vine, Katy. 2004, September. "Alive and Kicking." *Texas Monthly* 114–121, 220–21.

Waggoner, Catherine. 1997. "The Emancipatory Potential of Feminine Masquerade in Mary Kay Cosmetics." *Text and Performance Quarterly* 17: 256–72.

Waggoner, Catherine Egley, and D. Lynn O'Brien Hallstein. 2001. "Feminist Ideologies Meet Fashionable Bodies: Managing the Agency/Constraint Continuum." *Text and Performance Quarterly* 21, 1: 26–47.

Wallace, Amy. 2002. "Jamie Lee Curtis: True Thighs." *Ladies Home Journal.* Available at http://www.lhj.com/lhj/story.jhtml?storyid=/templatedata/lhj/story/data/jamieleecurti struethighs_08212002.xml

Ward, Cynthia. 1994. "Twins Separated at Birth? West African Vernacular and Western Avant Garde Performativity in Theory and Practice." *Text and Performance Quarterly* 14, 4: 269–88.

Watkins, S. Craig. 2001. "Framing Protest: News Media Frames of the Million Man March." *Critical Studies in Media Communication* 18, 1: 83–102.

Watts, Eric King. 2005. "Border Patrolling and 'Passing' in Eminem's *8 Mile*." *Critical Studies in Mass Communication* 22, 3: 187–207.

Weber, Carl. 1980. "Brecht in Eclipse?" *TDR: The Drama Review* 24, 1: 114–24.

Weeks, Jeffrey. 2003. *Sexuality,* 2nd ed. London: Routledge.

Weich, Dave. 2004. "Author Interviews: Laurie Notaro's Ongoing Adventure Series." Available at http://www.powells.com/authors/notaro.html

Weick, Karl E. 1979. *The Social Psychology of Organizing,* 2nd ed. Reading, MA: Addison-Wesley.

Weick, Karl. 1995a. "Definition of Theory." *Blackwell Dictionary of Organizational Behavior.* Ed. Nigel Nicholson. Oxford: Blackwell.

Weick, Karl. 1995b. "What Theory Is Not, Theorizing Is." *Administrative Science Quarterly* 40: 385–90.

Wendt, Ronald F. 1996. "Answers to the Gaze: A Genealogical Poaching of Resistances." *Quarterly Journal of Speech* 82: 251–73.

West, Rebecca. 2006. "From Happenings to Flash Mobs: The Evolution of a Form." Paper presented at Southern States Communication Association Convention, Dallas, TX.

Westerfelhaus, Robert, and Robert Alan Brookey. 2004. "At the Unlikely Confluence of Conservative Religion and Popular Culture: *Fight Club* as Heteronormative Ritual." *Text and Performance Quarterly* 24, 3/4: 302–27.

Wickstrom, Mauirya. 2001. "In the Body of the Commodity We Shall Triumph Over Ruin: Performance at the Forum Shops, Las Vegas." *Theatre Annual* 54: 63–94.

Wilchins, Riki. 2004. *Queer Theory, Gender Theory: An Instant Primer.* Los Angeles: Alyson Books.

Wiley, Eric. 2002. "Wilderness Theatre: Environmental Tourism and Cajun Swamp Tours." *TDR: The Drama Review* 46, 3: 118–31.

Williams, Raymond. 1958/1983. *Culture and Society.* New York: Columbia University Press.

Williams, Raymond. 1974/2003. *Television: Technology and Cultural Form.* London: Taylor and Francis.

Williams, Raymond. 1976. *Keywords.* London: Fontana.

Williams, Raymond. 1983. "Drama in a Dramatized Society." *Writing in Society.* London: Verso, 11–21.

Wimsatt, William K. 1954. *The Verbal Icon.* Lexington: University of Kentucky Press.

Wimsatt, William K., and Monroe C. Beardsley. 1946. "The Intentional Fallacy." *Sewanee Review* 54: 468–88.

Wolska, Aleksandra. 2005. "Rabbits, Machines, and the Ontology of Performance." *Theatre Journal* 57, 1: 83–95.

Wood, Andrew F. 2005. "'What Happens [in Vegas]': Performing the Post-Tourist Flaneur in 'New York' and 'Paris.'" *Text and Performance Quarterly* 25, 4: 315–33.

Worthen, W. B. 1995. "Disciplines of the Text/Sites of Performance." *TDR: The Drama Review* 39, 1: 13–28.

Worthen, W. B. 1998. "Drama, Performativity, and Performance." *PMLA* 113, 5: 1093–107.

Wuthnow, Robert. 1987. *Meaning and Moral Order.* Berkeley: University of California Press.

Yoffe, Emily. 2006, 15 May. "Tears of a Clown: I Bomb as a Kids' Birthday Party Entertainer." *Slate Magazine.* Available at http://www.slate.com/id/2141711/?nav=fo

Index

About the Author

Elizabeth Bell received her PhD in Communication, with an emphasis in Performance Studies, in 1983 from the University of Texas at Austin. She has taught at the University of Texas and the University of North Carolina at Chapel Hill and is currently Professor of Communication at the University of South Florida. She is the recipient of more than ten teaching awards from college, state, and national associations. Most recently, she was recognized for career-long teaching excellence with the John I. Sisco Excellence in Teaching Award by the Southern States Communication Association. In 2005, she received the Distinguished Service Award from the Performance Studies Division of the National Communication Association. She has published dozens of journal articles and book chapters and is the coeditor of *From Mouse to Mermaid: The Politics of Film, Gender, and Culture.*